Coalitions and Competition

The last decades have seen an overwhelming increase in the globalization of professional business services. As these become increasingly transnational, how can governments hope to gauge the success and influence of these? Is regulation possible?

Coalitions and Competition is the first attempt to analyse the forces behind the process. Based on contributions from leading authorities in international business, both academics and members of organizations such as GATT and UNCTAD, it looks at the opportunities for growth, environmental and regulatory problems, and the major problems of managing international expansion of professional firms. Crucially, it discusses such issues from the point of view of managers of such organizations, and the role of governments in negotiating multinational agreements on these operations in a world growing ever smaller.

This highly international book will be of interest to the international business community, particularly managers of professional business firms, and policy makers involved in international trade issues.

Yair Aharoni is a world-renowned expert on international business and strategic decision making.

Coalitions and Competition

The Globalization of Professional Business Services

Edited by Yair Aharoni

London and New York

First published 1993
by Routledge
11 New Fetter Lane, London EC4P 4EE

Simultaneously published in the USA and Canada
by Routledge
29 West 35th Street, New York, NY 10001

Typeset in 10/12pt Times by LaserScript Limited, Mitcham, Surrey
Printed and bound in Great Britain by
Biddles Ltd, Guildford and King's Lynn

British Library Cataloguing in Publication Data

A catalogue reference for this book is available from the British Library.

ISBN 0–415–08228–5

Library of Congress Cataloging in Publication Data
has been applied for.

ISBN 0–415–08228–5

Contents

List of figures

List of tables

x   *Tables*

List of contributors

Raj Aggarwal, The Edward J. and Louise E. Mellen Chair in Finance, School of Business, John Carrol University, Cleveland, Ohio

Yair Aharoni, Issachar Haimovic Professor of Business Policy, The Leon Recanati Graduate School of Business Administration, Faculty of Management, Tel Aviv University, Israel (J. Paul Sticht Visiting Professor of International Business, Fuqua School of Business, Duke University, North Carolina)

Andrew Anderson, Assistant Professor of International Business, Faculty of Management, University of Toronto, Ontario

Bernard Ascher, Director of Service Industry Affairs, Office of the US Trade Representative, Washington, DC

Charles Baden-Fuller, Professor of Strategic Management, Bath University

John H. Dunning, Emeritus Professor of International Business, University of Reading and State of New Jersey Professor of International Business, Rutgers University

Karin Fladmoe-Lindquist, Assistant Professor of Management, David Eccles School of Business, University of Utah

Stephen Guisinger, Professor of International Management Studies, School of Management, The University of Texas at Dallas

Seev Hirsch, Jaffee Professor of International Trade, The Leon Recanati Graduate School of Business Administration, Tel Aviv University, Israel

Jiatao Li, Assistant Professor, Strategy and International Management, College of Business, University of Hawaii at Manoa

Bente R. Lowendahl, Associate Professor Strategy, Norwegian School of Management, Sandvika (Oslo), Norway

Jan Maciejewicz, Central School of Planning and Statistics, Warsaw, Poland

Kalypso Nicolaïdis, doctoral candidate in political economy, Harvard University; associate, Center for Business and Government; associate, Center for International Affairs

Alan M. Rugman, Professor of International Business, Faculty of Management, University of Toronto, Ontario

Zur Shapira, Professor of Management, Stern School of Business, New York University

Richard H. Snape, Professor of Economics, Monash University, Melbourne

Yehia Soubra, First Economic Affairs Officer, United Nations Conference on Trade and Development (UNCTAD), Geneva, Switzerland

Viktor Vlasek, VUTESP, Research Institute of Technology and Economics in Light Industries, Prague, Czechoslovakia

1 Globalization of professional business services

Yair Aharoni

INTRODUCTION

Economic activities have been traditionally divided into primary, secondary and tertiary activities. In certain theories, either primary or secondary activities, or both, were seen as productive, others as less productive. The Physiocrats in France, for example, believed that land was the only source of value. Ricardo (and Karl Marx) ascribed such a role to labour. Services were long believed to be an unproductive and undesirable source of employment and an arcane area of economic activity. The result is that the service sector has been a neglected area in research and policy debates. In the last decade or two, however, the crucial importance of services to the economy has been increasingly recognized. One reason is the growing importance of services in national economies. The services' share in employment and GNP has grown in almost all countries in the last two decades (Shelp 1981, 1983; Daniels 1982; Gershuny and Miles 1983; Kravis *et al.* 1983; Riddle 1986); services account for about two-thirds of GDP in the developed countries and for almost half of GDP in developing countries (World Bank 1989). Another reason is the growing international trade in services (Leveson 1985; Giarini 1987).

The role of services in economic development is even greater than that represented by shares of GNP. Many services, e.g. research and development are of utmost importance for economic growth. Smooth business transaction depends on the availability of such services as accounting, auditing, insurance, transportation and legal services. Other services, e.g. after-sale servicing, advertising or telecommunications, determine the competitiveness of goods. The paramount role of services in creating and maintaining sustainable competitive advantage is increasingly recognized.

Services are often provided by large multinational enterprises (MNEs) on a global basis. By the end of the 1980s foreign direct investments (FDIs) in services accounted for 40 per cent (about $400 billion) of the world stock and more than 50–60 per cent (about $600 billion) of annual flows of FDI. The reasons for the growth in services FDI and the possible competitive advantages of MNEs in this sector have become of major interest. Clearly, the growth of MNEs in production has caused rapid growth and extensive transformations in business services; accounting, advertising, management consultants and lawyers followed the MNEs and generated more foreign income. Services also grew as a result of saturation of the demand for goods (Ott 1987: 13). The major reason, however, is technological: decreasing costs in the fields of data processing and telecommunications led to increased tradeability of these fields. Evidence is seen of more businesses franchising across borders, more people using highly modernized air transport, an increasing volume of tourism services and the innovative construction of fibre-optic transatlantic cables (Feketekuty 1988, UNCSE 1992).

In the early 1990s, the service sector has become the focal point of worldwide attention among both researchers and policy-makers. Interest has also shifted from analysis of the service sector in a national setting to an examination of the international trade and investment in services. Uruguay Round negotiators were grappling with the task of designing a multinational framework for trade in services, intensifying the interest in that topic. One result of the Uruguay Round negotiations was that many experts published their views on specific issues of international trade in services, with a wealth of data and publications also coming from the United Nations, the General Agreement on Tariffs and Trade (GATT) and the US government (UNCTAD 1984, 1985, 1989; UNCTC 1988, 1989a, b, 1990b; GATT Secretariat 1989).

The growing importance of services, their rising share in GDP and their increasing salience in international trade revolutionized international business, creating a vital need to examine the degree to which international trade and investment theories are applicable. Since the 1970s, it has been recognized that concepts and theories devised to explain the production of goods do not necessarily apply to the production of services, and that organization design paradigms applicable to manufacturing may not fit the special problems of a service organization.

Services include many and diverse types of activities. Some, such as the services of a doorman in an apartment building or a waiter in a restaurant, are low skilled and labour intensive. Others, such as air, rail, sea or road transportation and telecommunications, are capital intensive. Still others are highly human-capital-intensive operations. There have been many attempts to catalogue the characteristics of services and to propose schemes for classifying them (e.g. Lovelock 1983). Most research on services has focused on the whole sector (Richardson 1987), often suggesting some breakdown of the field according to different characteristics (Sapir 1982;

Gray 1983; Riddle 1986; Porter 1990). It was increasingly realized that services are a very heterogeneous area. Some are highly knowledge intensive, such as research and development. Others are not. It was also realized that the conditions of production changed, and that many services are complementary to the production of goods. Daniels (1985: xvi) warns that the diversity of the service sector 'defies applications of a principal theory, a particular analytical method, or a dominant mode of interpretation'.

In an attempt to understand the operations of a small but highly important subsection of services, an international conference was held on 19–20 October 1990 at the Fuqua School of Business, Duke University, on 'Coalitions and Competition: Globalization of Professional Business Services'. More than twenty scholars from all over the world attempted to shed light on different aspects of this topic. The conference participants found themselves identifying numerous areas in which facts were contradictory and differences were significant. It has also become clear that the participants had a variety of perspectives, often based on the field of their earlier studies.

This book is an outcome of the conference and includes revised versions of some of the papers. The purpose of this introduction is to pool the available state of knowledge, to enhance the existing understanding of global operations of professional business service (PBS) firms, to enumerate and categorize the major relevant issues and to propose some generalizations that may provide a platform for research issues of interest on the globalization of PBS firms and on the operations of these firms. We start by discussing differences between goods and services in general before enumerating the characteristics of PBS firms in particular. We then describe, as a background, the world market for professional services, review the principal modes of delivery and analyse the major barriers to globalization of PBSs. We also consider the extent to which concepts developed to discuss manufacturing MNEs are applicable to professional service MNEs.

SERVICES AND GOODS

Goods are tangible. Services are intangible. A consumer buying services is paying for information or quality of performance. While goods can be counted by physical quantities, service 'quantities' can only be measured by the duration and intensity of the service given to a user.

Most authors cite four characteristics of services: intangibility, perishability, inseparability and heterogeneity (Zeithaml *et al.* 1985). Intangibility is said to imply that a service is perceived in a subjective manner and it is frequently difficult to evaluate or define quality. Services cannot be stored;

consumption and production are generally simultaneous and inseparable. Moreover, except for the increased use of facsimile, computers and telecommunications, the products of most services remain embedded in the direct relations between clients and producers.

Although services are heterogeneous, in all of them the customer participates as a productive resource and does not simply *receive* the service. A seminal work by Hill (1977) conceived services as a change in the conditions of an economic unit which occurs as a result of the activity of another economic unit. This new definition has been widely quoted (on definitions see, for example, Siniscalco (1989), Kenessey (1987) and Smith (1972). One classification is between services that are primarily equipment based and those that are primarily people based. PBSs are in the latter category with highly skilled staff (Thomas 1978). Another important variable is the extent of customer contact required in the delivery of the product (Chase 1978; Kotler 1980). In high contact services it is extremely difficult to control product variability.

The conference concentrated on issues related to PBS firms. Yet, since these firms are a subsector of the services sector, the question of definition and characteristics of the services sector in general had to be discussed. In part, this discussion was a part of the analysis of the changing international environment – summarized below. In part, it concentrated on definitional issues. Seev Hirsch's chapter concentrates on the general question of differences between goods and services, stressing the service intensity. This notion, first developed as a result of an in-depth analysis of the electronics industry, is of utmost importance in understanding transactions with high levels of new technology or knowledge intensity. It is therefore of interest to those searching to understand the globalization of PBS firms.

Just as the industrial revolution caused division of labour and specialization in the production of industrial goods, the information revolution brought increased specialization of service sector inputs and outputs, particularly in technologically advanced economies. Services that were previously produced within the firm are now acquired from specialists outside it (Porter 1990). Bhagwati (1984: 19) refers to this phenomenon as the 'outhouse' versus 'inhouse' use of service inputs. For example, instead of internalizing the production of security services, many corporations hire local or transnational teams of security personnel to ensure the safety of their employees. One result is the expansion of professional business firms. These professional services are sometimes offered around the world by foreign affiliates of MNEs.

TRADEABILITY OF SERVICES

Services were generally believed to be non-tradeable, since they could be supplied only if producer and consumer were in close proximity. Perhaps because of this belief, only a small number of services, mainly investment income and tourism, were included in a country's current account in the balance of payments statistics. Further, statistics on international trade in services are highly aggregated, under-reported and inconsistent. Compared with over 10,000 product codes for manufacturing data, there are only forty service industry codes (Ascher and Whichard 1987). Today it is increasingly recognized that services are tradeable. Patients must be present to have a medical examination. However, medical records can be analysed in isolation and the results may be delivered on tape or video, or by electronic mail, thus obviating the need for face-to-face communication. In fact, many professional services are performed without the customer present (Riddle and Brown 1988). International trade in such storable services is said to be not very different from merchandise trade (Bhagwati 1984). Moreover, new information and telecommunications technologies have collapsed time and space and enabled many services to be produced in one country and consumed in another. Firms can move information across national borders with speed, accuracy, reliability and security. Data networks created the possibilities for interactive, instantaneous transactions across borders using a transnational communication–computer system. MNEs use their own data network systems: many firms are racing to create global private networks that virtually eliminate boundaries of time and distance. Data traffic in these networks has been growing at 20 or even 30 per cent per annum (*Business Week* 1986: 140–8). One public policy question is whether or not governments should force such closed groups to allow access to the network to anyone, and if so how. There are also problems of taxation on cross-border data transmittal and of the privacy of individuals. Bressand (1989) argues that the permanent links between actors across borders allows them to create value jointly instead of simply exchanging it. He therefore labels all participants in the network as prosumers (1989: 232). Despite improved communication linkage, advances in computer technology and enhanced ability to store inputs and outputs in a computer's memory, tradeability of services depends on international movements of factors of production (Feketekuty 1988) and/or of the receiver of services. The trade may or may not be carried out jointly with that of goods: consulting services may be separately commissioned, but a good may be sold including an agreement to train local engineers in its use.

Medical doctors can now join an electronically linked network, thus allowing smaller medical suppliers to be connected to the most modern diagnostic equipment and reducing the scale advantage of the large medical centre. In many other professional services, one can connect to a data base – even one in a different country – from a personal computer (PC). This allows even an individual professional to analyse extremely complex problems quickly and efficiently. A lawyer can connect to data bases, for example, completing in a short period of time an exhaustive background legal search. As a result, each firm can offer a wider variety of services, achieving economies of scope. The changing environment and the complex technological revolutions led to growth in international trade and investment in services. One result was the attempt to forge a new multilateral trade agreement and create a set of rules to govern trade in services in general, including the PBSs. Three contributions to this volume involve issues related to these negotiations: Bernard Ascher discusses the extent to which foreigners will be able to take advantage of opportunities to supply services in other countries; Richard Snape discusses the possible forthcoming rules for international trade in services and analyses the impact of these possible trading rules on PBS firms; and Kalypso Nicolaïdis focuses on the impact of the new concept of mutual recognition on the regulatory environment and therefore on the strategy of PBS firms.

PRINCIPAL MODES OF DELIVERY

Firms can offer their services internationally in one of three possible modes of delivery. First, they can offer services through pure cross-border trade, using telephone, mail, computer networks etc. Second, the clients may be enticed to come to the country in which the firm is located and purchase services there. Third, an employee of the firm (or a partner for that matter) can be moved temporarily or permanently to the place where the customer is located. In practice, business services are transacted by the firm moving to clients. Therefore, regulations on border movements and on immigration must be considered.

One should distinguish between temporary and permanent movements of factors of production, especially labour. The usual International Monetary Fund (IMF) rules for the balance of payments account are based on the definition of residence: those staying in a foreign country for more than one year are considered residents of that country. A Japanese computer technician travelling to Singapore to service imported ITT computers must still be a resident of Japan in order for this service to be considered a Japanese export. If a country attracts a lot of foreign students, the expenditures of these students in most of their learning experience would not be reflected in the balance of payments accounts. Conceptually, however, the movement of people to, say, the USA (often called 'brain drain') may be seen as international trade in services. A student who studies in the U.S. is as much an export of services as a tourist, and a professor who moved to an American university is a part of trade in services.

The three chapters in which the regulatory environment is discussed note several major differences between international services and goods. Thus, most trade barriers in services are embedded in domestic, not international, regulations. Such requirements as the licensing of professionals or the legal requirement to use the name of actual partners as the name of a partnership are barriers to foreign competition, even though they were not designed for this reason. Second, service trade requires international movement of factors of production. Third, the distinction between foreign investment and trade in services is not easily made. Finally, unlike trade in goods there are no natural barriers to service trade. There are no existing geographical barriers impeding the long-distance servicing provided by the technologically advanced communication and information sectors.

As in the case of the production of goods, a fourth mode of delivering services internationally is FDI. The high cost of transporting the final product through trade in services may be circumvented by the lower cost of moving factors of production through FDI (Gray 1983). Management consulting, advertising, accounting, public relations and market opinion survey work are all offered by multinational firms. The MNEs can employ local persons *or* use their own experts from the home country.

Several contributors to this volume touch on the age old question of the choice between export and FDIs in the specific contents of the PBS firm. Hirsch updates his earlier (Hirsch 1976) analysis of the choice between export and investment. Dunning expands on his eclectic theory, relating it to services in general.

These chapters set the background for a more focused analysis of the professional business firm. Let us turn to the definition of these firms and their major characteristics.

DEFINITION AND MAJOR CHARACTERISTICS OF PROFESSIONAL BUSINESS SERVICES

PBSs are services used mainly by other firms in the production process of these other firms. Feketekuty (1986) defines professional services as the application of knowledge and skills by experts to meet client's needs. Arkell and Harrison define PBS as:

> the provision of intellectual or specialized skills on a personal, direct basis, based on extensive educational training... some take a broader view and would include most forms of cultural, artistic, or intellectual

endeavor as professions. It is also recognized that the definition is not static, and that occupations over time can rise to a professional status.

(1987: 4)

Only very few researchers focus on the specific characteristics of the PBSs. Instead, much of the research on services looks at all services as belonging to one category, ignoring the differences.

The major characteristics of PBSs are, first, that they are highly skill or knowledge intensive and scale is achieved mainly by having a large number of partners or highly skilled participants. The key strategic resource of the PBSs is their ability to attract high quality and loyalty from their skilled individuals. The major strategic asset of the firms is their *reputation* – based on the availability of these professionals. There are great gains to be achieved from training of individuals, to inculcate a similar culture, similar ways of operation, systems and procedures and similar ways of problem solving among its many employees in different countries. Trained manpower can leave to establish their own firms. Indeed, several large audit firms faced a problem of the defection of management consultants who perceived their share in profits to be inequitable. This problem is also related to the rate of growth of these firms. If a firm is not growing, it usually faces difficulties promoting persons to partnership positions and therefore faces a high risk of losing talented and highly skilled personnel. This problem is important because PBS employees are able to use discretionary effort, defined as the difference between the maximum effort and the minimum effort required to avoid being fired (Zeithaml *et al.* 1990). These two basic characteristics of the PBS make human resource management extremely important. It also makes global operations based on hierarchical relations, as in most producing MNEs, much less likely.

Two additional characteristics of PBSs are the degree of customization of the service and the intensity of customer–provider interaction (Maister 1982). PBS firms focus on exploring and solving a particular problem for a client (Gummesson 1978). In so doing, they have to offer custom-made solutions rather than a standard service as exemplified in the fast food chain. Further, customization involves a high level of client–provider interaction on an ongoing basis and for a long time. Fladmoe-Lindquist emphasizes in Chapter 9 that these characteristics mean a high level of uncertainty and of negotiations. She claims that 'service delivery' is a misleading term: provider and client are working together and making decisions in a highly integrative mode. Fladmoe-Lindquist stresses that in these conditions it is impossible to negotiate all aspects of a contract *ex ante*. There is a need for a continuous bargaining under conditions of uncertainty. She provides several propositions on behaviour under these conditions, enumerating three sources of uncertainty: management uncertainty (e.g. quality control), contract uncertainty (i.e. incomplete contracts) and client uncertainty.

Customization increases uncertainty by making it difficult to achieve quality control but also increases the difficulty the customers experience in assessing the quality of the service they receive (Kotler and Bloom 1984). PBSs managers must rely on the integrity of the staff, making initial hiring and later training and socialization of utmost importance.

PBSs are supplied by interaction between a professional supplier and a client. Customers must be actively involved in the creation of the service – and with new computer networks may perform the action themselves (Bressand 1989). Because PBSs are consumed when they are produced, a quality control check cannot be performed before the product is delivered to a customer. Often the service cannot be evaluated after it is received either (Zeithaml *et al.* 1990). Most PBSs are advisory (Gummesson 1978) and depend on the client to implement the recommendations. This problem is exemplified by the information asymmetry between client and provider (Norman 1984).

Entry to some PBSs is restricted to licensed or accredited professionals. The licensing requirements are different in different countries. Some of the newer services, e.g. computer software, advertising or management consulting, do not necessitate a licence (Chapter 2 elaborates on these differences).

In many countries the professional must be willing to face unlimited liability for his or her actions (and for the actions of his or her partners). The combination of a high level of skill, very little economy of scale and much country-specific knowledge may mean a low probability of multinational operations. Yet at the same time several factors have made global operations necessary. These are the saturation of existing markets on the one hand and the pull of opportunities abroad on the other. In many cases, PBS firms had to expand abroad in order to serve their multinationally producing clients. Accounting firms who have to follow their clients tend to share profits within a national organization, not always worldwide.

Most of the services are organized and regulated by professional societies and associations. Two major changes affecting the mode of operations of PBS firms have been the deregulation in many service areas, particularly in the USA, and the relaxing of professional associations' standards, particularly in the EC, minimizing many constraints and barriers to entry.

A salient characteristic of at least some PBSs is the *uncertainty* inherent in the supply of the service. Many PBSs also offer customized service. Advice to one person is unique under a set of circumstances – the service is one of a kind. This uncertainty is the major basis for Fladmoe-Lindquist's propositions, already alluded to.

PBSs are also affected by *rules of ethics* of different professions. Regulations may be perceived as impeding globalization of PBS firms. However, these restrictions are all domestic regulations, not necessarily intended as trade barriers. Thus, professional licensing as mentioned earlier stems from domestic reasons.

David Maister (1986) notes that PBS firms can sell three things: their expertise, their experience or their execution capability (or efficiency). Any specific firm may specialize in one of these 'three Es'. The type of work done by the PBS firm would determine its economic structure, its human resources strategy, its growth strategy and its ownership structure.

The above discussion relates to PBS firms in a uninational situation. What about the multinational PBSs? An important question to be dealt with is: why should PBS MNEs *own* a subsidiary rather than entering an alliance with a local firm? A related question is why the customer would prefer an MNE to a local firm.

Porter (1990: 245), following Levitt (1976), posits that systematization and in some cases standardization of the process of service delivery is the major reason for the growth of the multi-unit service firm. In addition, the demand for certain services may come from mobile persons moving to other countries, as when US or Japanese firms offer services to US or Japanese tourists. The more people of a certain nationality that are mobile and the more the service can be supplied in a standardized form, the greater will be the firm-specific advantages of an MNE such as American Express, hotel chains or airlines. As shown above, PBS firms offer customized service. Thus, it is difficult to create systematic rules for offering architecture or legal services. Such rules are easier in consulting services, or for auditing. Indeed, there are significant differences among different PBSs with regard to the degree of globalization, the market concentration and the size of the firms. One extreme is auditing services, in which the 'Big 8' were reduced to the 'Big 6', and these firms control about 40 per cent of the US market. Another is legal services, in which literally tens of thousands of small firms operate. Law firms today operate in a highly atomistic structure while auditors are extremely concentrated. Moreover, auditing seems to have become a more global product than law or medicine. The top ten accounting firms had 3,156 offices and affiliates worldwide in 1988. An important question for research is the explanatory variables for these differences.

Even if the PBS sector is not composed of global industries, global firms have been able to flourish, developing expertise in a specific niche, as did Arthur Andersen in systems integration consulting, McKinsey in general management or BCG in strategy.

These questions are the focus of Charles Baden-Fuller's contribution to this book. Baden-Fuller distinguishes between the static and dynamic views of the world. He demonstrates, on the basis of several case studies, that PBS firms face an uncertain environment, forcing firms to integrate their international operations. Bente Lowendhal applies the theory of joint ventures to a case of an international PBS. Aharoni analyses different ownership patterns and their impact. All these authors emphasize organizational issues. In contrast, Li and Guisinger take a macro view, using a regression analysis to test different theories on the rationale of FDIs. Before turning to these issues, however, some statistical dimensions of the topic might be illuminating.

THE WORLD MARKET FOR PROFESSIONAL BUSINESS SERVICES

According to the official statistics, international trade in services grew in the 1970s at a rate of 19.6 per cent per annum – almost equal to the 21.4 per cent growth in merchandise exports (Trondsen and Edfelt 1987). Note, however, that when investment income is excluded from service exports, the similarity between growth in goods and growth in services dissipates (Kravis 1985). This could be due to the overwhelming under-reporting of much non-factor service trade, including education, insurance and telecommunication services.

International trade data on the magnitude of cross-border and other transactions in PBSs is virtually non-existent. Even domestic statistics on output and employment are not very easily available. The available data allow several points to be made. First, employment in the PBS field has grown much faster than employment in general. In the period 1979–86, employment growth in business services was 53.8 per cent compared with 13.1 per cent in all sectors; in France, the growth was 25.4 per cent compared with a reduction in total employment of 0.1 per cent. As a share of total employment in 1986, business services and real estate as a percentage of total employment ranged from a low of 3.3 per cent in the Federal Republic of Germany to a high of 7.6 per cent in the USA. In most of these business services, the US market accounts for at least half of the total world market. Thus, in accounting/auditing the US market, in 1987, was estimated at $26.5 billion and the world market at $50–60 billion. In management consulting the figures were $45.0 billion out of $80–90 billion. The US market in software/data processing was estimated at $60 billion and the world market at $100–120 billion. Billing in advertising was $215 billion worldwide and the US market was $110 billion. US market size for legal services for the same year was $75 billion, but no world market estimate is available (UNCTC 1990b).

Auditing and advertising have been low growth mature industries, while computer software services grew very fast. Indeed, all large firms in the first two services diversified into more growth fields (management consulting and software on the one hand and public relations and direct marketing on the other). Arthur Andersen, for example, is the largest management consulting firm in the world, the second largest audit firm and the fifth largest computer services firm.

COMPETITIVE ADVANTAGE OF NATIONS

When the importance of international trade in services in general, and PBSs in particular, was recognized, it was also assumed that developed countries, mainly the USA, would have a major advantage. This is because the USA exports manufacturing goods with a very high service content (research and development, marketing, after-sale service). The USA also exports services directly and, even more so, its large MNEs sell services characterized by a high human capital component (e.g. software, engineering, auditing services, legal advice or management consulting) all over the globe. Indeed the US Office of Technology Assessment (OTA) (US Congress 1986) used two concepts to assess the impact of service trade on the US economy. The first was exports, as defined for balance of payments statistics. The second was foreign revenues of US firms, including sale of foreign affiliates. The OTA estimated foreign revenues of US service firms in 1983 to be $160.5 billion, including $68.1 billion direct exports and $92.4 billion for sales through foreign-based affiliates. The OTA excluded from its estimates exports and foreign revenues of commercial banking and wholesaling (for reasons see US Congress 1986: 53–8).

Alan Deardroff (1985) demonstrated that management services are exported in large quantities from the USA despite their high cost. To be sure, if the price of management services is adjusted for differences in the quality of service inputs due to technology, the inconsistency with conventional trade theory disappears. Furthermore, management services are a necessary ingredient in a broader package of services that is produced more cheaply in the USA.

The United Nations Committee on Trade and Development was naturally concerned about the competitive position and export capacity of service firms from developing countries. Based on balance of payments statistics, developing countries export a low percentage of total service exports. The share of developing countries would be even less than that recorded by the IMF if income from affiliates of MNEs was also considered trade. However, liberalization of service imports may stimulate efficiency in key sectors, thus contributing to economic growth. Moreover, with growth in information networks, developing countries may be able to supply labour-intensive services. Indian programmers supplied software to IMI in Geneva through electronic networks. Gibbs (1989: 104) argued that the demarcation line is not between service and goods but between comparative advantage in knowledge-intensive goods (or services) and what he termed 'production that is not knowledge intensive'.

To be sure, the international division of labour, as noted by Gereffi (1989), has shifted from country-based comparative advantage in one product or another to intra-firm division of labour. MNEs can allocate skill-intensive operations to one country and low-skill labour-intensive operations to another. This development has been noted in manufacturing and has also become possible in services. A US-based insurance firm can transmit claims to Ireland to be processed there and returned through telecommunication–computer links to the home office; banks move the labour-intensive credit cards backroom operations to developing countries and so on. The role of PBSs in different countries was discussed only in one sense at the conference – that of the role of PBSs in Eastern Europe. The contributions of Maciejewicz and of Vlasek allow a glimpse into the role of PBS firms in Eastern Europe. Special attention was paid to banks. Agarwal analyses the role of Japanese financial institutions while Rugman and Anderson discuss the possible role of Canadian banks.

THE ROLE OF MULTINATIONAL ENTERPRISES IN THE SUPPLY OF PROFESSIONAL BUSINESS SERVICES

The operations of PBS firms may be studied from a macro point of view. Alternatively, one may look at the inside work of the firm to explain its multinational operations. These two points of view were clearly represented in the conference. They are also paramount in the general literature. The basic Heckscher–Ohlin comparative advantage model of international trade theory explains the sectoral distribution and geographical direction of trade in terms of factor costs and factor intensity. Countries export goods containing a high proportion of their relatively abundant production factors and import goods which contain a high proportion of relatively scarce production factors. All relevant costs are incurred in the exporting country, prior to the shipment of the goods to their foreign markets. Costs of transportation and other costs of transferring the goods to foreign destinations are assumed to be negligible. The implicit assumption in these theories is that manufacturing creates standard goods, so that they can be grouped into ISIC groups and assumed to compete against each other.

Modern versions of this simplistic model make allowance for imperfect product and factor markets, for declining cost functions and for international mobility of production factors, thus providing plausible explanations for real world phenomena such as the Leontief paradox or the MNE. However, even these models do not take explicit account of international service transactions. Several of the participants in the conference based their analysis on macro factors. Bernard Ascher, for example, provided a sweeping panorama of the increased international integration of markets for professional services. In discussing the extent to which foreigners will be able to take advantage of increased opportunities to perform services on a cross-border basis, or through the establishment of offices in other countries he stressed restrictions on entering and operating in foreign markets.

One way to reduce the national barriers is to allow professionals to practise their skills where they wish. The European Commission attempts to achieve this goal by proposing a general directive that would set up a system of mutual recognition of professional qualifications. Kalypso Nicolaïdis offers a succinct analysis of these developments in Chapter 4.

Richard Snape reviews the rules governing international trade in professional and other services and the possible changes in these rules – mainly related to rights of establishment, visas and work permits. He also focuses on the concepts derived from the GATT, such as most favoured nation and national treatment, and shows possible adaptations to services in terms of a draft framework for the new agreement. Snape also stresses the possible reduction of trade barriers.

The several macro papers all agree that, since international transactions in services entail movement of factors of production and the establishment of operations by the provider in the country of the receiver, any general agreement on services would have to include some international standards on issues such as the following.

1 The ability of a professional to give advice or information to a foreign client using telecommunications or electronic mail.
2 The recognition by the authorities of one country of the professional qualifications granted by another.
3 The ability of a professional of one country to enter and work in another country.

Because imports of PBSs are not easily detected by customs officers at the border, the major issues related to international agreements are on regulations, on rights of establishment and on movements of persons.

Seev Hirsch attempts to offer an approach to the analysis of services based on his service-intensity theory. In his analysis, however, he ignores the internal organization of the firm. Thus, Hirsch implicitly assumes a firm can grow but does not show how.

Other papers stress the internal decision-making mechanism of the firm, its organizational structure and power relationships within it. This does not imply that the macro analysis is not important. The macro analysis may point out some limits to organizational behaviour, but the ability to gain economic rents is based on strategy. Further, 'the firm' may be seen as a bundle of visible and invisible (or tangible and intangible) assets. However, one must explain how these assets are co-ordinated, how they are managed and how they are used to turn inputs into outputs.

Many researchers have attempted to explain the existence and operations of FDIs and of MNEs. Most of the new theoretical work has been done outside the framework of the general equilibrium market-based view of international trade and investment behaviour. Instead, the analysis of the MNE is based, following the seminal work of Hymer, on the market imperfections approach. Alternatively, the approach is one of recognizing the importance of transaction costs and the efficiency of internalizing activities (Hennart 1982). As Rugman (1980) pointed out, MNE activity is a substitute for market-based activities when either natural market imperfections or government-imposed barriers to trade occur. In these cases, market operations are inefficient or impossible and MNEs look for return on their firm-specific knowledge. Indeed, Rugman (1987) has argued that the returns on FDI should conceptually be included in the trade in services, being payments for 'trade in services' within the MNEs. Since services are generally considered to be non-storable and non-transportable, it makes sense to argue that FDIs transferred within an MNE system are services. It is also plausible that service trade can enter international transactions mainly by the operations of MNEs or by the movement of people across borders. (Therefore, the issue of freer trade hinges on the right of entry of such firms and persons to foreign markets.)

In PBSs, internalizing theory may not be a sufficient means of explaining the MNEs. As noted by Aharoni in Chapter 8, most PBS firms achieve their firm-specific knowledge and advantage by being part of a network, not by ownership and hierarchy. These networks cover only a few key factors of success. Firms also resort to strategic alliances, e.g. joint ventures, as discussed by Lowendahl in Chapter 11. More research is needed to explain which variables lead to which type of network, strategic alliance or full ownership, and how each can be made to work successfully.

PBS firms are typically knowledge intensive. The business they are in is based on the gap in knowledge between them and the client (Norman 1984). Much of that knowledge is created in the firm itself over time. These specific capabilities, termed 'invisible assets', by Itami (1987), may be reflected in the perception of clients, who believe the firm has a better knowledge, has a greater reputation, supplies reliable services, is responsive to clients' needs etc. To exploit these resources, obtain economic rents and sustain superior performance, the firm must be organized in a certain way and the capabilities it offers must be difficult to buy and sell in a market or to imitate. Unlike the view of industrial economics, the source of the economic rent is internal rather than exogenous to the firm. In other words, the source is a superior organization or culture, not necessarily market collusion or market structure. Indeed, many chapters in this book highlight these points, even if – as in Subra's chapter – the discussion is of a whole industry.

By understanding how PBSs achieve and maintain their reputation, one can appreciate the means by which firm-specific advantages are achieved. The importance of both is shown in several chapters.

The globalization of PBSs, argues Baden-Fuller, has also been demand driven: professional business firms were led, perhaps reluctantly, into a multinational route in order to serve best their important multinational clients. They 'have come under growing pressure to follow their transnational clients, wherever the latter have chosen to go and do business' (UNCTC 1990b: 145). An auditing firm, facing the need to audit an MNE, had to follow it to wherever it went. In the case of international banking, there are several studies that have demonstrated that banks follow their customers abroad so that they can service their business needs fully (Brimmer and Dahl 1975; Gray and Gray 1981; Ball and Tschoegl 1982; Yannopoulos 1983; Nigh *et al.* 1986; Goldberg and Johnson 1990).

From the demand side, it is also possible that for many clients the least risky path is to employ a large multinational PBS firm, thus avoiding the risk of being accused of using the wrong supplier. From the point of view of the service firm, it can contact a local reputable firm, asking it to supply the specific services needed (e.g. auditing of a subsidiary), thus avoiding the need for creating a fully owned subsidiary that would need much more work to cover its costs. It does need a strong international group to deal with international merger or taxation problems.

It is not clear that MNEs would indeed always want their professional service firms to be global rather than opt for a local supplier who is familiar with the peculiar conditions of each separate market. What are the advantages for IBM in using the same law firm all over the world rather than picking and choosing the best firm in each country? Why should an MNE pay higher prices for the services of another MNE, say in consulting, when it can hire a local consultant? MNEs do not acquire other inputs, e.g. computer paper, from a global firm on a global order.

Most PBSs have a clearly defined client: a doctor sees a patient, a consultant sees a client. In some PBSs, however, the number and the quality of consumers is not known. Auditors attest financial statements for use by shareholders, but never know the number or identity of shareholders who actually read the financial statements. This fiduciary role allows audit standardization and global operations. Because their services are really supplied to the outside shareholders rather than to the management of the firms, and because of the access to privileged information, a global audit firm may enjoy a competitive advantage. In contrast, lawyers generally give the kind of expert advice that is very local in character. Exceptions are legal advice on international tax or international acquisitions.

There are also supply-side reasons. With changing technologies there are some PBS firms that gain scale advantages in working globally. Management consultants who work on the global problems of a client may benefit from the availability of a global network of consultants that can be moved around. There may also be a benefit in taking advantage of the firm's *reputation* by diversifying both geographically and into new areas of expertise. Auditors may have more reasons to work globally to ensure minimum standards of quality and on-time delivery. The minimum standards are achieved by peer review. A PBS, once it operates globally, attempts to raise the switching costs of moving to other firms in any parts of the globe (see Noyelle 1989).

Dunning, following his eclectic paradigm, illustrates in Chapter 6 the ownership, location and internalizing advantages of MNEs in many service areas. In the case of both auditing and legal services, he sees the main ownership advantage in 'access to transnational clients' and 'experience' (and reputation for lawyers, 'brand image of leading firms' for auditors). As to internalizing, he notes for lawyers that many transactions are highly idiosyncratic and customer specific, requiring quality control and under-standing of local customers and legal procedures. Auditors' advantages lie in limited inter-firm linkages, quality control over international standards and government insistence on local participation.

As expected, conference participants found themselves identifying numerous areas in which present understanding is murky. It was also clear that the researchers came from heterogeneous backgrounds and operated from widely different value systems. Nevertheless all the participants found a great deal of common ground in identifying the major issues. The result of their research is presented in the following chapters for the reader to enjoy.

APPENDIX: BUSINESS SERVICES INCLUDED IN THE PROPOSED REFERENCE LIST OF INDUSTRIES

The following is taken from the *Reference list of sectors: note by Secretariat*, MTN.GNS/W/50 of the Uruguay Round Group of Negotiations on Services, 13 April 1989 (mimeo, p. 4).

Rental/leasing of equipment without crew
Transport: cars, trucks, aircraft, ships etc.
Non-transport: computers, construction/demolition etc.

Real estate service (not including rental of land)
Involving owned or leased property on a fee or contract basis
(e.g. property valuation, estate management)

Installation and assembly work (other than construction)

Maintenance and repair of equipment (not including fixed structures)

Services incidental to manufacturing

Professional services (including consulting)
Agricultural, forestry and fishing services
Mining and oil-field services
Legal services
Accounting and taxation services
Management and administrative services
Architectural services
Advertising
Market research and opinion-polling
Surveying and exploration services
Advisory and consultative engineering services
Industrial engineering
Engineering design services
Project management services
Urban planning services
Interior design services
Research and development, laboratories, testing and certification
Computer-related services (including hardware-related consulting, installation, data processing etc.)
Software development (including software implementation)
Travel agents and tour operators
Economic and behavioural research
Labour recruitment and provision of personnel

Investigation and security activities
Public relations services
Photographic services
Miscellaneous professional services
Business services not included elsewhere
Biotechnology services
Cleaning of buildings and similar activities
Packaging services
Waste disposal and processing
Translation services
Exhibition management services
Printing and publishing
Other

2 Business and professional services: competing in a more mobile world

Bernard Ascher

INTRODUCTION

Political, economic and technological developments leading to growth in international trade and investment should generate greater opportunities in foreign markets not only for producers of goods, but also for providers of business and professional services.

Among the factors contributing to the global expansion of opportunities are national deregulation and privatization of industries, integration of regional economies (e.g. the European Community (EC)), structural changes in the East European economies and liberalization of trade in services through bilateral and multilateral agreements.

Advancements in transportation, communications and computer technology, and the widespread easing of travel regulations, facilitate the spread of services on a global scale by overcoming impediments of time and distance. Exposure to news and information from other countries contributes to the growth in demand for access to products and lifestyles.

As product markets and financial markets become more internationally integrated, the markets for other business and professional services are bound to follow.

In the light of these factors, in this chapter we discuss the extent to which foreigners will be able to take advantage of increased opportunities to perform services on a cross-border basis or through the establishment of offices in other countries.

TYPES OF BUSINESS AND PROFESSIONAL SERVICES

Most papers on business and professional services focus largely on management consulting, accounting, law, architecture and engineering – and this chapter is no exception. These professions are among those most likely to be engaged in international business. They are the best known and account for a large number of gainfully employed professionals. As perhaps the most highly organized of the professions, more information is available about their international activities than for other professions.[1] In addition, businesses and professionals in these fields are generally confronted with numerous restrictions on entering and operating in foreign markets.

Not to be overlooked, meanwhile, are the many other lesser-known professional and business services.[2] Although most of these are domestically oriented small businesses or owner-operated businesses, they may have a high potential for international work or may already be serving foreign clients. More importantly, however, they probably face fewer barriers to entry in foreign markets than the more highly organized professional services.

Among those providing such services are computer and communications specialists, planners of business conventions and instructional seminars, weather forecasters, scientific advisers, investment advisers, economic analysts, newsletter writers and editors, political advisors and an assortment of business consultants. Although many of these enterprises are small, they may well be the types of businesses that can benefit from freer international mobility of persons, services, money, and information. Even though the individual enterprises are small, the cumulative total employed in such activities could be quite large.

A professional association for employees in the computer services field, for example, reports that US companies are competing in the $37 billion high-technology service market in Europe. The group has 6,000 members in forty-two countries. High-technology services are defined as services sold to support computers, such as the repair of hardware and software, managing and running a company's computer operations and consultations on how to build a computer room (Green 1990). As another example, US political consultants estimate that revenues from overseas political work have jumped several hundred per cent in the last couple of years[3] (Polman 1990).

OPPORTUNITIES FOR PROFESSIONAL SERVICES

Employment in business and professional services in the USA is growing more rapidly than employment in other service sectors. As laws and businesses become more complex and technical, the need for professionals with up-to-date knowledge and skills becomes more acute. Some companies are attempting to develop or upgrade their in-house capabilities, whereas others rely on outside contractors for these services.

For similar reasons, the conduct of international business requires more services of this kind. Not only do businesses need to deal with the complexities of their own home market but, in order to keep up with competition, they may need to become familiar with a variety of foreign markets as well. This calls for greater use of specialized expertise – lawyers, economists, marketing specialists, management consultants, financial and tax advisors and government relations and public relations specialists. Indeed, such specialized services are becoming more important as businesses strive for more efficient operations on a broader scale and in a more competitive environment.

Without question, markets for business and professional services around the world will be growing in coming years. The extent of growth will depend upon a great many factors – political, economic and social. The trends toward regional and international economic integration, buttressed by improved transportation and communication, virtually ensure continued demand for a wide range of technical advisors and specialists to assist manufacturers, distributors and investors. At the same time, the current Persian Gulf crisis reminds us how important peace and political stability are to the process of international economic integration.

TAKING ADVANTAGE OF OPPORTUNITIES

Newer methods of communications through computers, fax machines, video phones and conference calls make it possible to serve clients from remote locations. Jet travel, for example, makes it relatively easy to meet clients face to face periodically, to engage in negotiations on the spot when necessary or to conduct on-site inspections. Portable equipment (laptop computers, car phones and faxes) also aid the travelling professional. Time-sensitive documents and other valuables can be delivered promptly through air couriers. In addition, ongoing bilateral and multilateral trade negotiations hold the prospect for reduction of barriers to market entry that will make it easier for business consultants and other professionals to perform their services for clients in other countries.

The firms and individuals who will benefit from international business will be those with the required skills and knowledge, who are aware of opportunities, who are able to seek out or attract clientele and who can overcome the commercial and regulatory barriers that confront non-national professionals. Firms with established relationships with companies that become more international also stand to gain.[4]

Those hiring such services are likely to favour local (rather than foreign) firms or individuals if qualifications and all other factors are equal. Sometimes, however, a foreign-based firm with a well-known name and reputation for excellence may be favoured, particularly if its rates are competitive or if an 'outside' independent perspective is desired.

If the choice is between a large firm or a private individual, the client is likely to favour the firm (assuming no wide disparity in cost). If the choice is between the local office of a large, foreign-based international firm and a large domestic company, ordinarily the domestic firm is likely to be favoured, unless the foreign-based company has some special expertise.

Firms and individuals, domestic or foreign, with good reputations, special skills and expertisewill be able to compete successfully for business opportunities. Those with good international connections will have a considerable advantage over new entrants who can be expected to experience more difficulties in gaining clients.

American law firms, in particular, have obtained foreign business in recent years because of their skills and expertise in structuring and arranging corporate takeovers and privatizations of government-owned enterprises, as well as in international arbitration aimed at resolving disputes out of court.[5] World-class architects are in demand in Japan because of their new ideas and modern designs (Normile 1989).

RESPONSES OF FIRMS AND INDIVIDUALS

Firms and individuals can take advantage of growing opportunities in a variety of ways, depending upon the circumstances.

Firms may seek a certain level of commercial presence within the foreign market. They may do so by establishing their own office, by entering into a joint venture with a local partner or simply by contracting or subcontracting on major projects. International accounting firms generally operate through affiliations of general partnerships. Major law firms operate in several ways: independently, through partnerships with other law firms, through partnerships with non-law firms (cross-discipline conglomerates) and through loose affiliations. Some architectural and engineering firms maintain offices in foreign locations; some subcontract without establishing more permanent local offices. In advertising, companies enter foreign markets by acquiring existing firms and by establishing joint ventures with local firms (*Fortune* 1982; Galante 1984; Commins 1990; Crenshaw 1990; *Economist* 1990; Timberlake 1990).

Unlike firms, individuals are more likely to serve foreign clients from their home country, relying on cross-border communication coupled with occasional travel by the professional and/or the client, rather than assuming the expense of opening an office in the foreign market. An alternative for individuals or small businesses is to establish a commercial presence by arranging some kind of association with a professional located in the foreign country.

The market entry question itself has spawned new businesses that act as intermediaries between foreign and domestic companies or that serve as 'instant overseas operating divisions' for foreign companies (*Japan Economic Journal* 1984).

BARRIERS TO BUSINESS AND PROFESSIONAL SERVICES

To some extent, decisions on how to provide professional services internationally, i.e. through cross-border activities from remote locations or through offices established in other countries will depend upon conditions, attitudes and the nature of formal and informal barriers in particular countries.

Foreign-based companies and foreign individuals will probably find it easier to compete against domestic companies and individuals in the host country in fields that do not require professional accreditation or official certification.[6]

Conversely, it will be more difficult for foreign-based firms and individuals to compete against domestic companies and individuals in fields that require professional accreditation from a government or private body.

While many business services are relatively free of restriction and benefit from the trend toward growing internationalization of services, the accredited professional services (law, accounting, architecture, engineering) remain inhibited by numerous barriers to entry of foreigners.[7]

The barriers to individuals and firms in business and professional services have been outlined and discussed in various publications (US Government 1983; Feketekuty 1986, 1988; Noyelle and Dutka 1987). A brief description is pertinent here.

In attempting to serve foreign clients, individuals face licensing-type restrictions by government and/or professional bodies, including:

1 non-recognition of credentials and qualifications;
2 pre-conditions for licensing:
   (a) requirements for local education;
   (b) requirements for revalidation of college degrees;
   (c) requirements for additional education in the host country and practical experience in the host country;
   (d) the passing of an examination;
3 requirements for citizenship and residence in the host country.

Individuals who travel for temporary periods to visit foreign clients or to work in foreign branch offices may encounter visa or work permit problems. Those who seek to migrate to another country to practice their profession or establish a business service face immigration problems.

Firms face restrictions on foreign ownership (including licensing requirements); the use of the international firm name; the scope of practice;

the hiring of nationals and/or non-nationals; the temporary entry of personnel; the flow of funds (through exchange controls, taxation or other means) affecting repatriation of earnings and transfers to other offices; the flow of information; and government procurement.

In some countries, foreign individuals and/or firms may not be able to perform the same range of activities as in the home country.[8] The practice of foreign lawyers, for example, may be limited in a number of respects: they may be permitted to give legal advice only on international law or their own country's law or only on certain types of transactions (offshore) or only to certain clients (non-nationals); they may have to use the title legal consultant, rather than attorney or lawyer; they may not be permitted to appear before a court or to join the local bar association or, if they appear in court, they may have to be accompanied by a domestic/local lawyer; they may not be permitted to hire local lawyers or join a local law firm, or become a partner in a local law firm; they may not be able to use their home country law firm name; and they may be prohibited from advertising, while local lawyers are permitted to do so.[9]

Likewise, accountants may also face limits to their scope of practice in foreign countries; i.e. they may not be permitted to sign audits or they may have to represent themselves as bookkeepers or tax advisors; they may not be able to serve as management consultants or investment advisors etc. Foreign architects and engineers may not be permitted to sign building designs or blueprints for construction and would have to collaborate with local firms that are authorized to do so.

Practices of a profession may vary from country to country, which adds to the problems of international comparison. The USA has a single class of lawyers, whereas the UK has barristers and solicitors and Belgium has 'avocats', 'notaires' and 'conseillers juridique'. Within professions also there are numerous specialties. The American Medical Association recognizes seventy-nine medical specialty organizations and US universities confer 150 different baccalaureate degrees in engineering.

In the EC, under Article 52 of the 1960 Treaty of Rome, rights of professionals to practice their skills where they wish were to have been established within ten years of the formation of the Community. To carry this out, the European Commission originally sought to formulate directives that would harmonize the qualifications needed for specific professions. Such directives were adopted for doctors, dentists, nurses, veterinarians, architects, midwives and pharmacists (*Financial Times* 1985).

More recently, however, the Commission has changed its approach by proposing a general directive that would set up a system for mutual recognition of professional qualifications of degree or equivalent level. In the future, professionals such as lawyers, accountants, teachers, surveyors and engineers will have their qualifications recognized throughout the EC. At most, they will have to take a bridging course in the peculiarities of their new country (*Financial Times* 1988).

RATIONALE FOR REGULATION OF PROFESSIONS

Professions may be subject to self-regulation and/or regulation by governments. Self-regulation generally is for the purpose of assuring competence and quality for the public. Professional societies or associations set technical standards for education and experience and other criteria for accreditation of professionals, as well as ethical standards. Government regulations are intended to protect consumers.

Professional bodies are often criticized for discriminating against non-residents and for limiting the number of practitioners to keep income at a high level. The absence of regulation, however, could lead to abusive practices as in the case of doctors, telemarketers and others (Engel 1985; Quimpo 1990).

SERVICES TRADE NEGOTIATIONS

As part of the current GATT negotiations, known as the Uruguay Round, member countries are attempting to develop a set of internationally acceptable rules and principles that would apply to services trade – including business and professional services. These multilateral negotiations, launched in September 1986, involve the bulk of the ninety-seven member countries. After failing to conclude in December 1990 as originally scheduled, the negotiations resumed in February 1991.

A basic goal in these negotiations is to establish fair and non-discriminatory treatment of foreign suppliers of services selling from abroad or through local facilities. Establishing the right of foreign suppliers to sell their services in the national market under no less favourable conditions than those services sold by national suppliers ('national treatment') would afford non-discriminatory treatment *vis-à-vis* domestic firms. Assuring transparency of regulations affecting foreign suppliers by requiring due notice of pending changes in regulations and providing an opportunity for interested parties to comment also would facilitate the operations of foreign service providers. The agreement also would provide a procedure for identification and notification of discriminatory or unfair practices and 'protectionist' measures, along with a means of formal consultation and dispute settlement.

For regulated services, liberalization could be in the form of rules and principles asserting that the right of individuals to practise will be based on objective criteria. Criteria that automatically discriminate against foreigners, such as citizenship or residency requirements, would not be acceptable. While the sovereign right of a country to regulate would be recognized, it would be clear that such regulation should not be used as a guise to protect national practitioners from competing with foreigners.

In themselves, these principles and rules may not remove barriers and accord market entry. The establishment of technical standards for determining qualification or accreditation can still be controversial in government or private bodies that set the requirements. Thus, it will probably be necessary to seek standards that are mutually recognized or internationally recognized for a given profession.

A difficulty with regulation by private bodies is that it raises possible problems for governments where the need to deliver on international commitments could conflict with the need to respect the independence of private professional bodies (Barton 1986: 100).

The US–Canada Free Trade Agreement provides a mechanism for the development of mutually acceptable professional standards and criteria for architects. The agreement acknowledges that the Royal Architectural Institute of Canada and the American Institute of Architects are endeavouring to develop such standards and criteria on education, examination, experience, conduct and ethics, and professional development. Progress is being made along these lines, but the original target date of 31 December 1989 was not met. This mechanism has stimulated interest on the part of other professional groups in both countries (e.g. engineering).

Those performing services of an unregulated nature may encounter fewer problems in providing their services to foreigners. One problem they generally face – similar to those in regulated professions – is gaining temporary admission into some countries to perform their services. Liberalization in this area will be difficult because of the political sensitivity of immigration laws in most countries.

The US–Canada Free Trade Agreement facilitates, on a reciprocal basis, the movement of US and Canadian citizens across each country's border for business purposes by establishing provisions for certain business visitors, traders and investors, professionals and intra-company transferees. This may be too ambitious an undertaking in a multilateral setting, but the adoption of more flexible rules for temporary entry of certain professionals and specially skilled or key personnel would be a step forward in reducing these barriers.

France, Germany and Benelux signed an agreement in June (the Schengen Agreement) to remove all immigration controls between the five countries, effective at the end of 1991. This group of countries can be expanded to include additional signatories (Nelson 1990).

INFORMAL BARRIERS

A word about informal barriers is appropriate here. These comprise a variety of traditional practices, ethics and longstanding ingrained attitudes that tend to militate against dealing with foreigners. Differences in language and even foreign accents work against businessmen and others seeking to provide goods or services in another country.[10] These types of barriers, usually subtle and unwritten, cannot be overcome easily. International agreements would probably be ineffective in dealing with these types of barriers.

CONCLUSIONS

1 Continuation of the current political, economic and technological trends will make it easier to market business and professional services internationally, particularly for services that are unregulated.
2 Those engaged in unregulated business and professional services probably face fewer barriers than those in regulated professions.
3 Major trading nations are hopeful that current GATT negotiations will lead to the removal or reduction of barriers to international trade in business and professional services.
4 For regulated services, liberalization could be in the form of rules and principles asserting that the right of individuals and firms to practise will be based on objective criteria; that qualification or accreditation should not be based on nationality; and that country requirements should not be used as a guise to exclude competition from foreigners.
5 An international agreement that merely iterates a principle of non-discrimination and/or recognizes the need for international standards for professional services may not be sufficient to liberalize restrictive practices. Additional provisions would be needed to translate the principle into steps that actually confer equal treatment by removing requirements such as those that can only be met by residing, studying and/or practising within a given country.
6 Regulation to meet consumer protection needs will require some balance against the inefficiencies and other problems created when such regulation is used as a guise for discrimination against foreigners.
7 Those performing services of an unregulated nature face problems of gaining temporary admission in some countries to conduct their business or provide their service. Regulated professionals generally face the same problems. Liberalization will be difficult because of the sensitivity of immigration laws in most countries. More flexible rules for temporary entry of certain professionals and specially skilled or key personnel

would constitute a step forward to facilitating performance of services internationally.

8   Informal barriers are generally more difficult to overcome inasmuch as they involve longstanding traditions and personal attitudes in different cultures. Governments can deal more easily with matters reflected in laws and regulations than with subtle, unwritten forces that tend to impede transactions with foreigners supplying business and professional services.

FURTHER RESEARCH NEEDED

This chapter was intended to provide an overview of the prospects for providers of business and professional services in foreign markets.

Time did not permit an in-depth examination of various problems concerning international competitiveness. Three aspects in particular warrant further study and analysis.

First, of great interest to policy-makers are the potential consequences of growth in international sourcing of services. Common belief is that services, unlike goods, are not susceptible to separability in the production process. Under this assumption, functions that require less skill, less specialized knowledge and labour-intensive activities in producing services generally cannot be isolated and performed at different locations, including offshore. However, this is not true for all services. Office-type work is already being performed at locations far from the headquarters of many companies (e.g. key punching, insurance claims processing, coupon sorting, airline ticket recordkeeping etc.). This is occurring not only in labour-intensive services, but in some professional services as well (e.g. software development, engineering, medical testing).

Further analysis would be useful in estimating the job creation and job displacement effects of greater mobility of service production on an international scale. To be most effective, such analysis will probably have to review individual business or professional services or, perhaps, certain functions that may be common to several types of services.

Second, more information is needed on the great number and variety of business and professional services in order to assess their collective importance in domestic and international business. Many of these are small or individually operated businesses. Little or no official statistics are available on births, deaths, expansions or contractions of such enterprises and the extent of their international involvement.

Third, more work is needed to describe and analyse various informal barriers and to explore means of dealing with them. This subject sparked a lively discussion at the conference with participants contributing examples of practices and attitudes in various countries that create potential problems for foreign service suppliers (e.g. no-interest banking, 'capitalist devils', restrictions on advertising of products and services, attitudes toward the opposite sex, etc.).

Perhaps some of this work can be carried out for a future conference.

NOTES

The views expressed herein are those of the author and do not necessarily represent the views of the US Trade Representative or any other US Government agency.

1 This chapter does not attempt to define the term 'profession'. Discussions of what constitutes a profession can be found in Carr-Saunders and Wilson (1964), Coats (1985), Parsons (1968), Millerson (1964), Vollmer and Mills (1966) and Goode (1957).

2 Space does not permit a full discussion or description of business and professional services. This paper takes a broad, general approach. Lists of business and professional services can be found in Nusbaumer (1987b), Mallampally (1990), Schedule 2 to Annex 1502.1 of the US–Canada Free Trade Agreement, and US Standard Industrial Classification Manual (1987).

3 Also, see *The Economist*, (1990d) (re: Sawyer Miller Group, American consultants who helped run the campaign of Peruvian presidential candidate, Mario Vargas Llosa).

4 More than 2,000 consultants, mostly American, are established in Brussels to be close to the governing body of the EC and to advise their clients on European trade and investment policies and regulations (see *New York Times* 1989). Similarly, Japanese clients reportedly spent $100–150 million in 1989 for the services of Washington lawyers and public relations advisors to lobby the US Government on trade (see Pine 1990).

5 Examples of such activities of US law firms in a number of countries are included in Labaton (1988).

6 Richard Edwards observes that 'Mobility restrictions are least severe for the most unskilled workers (who may migrate clandestinely) and for the very top of the management ladder. But for employees in the broad middle categories of semi-skilled, skilled, and educated labor, the barriers are highly limiting.' This applies to the professions as well. Restrictions are least severe for world-class professionals and for those in non-accredited professions. (See Edwards (1990).

7 See the *Financial Times* (1985), which poses the question: 'What rights do EEC hairdressers, cemetery directors, and midwives enjoy which are denied to accountants, architects, and opticians?'

8 Note also that scope of practice may be a domestic issue as well as an international one. An American Bar Association panel, for example, has recommended that law firms with two or more lawyers be prohibited from owning or operating a subsidiary providing non-legal services. (See *National Journal* 1990.)

9 For specific restrictions applicable in Japan, including an American law firm's fear of using the company name on bowling shirts at a Tokyo Christmas party, see Feldberg (1990); for restrictions in France, see Schwartz (1990).

10 The *Economist* (1988c) discusses language differences as a problem in integrating the economies of the twelve member states of the EC, a land of 320 million people with nine official languages. One-third of the EC budget goes to pay for translation and interpretation. Languages and cultures are among Europe's greatest assets, but they also constitute a barrier. As an example, fewer than 2,000 of the EC's 600,000 doctors change country each year, although their qualifications are valid throughout the Community.

3   Effects of GATT rules on trade in professional services

Richard H. Snape

INTRODUCTION

As the Uruguay Round of multilateral trade negotiations approaches completion, it is appropriate to consider the manner in which professional service firms may be affected by the rules for international trade in services which may be forthcoming. And even if a full set of trading rules is not settled at the end of the Round, it is unlikely that the matter will rest there: 'Countries have no intention of letting four years of hard bargaining go to waste' (*The Economist*, 1990b, quoting a 'GATT insider').

Until now the rules governing international trade in professional and other services have been largely determined unilaterally or bilaterally. Those who have been pressing for international GATT-type rules have seen such rules as a means to reduce barriers to international trade. The GATT framework has been chosen for a number of reasons: unlike some other international fora, the GATT has succeeded in securing substantial liberalization. It has not been primarily a talking and posturing forum on the one hand; on the other hand it has a very broad coverage so that, in general, it has not been concerned with defending the interests of the producers of particular products or particular countries. There are, of course, exceptions. Agriculture, clothing and textiles have been problem products, while developing countries have received special and differential treatment. But nevertheless the GATT, as a *general* agreement (general with respect to country and commodity coverage), has been seen to be pretty successful in facilitating liberalization of trade in goods.

Those who have sought to have professional services in particular embraced by the trading rules for services have been concerned that the rules should liberalize existing modes of delivery, should open up modes where currently they are prohibited and should facilitate choice between the modes. Trade liberalization and well-defined and transparent trading rules will give firms more options for the international delivery of services than they have enjoyed in the past.

While the intention of those who have been seeking a GATT-type agreement to cover international trade in services is for it to facilitate trade liberalization, there is always the risk that the rules will turn out to be trade restricting. This can occur either because the rules themselves are essentially restricting (as in the Multifibre Arrangement, which largely removes clothing and textile trade from the coverage of the GATT, or the UNCTAD Liner Code for shipping, which seeks to allocate 80 per cent of the trade between any two countries equally between ships of the two countries), or because otherwise liberalizing rules provide machinery for exceptions or provide loopholes and the exceptions and loopholes come to dominate. The provisions of the GATT regarding anti-dumping and countervailing duties and balance of payments provisions for developing countries provide such exceptions, while 'voluntary export restraints' exploit a loophole. Of course, one can never be sure of the counterfactual: tight rules with exceptions and loopholes may facilitate more trade liberalization than weak rules with no exceptions, or no rules at all. Tight rules with no exceptions or loopholes may not be an option.

Trade in services and trade in goods are intertwined and so, therefore, are trade policies for services and for goods. For example, a restriction on the imports of automobiles may lead instead to imports of automobile design and engineering services to facilitate domestic manufacture. Conversely, a restriction on the imports of such services, or on the forms in which they can be delivered, may lead to increased imports of automobiles. Trade liberalization that embraces both goods and services provides less distorted choices for the delivery of services, including the choice of whether the services should be 'embodied' in traded goods or whether they should be traded as services *per se*. While this interconnection between goods and services is very important in practice, in the rest of this chapter we concentrate on trade policies and trade with respect to services themselves, and leave on one side the overlap with goods.

MODES OF DELIVERY AND BARRIERS

The manners in which professional services may be traded illustrate how services as a whole may be traded. Some can be traded at a distance without the service providers and receivers being in close proximity: the writing of computer software is an example. Some involve the movement of service providers, as in the case of an architectural firm or a surgeon. Others require the movement of capital, perhaps because equity is required as a condition of knowledge transfer, for example. In other cases it is the service receiver who moves, as in the case of many education services.[1]

Barriers to international trade exist for each mode of delivery. Some countries restrict the movement of their citizens abroad even for such purposes as education and surgery, as well as for lighter matters such as tourism. But among most of the major trading countries of the world, such barriers are of lesser importance as obstacles to trade in professional services compared with barriers to other forms of transaction.

Barriers also exist to trade in professional services which is conducted at a distance, through the electronic media or postal service for example, though it is often difficult to enforce such barriers, particularly in democratic societies. Some countries (e.g. Brazil) have restricted access to foreign information and information processing services in an effort to develop their own information processing industries. Many countries restrict the provision at retail level of foreign news services, for economic or political reasons. Again, many restrict the placing of contracts abroad for advertising and other services which would not involve the movement of the service provider or of the client. Even though technological development is reducing the impact and enforceability of many such barriers, they remain important for many services and particularly for those for which access to a local distribution system in the host country is essential.

But a great deal of the focus of those who would reduce barriers to trade in professional and other services has been in relation to trade for which the service provider moves to the country of the service receiver, on either a short- or a long-term basis. 'Rights of establishment' is an important issue here, and one for which the GATT does not contain any provisions with respect to trade in goods. The GATT has its most direct application to trade in services for those services which can be transacted at a distance. Such trade in services is very similar to trade in goods. Where the movement of factors of production is involved the GATT gives little direct guidance, though its principles can be applied. Important questions here on the one hand relate to visas, work permits and restrictions on practice including recognition of qualifications and prudential requirements, and on the other hand relate to questions of permitted business structures, direct investment, participation by locals and restrictions on placing contracts with foreign-owned firms. Questions relating to foreign investment and temporary migration are inevitably thorny, but they are by no means the whole of the matter of barriers to trade in professional services and much would be lost if disagreement on these matters were to hold up agreement on the simpler issues.

DEVELOPMENT OF TRADING RULES

Several documents have emerged on services from the Uruguay Round of multilateral trade negotiations. The first comprises the decisions taken at the mid-term review, finalized in April 1989, by the Trade Negotiations Committee; next was a draft developed by the Group of Negotiations on Services (GNS) titled 'Elements for a draft which would permit negotiations to take place for the completion of all parts of the multilateral framework' (referred to below as Elements). This modestly named document, dated December 1989, put flesh on the agreements made at the mid-term review and incorporated alternative positions on most issues. These alternatives were ensconced in square brackets; someone counted 167 sets of such square brackets. The third document was a draft agreement placed by the Chairman of the GNS, on his own responsibility, before the Trade Negotiations Committee in July 1990. Titled *'Draft multilateral framework for trade in services'*, this document has been revised as the negotiations have proceeded. At the time of the conference the latest revision of the whole document was dated 14 September 1990, though there are further draft revisions of particular Articles which are dated 9 October 1990. This *Draft Framework* (as we shall call it), together with these draft revisions, form the basis of the following discussion. While some of the details have been overtaken by subsequent drafts, most of the questions of principle remain.

Attention is now given to the broad principles which are being applied in these documents and the implications for trade in professional services of the main principles and the most important formulations of their application. The manner in which the overall structure has evolved is for a framework agreement to cover services as a whole and then for there to be sectoral annexes and schedules which will make such exemptions or applications as are deemed necessary to particular service industries.

A distinction is often made in trade negotiations between positive and negative list approaches. A positive list approach specifies those items to be included, all others being excluded. A negative list approach specifies those items not to be included, all others being included. Negative lists are generally regarded as being more trade liberalizing than positive lists in the framework of liberalizing trade agreements, particularly over time when new items (for example, new products or means of transacting) will be covered unless they are specifically exempted. In looking at the *Draft Framework* we give particular attention to whether it took a positive or negative list approach with respect to coverage and the manner in which trade is controlled. As will be seen it is not always clear which approach was taken.

Coverage

The mid-term review agreement stated that the multilateral framework may include all the forms of transacting services which were mentioned above: cross-border trade itself and trade which involves the movement of service receivers and/or producers. The Draft framework adopts this coverage quite explicitly. It provides that

> for the purposes of this Agreement, trade in services covers transactions involving the cross-border supply of the service as well as: (a) cross-border movement of consumers of the service; (b) cross-border movement of the providers of the service; (c) the establishment of commercial presence; for the effective production, distribution, marketing, sales or delivery of a service.

(Article I)

The coverage thus appears to be very wide. Permanent migration is, of course, not covered as migration changes the nationality of the migrant and it is thus in a sense trade in the owner of services rather than in the services themselves.

Coverage of all modes of trade does not imply that all these modes will in fact be allowed for all services: it simply states what the agreement can cover. It might be noted that Article I of the Draft framework appears to cover direct investment as well as other forms of investment. The draft coverage is much wider than that which was expressed in some earlier versions of the Article.

The nature of coverage of the particular rules of the agreement is specified in Article XIX and draft introductory sentences for the relevant parts of the agreement contained in the revisions of 9 October 1990. With respect to general obligations and disciplines, which are contained in Part II, Article XIX states that they 'shall be applied to all sectors by all parties in accordance with any relevant sectoral annexes'. For specific commitments, contained in Part III, it states that the provisions 'shall be applied by each party to the relevant sectors, sub-sectors and modes of delivery covered in its schedule, in accordance with the negotiated specific commitments set out therein'. With respect to Part II the thrust is a negative list: all parties and sectors are covered unless specifically excluded. The wording for Part III however, tends to leave open whether the lists should be positive or negative though, as we shall see later, the bias in the details appears to be towards positive lists.

The coverage of the agreement is greatly reduced, particularly for professional services, by the explicit exclusion of government procurement from coverage by the key Articles of the agreement. These Articles, which relate to non-discrimination and national treatment, are not to apply to procurement that is 'covered by public procurement laws and regulations', though the Draft framework states that parties should try to secure agreement to extend the coverage of the agreement 'in its entirety' to such procurement (Article XIII). This exclusion of government procurement is consistent with the GATT with respect to goods. However, the Government Procurement Code (GPC) (for goods), which was negotiated as part of the Tokyo Round of multilateral trade negotiations in the 1970s, effectively negates this exclusion for signatories to this code.

While it is understandable that in such new territory as a multilateral agreement on services a step-by-step approach would be taken and government procurement is a sensitive area in many countries (including federations), this exclusion could be particularly important for a whole range of professional services, for it covers government agencies as well as government itself and in many countries the government sector is the major purchaser of professional services. It may be that the view is being taken that government procurement is best handled through extension to services of the GPC, though such extension, draft or otherwise, has not yet surfaced.

There are several standard exceptions to coverage of the agreement: measures necessary for the protection of public morals, safety, health and the environment. But in the relevant Article (XIV) there is also a square bracketed exemption for the protection of cultural values. If this exemption were to be adopted it could affect the coverage of the agreement considerably, particularly in relation to cinema advertising, television, education and entertainment services. There is a very extensive range of industry protection which can be sheltered under the cultural values umbrella.

It has been reported that the USA, having been the prime mover in the whole GATT-for-services exercise, wishes to extract maritime, aviation, and telecommunication services. Such action could lead to other countries seeking to exclude other services which they deem to be politically sensitive in their countries; all the dominoes could fall. It is possible that sections of the first two of these industries will be excluded only from the most favoured nation (MFN) (non-discrimination) provisions of the agreement by means of an annex; such an approach would leave the industries subject to the other provisions of the agreement and to full incorporation into the agreement at a later date. A problem with telecommunications is the nature of competition between a privately owned partially competitive network in the USA and government-owned monopoly systems in other countries.

Concepts, Principles and Rules

The following concepts, principles and rules were considered relevant in

the mid-term review: transparency, progressive liberalization, national treatment, MFN (non-discrimination), market access (and this to be on the basis of
the preferred mode of delivery), increasing participation of the developing
countries, safeguards and exceptions, and the 'regulatory situation'. Most of
these 'concepts, principles and rules' derive from the GATT, though two do
not: market access and regulatory situation. 'Regulatory situation' recognizes
'that governments regulate services sectors' and that the right to regulate must
be taken into account. Even free trade in services then would not imply absence
of regulation of service provision or the prohibition of new regulations.
'Market access' has become very important in affecting the direction of the
negotiations: further comment is left until later.

We now focus on the concepts which derive from the GATT, as well as
those concepts which are imported from other sources, and the manner of
their adaptation to services. In so doing we note in particular the implications of these concepts for trade in professional services. All the specified
'concepts, principles and rules', except for market access, national
treatment and progressive liberalization, have been incorporated into the
'general obligations and disciplines' of Part II of the *Draft Framework*;
market access and national treatment comprise the specific obligations of
Part III, while Part IV comprises the progressive liberalization provisions.

Most favoured nation (non-discrimination)

Unconditional MFN is the GATT's expression of non-discrimination. Not
only is it at the core of the GATT, but many take the view that it is at the
core of multilateralism (Tumlir 1985). The MFN of the GATT is unconditional – any benefit given by one contracting party to another country
(and not just another contracting party) must be 'accorded immediately and
unconditionally to the like product originating in or destined for' all other
contracting parties (Article I). Exceptions exist for free trade areas and
customs unions and for preferences for exports of developing countries.
GATT's MFN is unconditional; i.e. benefits do not have to be 'bought'
one-by-one for them to be received by all members.

The essence of GATT-type MFN has been incorporated in the *Draft
Framework* (Article III), though there has been disagreement as to whether
benefits granted to countries which are not parties to the agreement have to
be extended to parties. Adoption of the GATT formulation would prevent
parties to the services agreement from making more favourable deals with
non-parties: some countries which may wish to strike deals with non-
members have opposed the imposition of this restriction.

Some difficulty has been encountered with respect to providing for the
mutual recognition of qualifications and standards and meshing this in with

non-discrimination. The *Draft Framework* (Article VII) contains the provision that where a system of mutual recognition or harmonization of qualifications etc. develops it should be open to all signatories and be applied in a non-discriminatory manner. In the 9 October draft revisions the provisions regarding harmonization are drawn into a new article which omits mention of non-discrimination but provides that any harmonization etc. agreements should be notified to the corporate body and be 'open for participation by any other party on the basis of negotiations'. Such a system could facilitate multilateral trade in professional services, though the test will be in how 'open for participation' it really is.

National Treatment and Market Access

It will be recalled that national treatment and market access comprise the two forms of specific commitments in the *Draft Framework* and that the 9 October draft revisions provide that they should be applied by each party 'in accordance with the negotiated commitments as set out in its Schedule, to the relevant sectors, sub-sectors and modes of delivery covered therein'. A great deal thus hinges on the Schedules and the manner in which the obligations are specified, these obligations being in some ways analogous to the bindings of tariffs under the GATT. It should be noted, however, that the obligations under the Article of the GATT which covers national treatment apply to *all* products and not just to the products for which the tariffs have been bound under the provisions of the GATT. Thus the national treatment provisions under the GATT are much wider than those being developed under the *Draft Framework*.

National treatment is not the same as MFN.[2] MFN relates to the differential treatment of foreign suppliers *vis-à-vis* each other, while national treatment concerns the treatment of foreigners compared with domestic producers. The GATT requires that 'internal' taxes, regulations etc. 'should not be applied to imported or domestic products so as to afford protection to domestic production' (Article III).[3] It has sometimes been implied that for some services national treatment means equality of treatment of foreigners and nationals. The word 'internal' in Article III could suggest that once a product has cleared the port of entry then no discrimination can be applied against foreign products. But what is the port of entry for services that can be traded in a disembodied or separated form – i.e. separated from the producer? And if they are 'embodied' so that movement of service providers or receivers occurs, the movement across the frontier of a service provider or receiver is not the stage at which the service is produced and traded. Thus, taxing services as they 'cross the frontier' is frequently not feasible or appropriate.

Perhaps a better way to approach the GATT provision with respect to national treatment is to note that the GATT authorizes or legitimizes certain forms of discrimination against goods produced by foreigners; the generally authorized form of discrimination according to source is an import tariff, though in some circumstances quantitative restrictions on imports are permitted. National treatment then implies that, once the authorized form of discrimination has been imposed on a product, there should be no further discrimination against foreign products.

When one views national treatment in this manner, a way in which it can be extended to services becomes apparent. As part of a general agreement on services there could be a provision for the specification of particular means of discrimination against foreign produced services. Sector-specific agreements could then identify the particular form or forms of authorized discrimination for the services in that sector, and particular levels of these forms of discrimination could be 'bound' by agreement between the parties to that agreement. National treatment would then imply that in all other matters domestic and foreign producers should be treated equally. A problem with this approach is that it could require a consideration of each service sector and of the barriers (or at least the barriers to be authorized) to trade in each. Life would be simpler if authorized forms of discrimination against foreigners, wherever possible, could be transformed into a common form such as a tariff-like impost (which in many cases could be collected at the time of production) and that, as with barriers to trade in goods, all other barriers could, in general, be proscribed in the services agreement.

The *Draft Framework* is not taking this 'tariffication' approach. And it is not at all clear whether it is calling for a positive or negative listing of barriers: i.e. a listing of those barriers which are authorized with others prohibited (negative list) or a listing of those means by which particular services may be transacted (positive list).

As noted earlier, the concept of market access is not one which is in the GATT. The concept was criticized by Arkell and Harrison at an early stage as not appearing to add anything to the GATT-derived principles. They state that

> market access appears to have been proposed for services, as an analogue to the tariff on goods, so as to provide the fixed point to which national treatment could relate, and it is proposed to specify or translate it in relation to how services are marketed. The danger with this approach is that it is an abstract and artificial construct which has been erected due to a start being made at the wrong logical standpoint. The key to the liberalization process for non-tariff barriers is more likely to lie in the principle of non-discrimination expressed in the concept of

national treatment developed so as to include both cross-border transactions and supplies from foreign owned or controlled enterprises
present or established in the market.

(1987: 14)

Although this criticism has substance, the 'market access' concept has
persisted. Its use appears to have biased the negotiations towards
negotiating access (which leads towards a positive list approach) rather
than negotiating away barriers, which steers towards a negative list.

Thus the Draft framework provides that

Parties shall make access to their markets available to services and
service providers of other parties *in accordance with the terms, conditions or limitations agreed and specified in the appropriate schedule
of each party* and in a manner consistent with the other provisions of this
Agreement . . .,

(Article XVI.I, emphasis added)

and

In conformity with other relevant provisions of this Agreement, and *as
set out in their appropriate schedules*, parties shall grant to services and
service providers of other parties, in the application of all laws . . . [etc.],
treatment no less favorable than that accorded to like domestic services
or service providers in like circumstances.

(Article XVII.1, emphasis added)

These provisions appear to suggest that it is the terms of access and national
treatment that have to be negotiated: a positive list approach. (A negative
list approach would have the word 'except' inserted in front of the italicized
sections of both Articles, with appropriate alterations after the italics.)
Further, Article XIX.2 states that

Provision relating to market access and national treatment shall be
applied by each party to the relevant sectors, sub-sectors and modes of
delivery covered in its schedule, in accordance with the negotiated
specific commitments as set out therein.

(Article XIX.2)

The draft 'Schedule of Commitments' itself, following Article XX, has as
its first column 'Limitations and conditions on market access' and a
heading 'Conditions and qualifications' with respect to national treatment
on the second column. These headings could imply open access unless
otherwise specified, this being a negative list approach. This is reinforced
by a footnote to this Article which states that

With respect to specific modes of delivery, the total absence of any limitations or conditions on market access would mean fully liberalized market access, and the total absence of any conditions or qualifications on national treatment would mean full accordance of national treatment.
(Article XIX.2)

A 9 October draft relating to initial commitments to be agreed in the Uruguay Round appears to allow either positive or negative lists. It speaks of negotiations on

commitments to bind the existing levels of market access and/or new market access undertakings, by indicating specifically limitations and conditions on market access, in its different forms prescribed in the Agreement and/or by positively indicating the specific liberalization undertaking

and

commitments to bind existing conditions and qualifications on national treatment, and/or to bind the total or partial elimination of such conditions and qualifications.

It appears that the choice is being left to the negotiators, with countries being free to choose whether they adopt a negative list or a positive list for market access and national treatment, with respect to both service coverage and the manner in which each service is traded. Given the rather mercantilist manner in which trade negotiations are conducted, including the reciprocal 'balance of concessions' approach (see below), it is unlikely that any major country would adopt a negative list for services to be covered, or for the manner of trade, unless its major trading partners do the same. The lowest common denominator – positive lists – is likely to emerge in this situation, and does.

What is the relevance of this for professional services? At issue is whether access, national treatment and every mode of access have to be negotiated for every form of professional services, current and future, or whether there is a presumption of access and national treatment with the exceptions being specified and, over time, being negotiated away. As it stands it appears that the former will be the approach adopted unless the major trading nations take a firm stance against it. If this is indeed so, then the adoption of the agreement is unlikely to be accompanied by any great reduction in trade barriers, at least in the first instance.

The *Draft Framework* provides for differential treatment between national and foreign providers of services so long as the treatment of foreigners in the host country is 'no less favorable' (Article XVII.2).

('Equivalent in effect' was the wording in an earlier draft.) For professional services this could allow for different paths for certification or for different prudential requirements for domestic and foreign suppliers, so long as the effects were no less favourable. This appears sensible. For example, governments may require the basic training of a lawyer to include a period of apprenticeship immediately after graduation. Such apprenticeship may be quite inappropriate for a senior foreigner moving to practice in another country: a test of competence and experience could suffice. But sensible or not there is plenty of scope for discrimination against foreigners and for dispute. What is 'no less favorable'? If prudential deposits are required, in which country do they have to be maintained? And so on.

Safeguards and Exceptions

Safeguard remedies under the GATT, apart from those related to balance of payments problems, are frequently classified into two types: those against 'fair' trade on the one hand and those against 'unfair' trade on the other. Before the remedies are invoked against members of the GATT, both types require injury to an industry to be caused by the trade in question. The level of injury required to permit action against 'unfair' trade is lower than against 'fair' trade. (The acceptance of these terms for expository purposes is not meant to imply that there is any economic content to the terms 'fair' and 'unfair'.) In relation to injury caused by increased but fair trade, the GATT permits the use of temporary tariffs with the possibility of compensation to foreign exporters who are harmed by the tariffs (Article XIX). Unfair trade refers to exports promoted by subsidies or 'dumped' exports: the remedies permitted by the GATT against these are countervailing and anti-dumping import duties respectively.

An important question here for both fair and unfair trade in services relates to the remedies which may be invoked. For services which are traded across borders the remedies could be similar to those for goods – an import duty determined by the nature of injury-causing imports – though the Draft framework does not address this. But what remedies should be invoked where factors of production have moved to the host country in order to supply the services? Should there be any remedies? Should expulsion and expropriation be among the remedies for injury caused by fair or unfair trading? Answers to these questions are not provided in the *Draft Framework* nor in the earlier document Elements but they are of major importance to trade in professional services as well as in other types of services.

In relation to fair trade the *Draft Framework* follows the GATT with respect to 'serious injury' being required or threatened to a domestic industry 'as a result of unforeseen developments and of the effect of a specific commitment of a party under this agreement' in order for a remedy to be invoked. And like the GATT, it allows for the suspension of commitments to the extent and for the time necessary to remedy the injury. But there is dispute as to whether these actions can be taken only as a consequence of a service 'imported into the territory' of a party (presumably this means the cross-border movement of the service) or in relation to such imports *and* supplies from 'a foreign service supplier' (presumably located within the territory of the party seeking to take remedial action). If it were to include the latter form of provision, then presumably a 'commitment' which could be suspended could be one in relation to local establishment – a form of remedy which is not relevant under the GATT. There is much yet to be sorted out here.

In relation to the safeguard measures the Draft framework speaks of injury to a 'like service'. One may ask what is a 'like service'. The term 'like product' has been used in the GATT in relation to safeguards for fair and unfair trade, and occasionally problems have arisen in defining 'like' when products are differentiated. Services are frequently personalized for the particular demander or market and are generally much more differentiated than goods. So one can expect the term 'like service' to add significantly to the income of trade lawyers.

Subsidies

Many governments have been concerned to constrain those subsidies of foreign governments which promote the exports of goods, particularly agricultural products. It is not surprising that those governments sought to have constraints on export-promoting subsidies built in to a services agreement. While other remedies exist against export promoting subsidies for goods, under the Subsidies Code of the GATT in practice the main remedy, and the only really effective one, is the levying of countervailing duties.

The Article (XV) relating to subsidies in the *Draft Framework* provides for notification of trade-affecting subsidies, for consultation and for parties to 'enter into negotiations with a view to developing the necessary multilateral disciplines to avoid the distortive effect of subsidies on trade in services'. This appears to be innocuous, but it pays to consider the provisions with respect to subsidies in the GATT and how they have been interpreted.

A key element in determining whether a subsidy is countervailable or not under the GATT, particularly in the USA which is the main user of this provision, is the specificity of the subsidy. An important US judicial decision on this matter occurred in relation to the import of fresh-cut roses from Israel (Mundheim and Ehrenhaft 1984: 106). Injury to the relevant US industry was established but it was held that the subsidization in question – being that of horticultural research in Israel – was not specific enough to the cultivation or export of roses to be regarded as an export-promoting subsidy.

For exports of professional services the subsidies for professional education which exist throughout the world, and even in the USA, could be regarded as export-promoting subsidies under the principles that have been adopted in the US courts. The implication of this is that firms in those countries in which education of a fairly specific nature is provided by the state may find it difficult to determine prices for the provision of their professional services which will not make them targets for remedies (the remedies are yet to be determined in the agreement), or at least make them targets for harassment in this regard. Similarly, those firms which are engaged in employing the professional services of foreigners in supplying their own market, or in exporting, may need to be cautious in regard to the hiring of labour which has not had to pay the full cost of the specific training which is being utilized.

Dumping

Under the GATT, dumping is defined as exporting at prices below those prevailing for a 'like product' in the home market of the exporter (Article VI).[4] If the appropriate level of injury is sustained as a consequence of dumping, anti-dumping duties can be imposed. The extent of the anti-dumping duties is limited by the extent of the dumping. Under the Anti-Dumping Code (ADC) negotiated in the Tokyo Round of multilateral trade negotiations, which purports to interpret the relevant GATT Article, a preferred means to deal with dumping is to form an arrangement between the parties under which the exporter raises the price above the 'dumping' level through price undertakings (Article VII).

When applied to professional services these provisions have some striking implications, many of which are analysed by Hoekman and Leidy (1991). The provisions would imply, for example, that if a US accounting firm, for services provided from the USA, charged less for the same service (i.e. a like product or service) for an Indian company than it did for a US client, it could be subject to anti-dumping action in India. An anti-dumping duty may or may not be appropriate but it is quite reasonable to assume that the 'arrangements' favoured by the ADC could be forthcoming under threat of some form of anti-dumping action. Many countries have not been users of the anti-dumping provisions with respect to goods, often having other instruments with which to restrict imports. But if other barriers are constrained with respect to trade in services, anti-dumping actions could be a significant barrier to the export of professional services. This would apply particularly to those services for which the demand is more elastic on the export than on the domestic market and for which the exporter would normally wish to charge a lower price on the export market.

As it stands the *Draft Framework* does not contain any provisions with respect to dumping, but it is incomplete, and the earlier Elements document contained a square bracketed section that stated that the framework should cover dumping. Dumping could yet be incorporated; indeed with the concern in many countries regarding unfair trade and the action which the European Economic Community took against the 'non-commercial' advantages of the shipping services of a Korean shipping firm, Hyundai (Messerlin 1990: 139), it would be surprising if a provision relating to dumping were not to be included. But if it is it will create many problems, not least for professional services, as noted above.

Reciprocity

One principle running through the GATT which also has run through the negotiations for a services agreement is that of reciprocity. Although it was not listed explicitly as one of the headings of the mid-term review, it surfaces in Elements and the *Draft Framework*. Any analysis of a services agreement, its relation to the GATT and its implications for professional services would be incomplete without consideration of reciprocity.

The term reciprocity has many meanings and applications (Bhagwati 1988a: ch. 2; Cline 1983). At one end of the spectrum is product-specific bilateral reciprocity. This would imply that, for example, the USA would only allow the import of Korean shoes if Korea allowed imports of US shoes under the same conditions. Applied to professional services, the USA would allow Korean lawyers to practise in the USA if Korea allowed US lawyers to practise, on the same terms, in Korea. At the other end of the spectrum is a much broader approach to reciprocity, that which is the GATT norm. Under this there is a balance of concessions, both as an 'entry price' to the GATT and as part of the ongoing barrier reduction under the GATT. Deals are concluded across goods in general, with exchanges of concessions (barrier reductions or bindings – i.e. commitments not to increase barriers) ranging widely over products and sectors and, under unconditional MFN, with concessions being automatically extended to all members of the GATT. The concessions are in terms of reductions of trade barriers and guarantees against increases of the barriers beyond specified levels (binding), rather than in terms of equality of access: this has been termed 'first difference reciprocity' (Bhagwati 1988a: 36).

Concern over foot-dragging and free-riding in negotiations and over the US trade deficit has led, over the last decade or so, to pressure for a more bilateral, product-specific approach to trade policy, with more of a focus on equality of access rather than a first difference approach to reciprocity. Thus the benefits under the Subsidies Code of the GATT are extended only to those who have signed the code and (in the case of the USA) are judged to have complied with the terms of the code, rather than being extended to all members of the GATT. Further actions under Super 301 of the Omnibus Trade and Competitiveness Act of the USA are aimed at market opening quite outside the terms of the GATT and are inconsistent with obligations under the GATT.

The Draft framework appears to follow the GATT in a broad concept of reciprocity and, referring to negotiations that would follow after an initial agreement, Article XVIII.1 speaks of 'an overall balance of rights and obligations', as does a 9 October draft relating to initial commitments. But the real test is probably in the manner in which the agreed Schedules of commitments are developed and specified. It might be possible for these to be specified on a bilateral reciprocity basis: e.g. that a particular country would agree to allow foreign lawyers to practise under certain conditions, one of the conditions being reciprocal recognition of qualifications. The pervading influence of regulations regarding registration, qualifications, standards, prudential requirements etc. in services provides considerable scope for regulation-, product- and country-specific reciprocity to develop, even within an agreement whose general thrust is towards a generalized balancing of commitments, unless a firm stance is taken.

Transparency

Transparency with respect to the existence and forms of barriers to trade is an essential element of the GATT, as is transparency of the procedures in relation to the invoking of safeguards and dispute settlement. These provisions have been carried into the *Draft Framework*. Article IV provides that relevant laws, rulings and so on should be published and relevant information be made available on request from other parties. It also provides for enquiry points. The regulations etc. referred to include not only those of central governments but also those of local governments and non-governmental agencies which affect trade in services. This is a very wide provision which, unless amended, can be expected to have major implications for trade in those professional services for which obscurity and imprecision of regulations have been barriers to trade.

Progressive Liberalization

The *Draft Framework* (Article XVIII) provides that the parties 'shall enter into successive rounds of negotiations' and a deadline date is to be specified. The process is to be one of progressive liberalization of restrictions on market access, qualifications on national treatment and so on.

Developing Countries

The GATT provides for special treatment and differential treatment for developing countries. Indeed it has been argued (Wolf 1987) that the effect of this treatment has been to free many developing country members of the GATT from most obligations under the GATT. This low level of obligation particularly applies to those ex-colonies which rode into membership of the GATT without undertaking commitments for themselves as a consequence of the prior membership of the metropolitan powers. Also, many developing countries (including these ex-colonies) have bound few of their import tariffs and thus are not constrained from raising them.

Many developing countries were very wary of entering into negotiations on international trade in services (Bhagwati 1987a). *Inter alia* they feared that the result would be the opening up of their services sectors, which in many cases are in an embryonic state, to highly developed providers from other countries, without concomitant export opportunities for themselves. But they were persuaded to enter into negotiations and have remained in them – to the surprise of many.

This retention of developing countries in the negotiations has not been achieved without significant effects on the *Draft Framework*. Rather than 'special and differential' treatment for developing countries being an 'add-on', provisions for developing countries are sprinkled throughout the *Draft Framework*. There are provisions for them to form preferential arrangements among themselves with no requirement (as there is for other countries) that most of service trade be covered, while the 'particular need' they may have to introduce new regulations (consistent with the *Frame-Work*) is recognized, as is their 'need' to introduce restrictions on trade for balance of payments reasons and to provide subsidies for service industries. In the process of liberalization, the *Draft Framework* states that developing countries may open fewer sectors and fewer modes of delivery and access and may move slower on all of these than other countries. Least developed countries have even softer treatment. Whether all this adds up to fewer or more obligations for developing countries than under the GATT seems to depend on what is written into the Schedules. If there are firm commitments, even though they are softer commitments than those entered into by developed countries, then the services agreement will probably be tighter than the GATT has turned out to be for most developing countries. There could be firm and bound commitments for some forms of access for some professional services for example, whereas many developing countries have virtually no bound tariffs on goods under the GATT. But, as stated, this will depend on what is negotiated in the Schedules and whether other potential parties judge that sufficient commitments are being entered into to warrant membership of the services trading club.

Monopolies

Provisions with respect to monopolies were not required by the mid-term review nor are they part of the GATT except in relation to state trading. But Article VIII of the *Draft Framework* requires government-designated monopolies (such as post and telegraph authorities) to provide the same facilities and treatment for the service providers of other member countries as they do for the service providers of their own countries. This should have implications for the access to distribution systems etc. of the providers of professional services such as actors and other performers.

SUMMARY OF IMPLICATIONS FOR PROFESSIONAL SERVICES

It is still too early to say how liberalizing a services agreement will be for professional, or other, services. Much will still depend on the Schedules, including whether they are constructed as positive or negative lists. This central issue still appears to be unresolved at the level of principle and is likely to be left to the negotiations of the Schedules themselves. As noted above there is a real risk that it will be solved at the lowest common denominator level. It is perhaps too late for negotiators to switch away from negotiating 'market access' to negotiating which barriers may remain. And the risk of bilateral, sector-specific reciprocity is still present, particularly in professional services through the recognition of qualifications and similar matters.

The most likely development is perhaps for very wide coverage and potential with respect to the agreement as a whole, but with a modest set of initial commitments or bindings on market access and national treatment and with MFN and other general commitments being applied widely though not universally.

Of particular concern to professional services is what will happen to the provisions with respect to subsidies and dumping. Constraining both appears at first blush to be a reasonable thing to do, and yet if the triggers for remedies are anything like those that exist under the GATT they are likely to have the most serious implications for trade in professional services: an inability to price differently in different markets and a fear of countervailing actions against subsidized education (for example), making trade in the professions very risky.

On the other hand the provisions with respect to transparency, for example, which apply to barriers in all sectors, should significantly reduce the costs of acquiring information relating to the supply of professional services, should make for more confidence in such information and should facilitate trade.

NOTES

1 Sampson and Snape (1985) provide an extensive discussion of the classification and associated barriers.
2 The next three paragraphs draw on Snape (1990).
3 Article III explicitly permits subsidies on domestic production.
4 There are other provisions in the absence of a domestic price of a 'like product'.

4 Mutual recognition, regulatory competition and the globalization of professional services

Kalypso Nicolaïdis

The global competitive strategy of multinational services firms is influenced by a whole host of factors which are investigated at length in other parts of this volume. This chapter focuses on the regulatory environment – both domestic and international – in which the strategies take place as one such factor. Decisions on whether to penetrate a new market, whether to do so through cross-border network delivery, licensing, joint ventures or foreign direct investment in order to provide a homogeneous service to a global client are often constrained by the features of respective national laws and regulations. In the context of progressive globalization of their activities throughout the 1970s, service providers have been increasingly concerned with the effects of regulatory impediments to trade and, under the Uruguay Round, governments have been negotiating a new trade in services regime meant to address such concerns. The signatories of the General Agreement on Trade in Services (GATS) and its annex on professional services will be under obligation to provide effective market access to foreign service providers on their national territories on the basis of the so-called national treatment principle.

Yet, as the debates within the Group of Negotiations on Services (GNS) have already underlined, effective market access for service providers requires not only that the *discriminatory* nature of national regulations be dealt with by governments but also the *fragmented* nature. Such a diagnosis has already led to a radically new approach to services liberalization within the European Community (EC) in the context of the 1992 single-market initiative through the adoption of a norm which is meant to deal upfront with regulatory fragmentation, namely the norm of mutual recognition. Whether and how such a norm can be envisaged as a next step of the liberalization process under the GATT is beyond the scope of this chapter (for background on the GATT services negotiations, see, amongst other publications, Feketekuty 1988; Bressand and Nicolaïdis 1989; and Drake and Nicolaïdis 1991). Instead we shall point to the relevance of mutual recognition as a new factor in the competitive environment of professional service providers.

The first section will highlight the specificity of mutual recognition in providing for a global regulatory environment congenial to the needs of global service providers. In the second section we ask under what conditions and to what extent does mutual recognition affect modes of globalization of transnational service providers. Such relevance will be assessed on the basis of a taxonomy of modes of globalization, taking into consideration in particular the observed importance of network-based modes of service delivery. The last section will point to new constraints of global competitive strategies under 'regulatory competition'.

MUTUAL RECOGNITION: FROM REGULATORY FRAGMENTATION TO REGULATORY COMPATIBILITY

Why have EC countries moved beyond the issue of regulatory discrimination in order to deal with the second source of impediments to the development of truly global strategies, namely regulatory fragmentation? What can we learn from this experience?

Under national treatment obligations, governments commit to do away with discriminatory measures implemented at the border or within their national territories. Meanwhile, states continue to hold sovereign prerogatives to regulate market interactions taking place on their respective territories. Such prerogatives in turn make it legitimate to require the apposition of national regulatory stamps to incoming people, services, firms or goods. The application of local requirements as called for by the mission of governments to 'protect the public interest' is indeed totally compatible with national treatment obligations, short, that is, of discriminatory intent of such government measures.

Under the logic of a 'single market' characterizing the so-called 1992 project, the aim is not only to identify barriers so as to be able to bargain over their withdrawal, as traditionally done under GATT trade rounds, but also, and much more ambitiously, to create an environment within which economic agents can operate across borders as if they were operating within national borders. This implies minimizing the costs associated with the shift from one type of regulatory control to another, which we might term *switching costs*. The GATT approach to 'free trade' does not take into consideration such a cost of collecting regulatory stamps. Under the 'single market' premise, on the other hand, when regulatory switching costs exceed expected benefits from trade they need to be considered as trade barriers in spite of the non-discriminatory nature of the regulations *per se*. In other words, it is recognized that regulatory boundaries, even given national treatment, can become a *de facto* impediment to freer trade. The national character of national laws and regulations – over and above the discriminatory character – hampers economic integration. What does this imply for services liberalization?

As we ask what 'freedom of movement of services' actually entails, we must first point out that the notion of a movement of a service across a border is actually an imaginary construct, a convenient shorthand for trade law typologies. Services never actually 'cross' a border as such: what we see is (a) the movement of people, capital, goods or information which embody a given service, a service which either has been received in the exporting country or will be provided in the importing country; or (b) the existence and management of infrastructure services, such as transport or telecommunication, which provide the support for the movement of people, goods, information or capital.

Services liberalization is based on facilitating such movements in part by recognizing their nature as *flexible modes of service delivery* rather than movements of factors of production.[1] Hence, for instance, in the case of people moving to provide or receive professional services, the issue is not one of freedom of migration nor free movement of workers. Rather, the freedom to provide services is based on the actual availability of communi-cation channels and transportation, the right for short-term movement of persons and the right to operate under home country requirements and accreditation. In other words, 'access' implies that the credentials of service providers be recognized as valid in the territory where the ultimate transaction takes place, even when not bearing the stamp of the territorial authorities concerned.

In the same vein, service firms often operate simultaneously under more than one jurisdiction. Again, requiring incorporation (i.e. movement of capital as a factor of production) in every country where they operate would preempt the freedom of these firms to choose to access neighbouring markets through branches or offices, rather than through subsidiaries which are national by definition. Moreover, these firms operate across different systems and seek to do so in an integrated manner, as is the case for global or regional service delivery through electronic networks. Information tech-nologies have made possible network strategies based on cross-border exchange of information, which in turn allows firms to reap increased economies of scale and scope. In other words, a full local presence, in the legal sense of the term, implies forgoing economies of scale from de-livering services on the basis of enhanced information and communication technologies (Bar and Borrus 1987).

In short, the competitiveness of international service providers is often based precisely on *partial* rather than *total* movement of factors of production, while applying national regulations often amounts to requiring the latter.

More generally, it has become commonplace in the field of 'service economics' to point out that, for services, production and sale are not two neatly separable economic phases (see Giarini 1987; Bressand and Nicolaïdis 1988). A service is often jointly produced through the inter-action of provider and buyer, i.e. at the point and time of consumption. As a result, regulatory control at the local marketing stage is paramount to regulatory control at the 'production' stage. The imposition of trade barriers – or withdrawal thereof – as related to services most often concerns the provider of a service and not the service itself. Given that a service provider, when engaging in international trade, operates mostly from his country of origin, regulations at the point of sale apply back in effect to the whole 'production chain', e.g. the way a service is originally designed. As in the case of goods, barriers created by differences in national regulations have a double-edged effect as they add extra costs (switching costs) and distort location patterns (location in the importing country to conform to regulatory requirements). But in addition, they may often preclude ex-change altogether as service providers are unable to switch to different regulatory jurisdiction. In an environment where the mobility of the factors of production which could allow a service to be provided entirely locally is not very high, or if such mobility leads to major efficiency losses, 'frag-mented' regulatory supervision is all the more detrimental.

In a nutshell, globalization strategies imply a new mode of territorial *presence* which plays hide and seek with traditional geographical patterns of regulatory control, whereby regulatory and territorial boundaries coin-cide. It is clear that the need to ensure 'access' is increasingly at odds with a national territorial logic of control. In any case, global service providers develop their competitive advantage by increasing their degrees of freedom relative to regulatory constraints. It is therefore necessary that regulatory policies catch up with the strategies of private actors. Up to now, govern-ments have been able to maintain the fiction of an approximate coincidence between territorial and regulatory boundaries: local incorporation of subsidiaries of multinational firms brings them under national regulatory control and service transactions are regulated at the point of sale, i.e. by the host country. But as actors adopt new modes of presence and delivery, such a territorial fragmentation of control becomes not only increasingly cum-bersome from their point of view, but increasingly difficult to implement for governments. Conditions governing foreign access to national markets can no longer be envisaged for each given territory separately but depend on the interrelationships between national systems of law, regulations, technical norms, standards and the like.

Regulatory fragmentation, which is the flip-side of national treatment, therefore needs to be considered as the next target of services liberalization in order to allow actors to operate under a 'single jurisdiction'. The experience of liberalization in the context of the 1992 internal market suggests that this may be done through a combination of approaches which all amount in effect to the 'denationalization' of national treatment.

Regulatory privatization amounts to decreasing the overall level of governmental regulation, and hence control, associated with the national treatment of transterritorial activities. It may be the result of pure de-regulation, the failure by governments to regulate new types of activities or the transfer from public regulation to self-regulation on the part of private professional bodies. Yet national regulatory privatization does not necessarily amount to transnational regulatory compatibility. Governments are often tempted to restrict access to deregulated activities to domestic actors; *de facto* standardization may increase barriers to access in a given national market owing to higher market power on the part of a few strong players; private actors may fail to agree on norms which facilitate trans-territorial transactions; and last but not least, if deregulation occurs in only one country, or at least to a much greater extent in one country, switching costs are reduced *to* and not *from* the deregulated country. Regulatory privatization will therefore help bring about a 'single jurisdiction' from the point of view of international service providers only to the extent that deregulation is non-discriminatory and private bodies do not themselves erect barriers which are discriminatory (for a discussion of the relationship between liberalization and deregulation, see Nicolaïdis 1988). But in any event, in spite of the prominence of deregulatory policies in the 1980s, there are limits to this first option: governments are likely to continue to regulate services which are characterized by a highly asymmetric distribution of information between buyers and sellers. In this vein, most observers agree that deregulation processes are to some extent better characterized as re-regulation processes (see Disstler 1987; Vickers and Yarrow 1988).

Regulatory harmonization involves keeping the national treatment norm as is but in conjunction working on the convergence between laws, standards and regulation through progressive *harmonization*. Systems are made similar in order to be compatible, by creating a significant overlap between the realm of control of different governments. The advantage of this approach is that it creates a level playing field for market players. Above all, governments can collectively pursue 'public interest' concerns in a systematic manner. Its pitfall is that it is obviously a cumbersome process, the more so the more national systems initially differ. Yet harmonization or, in the Treaty of Rome's terms, 'the approximation of laws and regulation' has traditionally been the route taken by European governments towards free cross-border services provision. Observers of current European integration in the field of services stress harmonization or, more generally, the co-ordination of regulations as the core to liberalization in this area (Roth 1988; Gatsios and Seabright 1989; Kay and Posner 1989; Bressand and Nicolaïdis 1991).

Regulatory competition involves actually breaking away from the very assumption on which the concept of national treatment is based: in other words delinking locus of presence and the authorities of control by allowing for the coexistence of different regulatory authorities on the same territory. Very broadly, regulatory competition is most typically exemplified by the proliferation of all sorts of 'heavens' which seek to attract economic actors on the basis of their less stringent rules and taxes. It may refer to the unilateral enforcement of a country's law in other countries as a signal that the regulation of the competitive environment can no longer be constrained by national borders. After all, extraterritorial application of national law and regulations is a traditional attribute of power.[2]

In the context of Europe 1992, European governments have come to adopt directives in the field of professional services implementing what we may see as a consensual form of regulatory competition, namely the norm of mutual recognition.[3]

The regional regulatory framework being developed, however, is a much more complex regulatory fine-tuning than all-out regulatory competition, based on an agreed upon 'division of labour' among national regulators. Actually, and in order to avoid the threat of what is often referred to as competitive deregulation (stemming from regulatory competition), regulatory co-operation is usually a prerequisite to mutual recognition. The emphasis, however, has definitely shifted from the former to the latter. In addition, regulatory privatization and regulatory competition tend to come together as countries turn to what Kay and Vickers (1988) refer to as 'parallel regulations'.

Mutual recognition as operationalized by the EC can therefore be defined as *a norm binding government behaviour, by which these governments agree that laws, regulations, standards or administrative practices of other parties to the agreement (or standards developed by private actors under the jurisdiction of these other parties) are to be considered as equivalent to their own.* Provided there is minimal harmonization of essential rules, governments therefore agree to the transfer of supervisory authority from the host country where a transaction takes place to the home country from which a product, a person, a service or a firm actually originates.

In this context, as will be explored further in the third section, mutual recognition creates the setting for regulatory competition to the extent that customers and suppliers make decisions based upon choices between different regulatory environments. Regulatory competition in turn may induce an increased degree of regulatory convergence among national systems of rules. Holding such variance constant at the political level, let us now turn with more specificity to the ways in which the adoption of home country control of the global operations of professional service providers changes the competitive environment of transnational service providers.

MODES OF GLOBALIZATION AND RELEVANT 'RIGHTS'

What is the actual relevance of mutual recognition for the globalization strategy of service firms? What are the actual efficiency gains to be expected? In the first section we presented in broad terms the general rationale for adopting mutual recognition as a mode of services liberal- ization. As the discussion has already indicated mutual recognition is not the only approach, and not necessarily always the most optimal approach, to ensuring regulatory compatibility. In addition, variations in levels of regulations of professional services across sectors and across countries should also be taken into account. Clearly, this is an attempt to provide a preliminary framework for enquiry and is not in any way a systematic investigation.

Let us start with the following broad assertion: the extent to which regulatory fragmentation is actually considered an important variable from

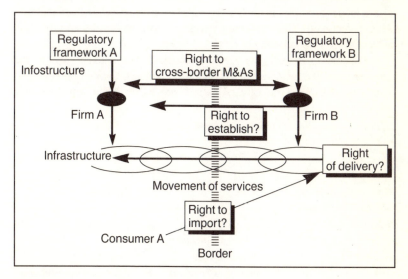

Figure 4.1 Globalization strategies and rights of access

the point of view of firms will depend on their actual globalization strategies. As widely explored in the literature and in this volume, modes of
internationalization for service firms can take many forms. Figure 4.1 is a
schematic description of this strategic map which stresses the fact that such
internationalization always involves a move from one regulatory framework to another. As shown, firm B can 'buy' its market share through
merger with or acquisition of firm A, it can develop an alliance with A or
grant A a franchise for selling its products, and it can deliver its services
through establishment or through communication infrastructures, although
the latter may sometimes be the result of the buyer of a service taking full
initiative for importing the service. The criteria guiding such choices have
been explored by business analysts. To be sure, one of the major differences
between goods-related and services-related globalization is due to the
greater choice of modes of cross-border delivery for goods than for
services. For our purposes we may distinguish these strategies further on
the basis of a simple taxonomy following two criteria (Table 4.1).[4]

The first criterion is the share of the service's value which must be produced
locally as a function of technological constraints and demand factors (e.g. to
what extent is proximity and simultaneity of production/consumption a
constraint). At one end, all or most of the value added must be locally produced
by locally constituted firms, e.g. subsidiaries, branches etc. At the other end the
sale of the service will only require a local 'conduit', e.g. an agent, or even only
local communication channels and a computer terminal. In between are
'mixed' modes of production whereby a somewhat comparable share of the
value added is produced in the home country (e.g. the processing and interpretation of data) and in the host country (e.g. gathering of country-specific data,
interaction with the customer).

The second criterion is the degree of ownership or actual control by the
service firm of the local unit in the importing country. Crossing this second
criterion with the first, globalization strategies based on retaining

Table 4.1 A taxonomy of modes of globalization

| Share of local value added | Degree of ownership and control of local units | |
	High	*Low/none*
High	Foreign direct investment; mergers or acquisitions	Partnerships
Mixed	Branching out	Franchise
Low	Proprietary networks	Public network delivery

ownership and control of local units consist of (a) multinational investment/ establishment or cross-border merger or acquisition (a high share of local production of value added); (b) local commercial presence through branches or agencies which are an integral part of the multinational firm (mixed source of value creation); and (c) local sale through proprietary communication channels (low local share of value creation).

On the other hand, service firms can seek a global presence without extended or ongoing control from headquarters (in cases when global availability of a given service plays a crucial role for instance). Globalization strategies are then based on a somewhat loose interconnection between independent profit centres which produce most of the service value added locally through global franchising or partnerships. Conversely, they can be based on giving a licence to a local agent to sell a given product. Finally, local sale can be carried out through universally available communication networks such as Minitel in France.

Implicit in this categorization is the recognition that no clear-cut distinction can be established between trade and investment in the realm of international service transactions. 'Pure trade' and 'pure investment' only constitute two ends of a spectrum and the features of globalization strategies are a matter of degree between two major criteria. This in turn explains why devising rights associated with traditional notions of cross-border trade has proven so intractable in the context of the GATT negotiations. There actually exists a more complex mapping implicit in the negotiations between relevant rights and modes of globalization, as indicated in Table 4.2.[5]

Depending on their strategies, service firms will be concerned with different types of rights and, in turn, with whether or not regulations have

Table 4.2 Relevant rights according to modes of globalization

| | *Degree of ownership and control of local units* | |
Share of local production of the service	*High*	*Low/none*
High	Right of investment Right to cross-border Mergers and acquisitions	Rights related to partnerships and global franchise
Mixed	Right of 'commercial presence' Right of establishment	Right to franchise Right to import
Low	Right to deliver, e.g. of non-establishment	Right to import

been mutually recognized. The need for mutual recognition ranges from cases where mutual recognition is a prerequisite for the exercise of these rights to cases where mutual recognition may be irrelevant. In between there exists a wide array of cases where mutual recognition leads to various degrees of efficiency gains, from significant gains to marginal gains. When the level of local production is high such efficiency gains may depend on the balance between professionals trained and licensed locally or abroad, or on how different are the features of the services required by the regulations of the respective countries (from accounting methods to types of financial products). In cases of a low level of local production, the need for mutual recognition arises not so much at the level of definition of rules applicable in the host country but rather in terms of the supervisory requirements (ongoing enforcement) applied by the respective countries. Assessing the complex mix of underlying legal and economic factors for the demand for mutual recognition is beyond the scope of this chapter. Instead we raise two central questions, namely whether there is a need for a single applicable rule and whether globalization strategies are based on network modes of delivery.

The need for a single applicable rule

The extent to which globalization strategies require a single rule applicable to their operations across national territories depends on both supply and demand factors. On the supply side the question is how high are the switching costs associated with adapting the service to local regulatory requirements. On the demand side we must first distinguish between service categories and in particular between two broad categories of professional services. On the one hand there are business services which are sold to firms as inputs (such as legal, advertising, management consulting or accountancy professional services) and on the other hand there are consumer services (including health and educational professional services). The fact that many services obviously fall into both categories (including financial and insurance services, software services, architecture and engineering services) has meant that the demand push on the part of business services has trickled down to services provided to individual consumers. Yet, as has been widely acknowledged, professional service providers started to internationalize their activities in an increasingly systematic way in the mid-1970s, mainly owing to a demand push on the part of their clients, e.g. multinational manufacturing firms (this is the so-called phenomenon of the cohort of multinationals). If service firms follow their transnational clients to various locations around the world in order to generate scale economies, they must consider the extent to which those global clients value the fact that the services provided are designed on the basis of the rules of their country of origin. Finally, services providers will need to examine whether potential mutual recognition of rules may constitute an incentive for re-internalization of business service production on the part of their global clients.

Network-based service delivery and the 'right of non-establishment'

As stated in the first section, mutual recognition is a necessary prerequisite for network-based modes of delivery. In this case, mutual recognition amounts to a 'right of non-establishment', as most of the value added is provided in the country of origin and is therefore under its regulations. Coming back to the distinction between business and consumer services, again network-based delivery is highly correlated with the level of sophistication of the client and the extent to which it itself is a global player. In this light, business services will tend to be more based on network delivery than consumer services.

In considering the relationship between service firms and their clients we must differentiate between cases where the service firm will directly access the local branches of global clients and cases where the service provider must operate with the central management rather than on the operational premises of its client. In other words, what is the locus of interface between global companies and is this interface likely to shift from the headquarters to local affiliates? These strategies will depend in part on the extent to which locally based branches of the service providers can use their access to the global networks of their firms to enhance the value of the service they provide locally. Depending on the chosen mix, networks as modes of delivery will be used in combination with the movement of individuals across borders.

Obviously, the potential for network-based delivery is related to the technological proximity constraint, in addition to regulatory constraints, and the former may override the latter. In this regard, the sharing of information on a global scale within companies can be plagued by cultural and technological incompatibility. When information systems cannot be deemed reliable, connection protocols not always consistent, capabilities in different sites disparate and staff training decentralized and differentiated, sharing data files with remote locations can be an expensive proposition. On this basis, local service providers may or may not want to externalize some of their functions depending on the type of risk and upfront investment costs they decide to bear.

In summary, the competitive advantage provided by the ability to operate under the regulations of the service provider's country of origin will depend on the modes of globalization adopted by the various service providers under consideration. Indeed, regulatory constraints may be considered as one of the variables underpinning chosen modes of globalization in the first place. Yet globalization strategies are based on a host of other factors linked to the types of interactions prevailing between service providers and their clients. In this light, the impact of the adoption of mutual recognition ranges from being a *prerequisite* for certain modes of internationalization to being an *ex post* environmental change which may contribute in shifting incentives for one type of globalization strategy to work against another.

COMPETITIVE STRATEGIES UNDER REGULATORY COMPETITION

The implementation of mutual recognition between countries in which global service providers operate may *ex ante* be considered more or less necessary to effective market access worldwide. Yet, once it is implemented, mutual recognition definitely introduces a new layer in competitive strategies of firms as competitive moves come to integrate the regulatory dimension of global competition. In this last section we consider how demand patterns and government policies are likely to be affected by this new phenomenon.

Mutual recognition introduces the possibility for the public to choose how and by whom its 'interests' will be protected. In other words, the act of consumption will henceforth grant access, albeit indirectly, to multiple jurisdictions. For the first time, services available on a given territory may alternatively embody different regulatory features. As domestic rules of exporting countries become an actual feature of the product influencing consumer choice in the importing country, this creates a dynamic which may be termed regulatory competition.

There are two dimensions of 'regulatory competition', in that it refers to 'competition' at two levels. First, it refers to competition between suppliers who see their competitiveness affected by the characteristics of their regulatory control 'of origin' (customers and suppliers make decisions based upon choices between different regulatory environments). To the extent that economic actors are regulated according to their origins, market transactions pit regulatory systems against one another. This dimension may be termed *structural* in that it stems from the given regulatory differential at the time of implementation of mutual recognition and is present independently of the way in which regulators respond to this (structural) feature of their environment.

The second dimension is that of competition between regulators who seek to favour their own producers as well as attract economic activities on their soil by tampering with their domestic regulations. Regulatory competition may become part of 'strategic trade' policies, as governments are likely to use their regulatory prerogatives in order to improve their balance of payments. Henceforth, this second dimension is the *strategic* component of regulatory competition.

Under such a dynamic, market forces may override political compromises in yielding the 'level' of protection that will prevail. Whether this is paramount to a deregulatory spiral stemming across the border from the least to the most regulated countries is open to question. In other words, the extent to which economic actors do actually 'vote with their feet' or 'vote with their modems', and when they do, according to what incentives, needs to be the object of further thorough analysis than has been carried out to date. Under a rational actor model, governments would try to assess potential market response to high regulatory differentials, i.e. in situations where mutual recognition is implemented with remaining important disparities between national rules.

In summary, we can differentiate between two competitive effects of regulations, namely *cost-related* effects and *signalling* effects. Under the assumption that less stringent regulations actually decrease the costs of providing a service, mutual recognition will most probably constitute a deregulatory incentive. Yet elasticity of demand with regard to regulation is only partly correlated with price elasticity. Regulations also serve as signals about the overall quality, security and specific features of the services and service providers who are known to abide by them. Consumers may favour more stringent regulations and may therefore choose their insurance policies or doctors accordingly. If the latter effect appears to override the former, regulatory competition may actually induce more regulation, either unilaterally or through demands for increased harmonization. Only in the event that cost effects prevail will governments worry about – or welcome for that matter – competitive deregulation. In the light of these dynamics, governments will have more or less incentive to make their preferred level of harmonization a prerequisite for mutual recognition. But in any event both governments and private service providers will progressively take greater account of the dynamic of regulatory competition in designing their policies and strategies.

CONCLUSION

Mutual recognition is a norm which today is only relevant in the context of 'Europe 1992' and even then its implementation is only starting. At the multilateral level it is only a long-term prospect, 'beyond the Uruguay Round'. Yet bilateral negotiations between the EC and its trading partners already show that the emergence of 'mutual recognition zones' creates a new context for liberalization negotiations in which each negotiating partner needs to consider the internal regulatory context of its counterpart and design means to render its regulatory system compatible with it.

International service providers will need to assess not only the benefits but also the competitive adjustment costs induced by having to operate in a global regulatory environment whereby the progressive adoption of mutual recognition creates both regulatory convergence and regulatory competition. In particular, will they lose their traditional channels of influence *vis-à-vis* regulatory authorities in a context where the regulations which affect their home market's competitive environment are not necessarily those designed by their home governments? How can they make use of the increased authority of private professional bodies in bringing about regulatory compatibility across borders? How will their 'regulatory learning curve' compare with that of their competitors? How will they go about marketing the home country 'regulatory quality' of their products as part of these products' intrinsic characteristics? What will be their consumers' sensitivity to this new strategic environment? With the emergence of mutual recognition as a central norm governing international service transactions, these questions and many others will need to feature high on the checklist of global strategic planners in the decade to come.

NOTES

1 The extent to which the movements of people and capital which are intrinsic to services trade should be considered as factor movements is itself a major point of controversy. For a discussion, see Nicolaïdis (1987). The point here is that if and when such movement is considered as 'investment' or 'immigration' rather than 'trade' there is no question that host country rules apply. It is only to the extent that this is not the case that the norm of mutual recognition is relevant.
2 The rising instances of extraterritorial application of anti-trust laws pertain to this logic. American judges have been very prone to seek to extend US laws outside its borders. The latest example is that of the Minorco bid on Gold Fields – two European companies – blocked by an American judge in May 1989 on the basis of a complaint by the US subsidiary of Gold Field and in spite of the go-ahead previously granted both by the British Mergers and Monopolies Commission and the European Commission. The European Court of Justice has followed this route in its September 1988 ruling against price fixing by wood pulp manufacturers from North America.
3 *The General Systems* Directive adopted in 1988 has been the first directive to extend mutual recognition of educational requirements across professions.
4 The proposed taxonomy is expanded from Gadrey (1990). Obviously, real distinctions are not as clear cut and those presented are ideal types.

5 It must be noted upfront that this categorization, by merely referring to the 'rights' which may underlie obligations of governments towards foreign firms, does not exhaust the range of issues which would need to be addressed under a comprehensive international services regime. In particular, it does not directly address the question of 'obligations' which could be imposed on firms themselves to correct for effects of exclusion, limited access to infrastructures, monopolistic behaviour and the like. Issues of 'competition' policy and global anti-trust rules are likely to be prominent on the post-Uruguay Round agenda.

5 The globalization of services and service-intensive goods industries

Seev Hirsch

INTRODUCTION

It is rather surprising that services which account for such a high proportion of world output and world employment have only recently begun to occupy a significant position on the agenda of both policy-makers and researchers. International transactions in services have not fared much better, though the inclusion of services in issues covered by the Uruguay Round of the GATT has helped to increase public awareness of services and their growing importance in world trade and investments (see Bhagwati 1988b; Messerlin and Sauvant 1990). The omission is probably due at least partly to analytical problems. Economists and business scholars have found it difficult to offer meaningful characterizations of services and to distinguish between goods and services in a manner which will make analytical and empirical sense.

This chapter represents a third attempt by the author to offer an approach which facilitates the analysis of goods and services within a single analytical framework (see Hirsch 1989a, b). Unlike its predecessors, which focused on definitions and dealt mainly with trade, the present chapter focuses on the factors which determine the mode of operation chosen by goods-producing and service-producing firms in the domestic and inter-national markets.

Received theory suggests that goods and services are influenced by the same economic factors. Implicit in this approach is the view that there is no need to develop specific service-related models and paradigms. In this chapter we arrive at a different conclusion. We start from a premise that goods and services do indeed differ in several important respects. We go on to show that, when viewed by the market, all transactions involving goods have a significant service content, and we conclude by arguing that it is the service characteristics which determine the entry and operating policies of both goods producers and service providers.

In the following section we review and update the analytical concepts developed in the earlier papers. In the third section we discuss service characteristics and their impact on the institutional options available to producers of goods and of services. In the fourth section the analysis is extended to incorporate international transactions. Dynamic factors and policy implications are discussed in the concluding section.

GOODS, SERVICES AND SERVICE INTENSITY REVISITED

Services differ from goods in several respects which are of little relevance in the present context.[1] However, a difference which is important for the subject of this chapter concerns the manner in which they are absorbed (or consumed) by the users.[2] Absorption of services requires interaction between producer and user. Absorption of goods can be carried out by the user in isolation. This difference is crucial since it means that goods can be inventoried, they can be produced for the shelf to await absorption at a later date. Services cannot be inventoried. Production and consumption are at least partly simultaneous (for a detailed discussion see Hirsch 1989a, b).

Note that the specification of the distinction between goods and services offered above does not contain any reference to tangibility. This omission is not an oversight. While services are indeed intangible, goods may be either tangible or intangible.

For example, the 'production' of scientific or commercial information does not require interaction with the user. Thus, information and knowledge, regardless of the particular form in which they are stored, are not services; they are intangible goods which happen additionally to have characteristics of public goods.

While information is not a service, transmission of information, an activity which does indeed require direct or indirect interaction with the user, is properly regarded as a service. The two activities must not be confused with each other.

Tangible and intangible goods are thus distinguished from services in one very important respect: while all goods can be produced in isolation, the production and absorption of services require some form of interaction between producer and user.[3]

Analysing the activities performed by service organizations such as consulting, accounting and engineering, we note that the 'production process' is broken down into those segments which require producer–user interactions and those which can be performed in isolation.

A significant proportion of the costs involved in producing a consulting report, a company audit, engineering plans etc. is in fact produced in isolation. We may therefore conclude that the output of these organizations is not a pure service; it is a combination of intangible goods and services.

Closer examination of the process of production and absorption reveals, however, that the sharp conceptual distinction between goods and services may be blurred in practice. While goods may in principle be absorbed in isolation, 'post-production' services must be added to them before the process of absorption can commence. Goods cannot be absorbed without being packed and transported. Frequently, numerous other services must accompany them before they are ready for absorption.

Empirical evidence suggests that these post-production services account for a high proportion of the value of typical goods and in cases where independent distributors and additional channels of distribution are employed the ratio of the ex-factory price to total cost incurred by the user declines even further (Hirsch 1987b).

Hirsch (1989a, b) outlined a formal model which characterizes the process of providing a typical service. The model distinguishes between two types of activities performed by the producer, denoted by P_i and P_s, and two types of activities performed by the user, denoted by R_i and R_s. The subscripts i and s characterize the nature of these activities. Activities performed in isolation are denoted by the subscript i and simultaneous activities by s. Simultaneous activities pertain to those activities which require interaction between the provider of the service and the user. The total value of a service transaction (denoted by U) is obtained by summing the cost of the four components defined above over all the relevant activities:

$$U = P_i + P_s + R_i + R_s \qquad (5.1)$$

This definition focuses on a number of economically important service characteristics. Note first that both producer and user incur costs in the course of producing and absorbing a service. Both spend time and use up economic resources such as labour and capital which are reflected in the cost of the service which must ultimately be borne by the user. Note also that the value U of the service to the user is not the same as the price paid to the producer which, under conditions of perfect competition, would equal $P_i + P_s$.

Next, consider the 'simultaneity factor' denoted by S, which is formally defined as follows:

$$S = (P_s + R_s)/U \qquad (5.2)$$

From the definition of services it follows that S is always positive since provision of a service requires some form of producer–user interaction. However, S can be relatively small, e.g. when the interaction is brief, and it does not involve costly face-to-face communications.[4]

The definition offered above need not be restricted to services, it can also be employed to denote transactions involving goods. To be useful to the user, transactions in goods must be accompanied, as was noted above, by associated services. The user therefore requires interaction with the provider of the service. The mode of interaction, whether face to face, by telephone, by computer terminal or by letter, depends on the nature of the service to be provided and not on the characteristics of the good with which the services are associated.

Equations (5.1) and (5.2) can thus be employed to characterize any kind of transaction from the user's point of view. S will be relatively large (i.e. close to unity) when producer–user interaction accounts for a high proportion of total transaction value. Typically, it will be small when the transaction involves a tangible good which has few associated services. However, even when the transaction has no tangible contents the S factor need not be significant. This is so when producer–user interaction is both brief and inexpensive.

In conclusion, the value of S does not in itself provide an indication as to whether a given transaction involves a good or a service. A low S factor can be indicative of a transaction involving a good which has few associated services. It could also indicate a service transaction which requires only a low level of producer–user interaction. Conversely, a high S factor might be indicative of a pure service or of a service-intensive good requiring a high level of producer–user interaction.

It is the S factor and not the tangibility of the object being transacted which is of interest to us since, as will be shown in the following sections, it affects the mode employed to effect both domestic and international transactions in pure services as well as in goods with varying service intensities.

SERVICE CHARACTERISTICS AND OPERATING MODES

Provision of services requires interaction between producer and user, as was repeatedly noted above. This characteristic and its corollary, that services cannot be inventoried, determine the mode employed to provide services. Services must be provided directly; they cannot, be produced by one organization and delivered in whatever sense by another. Services cannot in other words, be provided by intermediaries.

Contrast this with the supply of goods. In this case intermediaries can of course be employed. No direct interaction between the producer and the ultimate user is required. Ownership can in fact be transferred through several organizations such as wholesalers and retailers before the good reaches the ultimate user.

What can be said about the mode employed to provide what was termed above post-production services, i.e. services which must accompany tangible and intangible goods before they are useful to the buyer?

To address this question we find it useful to distinguish between two generic groups of services: 'universal services' and 'specific services'. The first group includes transportation, warehousing, finance and insurance. The second group includes instruction, installation, maintenance, repairs etc.

The 'universality' of the first group derives from the fact that the services it contains are supplied by specialist organizations (banks, transportation companies, insurance brokers etc.), organizations whose professional expertise relates primarily to the service they are providing. Their interest in the product with which the service is associated is in most cases marginal or incidental. By contrast, providers of the second group of services must have an intimate knowledge of the product.

This proprietary knowledge will be shown to be a major factor in the determination of the mode of operation adopted by producers of service-intensive products. To show why this is so we consider once again some of the major service characteristics. Services defined above as universal, i.e. finance, transportation, warehousing etc., can be provided by independent specialized service organizations which need have no contact with the user or, for that matter, with the producer. Other services, those labelled above as specialized, cannot be provided by organizations wholly independent of the producer. Services such as training, installation, maintenance and repair require specialized knowledge. This knowledge originates with the producer of the associated product. Consequently, the services in question cannot be supplied without the involvement of the producer.

The manufacturer may choose to provide some or all the specialized services through organizations partly or wholly controlled by him or her. Alternatively, he or she may choose to authorize independent organizations to provide the services to the final user. In either case, provision of the services depends on the decision of the producer of the good and on his or her willingness and ability to transfer proprietary knowledge to independent organizations.

The operating mode chosen to provide the specialized services depends on a number of factors, including the ability of the producer to control the diffusion of the relevant service know-how, the importance of the services to the users, the resources required to control and manage different service organizations, the size of the market etc.[5]

Note that several of the factors listed above as determinants of the operating mode chosen to provide the specialized services are associated with the different phases of the product cycle. New and particularly high-tech products tend to be associated with specialized services. Detailed specifications must be made available to the users. The users also require training, installation, running-in and assurance of maintenance and repair services before they can make proper use of the product. These services, as was noted above, are normally provided by the producer of the product or by organizations explicitly authorized by him or her to provide the services.

Mature products may also be service intensive in the sense that associated services account for a high proportion of total transaction value. However, the associated services are more likely to be available on the market from independent organizations. This is because the relevant know-how becomes diffused over time and ceases to be proprietary.

INTERNATIONAL TRANSACTIONS

Thus far no distinction has been made between domestic and international transactions. In this section we consider the choice of the operating modes in the international environment. As in the last section, comparisons between goods and services are used to emphasize both the differences and the similarities between the two types of transactions.

We start with a brief discussion of a model developed by Hirsch in an earlier paper for the purpose of analysing the choice between exporting and international foreign direct investment (FDI) (Hirsch 1976).

The choice is faced by a firm with a head office in country A where it has an established market position. The firm seeks to enter a new market in country B. It was shown in the paper that the decision is determined by the relationship between the following variables: P_a, P_b; M_x,M_d; C_x,C_d;K. P_a and P_b stand for the outlays related to manufacturing in countries A and B respectively. It is assumed that if the firm in A chooses to export to B then an expansion of output capacity is required. If the FDI alternative is preferred then production facilities in the target country are needed. In either case, capital expenditures are required. P_a and P_b (as well as the other variables) should therefore be viewed as expressing present values of costs extending over the entire lifetime of the investment project. They include outlays on capital and on current inputs such as labour, raw materials and other supplies. Note, however, that the costs of acquiring technological and marketing know-how are not included in P_a and P_b. Assuming that A is the high-cost country we define $p = P_a - P_b$, where p has a positive value.[6]

P_a and P_b represent in a sense the traditional comparative advantage variables familiar from the Heckscher–Ohlin classical trade model. Their level is determined by the relative abundance of the production factors which they embody. Employing Dunning's (1988a) terminology, P_a and P_b

may be labelled 'location advantage factors'. While these factors are internationally immobile, they are universally available to all producers who might be either domestic firms or foreign firms engaged in FDI.

M_d and M_x represent domestic and export marketing costs respectively. Marketing costs in the present context should be viewed in the broadest sense. They cover a wide array of services including information and logistical services and, when necessary, other sales-related services such as instruction, installation, running-in and even maintenance, i.e. services which in the last section were labelled 'post-production services'.

M_x is assumed, on empirical grounds, to exceed M_d by a margin which is an increasing function of the economic distance between A and B. Economic distance in this case has physical, cultural and political components. Physical distance raises the cost of transportation, whereas cultural and political distance raises transaction costs pertaining to functions such as communication, finance, insurance and other costs of operating in more than a single environment.

We assume the excess of M_x over M_d to be symmetric. This means that the cost of M_x can stand for exporting from A to B or from B to A. Similarly, M_d stands for domestic marketing costs in either A or B.[7] Defining m as M_x - M_d we conclude that, as long as our assumptions hold, m is positive.

C_d and C_x represent costs of monitoring and controlling domestic and foreign operations respectively. It is assumed that the decision to serve the B market entails expenditures on the design and operation of an expanded control and monitoring system capable of handling international business operations. Defining c as C_x - C_d we assume that c, like m, is positive.[8] Costs of controlling and monitoring foreign operations are higher than similar costs incurred in the domestic market, because international operations involve, by definition, more than a single legal, cultural, economic and political environment.

K is a firm-specific revenue-generating intangible asset. Strictly speaking it is measured by the costs which a firm in B would incur in order to acquire the know-how needed to produce and market the product which the firm in A seeks to market in B. To the firm in A, K is a sunk cost incurred in the past, when it first introduced the product in the market in A. Again using Dunning's terminology, K stands for the value of his 'ownership advantage'. This advantage can be costlessly transferred internationally between different entities belonging to a single firm.

The choice between exporting and engaging in FDI is determined by the relationship between the cost elements listed above. Thus, exporting is preferred if

$$P_a + M_x + C_d < P_b + K + C_d \tag{5.3}$$

and

$$P_a + M_x + C_d < P_b + M_d + C_x \tag{5.4}$$

and investing is preferred if

$$P_b + C_x + M_d < P_a + M_x + C_d \tag{5.5}$$

and

$$P_b + C_x + M_d < P_b + K + C_d \tag{5.6}$$

In plain words, the following two conditions must be satisfied if exporting is to be preferred.

1 Landed costs at B (production costs in A plus export marketing costs plus domestic monitoring costs) are less than the product entry costs of a potential competitor in B (i.e. production costs plus domestic marketing and monitoring costs plus outlays on the acquisition of the relevant production and marketing know-how).
2 Landed costs at B are less than the foreign operating costs incurred by the firm in A (production costs plus foreign monitoring costs plus domestic marketing costs).

Similarly, the following two conditions must be satisfied if the FDI option is to be preferred.

1 Inequality (5.4) is reversed.
2 The foreign operating costs of firm A are less than the product entry costs of firm B.

To emphasize the decision variables which the choice between exporting and FDI entails, inequalities (5.3)–(5.6) are rewritten as follows.

export:

$$p + m < K \tag{5.7}$$
$$p + m < c \tag{5.8}$$

invest:

$$c < p + m \tag{5.9}$$
$$c < K \tag{5.10}$$

Note that the various components of the marketing function discussed above require interaction between producer and user. M_x and M_d can therefore be viewed as representing the simultaneity factor discussed in detail in the second section of this chapter and m, which stands for the difference between export and domestic marketing costs, represents the export cost premium incurred in the process of engaging in international interactions. C_x, C_d and c can likewise be viewed as representing interactions. In this case, however, the interaction is internal; it takes place within the organization. C_d in this case represents the interaction between the head office and domestic-operating units and C_x represents interactions with foreign-operating units. The positive value of c, like that of m, indicates that international interaction is more costly than domestic interaction.

Service providers, like producers of tangible goods, who seek to serve foreign markets, must choose between exporting their services and providing them from a location in the target market. Country A exporters, who by assumption are located in a high-cost country, suffer from a double cost disadvantage compared with domestic service providers – their production costs are higher and they incur an interaction cost premium. Their domestic competitors, on the other hand, must bear the costs of acquiring the technological and marketing know-how required to provide the service. If the firm in A chooses the FDI route, it must accept the interaction cost premium associated with international interactions compared with domestic intra-firm interactions. Inequalities (5.7)–(5.9) provide the appropriate decision rules.

The choice actually made in concrete situations between FDI and exporting depends of course on specific conditions prevailing at the time in question. Certain general observations can be made however.

Note that K appears in inequality (5.7) as well as in (5.10). This implies that a firm's proprietary knowledge may be used to generate exports in some cases and FDI-based revenues in other cases. The difference between production costs at home and abroad can similarly favour exporting in some cases and FDI in other cases. The possession of firm-specific know-how is thus a necessary but *not* sufficient condition for FDI.

The relationship between m and c is the factor which appears to be more consistent. A high m favours FDI and a high c increases the attractiveness of exporting. FDI is preferred in those cases where c can be kept low in relation to m.

Next, let us relate these conclusions to the S factor framework. To provide specialized services and service-intensive goods the producer must interact intensively with the user. When the interaction is across national boundaries international cost premia must be incurred. In this case FDI is the preferred mode of operation.

This explains the prevalence of FDI in a number of service industries, especially in the business service sector, such as consulting, engineering and accounting which were mentioned earlier. Firms in these industries possess marketable proprietary knowledge which can be effectively denied to their competitors. While some of the work involved in providing these services can be performed in isolation, interaction between producer and user inevitably accounts for a significant proportion of the total time spent on the provision of the service. When the export cost premium is high, as is inevitably the case when face-to-face communications are required, FDI will tend to be preferred to exporting.

Thus, it is the *S* factor which determines whether services are 'produced' in the home or the target country. When the S factor is negligible or small, services for the market in B can be produced in A if the firm in A enjoys an ownership advantage large enough to compensate for its production cost and export marketing cost disadvantage. A's advantage becomes eroded and approaches unity as the S factor increases in value. The firm in A, in this case, will opt for the FDI mode and use a market base in B to provide the service to the local users.

The same considerations apply to the mode used for transactions in goods. In this case too the mode is determined essentially by the characteristics of the associated services. FDI will tend to be preferred to exporting when the associated services are dominated by specialized services, i.e. services whose provision depends on proprietary know-how possessed by the producer of the good. Such services tend to have a significant *S* factor which gives rise to a high export cost premium. Exporting will be preferred when the associated services are universal. The manufacturer in this case need not be involved in the provision of the services which can be obtained from independent service organizations located in either A or B.

DYNAMIC FACTORS AND POLICY IMPLICATIONS

Having the characteristics of a public good, every kind of knowledge, even proprietary knowledge, becomes widely available over time through experience, turnover of employees, expiry of patents and other processes of diffusion. This process affects the economic value of ownership advantage which diminishes as the know-how gets diffused. The decline in the value of proprietary knowledge applies to both goods and services. As the relevant knowledge becomes diffused, services tend to become less specialized and the link between products and associated services weakens. Universal service providers can enter the market and capture a growing share. Consequently, the entry costs of potential competitors, whether in A or B, decline over time.

As already noted, these changes are related to the well-known product cycle. As goods mature, the associated services, while not necessarily diminishing in relative importance, change their characteristics. They become less specialized and more universal. Consequently, the product manufacturer ceases to enjoy an advantage in the provision of the associated services, which may be competitively provided by independent service organizations. The links in the value chain, which in the early phases of the cycle are held closely together by the manufacturer's monopoly of know-how, are gradually loosened, facilitating the break-up of the chain into more or less independent (or unbundled) activities.

As the product matures the ownership advantage enjoyed by the producer in A in the market in B diminishes. As the associated services change their characteristics, entry barriers faced by potential competitors in the market in B are lowered and dissociation between the provision of the goods and their associated services becomes feasible. This trend reduces the attractiveness of the FDI mode. Following the 'universalization' of the associated services, firms in A will tend to exploit their ownership advantage by exporting rather than by engaging in international investment.

The implications for pure services are in a sense rather different. In this case the 'universalization' of previously specialized services will tend to transfer the competitive advantage from firms in A to firms in B. Particularly affected in this case are, of course, services characterized by a high S factor and its associated export cost premium. We can therefore expect FDI to figure prominently in industries which provide services which have not yet lost their specialized characteristics, i.e. where the trade-retarding S factor is high. Universal services, as has been noted already, will be provided by domestic organizations. Conventional international trade will be employed only in those rare cases where the S factor is insignificant.

It should be borne in mind that several of the policy implications discussed above are applicable primarily to the entry decision. They do not necessarily apply to the competitive situation facing firms which are already present in the market. These firms benefit from learning by doing, from consumer loyalty, from the high cost of switching faced by customers and from other entry barriers which potential competitors have to overcome. These factors help to neutralize the impact of universalization.

In interpreting these conclusions, distinction should be made between the firms and the services or the service contents of the products which they produce. Pure services, like services associated with specific products, will indeed tend to become universal as they mature. However, it is important to recall that the very essence of innovation consists of introducing new products and/or new services on a continuous basis. Hence, the innovative firm can avoid the undesirable consequences of the universalization process which affects their services by introducing new products and new services on a systematic basis.

This policy is particularly appropriate for pure service organizations because services are in a certain sense tailor-made. This means that each service transaction has a unique component, a factor which when properly exploited can delay or even permanently neutralize the process of universalization.

We started this chapter by disagreeing with the notion that goods and services do not differ from an economic viewpoint. We end up by arguing that goods manufacturers and service providers would be well advised to ignore these differences when addressing the issues of domestic or international operating modes. This advice is based on the empirical observation that goods are worthless unless they are associated with post-production services which, almost invariably, account for a high proportion of total transaction value. Our analysis leads to the conclusion that the nature of the interactions between producers and users of specialized services provided on their own or in association with goods is a major determinant of the mode employed to provide both goods and pure services in domestic as well as international markets.

NOTES

1 For a detailed discussion of the different definitions of services, of the differences between goods and services and of their implications see Hirsch (1989a).
2 Sampson and Snape (1985), and other writers on services such as Sauvant (1990), use the term 'receiving' to denote consumption of services and 'providing' to denote production. See also Sauvant *et al.* (1990).
3 Some writers erroneously imply that producer–user interaction takes place during the entire time required to produce and absorb a service. Sauvant, for example, says: 'Services have to be produced when and where they are consumed. For this reason, the possibility of transporting, and hence of trading many services may be limited, and foreign direct investment or labour movement are often required to bring them to foreign markets.' See Sauvant (1990: 114). On this point see also Grönroos (1985). This view is clearly incorrect. A legal consultation, for example, requires interaction between the professional in question and the user. A substantial part of the transaction consists of both the user and the producer working in isolation.
4 Legal, medical, accounting, consulting and engineering services are examples of services whose *S* factor is typically quite modest. These services require producer user interaction; however, the activities performed in isolation may well account for a high proportion of the total value of the service.
5 For a detailed example see Hirsch (1987b).
6 This assumption is made for convenience and clarity of the presentation. It does not affect the outcome of the analysis and can be omitted when necessary.

7 The assumption that M_x and M_d are symmetric is made only for convenience. The conclusions remain unaffected if M_x is replaced by M_{ax} and M_{bx} and M_d is replaced by M_{ad} and M_{bd} respectively, as long as export marketing costs exceed domestic marketing costs.

8 Note that the statement in note 7 regarding the relationship between M_x and M_d holds in this case too.

6 The internationalization of the production of services: some general and specific explanations

John H. Dunning

INTRODUCTION

Mark Casson (1987) has defined a multinational enterprise (MNE) as a firm which internalizes international markets for intermediate products. These products may take the form of either goods or services. Critics, however, assert that scholars have paid insufficient attention to the determinants and impact of foreign-owned output in services. They are more concerned with the *final* products supplied by the affiliates of MNEs, and argue that the focus on goods-producing activities is unjustified as the value of the output of foreign-owned services has been as great as, or greater than, the output of foreign-owned goods. Moreover, services are currently the fastest increasing component of MNE activity both in developed and developing countries (UNCTC 1988).

It should be emphasized that some 85 per cent of all international direct investment in services is in two groups of services – namely trade-related activities, and banking and finance (UNCTC 1988). As regards the former group, two points should be made. First, the purpose of foreign direct investment (FDI) in trade is to create or acquire markets for the export of goods and services of the investing company or to assist in acquiring imports for the investing company on the most favourable terms. Also, some trade-related investment represents a stage in the internationalizing process of the firm, which might subsequently be followed by production of the goods being traded.

There have been numerous studies of the internationalization of banking and financial services, some of which have specifically sought to explain the extent, pattern and ownership structure of international production. These include those of Grubel (1977, 1989), Gray and Gray (1981), UNCTC (1981), Yannopoulos (1983), Cho (1985), Casson (1989) and Campayne (1990).

There have also been a few publications on the internationalization of different types of services. These include those on the international construction and design engineering industry (Seymour 1987; Rimmer 1988; Enderwick 1989; UNCTC 1989c), the hotel industry (Dunning and McQueen 1981), multinational news agencies (Boyd-Barrett 1989), the advertising industry (UNCTC 1979; Terpstra and Yu 1988), the accounting industry (Daniels *et al.* 1989) and trans-border data flows (UNCTC 1984, 1990a). Some of these studies have been directed to theorizing about the determinants of foreign production.

There has been no substantive work, however, on the internationalization of management and business consultancy, education and medical services, motion pictures, legal services, and transportation services, and much less than might be expected on FDI in the telecommunications and computer software sectors.

Many services are supplied by goods-producing firms. It is, indeed, important to distinguish between specialized *service MNEs* and *MNEs that produce services*. According to the UNCTC (1988), in 1982 about one-half of all foreign service affiliates of US origin were owned by industrial companies. In that same year, 55 per cent of US direct invest- ments in banking and finance and 82 per cent of those in wholesale trading were undertaken by companies whose main activity was the production of *goods*. It is possible that, since the production of services by these com- panies is usually considered to be a secondary activity to the production of goods, they have not gained the attention that they might have done had these same services been supplied by specialist service firms.

The degree of internationalization of services is generally less than that of goods. Again, trade is an exception. Some relevant data drawn from a variety of sources, but first published by the UNCTC (1988), are given in Table 6.1. Here we come closer to the possible reasons for the relative neglect of services, which we shall examine in more detail in the next section.

DIFFERENCES BETWEEN MULTINATIONAL ENTERPRISE ACTIVITY IN GOODS AND SERVICES

There are six characteristics of MNE activity in services. First, the distribution of most services (with the notable exception of tourism) is less geographically concentrated than that of goods.[1]

Second, some goods-producing industries are truly international by nature. At least some of the major markets of the world are necessary to finance the ever increasing fixed costs of research and development which, in turn, are required to generate the innovations upon which dynamic competitiveness rests. Most service firms, however, do not need global markets to be competitive except those which are internalized by MNE

Table 6.1 Degree of transnationalization of US non-bank transnational corporations, 1984[a]

Industry	Percentage share of foreign affiliates in			Number of +		
	Sales	Assets	Employment	TNCs	Foreign affiliates	
All industries	26.2	19.7	25.9	2,088	16,892	
Manufacturing	27.3	24.4	30.3	1,221	11,075	
Petroleum	41.7	34.2	31.1	77	1,644	
Other industries	25.3	21.7	39.7	24	98	
Services	16.6	11.3	16.9	673	3,943	
Finance, insurance, real estate[b]	12.0	9.7	27.9	127	999	
Finance	16.3	13.2	14.6	34	227	
Insurance	10.2	7.3	24.8	77	733	
Trading	18.0	14.7	16.5	217	904	
Wholesale	24.8	23.6	21.6	165	685	
Retail	11.6	10.7	15.6	52	219	
Transportation, communcations, public utilities	6.5	7.1	10.7	83	437	
Construction	23.6	22.5	16.3	33	173	
Business and other services	11.6	12.7	10.9	158	758	
Hotel	7.6	11.1	6.5	8	67	
Advertising	20.3	24.2	29.4	22	179	
Motion pictures	20.0	13.9	11.5	9	79	
Engineering etc.	23.9	20.5	15.3	23	72	
Management consulting and public relations	14.2	15.4	15.6	18	43	
Equipment rental (excluding autos and computers)	3.2	3.8	8.1	7	7	
Computer and data-processing services	10.3	11.9	8.9	13	37	
Health	3.1	7.4	4.4	9	26	
Accounting	–	5.3	–	6	31	
Other	10.6	11.6	12.3	49	238	
Petroleum-related services	28.7	20.5	25.6	55	663	

Source: UNCTC 1988
Notes: [a] Measured by the share of foreign affiliates in total TNC activities.   [b] Including holdings, excluding non-business entities.

goods producing firms where the global output accounted for by foreign production is highest, noticeably in finance and investment banking, some kinds of consultancy, up-market hotels and advertising.

Third, and related to the second factor, is the growth of the international division of labour in goods which the MNE has, itself, helped advance. As one example, the elimination of all intra-Community tariff barriers has enabled foreign-owned firms to engage in product and process specialization in particular countries in the European Community (EC), and to supply other European markets from there. Such intra-firm specialization has not occurred to the same extent in the services sectors. This is because of the limited opportunities for trade in some services; and also because the presence of non-tariff barriers within the EC has impeded both trade and investment in services much more than it has in goods. Hence, the amount of rationalized investment in the service sectors is lower than that in the manufacturing sector, as is the proportion of world output produced by foreign affiliates.

Fourth, as shown in Dunning (1988b), foreign affiliates of MNEs may enjoy three types of advantages compared with indigenous competitors: (i) privileged access to intangible assets; (ii) advantages associated with being part of a larger organization; and (iii) advantages stemming from the multinationality of a company *per se,* referred to by Kogut (1983) as 'sequential' advantages, e.g. the ability of MNEs to engage in cross-border arbitrage operations, to spread exchange, political and other geographical risks and to minimize environmental volality (Kogut 1985). We contend that the competitive advantages of specialized service MNEs, derived from their multinationality, are likely to be less than in the case of goods-producing MNEs.

Fifth, while some service activities by MNEs *precede* those of goods activities abroad, these are often likely to be financed by loans or grants from international banks, development agencies or governments, rather than by direct investment from corporations. Examples include transportation and communication networks and some social infrastructure, e.g. housing, hospital, public utilities and schools. Exceptions include some pre-production commercial activities by goods-producing MNEs (e.g. research and development, employee training, construction and consultant engineering) and some infrastructure activities necessary for an efficient market to operate which firms are prepared to finance themselves, (e.g. some kinds of education, housing and health care activities).

Nevertheless, a sizable proportion of direct investment in services *follows*, rather than *leads*, investment in goods. These include support activities such as business and professional services, finance and insurance, as well as consumer services which have a high income elasticity of demand, e.g. insurance, leisure and travel-related services and specialty retailing. Also, the service component of goods-producing activities by foreign affiliates tends to increase as the local content of the sales generated by them rises.[2]

Sixth, and lastly, many services are not capital intensive, and their contribution to the value added process is better measured by their sales, net output or employment rather than by their assets. The difference this makes is well illustrated by the data set out in Table 6.1, and also by the more general statistic that, in most countries, the share of services in GNP has risen much less dramatically since the mid-1970s than the share of employment (World Bank 1987).

THE THEORY OF FOREIGN PRODUCTION IN SERVICES

Introduction

We now look at the implications that the characteristics of MNE activity in services have for the theory of foreign production in services.[3] The existence of this theory poses two sets of questions. First, do we need a different general paradigm to explain initially the foreign value added activities production in goods? Second, do we need a different set of specific theories to explain foreign production of particular services or groups of services compared with those put forward to explain the foreign production of particular kinds of goods?

General paradigms

The international production literature identifies four reasons for engaging in foreign based value added activity. The first is to acquire inputs for further processing activities in other parts of the investing firm's operation, or for export to external markets, e.g. the activity of oil exploration, whose main locational requirement is the presence of the natural resource. Examples of supply-oriented or resource-based service investment are tourism, car rentals, resort-based hotels, some construction, news agencies and relating services, film making and entertainment. Almost by definition, cross-border transport services also fit into this category.

The second motive for FDI is to supply a foreign market with goods and services more beneficially than by alternative routes, e.g. by exports. This investment may be initiated as a *defensive* response to protectionism by importing countries, or to the actions of competitors, or as an *aggressive* strategy to relocate existing production to where it is likely to be more profitable in the future, or to steal a march on competitors. The customization of products to local sourcing capabilities or market needs and after-sales maintenance is another motive for market-based investment. Examples of such service sectors which attract such FDI include most business and professional services, commercial banking, insurance, telecommunications, some educational services, restaurants and telecommunications.

The third kind of FDI grows out of one or the other of the first two. It represents an international division of labour of the production of MNEs so as to maximize the benefits of differences in factor endowments (both natural and acquired), to exploit the economies of specialization and scope and to minimize environmental volatility (Kogut 1985). The most noticeable manifestation of MNEs practising a 'rationalized' rather than a 'resource-based' or 'market seeking' investment strategy is the extent and pattern of cross-border trade within their own networks.[4]

The fourth type of MNE activity is primarily motivated to *acquire* assets or some kind of competitive advantage rather than to exploit the use of an existing competitive advantage, so that the complementarity between the asset acquired and those already owned by the purchasing firm will improve the firm's *overall* competitive position in a particular market or in a group of markets.

Data available suggest that acquisitions and mergers among accounting firms, banks and finance and security analysts (particularly those involving Japanese firms) appear to have some of the characteristics of strategic asset seeking manufacturing investments. There have also been substantial cross-border purchases of service firms by manufacturing firms to gain access to distribution channels and marketing outlets. Examples include the purchase of Columbia Records by the Sony Corporation. In some technology and marketing sectors, the major *fixed* cost of production is increasingly *service* rather than *goods* based. Examples include the biotechnology and the semi-conductor industries. But, in almost all goods-producing sectors, the proportion of service-intensive inputs and 'created' factor endowments is rising fast. This, then, might suggest that new investment by information or capital-intensive service firms might be increasingly motivated by the desire to acquire, protect or advance a competitive position.

Two core paradigms have evolved from the literature on goods-producing MNEs. The first is the internalization paradigm. The proponents of this approach,[5] essentially viewing the MNE as a particular form of multi-activity firm, attempt to identify advantages which MNEs may have over uni-activity firms which specifically arise from their being multi-activity, and to explain why the location of the plants may be outside the home country of the owning company.

The entry of multi-activity firms is explained by the presence of market imperfections in intermediate product markets which give rise to certain transaction costs. Firms replace or bypass the markets by undertaking themselves the production leading to the goods or services being transmitted.

The internalization paradigm has also been applied also to the service sector, e.g. Mark Casson's analysis of the banking and information services sectors (Casson 1989, 1990a), and Peter Buckley's analysis of tourism (Buckley 1987). Each offers a persuasive explanation of *why* MNEs may engage in FDI rather than in some other form of international involvement, e.g. licensing. In the case of some kinds of investment, i.e. those made to acquire a competitive advantage, the gains anticipated from internalizing foreign markets may provide a sufficient *raison d'être* for the investment.[6]

The internalization paradigm, however, cannot provide a full explanation for all foreign value added activities undertaken by MNEs. This is because it regards ownership specific assets of MNEs as exogenous variables which have nothing to do with the internalization of cross-border intermediate products. The advantage is the ability of a firm to supply consumers efficiently with the products they require independently of *where* it locates its plants or whether the cross-border markets for products exported from the home country are internalized or not.

Take, for example, a Swiss drugs company that finds an effective and affordable cure for AIDS and has undertaken all the research and development which led to the discovery of an AIDS curing vaccine in Switzerland. The successful discovery of this new drug obviously gives the company a substantial competitive advantage over its competitors. If the corporation wishes to sell its drug to US consumers, how is it going to do it? One way is to produce the drug from the company's Swiss factory and to export the final product to the USA. Another is to export the know-how on how to produce the drug to a US-owned company for it to manufacture. A third is for the Swiss company itself to acquire or set up a factory in the USA or to increase the output of either its or someone else's factory. Suppose it opts for the third alternative. The value added in the USA by the Swiss subsidiary is foreign production. What explains the amount of this value added? The internalization economist would assert that, without the incentive to internalize the market for the drug technology and to locate production in the USA, no foreign investment would take place. However, if the Swiss firm had not discovered the drug in the first place, no foreign production would have been possible.

The eclectic paradigm of international production seeks to overcome this particular problem. It argues that at a given point of time the propensity of firms is to invest and produce outside their boundaries. This reflects three things. The first is their abilitiy to produce saleable goods and services to intermediate or final consumers profitably, *vis-à- vis* their competitors or potential competition. The second is the extent to which it is profitable to combine these advantages with factor endowments in a foreign country, rather than undertake further value adding activities from domestic plants for export. The third is that the firm possessing the capabilities may find it profitable to add value to these assets, rather than to sell the right to do so to other firms.

The eclectic paradigm of international production asserts that it is the interaction between the competitive or ownership (O) advantage of MNEs, or potential MNEs, and the competitive or locational (L) advantage of countries which will decide the structure of the foreign value activities of firms. In addition, the way in which these activities are organized, e.g. by hierarchies or markets, will depend upon the extent to which there are imperfections in cross-border intermediate product markets and the extent to which there are economies of scale or scope and risk-reducing economies which might be derived from the common ownership of cross-border activities, i.e. internalization (I) advantages.

The OLI paradigm is, perhaps, the dominant paradigm of international production. The ownership advantages (apart from those arising from internalization of cross-border markets) are assumed to be a determinant of foreign production, while in the internalization model, which is interested in explaining why firms choose to become MNEs rather than grow in some alternative way, they are regarded as exogenous variables.[7] The configuration of OLI advantages will vary according to *industry-*, *country-* (or region) and *firm-* specific characteristics. Applying the paradigm to the services sector, the lower propensity of the hotel industry to engage in FDI relative to the advertising industry (see Table 6.1) is hypothesized to be either because multinationals have fewer unique competitive advantages *vis-à-vis* domestic firms, *or* because hotel firms believe that they better appropriate the rent on these assets by way of using the external market than can advertising firms; *or* because, relative to hotel firms, the value added activities of advertising firms are better undertaken from a home rather than a foreign production base. Or more likely it is a combination of all three factors. Note that two firms faced with an identical OLI configuration would not necessarily react (as far as their foreign value activities are concerned) in the same way. Indeed, there is no homogeneity of competitive strategies or of modes of servicing global markets among, for example, the big accounting, advertising, money management, engineering and architectural consultancy, and hotel MNEs. Any paradigm of international production of services must take these firm-specific differences into account.

One way is to incorporate strategic behaviour as a specific and dynamic add-on variable to the OLI tripod of factors. For example, the amount of international production undertaken by a firm in time *t* is a function of the OLI configuration facing that firm at that time, together with the strategic response of the firm to past OLI configurations and any changes in the value of the OLI variables and the strategy of the firm between the past and present time.

Similarly, international production at any future time *t* + 1 can be considered as a function of the OLI configuration at time *t*, of any changes in the strategy of the firm, given that configuration, and of any reconfiguration in the OLI variables together with the effect which these, in turn, have on strategy between that time and time t + 1. Thus, any satisfactory incorporation of both economic and behavioural explanations at a general or paradigmatic level requires, in addition to a theory of economic organization (including a theory of the firm) and a theory of the (international) location of economic activity, a theory of business strategy which is able to predict the likely response of firms to any given OLI configuration, given the existence of market imperfections.[8]

Economists such as Caves, *et al*. (1980), Buckley (1989), Casson (1987 1990a), Teece (1984) and Kay (1991) and business analysts such as Chandler (1962, 1977), Kogut (1989) and Bartlett and Ghoshal (1989) have attempted to identify and/or evaluate the significance of strategy-related variables as factors influencing not just the decision of a firm to adopt a hierarchical structure rather than a market solution to reduce transactions and/or production costs, but the *form* of organizational structure which optimizes decision taking. Similarly, marketing scholars have given some attention to the role of strategy-related variables in influencing the modes of entry (or expansion) into particular markets; while the main thrust of business analysts has been to evaluate not only why certain kinds of firms build up and/or sustain a competitive advantage, and why they choose a particular strategy towards, for example, product development, product diversity, manufacturing, purchasing, marketing, research and devlopment etc., rather than another strategy, but also the factors determining the strategic postures adopted by firms.

Out of all this research, a sense of a generic or core strategy is beginning to emerge; but as yet it tends to be confined to particular functional areas of the firm (e.g. product development or marketing policy). Examples include Michael Porter's cost reducing and product differentiation strategy (Porter 1980) and Susan Douglas's five kinds of marketing strategy (Douglas and Rhee 1989).

Two exceptions might be noted. The first is the distinction made by Mintzberg (1978) between *intended* and *realized* strategy. Whether they accept it or not, all firms do have a strategy (even if that strategy is no strategy). When firms review their achievements and performances over the past year, for example *vis-à-vis* that of their competitors, and there is some dissatisfaction about their performance, the usual course of action is to try to do something different; in other words, change strategy. The *incremental* effect of such a change can often be monitored more easily than the effect of the strategy as a whole.

The second exception is to do with internationalization strategy *per se*. Distinct progress has been made from the time of Perlmutter's classic article on the evolution of the organizational form of MNEs (Perlmutter 1969) to Bartlett and Ghoshal's examination of the changing organizational needs of corporations as they become more globally oriented (Bartlett and Ghoshal 1989). Even in these cases, there has been no real attempt to formulate any general model of the MNE. Perhaps, indeed, such a model is a contradiction in terms, for the more generic the subject to be explained, the wider the strategic options become and the greater the difficulty of identifying the most significant strategy-related variables.

The possible responses are numerous and varied. We shall mention just three. The first is to construct a framework of variables which embrace all strategic options and then to consider, for each main type of international production, the particular options most likely to influence decision taking specific to those kinds of production. The second is to reclassify types of international behaviour by the commonality of strategic responses. The latter response is consistent with the concept of strategic groups (McGee and Thomas 1986). The third possible response is to relate sources of OLI advantages to particular strategic objectives. Ghoshal, for example, has identified three main types of competitive advantages enjoyed by firms, including those associated with the location of their production,[9] to three strategic objectives, namely achieving efficiency in current operations, managing risks and innovation learning and adaptation (Ghoshal 1987).

We have introduced the strategic dimension into an analysis of the determinants of international production mainly because, with the growing plurality of forms of globalization and especially the explosive growth of cross-border collaborative alliances, strategic decision taking has become an increasingly important component of competitive success. It is also an area which seems to have escaped the attention of most scholars interested in the globalization of services.

More recently, however, some attention has been given to the application of overseas market entry strategies to the services sector (Shamia and Johnson 1987; Erramilli and Rao 1990). Erramilli and Rao, for example, suggest that it is possible to relate the entry mode (graded by the degree of resource commitment) to the motives for entry, and these, in turn, to different kinds of service firms. In particular, the authors distinguish between *client following* (CF) and *market seeking* (MS) entry strategies. The first of these strategies is self-evident. Service firms go abroad to service their clients who have preceded them abroad. Thus, many professional service firms initially followed their goods-producing clients to the countries in which they set up their factories. Today, firms are expected to offer global services to their global clients. The second strategy of service firms is to enter foreign markets to supply new foreign (or foreign and domestic) clients.

These two strategies can be related to different typologies of MNE service firms. One classification is by the kind of service provided; another is whether or not the production of the service can or cannot be separated from the consumption of the service (Hirsch 1989a). Table 6.2 reproduces the table compiled by Erramilli and Rao, who theorized that, compared with MS strategies, CF strategies are most likely to be associated with 100 per cent equity ownership rather than a joint venture or some form of non-contractual form of involvement; and that there would be a greater tendency among firms pursuing MS strategies to conclude co-operative alliances with other firms than in the case of firms pursuing CF entries.

The hypotheses were tested separately for coupled (soft service) and decoupled (hard service) firms and controlled for country-specific effects. In all, 286 firms provided data. The first hypothesis held well across the board for soft service firms, but not for hard service firms. Part of the reason for this may be differences in the factors influencing entry models of the two groups of firms. As regards the second hypothesis, firms pursuing an MS strategy showed a far greater inclination to team up with external entities than did firms adopting a CF strategy.

This study is an example of the way in which strategy-related variables might be incorporated into economic explanations of international production. For the most part, however, strategic management applied to

Table 6.2 Examples of entry strategies associated with two types of service firms

	Soft-service firms	*Hard-service firms*
Client following	An advertising agency sets up an office abroad to serve a domestic client's foreign subsidiary	A software company provides software support to the foreign subsidiary of a domestic client
Market seeking	A fast-food chain appoints a franchisee in a foreign market to serve the local customers there	An architectural design firm sells blueprints to foreign customers

Source: Erramilli and Rao 1990

services remains at a conceptual stage. Thus, Quinn and Pacquette (1990) argue that there is no conflict between a low-cost strategy and differentiated product strategy to achieve maximum value from service technology, and that a new strategic focus is needed to ensure and manage the efficiency, flexibility and responsiveness which the technology demands. In a companion article, Quinn *et al.* (1990) also suggest that these new service technologies will impact on corporate-strategy-involving activities through the value added chain.[10]

Earlier (Dunning 1989a) I attempted to identify the main *economic* variables which might determine international production in services. I also tried to pinpoint those OLI variables likely to be particularly significant in explaining the activities of MNEs (or transnational corporations (TNCs)) in the service, and to review some of the more significant changes in the OLI configuration affecting these activities over the last decade.

The following section briefly summarizes (and, where appropriate, develops further) the main conclusions of this earlier study.

THE OLI ADVANTAGES OF SERVICE-BASED FIRMS SUPPLYING SERVICES IN INTERNATIONAL MARKETS

Ownership advantages of firms

We can identify five competitive or *ownership advantages* in the case of service-supplying firms. They are as follows.

1 *Quality consistency, reputation and product differentiation*: Examples include customer-specific services associated with the ability of the selling firm to create and sustain a successful brand image and/or to build up a personal reputation with a client, e.g. legal or accounting and management consultancy services.[11]
2 *Economies of scope*: These include most large multiple retail establishments, investment analysts, travel agents or business consultants.
3 *Economies of scale and specialization*: These include airlines, cruise shipping, re-insurance, health and education establishments and industrial cleaning.
4 *Access to, control of and ability to process and disseminate information effectively*: Examples include stockbroking, foreign exchange and securities dealing, commodity broking, various data-providing processing and service bureaux and data transmission networks. The ability to provide these and similar kinds of services is often complementary to the supply of equipment and physical goods, and the knowledge of how to produce and disseminate data is itself a service.

However, the outlets depend upon the simultaneous use or part-use of equipment and physical facilities which might be owned or leased.

5 *Favoured access to inputs and/or markets*: The need to gain access to inputs and to sustain or preserve a competitive advantage is noticeable in highly competitive information-intensive industries where firms such as executive search companies, consultant engineers, investment banks, insurance firms, airlines and shipping companies tend to cluster their offices in the same location. Because of their size and reputation, some firms may have a better access to quality inputs than their competitors. Examples include Ivy League universities or medical schools, the more prestigious advertising and public relations companies and the top accounting and legal firms.

As regards market access, some service firms initially followed their clients abroad. The East Asian general trading companies advantages arise from the global network of their activities, their immense bargaining power, their unsurpassed experience and knowledge of international market conditions, their control of wholesale outlets for the products they buy and sell and their ability to reduce foreign exchange risks and environmental turbulence by diversifying their trading portfolios. Such trading companies are a good example of multinational service companies whose advantages tend to be correlated with their degree of multinationalization.

Locational advantages of countries

Many of the factors affecting the location of goods-producing activities help explain the location of services. There are two variables of particular significance, however, in the siting of the production of services.

1 The first is the extent to which the service is tradeable – either in its own right or embodied in goods or people. Many services are location bound, i.e. immovable across space. Examples include many public utility services, most forms of public administration services and personal services which require a face-to-face contact between buyers and sellers. Such services can only be provided to consumers by a foreign firm via inward direct investment or by an indigenous firm under licence to the foreign producer, whereas the tradeability of other services rests on the availability and cost of the right kind of transportation facilities by which the services can be imported or exported. Technical advances, in the form of the computerization of a wide variety of cross-border telecommunication facilities, have dramatically affected the ease with which knowledge and information can be transmitted across the world and have proved especially important in the case of business and financial services.

2   The second factor, especially relevant to the location of services, is the regulatory environment of host countries. Countries have greater controls on trade and investment in services than in goods. In the past, entry or performance requirements have been widespread in the provision of business services and in the operation of financial and commodity markets. Country-specific laws and regulations tend to govern entry into many professional trades while price fixing and/or market sharing is common – and often upheld by governments – e.g. in the air transport, education and training, and public utility sectors. Though there has been some movement towards the privatization and deregulation of markets, non-tariff barriers (NTBs) continue to be a major factor influencing the mode by which markets are serviced by foreign-owned firms (Enderwick 1989). This is why the completion of the European internal market in 1992 is likely to have a particularly significant effect on the location of production by service MNEs and of goods-producing MNEs which are highly service intensive, e.g. pharmaceutical and telecommunication companies.[12]

More generally, the locational variables affecting the siting of service activities by MNEs will depend upon the type of services being provided. The distribution of location bound natural and cultural resources, including climate and topography, largely determine the siting of tourist activities. Geography also partly explains Singapore's strength in ship repair facilities and London's preeminence as a financial and trading centre. The ability of the Philippines and Turkey (and at one time South Korea) to supply construction services to the Middle East rests on the transportability of their abundant unskilled or semi-skilled labour force.[13]

The location of most import substitution and rationalized service investment is motivated by very different factors, including the availability of adequate infrastructural facilities. The role of government may also be important, particularly in the encouragement of research and development, labour training and mobility and the provision of information to small businesses. Other work by the present author and a colleague has shown that *transaction cost* related factors (which might best be described as the costs of doing business effectively) are far more important in influencing the choice of location of business-related services within a broad region (e.g. in the EC) than are the costs of actually producing the services in any particular country (Dunning and Norman 1987).

The locational advantages offered by countries, both as home and host to service-based MNEs, are likely to vary according to their resource capabilities and the demand patterns of their consumers. The need for customization or adaptation of services supplied by MNEs to the needs of domestic purchasers is likely to be the greatest in host countries with different cultures, tastes, living habits and industrial needs from those of the investing countries.

While an above average proportion of MNE activity in finance and investment banking, insurance business and professional services (indeed most industrial services apart from the supply of technology) tends to be between developed market economies, the services of tourism, building and construction, and trade and distribution are relatively more concentrated in developing countries.

Table 6.3 gives Michael Porter's estimates of the comparative advantage of different countries in supplying a range of services (Porter 1990). Porter argues that the advantages so revealed have less to do with the availability and cost of *natural* factor endowments and more to do with the characteristics of domestic demand, the presence of complementary and supporting industries,[14] and the extent and form of domestic rivalry among indigenous service firms. Surrounding and influencing these variables is the role of government, particularly in stimulating entrepreneurship and innovation, in upgrading human capital and in helping to provide the infrastructure and complementary assets necessary to ensure the competitiveness of service sectors in international markets.

Internalization advantages of firms

The exchange of intangible services through the market is likely to involve higher transaction costs (relative to total costs of production and transaction) than those of goods. The reasons are sixfold.

1 Most services contain a larger element of customer tailoring than do goods, and they are more idiosyncratic.
2 Owing to a greater human element in their production, their quality is likely to vary much more than that of many goods.
3 A major proportion of information provided, and, until recently, knowledge and experience connected with interpreting and evaluating the information, was tacit and non-codifiable.
4 Owing to 3 above and the fact that information or knowledge related to service activities may be inexpensive to replicate, the possibility of an abuse of that knowledge is a real threat to the firm possessing it.
5 Since markets for many services are highly segmented, the opportunities for price discrimination, which can be best exploited via hierarchies, are considerable.
6 The control of some service activities may be perceived to be a decisive element in the success of non-service-producing companies. For example, some shipping lines may be owned by manufacturers to ensure delivery of

Table 6.3 Estimated patterns of national competitive advantage in international service industries

Industry	Denmark	Germany	Italy	Japan	Korea	Singapore	Sweden	Switzerland	UK	USA
Food										
Fast food										xx
Food service/vending										x
Retailing										
Convenience stores										x
Specialty stores			x						xx	
Education and training										
Secondary and university education		x						x	x	xx
Graduate education										xx
Corporate training										xx
Leisure										
Entertainment									x	xx
Auctioneering									xx	
Medical										
Health care services								x	x	xx
Hospital management										xx
Travel related[a]										
Hotels								x	x	xx
Car rentals										xx
Airline		x				x			x	x

	1	2	3	4	5	6	7	8	9
General business									
Accounting	×							×	××
Legal services								×	××
Advertising								××	××
Public relations								×	×
Management consulting		×					×	×	××
Engineering/architectural[b]	×	×	×	×	×	×		×	××
Construction			×	×	×		×	×	××
Construction research								×	×
Design services			××						
Temporary help							×		××
Industrial laundry/apparel supply	×							×	××
Industrial cleaning (facilities, tools, equipment)						×	×		×
Security services						×	×	×	×
Building maintenance services	×					×		×	×
Equipment maintenance and repair						×			
Wages support and management									××
Trading				×			××	öö	öö
Financial									
Credit card									××
Consumer finances									××
Credit reporting									××
Merchant/investment banking								×	××

Industry	Denmark	Germany	Italy	Japan	Korea	Singapore	Sweden	Switzerland	UK	USA
Commercial banking				×				××	×	××
Leasing									×	××
Money management		××						××	××	××
Re-insurance				×				×	××	××
Information										
Information processing										××
Custom software[c]									×	××
Information/data									×	××
Transport										
Air cargo		×								
Airport terminal		×				×		×	×	×
Shipping	×			×			×			
Port services		×				×				
Ship repair						×				
Logistics management								×		
Service stations									×	×

Source: Porter 1990
Notes: ×, position; ××, leading position.
a   Excludes tourism attracted to a nation.
b   National positions in engineering tend to be in different types of projects.
c   France also had a significant position in custom software.

goods on time, while the prosperity of large retail outlets may be dependent upon the expertise and goodwill of their buyers of foreign goods.

Together with the fact that many services are impossible or difficult to trade over space, the above reasons explain both the presence and the rapid growth of MNE activity in this sector. As suggested earlier, both people and firms tend to spend more on services as incomes rise. Non-service firms are becoming increasingly involved in service activities and new specialized service companies are being set up as the provision of some services becomes more complex. All these trends are making for an intensification of international activity in its varied forms.

Some changes in the organizational strategies of multinational enterprises in the 1980s

There have been forces encouraging both FDI and cross-border collaborative alliances in services over the past decade or so. The main factor encouraging increased MNE activity has been the deregulation of national markets and the liberalization of policies towards trade and inward MNE activity by several developed and developing countries, particularly in the airline, financial, insurance and telecommunication industries, which has impinged on the location and organization of some service-intensive goods sectors, e.g. health care products.[15]

The second factor has been the dramatic developments in the technology and management of information collection, handling and storage (e.g. system integration services, facilities management, remote computing services) and of data transmission (e.g. satellite and optic cables). By reducing the cost of co-ordinating decision making across national boundaries, these innovations have tended to increase the scope for, and advantages of, centralized control (Sauvant 1986a). Some excellent examples of the ways in which this is being achieved are given by Feketekuty and Hauser (1985).

Service firms have also been prompted to conclude cross-border joint ventures or collaborative non-equity arrangements, for the following main reasons. The first is the increasing specialization among suppliers of finance capital, information and people-related services (e.g. employment agencies). Second, owing to economic development the necessary indigenous infrastructure required by foreign MNEs in the service sector to conclude joint ventures or non-equity agreements is also improved.

The third reason is that the assets required to provide some services, particularly those which are data intensive, are either too costly or require a range of skills and technology which no one firm can be expected to possess. In consequence, some service firms are either merging or collaborating on particular projects. (Some of these are described in UNCTC (1988), Porter (1986) and Contractor and Lorange (1988b).) They are less numerous, however, than in the goods-producing sectors. About 17 per cent of some 839 agreements concluded between 1975 and 1986 were in the telecommunications sector (Hergert and Morris 1988). Cross-border acquisitions and mergers have been particularly marked in the insurance and advertising sectors (UNCTC 1988). Co-operative arrangements help their participants to reduce risks while capturing the advantages of joint information and technological synergies.

The fourth reason (and this is the same as the second reason for encouraging more FDI) is the reduction in market failures brought about by improved data flows. The hypothesis here is that this could ease the possibility of non-equity arrangements for specific projects, even though improved data flows could encourage more equity involvement by large and diversified TNCs pursuing global strategies.

The technological events of the early 1990s suggest that service firms are increasingly becoming more specialized in their final outputs, but are also engaging in co-operative ventures both with other service firms and with goods producers along a particular value added chain. The larger service companies are also becoming increasingly internationalized. This is especially the case in those sectors where globalization brings its own dynamic advantages. Perhaps the most obvious examples are investment banking and finance, accounting, advertising and management consultancy, re-insurance, hotels,[16] car rentals and arbitrage-related activities, where all the major players are large international companies, many of which have an extensive network of both foreign affiliates and non-equity associations with foreign firms.

Finally, we would emphasize the growing interdependence between the services and goods sectors. Not only is the service intensity of the production of goods rising, but the cost and quality of external services bought by both goods- and service-producing firms are becoming an increasingly important determinant of the competitiveness of such firms. Moreover, the linkages between service- and goods-producing activities are becoming more and more complex. The locational decisions of manufacturing MNEs are often strongly influenced by the quality of transport, telecommunication and educational services. The competitive advantages of firms supplying durable consumer goods, e.g. colour TV sets and automobiles, are increasingly influenced by the extent to which they provide information for the purchaser, and/or require after-sales maintenance.

Because of these and other interdependencies, it makes little sense to try to develop a new paradigm to explain the international production of services or service-related activities. Scholars of the MNE would do well to acknowledge that the growing service intensity of FDI and the cross-border collaborative alliances may require certain modifications to their existing explanations of these phenomena. This is simply because the OLI configuration facing firms, and the strategic response to that configuration, is likely to vary according to the service intensity of the output being supplied.

CONCLUDING REMARKS

While partial theories of FDI and international production may be relevant to explaining some kinds of service activity by MNEs,[17] only a generalized paradigm, such as that outlined in the previous section, can provide an adequate analytical framework for examining all kinds of MNE service activities. In the present chapter we have sought to identify the main ownership-specific advantages of MNEs in providing services, the way in which those advantages are used to best advance the strategic goals of MNEs and the reasons why, at least some of the value added activities which those advantages generate are undertaken outside the home country of the MNE.

We have also identified some of the reasons for the growth of international production in the services sector over the last two decades and, in particular, why FDI has been the preferred route for organizing cross-border activities involving services. Special attention has been paid to the increasing need of firms, both in service and non-service sectors, to integrate vertically or horizontally their domestic activities with services obtained from, or sold to, foreign countries. Some emphasis has also been given to the fact that, over recent years, both demand and supply-led forces have intensified the advantages of common governance for interrelated activities involving services. Moreover, new opportunities for industrial and geographical diversification have created their own locational and ownership advantages which have strengthened the position of MNEs in an increasing number of service industries. That trend is likely to continue throughout the 1990s, assuming that governments do not impose substantial new restrictions or regulations on trade and investment in services and service- related activities.

Finally, we would suggest three possible directions for further research on the theory of international production in services. The first is the interaction between the production of services and that of goods, and the implication of such interaction for the configuration and co-ordination of value added activities. The second relates to the strategies of service-producing firms. The third is to identify and evaluate the competitive advantages of countries in service-producing activities and the ways in which governments, directly or indirectly, may help their own firms to improve their international competitive position and to attract more service-type investment by foreign companies to their shores.[18]

NOTES

1 *Inter alia*, this is shown by the fairly stable share of services in the GNP of countries. Although this varies from 32 per cent in low-income developing countries to 55 per cent in developed countries, the spread is far smaller than in manufacturing industry and even more so in particular manufacturing industries.

2 Normally, high-value activities are service intensive; the best example is research, development and design, which tends to be one of the last activities undertaken by goods-producing affiliates of MNEs.

3 Foreign production is defined as production financed by FDI and undertaken by MNEs.

4 For example, some 75 per cent of exports of US manufacturing affiliates from EC countries are to US affiliates in other EC countries.

5 For some recent analyses, see Hennart (1990) and Casson, (1990b).

6 Although such gains only arise as a result of the common governance of both existing and newly created or acquired advantages.

7 The argument being that the O advantages of MNEs may not arise from the fact that they are multinationals and may apply equally to firms who choose to exploit such advantages by routes other than FDI.

8 Like the student of the MNE, the business strategist is only interested in situations in which managers of firms have a choice of behavioural options. In a perfect market, a firm's behaviour is entirely deterministic; managers have to take certain decisions on resource allocation and pricing if they are to remain in business. The introduction of market imperfections in the form of uncertainty, externalities, barriers to entry, fewness of producers, economies of scale and the common governance of internalized markets (e.g. which gives rise to product diversification and/or vertical integration) extend the options for strategic behaviour – even assuming that firms have the general goal of maximizing the value of their assets over the long run.

9 Whilst the eclectic paradigm considers all OLI variables affecting international production separately, it fully acknowledges that, over time, these variables are inextricably interlinked. Thus, the O advantage of a firm at time $t + 1$ may be related to how it responds to the advantages at time t. And, indeed, the O advantage of firms may influence their ability to affect L advantages by, for example, their impact on government behaviour.

10 The authors define these new technologies as those including all information technologies and other systems operations, software or hardware technologies developed specifically for, or applied to service functions. Examples include diagnostic techniques, treatment devices and specialized procedures for health care; advanced cargo handling or passenger movement for transportation; automatic teller machines or satellite communications systems for banking and so on (Quinn *et al.* 1990).

11 Often the advantages just described were built up in the domestic market. Because of its widely spread borders and the size and prosperity of the USA, US

hoteliers, car rental companies and industrial laundries all gained experience from a multiplant network of activities within the USA, which could fairly readily be transplanted abroad.

12 Such service intensity might relate either to pre- or post-production, e.g. after-sales activities.

13 Which, in turn, depends on the willingness of host labour to accept such labour.

14 A good example are the economies associated with the clustering of banking, finance, insurance and shipping firms in the City of London (Dunning and Morgan 1971).

15 For example, the removal of intra-EC non-tariff barriers is likely to affect the strategy of both EC and non-EC pharmaceutical MNEs towards the location and organization of the service-intensive stages of their value added chain, e.g. research and development and marketing activities, just as the earlier removal of tariff barriers dramatically affected the location of the goods-intensive stages of the value chain, e.g. the production of the drug ingredients and dosage preparation activities.

16 For example, in the early 1980s, about 30 per cent of the hotels managed by the leading US hotel chains were owned by them, about 40 per cent were managed by them and the balance were managed by local hotels under franchise to the US chains.

17 For a summary see Dunning (1989a).

18 See, for example, Porter (1990; ch. 6) and Dunning (1992).

7 The globalization of professional service firms: evidence from four case studies

Charles Baden-Fuller

Over the last few decades there has been a great increase in the international activities of professional services firms such as those provided by lawyers, accountants, engineering consultants, management consultants, advertising agencies and surveying firms (UNCTC 1988). To be sure, many firms have been international for some time, some even as early as the Victorian age (Jones 1981). However, the number of firms going abroad or doing international work in those days was a trickle in comparison with today's flood. Now, for most large professional firms, becoming international is no longer a marginal activity – it is central. But there remains an unresolved issue: what is the best path to take?

Looking at what firms have done provides no obvious clues as to the best way to become international, for the choices taken have been many and varied. Some have been content to accept overseas clients and service them from their home territory, some have used roving teams to do overseas business, others have forged alliances or joint ventures with overseas practices and some have devoted substantial resources in building overseas branches or buying overseas firms. The differing approaches are noticeable both across the professions and within any one profession. For example, Aharoni (Chapter 8) notes that Arthur Andersen has taken a different approach to its international practice than those of the other major accountants. Arthur Andersen has formed a single world-wide partnership of which each country is in effect a separate branch, whereas the other firms have formed complex alliances. In advertising, some of the largest firms such as Saatchi and Saatchi have set up branch offices the world over, whereas some others such as Lopex have formed a myriad of alliances and minority investments. In property consulting (surveying), the largest firm, Jones Lang Wotton, has set up branches, whereas its nearest British rivals Richard Ellis and Hillier Parker have used a combination of branches, minority interests, alliances and joint ventures. Law firms have also differed: Clifford Chance has set up a world-wide network, whereas many others such as Baden Oppenhoff, De Bandt, De Brauw, Jeanet and Urai and Mendez have set up multinational alliances (UNCTC 1988; Rice 1990).

Not only do firms differ both across professions and within a profession, but there are also differences over time. Firms have changed strategies: some have initially gone with branch offices only to follow with a spate of mergers; others have done the reverse. Joint ventures have been bundled and unbundled.

It is extremely hard to gauge the success of professional firms' international activities. Unlike their manufacturing counterparts which are required to disclose financial figures, most professional firms are closed companies, partnerships or other such entities. In general they are neither required by law nor willing to disclose their financial results; even obtaining data on their international activities is not always easy. In a recent survey of ten chief executives (senior partners as many were called), covering such diverse professions as advertising, management consulting, surveying and consulting engineering, it was revealed to the author that international activities were neither universally profitable nor easy to manage. Although reluctant to speak in public, many privately admitted that they were perplexed.

The myriad of responses to international pressures and the evidence that at least some large firms have experienced less than fully satisfactory financial results opens up two alternative explanations of events. Stated as extremes, the first interpretation is that professional firms are responding to a single major force encouraging increased internationalization, which at present they understand rather poorly. This explanation does not necessarily require the response to be the same for all professions nor even for all firms within a profession. However, it does suggest that, by a process of trial and error, firms are identifying the critical factors in achieving success in an increasingly international arena. If internationalization is driven this way, then the tasks of managers and researchers alike are clear: the key force, or set of forces, needs to be identified and agendas constructed for coping with the pressures.

The second and sharply contrasting explanation is that in most professions the conditions of competition are turbulent. This turbulence is not confined to superficial notions of competition for customers, staff and profits, but involves something more significant. In particular, the customer segments may be changing, the technology may be changing and there may be new forces from foreign and domestic competition. This, along with changes in government and professional regulations, adds up to turbulence in the fundamentals of competition. Firms should not be seen as searching for the single nirvana, but as adjusting their activities to cope with the complexity of the international market place. The various responses by firms can be seen as competition for different solutions to cope with current and future uncertainty. The second explanation sets a different agenda for researchers and managers: rather than looking for the single force or set of forces, we need to understand the dynamics of the market place and identify ways to cope with the inevitable change.

There is a third explanation which is complementary to both of the above. Many firms may be acting defensively in response to the initial moves of a few. The herd fears that if it does not follow its more sophisticated rivals and become more international, it may be at a strategic disadvantage (see, for example, Graham 1975; Hamel and Prahalad 1985; Kogut 1989). As this explanation does not explain the initial moves (in weakly concentrated industries such as professional services) it will not be discussed further.

In this chapter, I argue that, for many firms, the second condition prevails. By examining the forces for change and giving four case studies I present some evidence to support this view.

COMPETING THEORIES

Let us begin by looking more carefully at the competing explanations of international activity. Many believe that the basic economics of an industry changes slowly over time, and that changing patterns of international trade represent responses by firms to changes in factor costs and trade barriers rather than to a fundamental realignment of economic circumstances. For example, the economists' doctrine of comparative advantage can explain shifting patterns of trade by reference to changes in relative wage costs and tariffs. Trade in professional services, although still small, has enormously increased over the last few decades. Since trade in professional services is usually confined to the developed nations, changes in wage costs are unlikely to be a crucial factor affecting trade changes (Caves 1982), but tariffs and other government or professionally imposed restrictions are likely to be important (UNCTC 1988). An increase in the trade of professional services can be seen as a response to falling tariff barriers and other restrictions. If this were so, then undertaking international business could be seen as merely an extension of traditional domestic business to overseas customers.

The theory of the multinational enterprise (MNE) explains foreign direct investment (FDI) activity using the transactions costs approach: increases or decreases in the activities of MNEs can be explained by reference to changing rules on investment flows and changes in transactions costs. In the context of professional service firms, the increases in overseas investment in branches, acquisitions and the like can be explained by reference to the falling costs of monitoring services delivered overseas. The most notable cost reductions have occurred on account of the fax, the falling costs of air travel and the reduced controls on inward and outward investment following deregulation. Again, if this were so, then the creation of foreign branches could be seen as an extension of domestic branching and overseas mergers as an extension of domestic ones.

Strategy writers, especially those whose background is in industrial economics, such as Porter (1980) and Harrigan (1988a), suggest that established industries show patterns of stability and suggest that firms will follow generic strategies. They go further and suggest that international strategies are extensions of domestic ones (Porter 1990; ch. 3). Increases in international activities can be seen as the response to forces which change the industry at the margin. In the case of professional service firms, one would not only include the falling barriers to international activities mentioned above, but also mention the pull effect from overseas investments of the firms' major customers (see Chapter 5 and UNCTC (1988)). Like changing tariffs, such moves could be seen as marginal shifts to which firms can respond without major changes in the business philosophy.

In contrast, Schumpeterian and Knightian views of the world suggest that firms are operating in a highly uncertain environment where the fundamental forces driving competition are constantly changing (Schumpeter 1934). In particular, the nature of demand and the technology of supplying services (or goods), as well as the conditions of government and the role of competitors, are always shifting. In such a world, the rules of the game are never stable, moves abroad are not extensions of domestic strategy but indications of firms' responses to more fundamental shifts. The firm, far from being a simple cost minimizer, is portrayed as a dynamic organization involved in continuous adaptation and learning (see for instance Mintzberg and Waters 1985). Whilst not cast in Schumpeterian terms, contributions such as Aharoni's (Chapter 8) view the greater internationalization of professional service firms as a response to a complex set of forces. He emphasizes not only traditional factors such as the deregulation and movement of customers, but also important influences of factors such as the continuous drive for economies of scale, high standards and the problems of monitoring and motivation of increasingly sophisticated employees.

Such a view of the world suggests that firms' international activities are not a response to a single force, such as the removal of restrictions on foreign investment or the movement of their customers, but rather a response to multiple forces whose relative strength constantly alters. In strategy terms, there are no generic strategies, but firms compete using different approaches. Strategic innovation is a crucial method of gaining advantage, innovation being in the ways in which problems can be approached or dilemmas resolved (Nelson and Winter 1982; Hampden-Turner 1990; Stopford and Baden-Fuller 1990).

Whilst the two schools of thought would agree as to some of the fundamental underlying economic models of trade and investment, there are great differences in the interpretation of what management should and can do. In the static world, the job of the manager is first problem identification and then implementation of the solution (Hofer and Schendel 1978; Porter 1980). Goal congruence is important and the job of the managers in the centre is to direct and monitor the subsidiaries (Chandler 1962; Williamson 1975). In this world we would expect the centre to replicate its domestic operations in overseas markets with relatively few feedback loops. In contrast, in the Schumpeterian world the role of managers is not to identify the holy grail of a simple single solution but to operate like corporate entrepreneurs encouraging the organization to explore and learn (Burghleman 1983a, b; Kanter 1983, 1989; MacMillan and Day 1987). Sustained investments in style rather than specific solutions are needed (DeGeus 1988; Tichy and Charan 1989). Here we would expect overseas investments to influence the whole firm.

Posed as extremes the two sides appear to have no middle ground, yet each side recognizes that some middle ground exists. For the static school, radical shifts occur but they are infrequent. For the dynamic school, stability is the exception not the rule. Nonetheless, the schools of thought remain different. Because of these differences we can generate some testable hypotheses.

Generating some hypotheses

The Direction of Learning

The immediate conclusion from comparing the static and dynamic models concerns the relationship between the centre and the periphery. In the static view, the peripheral units will replicate the experience of the centre. There may be some interaction as the centre learns about local conditions and needs to modify its views of the world, but feedback loops which alter the centre's view of the overall business are likely to be limited. In contrast, in the dynamic model we would predict active dynamic feedback between the centre and the periphery. We can summarise this as a crude proposition.

Proposition 7.1
In the static view of the world, information giving rise to learning moves generally in one direction, from the centre to the periphery. In contrast, in the dynamic model there is significant two-way learning.

The initial steps

It is commonly agreed that firms operate in a world of less than perfect information and that the high costs of obtaining information on overseas markets and other international activities often forces firms to make initial investments with less than full information. Indeed, Aharoni (1966) suggests in some cases that the amount of information may be only slightly greater than total ignorance! Any initial move into a country would be proceeded by a series of steps with uncertain returns in the early stages (Paschale 1984).

There would be a significant difference, however, in the way in which firms should interpret the results of their initial investments. Those who subscribe to the more static and definable view of the world would see the initial activities as ways of making the world reveal itself. If the initial investments were successful then this would give a good guide to how future investments should be made and longer-term success ensured.

In contrast, those who subscribe to the more dynamic view of the world only see a limited connection between initial success and longer-term advantages. Conditions which made the initial move a success may change and the initial moves may not be good predictors of future success.

We could summarize the two alternatives in another proposition.

Proposition 7.2
The static view of the world suggests that initial success of an international operation is a good guide to future success plans, whereas the dynamic model suggests only tenuous connections.

The organizational form

Both the principal–agent approach (Jensen and Meckling 1976) and the transactions costs approach (Williamson 1975) can be used to examine the relative benefits and costs of differing kinds of contracts (organizational arrangements) between the parent organization in the home country and the branch office or overseas organization. Much of this literature poses the problems in terms of monitoring and incentives, with shirkers being the branches and the monitors being the head office or parent organization. Whilst the approaches do differ there are areas of agreement. When a head office is seeking to control an overseas operation or make it more effective, one must look at the contracts between the two organizations. Using this framework one can analyse the relative merits of joint ventures, wholly owned subsidiaries, simple alliances or pure market relationships (e.g., Buckley and Casson 1985; Dunning 1988b; Hill *et al.* 1990; see also Chapters 9 and 10 of this volume).

In the case of professional service firms, an ambiguity arises. The crucial assets of the organization are not the tangible assets of furniture, fittings, computers or buildings, but rather the staff. Maister (1982, 1985b) argues that the professional service firm is only a piece of architecture which links staff to clients more efficiently than the staff could do themselves. This poses an important question: should one examine the organizational arrangements between the head office and the local entity or are the implicit or explicit contracts between the local staff and the head office staff more important?

We can pursue the point with a hypothetical example. In the particular case of the professional service firm, does the fact that firm A buys 100 per cent of firm B mean that a professional staff member in B feels loyal to the head of firm A? Vice versa, can a staff member in firm B have loyalty to the head of firm A where there is an alliance and no ownership occurs?

The principal–agent and transactions costs approaches see the contracts of the parent to subsidiary as crucial. Because each individual is bound to its firm in the first instance, the parent-subsidiary relationship determines the binding relationships of individuals in the different organizations. In contrast, in the Schumpeterian model, the formal relationships between parent and subsidiary organization are not considered critical. Since the organization is seen to be a group of people responding to changing economic circumstances (Quinn 1980), the informal relationships are more important. It is the informal arrangements which determine how the firm behaves in unknown states of the world (Nonaka 1988; Imai *et al.* 1985). Jarillo (1988) and Lorenzoni and Ornati (1988) go further: they argue that it is the implicit relationship between the actors in the whole 'network' which ensures its efficient operation and survival. This set of relationships may transcend both the institutional and the individual contracts. Lorenzoni (1988) describes network relationships in Benetton which are not linked by ownership, but which are very close.

Since the staff of the firm are its most crucial asset, the question of implicit contracts is not a trivial point. Monitoring the staff of professional service firms is extremely difficult and expensive. It is so difficult that most firms undertake little or no monitoring amongst their partners, preferring to rely on the pre-partnership stage of training and experience. Even below the partnership level, monitoring is hard as much work is done by staff members alone. Monitoring usually means that someone more senior has to do the same job again to check if it was done right, and this is costly.

This leads us on to another proposition.

Proposition 7.3

The static model leads us to conclude that the important relationship exists between the parent organization and the local organization. In contrast the dynamic model suggests that it is the implicit contracts between the actors which are crucial.

The importance of teams and inter-office co-ordination

Leading on from the above point, there arises the issue of investment in building information networks and teams. The more static view of the organization suggests that the job of the managers is to identify the crucial synergies and invest in building these linkages (Prahalad and Doz 1987). For example, if synergies exist between customers, then the organizations need to build links which exploit and promote marketing and selling to these common customers. In this model, unnecessary co-ordination outside the crucial activities can be wasteful and counterproductive. Its costs are not worth the benefits.

In contrast, in the dynamic view, inter-office co-ordination and inter-functional co-ordination are crucial activities to improve the effective workings of the whole enterprise (Kanter 1983, 1989). Investment in these activities, whilst having no easily definable short-run benefits *ex ante*, can provide crucial benefits in the longer run (Stopford and Baden-Fuller 1990).

This leads us on to another proposition.

Proposition 7.4

In the static view of the world, building inter-office teams should be confined to those areas where definable benefits accrue. In contrast, in the dynamic view, a general investment in inter-office communication will be observed without any obvious short-run benefits.

THE DYNAMICS OF COMPETITION.

There are two ways in which we can test our propositions. The first is to observe the context in which the firms operate and note whether it is one which reflects static or dynamic competition. That is what we shall do in this section. The second method is to examine what individual firms do, and we shall examine four cases in the following section.

In recent years there has been a significant increase in the level of international trade and investment in professional services. Figures complied by the United Nations Centre on Transnational Corporations suggest levels of trade of the order of 10 per cent of domestic turnover.

These figures concur with data drawn from three firms in three different sectors (hardly a large sample, but all firms were significant in their sectors). They revealed that, among their European operations, about 10–20 per cent of customers came from other branches and about 5–15 per cent of the business of any one office was international and required the use of roving teams either to get the business or to execute it. Whilst the percentages were lower for those firms trading intercontinental (e.g. the UK to the USA) trade was growing.

Although international activity has been on the increase, it is still small and one might be tempted to feel that this supports the static view. However, closer analysis shows that many changes are going on – more than the few indicated by the static model.

The changing legislation regarding partnerships and incorporation has been a necessary precursor to international growth. Let me explain the UK context: at one time most UK professional practices were required to be partnerships and were limited to twenty partners. Most of the major professions have changed their rules – the modern professional service firm can be a partnership not limited in size and in some sectors it may be a corporate entity. The modern firm is much larger than its counterpart of even a few years ago, let alone those of the last century. Many have more than fifty partners (directors for a limited company), some more than 500. Deregulation has not only permitted larger practices but has also allowed the range of services offered by any one firm to grow significantly. In the UK, chartered surveyors are allowed to offer financial advice, banks are allowed to sell buildings, accountants to offer consulting services. There have been similar trends elsewhere in the world. Whilst size alone is not sufficient to force a firm to expand overseas, restraints on size have certainly been a force hindering international expansion.

For various institutional reasons the owners of a professional firm may be better placed to invest overseas through the firm's corporate or partnership structure rather than through other market mechanisms. In many countries, outside investors are restricted to those in the same line of business, thus preventing the stock market from having a role. In addition, the investing firm may have access to better information and may benefit from many tax and other advantages.

The pressure from international clients has been another force stimulating greater international activity (see Chapter 8). This force is most obvious in the accounting profession, where the firm which audits the head office of a multinational company has an obvious demand for activities which relate to the auditing of the client's overseas activities. Whilst it can use affiliate organizations in other countries to undertake this work, there is pressure from the client, its staff and its own internal management to 'internalize' many of these activities into the firm. In the case of accountants, only a few have set up truly multinational firms with most preferring to enter into complex alliances.

As indicated earlier, both these forces are consistent with the static school. However, other changes have been going on which are consistent only with the dynamic school. These changes have been of differing importance across different professions and different firms. One has been in the nature of the demand from the clients. Until recently, many firms have perceived their offerings to be rather standard in type and directed at a client base whose chief segmentation has been by size. Increasingly, new segmentation is emerging. There are sophisticated clients who are looking for highly skilled advice on particular issues, and who have highly skilled internal departments to provide basic services. There are also clients who are looking to contract out all their professional service needs in an attempt to reduce the size of their corporate head offices. The new segmentation may not distinguish clients by size but rather by their own internal corporate strategy. Such changes could alter the basis of competition, especially when added to supply-side effects.

On the supply side there are changes too. Whereas several years ago large firms sought to do the same as small firms but on a larger scale, now things are different. Increasingly the large firms are building up highly specialized skill bases and creating subdivisions of expertise. Far from creating economies of scale which lower costs, this activity is aimed at gaining possibilities for greater differentiation and the charging of higher fees. Table 7.1, documenting different charge-out rates for large and small accounting firms, neatly illustrates this point.

These supply and demand changes are altering the rules of the game in many professions. For example, in the property advisory sector large firms no longer gain their greatest margins from straightforward sales, valuation or advice: the biggest margins are to be earned from arranging the

Table 7.1 Comparative charge-out rates for differently sized UK accounting firms (pounds per hour)

	Big eight	Medium sized	Small sized
Senior accountant	40–60	40–70	40–5
Manager	100–30	100	n.a.
Partner	150–200	150	80

Source: Davis *et al.* 1990
Note: n.a. not applicable.

construction of large office or shopping complexes. These deals are not only larger in size but involve more players and more services. Together with the size and scope of the deal comes complexity and long gestation times: deals may take years rather than weeks to consummate. The pay off to such deals is likewise spectacular. In consulting there has been a corresponding increase in complexity. Whereas several years ago a firm might deliver to the top management a strategic plan and leave the management to implement the ideas, now consultants are expected to do much more difficult and complex work. They may be required to teach the management to solve problems (as opposed to providing solutions), they may be required to design data systems (rather than just producing data) and advise on all aspects of implementation. In the advertising business, complexity has grown too. No longer is the agent producing one campaign for one product in one country: now there is a range of products to be sold in a range of countries, each with their own cultural differences. Moreover, there are feedback linkages between the work of the firm and the work of the designers.

This kind of innovation requires the professional firm to devote resources to developing skills and people for the new kinds of services. Their investments need to be amortized. Typically the home market is not big enough, especially if it is a state within Europe. Senior executives and other professional staff often ask the question 'Maybe we can do what we have done again for an overseas client or in an overseas location?'.

Other factors are also pressuring firms to become multinational in some way or another. The most obvious is the competition among firms for staff. Many say that competition in the staff market is even fiercer than in the client market. Potential staff (and existing ones too) are increasingly asking the question: is the firm international? Can I go abroad? Will I do international work? They perceive that international firms are more glamorous, offer more interesting work, have better prospects for growth and offer staff more mobility.

If these forces are as strong as suggested, then the move to greater international activity, both by trade and by investment, is an indicator of substantial changes in the basis of competition among firms. Firms would not be expected to follow a single strategy but rather a variety of strategies as they seek to achieve competitive advantage in both the staff and the client markets.

FOUR CASE STUDIES

In this section I report on four case studies of overseas investments made by three firms drawn from three different professions.[1] Over 1990 ten

detailed interviews were held in the three firms discussing the four investments, together with several informal discussions and an analysis of some
internal and external documentation. In each of the three firms, a member
of the top management team, the chief operating officer of one of the
overseas operations and another person who was lower down the organization were interviewed separately. Each of the three firms was in the 'top
ten in the world' in their profession, and two of the firms employed more
than 2,000 professional staff world wide. All three firms had involvement
in at least two continents and one of them in all the major continents. All
had operations in more than ten countries and so had considerable experience of 'multinational' activities.

Each of the four overseas investments was initiated since the late 1970s
but no later than the mid-1980s. Each of them is now a substantial operation
employing at least thirty and up to several hundred people. Each has a
significant position in its domestic market. Each of the investments was not
the first overseas move by the firm in question: those had occurred several
years earlier. The four overseas investments were as follows.

A An investment in Italy. This investment was, and still is, a minority
ownership in a local established firm. The original partners of the local
firm still manage the business. The investment has been successful
although there are some tensions between the periphery and the centre.

B An investment by another firm in another sector in Italy, initiated in the
early 1980s. This investment was originally on the back of a client
project. The project was for a major Italian enterprise and locally based
staff were seen to be at an advantage. Since the project ended, the
location of the office has been moved and the business greatly expanded.
The business is successful.

C An investment by another firm in yet another sector in the USA. Initiated
in the late 1970s, this investment was originally undertaken in conjunction with five other partners and was an acquisition of a local well-
established firm. The initial move was a great success, yielding high
profits and an attractive offer to sell out at several times the original cost.
Since that time, the company has had mixed fortunes: the ownership
structure and the nature of the operation has been changed several times
and the firm now has majority control over a slimmed down operation.

D An investment by one of the above firms in Australia, initiated in the late
1970s. This investment was originally in the form of a small team wholly
owned and controlled from the UK head office. The business was very
successful in the early years, serving UK clients' interests in the
Australian market. The business grew in size and became more locally
focused. The business is currently being reorganized.

Summary of results

I begin by examining the data for Propositions 7.2 and 7.3 – the initial steps and the nature of the implicit contracts – before going on to Propositions 7.1 and 7.4 which concern the ways in which the organizations are bonded. A summary of the four cases is given in Table 7.2.

The initial steps

All four of the investment projects were preceded by documented plans and these served to justify the investments required. In case A the proposal was justified purely on an investment basis. In cases B and D the proposals were couched as a need to follow or serve a particular customer. Case C was put as an investment but with business spin-offs.

For each case these investments were not the parent company's first moves overseas, but for three of the cases the proposals deviated somewhat from the earlier (sometimes formal) plans. The proposal which did not deviate was case A. It followed the firm's usual pattern of selecting a country, going to that country and looking around to see which firms were for sale. When potential candidates were identified, investment criteria rather than business criteria were the highest priority in making the final bid and setting the price.

Case B at first sight followed its strategic plan. The firm's centre always wished to have a set of world branches and initially conceived of London as the European headquarters. However, they opened up in Spain long

Table 7.2 Summary of case studies

	Case A	Case B	Case C	Case D
Location of Parent	UK	UK/USA	UK	UK
Subsidiary location	Italy	Italy	USA	Australia
Structure of investment	Minority	Branch	Minority (now) Majority	Majority
Initial step success?	Yes	No/Yes	Yes	Yes
Changed operations?	No	Yes	Yes	Yes
Integrated reward structure	No	Yes	Yes	Yes
Inter-country team building	Yes	Yes	Some	Some
Subsidiary operations influencing the parent	Yes	Yes	Yes	Yes

before they opened in London and the Spanish branch is still the largest European office. Spain was chosen because the senior partners had close affiliation with the Spanish, closer than the UK. Italy came before Germany, although the strategy called for the sequence to be the other way around. The Italian connection came about because there was a junior partner who was an Italian, well connected with local business, and wanted to head an operation there. The initial move to Italy was not a tactical success and early plans had to be modified several times before the operation was running 'right'.

Case C was a move to the USA. The firm had identified the USA as a place to invest on the basis of some earlier successful transatlantic deals. They sent two partners to New York to examine the market, these partners recommended investment in an existing firm rather than a new branch, but were unable to identify a target. The actual investment arose shortly afterwards by pure coincidence. A London senior partner was told that there was a New York firm for sale and so he took the initiative and put together a consortium to buy it, the price being too high for his firm to do it alone.

Case D was similar to C. The firm knew about Australia because of some deals it had done there, there was a partner who wanted to go out and start the operation and there was a local client who was willing to help set up the operation.

The initial success

If one looks at the initial returns on investment (ignoring the unallocated costs of top management time), all four investments were a financial success. In case A, the investment was a success and the minority firm is profitable. In case B, the firm did not keep (or reveal) its calculations of cash flows. Although its original ideas had to be modified, in a short time profits were flowing in. In case C, not only did the firm receive more in dividends in the first few years than it initially paid out, but it was also offered many times its initial investment by a third party wanting to buy it out. In case D, the profits greatly exceeded the initial investments. In cases C and D subsequent events adversely affected the profitability of the enterprises: more will be said later.

The subsequent moves

None of the firms felt able to leave the initial investment unaltered over the ten or so years after the initial investment had been made. In case B, it was apparent from the very beginning that the details were wrong. The location of the branch was moved, twice: once to Rome and then to Milan with

Rome as a branch office. The kinds of business were also changed, for it was clear that they were ill equipped to serve their initial client group in a satisfactory manner. However, the other firms also changed their strategies. If expansion internationally were to be seen as primarily 'domestic with some international add-on' such changes would not seem to be necessary: in cases A, C and D the initial moves were very successful. Why were changes necessary?

Case A was particularly interesting. The firm realized that its initial strategy needed modification. 'Our initial strategy was investment and acquisition, to achieve profits growth. However, we realized that when approaching potential targets in other countries we needed something more. We therefore devised a strategy for tying together all the investments.' In this case, the inability to fulfil the original strategy to the full, together with the realization that the market place was not 'multi-domestic' but international, forced the firm to revise its strategy.

In case C, the US operation was initially being run very successfully at a distance, without great intervention. Yet changes were necessary. In part some of these changes came about because other parties to the joint venture decided to quit for strategic rather than profit-related reasons, and in part the changes came about owing to the retirement of the original owner–manager in the US business. However, neither of these could explain the radical nature of what happened over the ten years. The firm has been split with different parts being sold to different investors. The constituent parts have been reformed and their direction reshaped. The extent of the changes suggests that the fundamentals of the business were changing. Similarly, in case D there was also radical restructuring, indicating a shift in the fundamental economics of the domestic business.

The extent to which the firms, although initially successful, were forced to revise their strategies suggests that international activity has not been conducted in a stable environment.

The nature of the contracts

The number of interviews was too small to determine properly the nature of the relationship of the professional staff in an overseas branch to the staff of their parent organization or the staff in the other offices. However, an answer to this question can be inferred from the employment packages.

In case A, the overseas firm was a minority holding and all staff were paid by the local firm on the basis of local profits as decided by the local management. In wholly owned subsidiaries, the parent firm acts differently: the parent company determines pay scales. However, the exact details were not revealed.

Case B was the opposite to case A: the top manager of the overseas operation was remunerated on the basis of a share of the world-wide profit pool, and this was not directly tied to the performance of the local unit. In addition, all promotions and salaries of senior professional staff were agreed with the world-wide partnership.

In cases C and D, the local units were in another continent from the head office. In each case the majority of employees were paid and promoted on the basis of local decisions. However, the position of the local chief executive officers (CEOs) had changed over time. At first, they were paid exclusively on the basis of local profits. Now things are different. Local CEOs are paid on the basis of their respective firms' world-wide profit pools.

These remuneration packages suggest that the degree of bonding between the subsidiary and the parent organization initially varied across the sample from very high to quite low. Recently, moves have been made to create closer bonding, especially among the heads of the professional staff.

Managing the integration process

None of the three firms studied in detail now believe that they can operate their overseas activities at a distance – that is, by treating them as autonomous units. In three cases the parent company had tried this but for various reasons had come to the conclusion that integration of some kind was essential. In only one case (B) did the parent organization start out integrating its operations. The issue facing all three firms was *how* the integration should be managed. Here their attitudes differed.

All the firms agreed that it was essential to integrate the top management of the local operation. The methods of doing this were varied, but the purpose was clear: to keep a close sense of what was happening in the local unit and create a two-way dialogue. This integration is far more extensive than the minimum necessary for financial control in a diversified firm (Goold and Campbell 1988).

In case A, all the managing directors met two or three times a year for two days to discuss matters of mutual interest. The cost of the meetings was borne by the corporate headquarters and the locations varied. In general, one day was devoted to discussing tactical issues such as the state of the market, and one day was devoted to more strategic questions such as new approaches to getting multinational clients and the long-term issues facing the industry.

In case B, the local top manager spoke of the tremendous personal rapport he had with the CEO. 'I do not actually need the money: and there is no formal sanction to doing badly. However, the results of each office are known throughout the firm. Most important, if I do badly, I feel I have personally let him [the CEO] down. I feel bad. This forces me to talk to him about what is going on.' In this firm, the top team of all the branches met regularly for European board meetings, and they put aside time to deal with longer term strategic questions.

In cases C and D, the parent organizations had decided that top management of overseas operations had to be drawn from the top team of partners based in the UK. Furthermore, there had recently been a commitment to sending some of the best people. The costs of such moves were considered to be high but the integration was effected naturally 'as they are our people'.

Exploiting client linkages

The firms differed significantly over how they pitched for international business. In case A, the firm was highly organized, having a system for setting up the meetings and rules about requests for information. The system for making the initial moves was based on trust: 'we could all cheat so easily and ask for the moon and give nothing' but there was a carefully constructed reward system for dividing profits after deals were done. In case B, the system was highly informal. Sometimes it worked well, for instance for clients in the financial service sector; in other sectors it was more haphazard.

In cases C and D, the system for joint efforts was much more informal, but seemed to work well. There were clear rules for sharing the fees from the work, which were adhered to strictly.

The staff linkages

Only in case B was the parent firm really committed to large-scale team building across borders. This firm spent very substantial sums on this activity. For instance all members of the staff were expected to spend several weeks each year on training courses, recruitment drives and other similar activities organized on a regional or global basis. In addition, once every two years the whole firm met for a week to discuss wide ranging issues. These activities were reinforced by an unquestioning culture of inter-office mobility. As one person explained: 'I wanted to go to . . . , and they agreed. The cost was borne by the office I was visiting, and they did not complain. This is part of our culture, for it is clear that I cost that office money as I was unproductive.' The costs of these moves were high in terms of air fares, hotels and lost billing hours. Yet this firm was one of the most profitable of all those I had contact with.

The other firms had started the process of integration but undertook it on a much smaller scale. Moving staff around, except on special assignments, was rare: invariably questions arose as to which office would bear the cost. However, one manager explicitly had greater mobility as his goal, and he was determined to introduce the idea 'by stealth if necessary'.

The evidence from the integration process is that all firms were committed to a greater or lesser extent to cross-border learning activities. This is consistent with the idea of a dynamic model of internationalization.

Parent and subsidiary interactions

Without exception, all the firms admitted that international operations had affected the way they ran their domestic businesses, despite the fact that international trade and international clients represented only a small part of their activity and that international business was not intrinsically more profitable. The influence of international operations was most obvious in case B where the firm had integrated its overseas activities very closely with its domestic operations. But the influence was also noticeable in cases A, C and D. This story illustrates the general point.

In one case, the firm undertook a full review of its international operations: it was concerned that if it took account of all the hidden costs, international activities would not be so profitable. The review found that the share of the overall firm's profits from overseas operations was less than the amount of time devoted to the international activity by the senior partners. At first sight, international activity was not as profitable as it should have been. In a wide-ranging partnership debate, many partners pointed out that the international operations produced intangible benefits. For instance, a very substantial proportion of the UK profits could be attributable to business from clients who were not UK based. It was agreed that much of this business would not have been done if the firm had not had an international presence, even though the foreign operations did not directly contribute to the getting of the business or its execution. The domestic partners further argued that the existence of the international network 'makes us more aware of the international dimension and more able to be responsive in our home market where the clients are increasingly international'.

Conclusions

Case study evidence is always open to mixed interpretation; and a case study based on four firms, albeit large and sophisticated firms, is limited in scope. However, the results are indicative. Whilst the firms approached international investments differently, using different ownership structures and different ways of operating, all show strong evidence of integrating their international operations in a significant way into their overall businesses. The extent of this integration is far greater than one would expect from the 'static model', although less than that advocated by the full dynamic model. A longitudinal study involving more firms is likely to reveal clearer results.

NOTE

1 The names of the firms cannot be released, nor can their industries as identification would be easy. However, they were taken from three of the following five industries: advertising, chartered surveying, engineering consultancy, law, and management consulting.

8 Ownerships, networks and coalitions

Yair Aharoni

INTRODUCTION

The service sector has been a neglected area in research and policy debate. In the last few decades, however, the crucial importance of services to the economy has been increasingly recognized. In recent years, interest has also shifted from analysis of the service sector in a national setting to examination of international trade and investment in services.

A subsection of the service sector is that of professional business service (PBS) firms. These are firms supplying services to other businesses in areas such as architecture, accounting, advertising, engineering consulting, surveying, legal services, management consulting or software consulting. Feketekuty (1986) defines professional services as the application of knowledge and skills by experts to meet client's needs. Arkell and Harrison define PBSs as

> the provision of intellectual or specialized skills on a personal, direct basis, based on extensive educational training . . . some take a broader view and would include most forms of cultural, artistic, or intellectual endeavor as professions. It is also recognized that the definition is not static, and that occupations over time can rise to a professional status.
>
> (1987: 4)

PBSs constitute only 10 per cent of service trade, but their importance to the economies is much greater. In their global operations, PBSs are based mainly on foreign direct investment (FDI). From the end of the nineteenth century to the 1980s, almost all FDIs were in resource-based activities. FDIs were often vertical integrations of manufacturing firms from developed countries and associated with colonial ties. Trading companies followed colonial lines too, e.g. British trading firms in India.

By the 1950s, the major FDIs were made to establish or acquire subsidiaries, producing goods. The increasing size of minimum efficient scale, the growing homogeneity of consumers' demands and the rising value of the ability to control and co-ordinate a myriad of activities have all helped the growth of multinational enterprises (MNEs), whose cross-border activities created a major new form in international business.

The tradeability of PBSs has long been limited because of the simultaneous nature of production and consumption. Today, developments in both telecommunications and computer technologies (and the merger of these two technologies) allows the production of a service in one location and its simultaneous consumption elsewhere. Today, business services are supplied internationally, mainly, by affiliates of MNEs, supplemented by the movement of people. These MNEs, however, are rarely a cluster of fully owned subsidiaries of one headquarters, as is commonly found in manufacturing MNEs. In most cases, one finds various types in an informal network of independent firms.

The theory on MNEs is dominated by transaction cost analysis, explaining the choice of market *or* hierarchies, but much less so the formation of a network. In this chapter some hypotheses are proposed on reasons for using networks, coalitions and ownership structures. Its major proposition is that the organizational structure chosen by PBS multinational operations is a joint function of (a) the key factors of success (KFS) needed to achieve distinctive competence; (b) the best means management has to achieve competitive advantage in these factors; and (c) legal and other environmental constraints, risks and demands on managerial time that impede international operations but also determine the KFS.

The choice is hypothesized to be based on top decision-makers' perceptions of certain trade-offs. These trade-offs are not necessarily the same for all firms in a particular industry. In other words, this chapter does not propose another contingency theory for the design of organizations or for the existence of the firm's governance relations. It is recognized that firms in the same industry may pursue different strategies and therefore have different structures. Rather, the chapter lists the various variables taken into account by top management in making decisions on organization design. The saliency of any specific variable and the trade-offs may be different for different managers either because of differences in their willingness to take risks, their perception of the risks and their ideas about the firm's culture and history, or because of differences in the competence of the firms, which make certain variables difficult to achieve for one firm but relatively easy for another. A better understanding of these choices will enhance the creation of an integrated theory of MNEs.

This chapter is exploratory in nature. It is laid out in the following manner. The first section reviews traditional theories of FDI. The second enumerates the possible forms of international business collaboration found in PBS firms. To explain these forms, the major characteristics of PBSs are outlined in the third section. Obstacles to globalization and the reasons for increased demand for global-type services are enumerated next. The last section proposes an explanation for the use of various forms of organization, most of which are between markets and hierarchies.

TRADITIONAL THEORIES OF FOREIGN DIRECT INVESTMENTS

In this section we survey the major attempts to explain the phenomenon of FDI. It is not an exhaustive review, as such attempts have been made several times before, e.g. by Lall (1976) and Caves (1982). It is intended, however, as a short background to the problem under review.

Business firms can supply foreign markets in many more ways than those traditionally postulated by international trade theory. One of these is FDI. The theories of FDI attempt to explain why business enterprises invest in other countries, rather than trade in goods and services. Some of the theories explain why firms invest, others explain why a particular firm is able to gain advantage through investment. Some authors also concentrate on explaining specific investment in specific periods or specific industries, e.g. resource-based investment. Certain economists attempted recently to embed theories of FDI in formal models of international trade (e.g. Helpman and Krugman 1985).

Attempts to explain FDIs started in the 1960s. Aharoni (1966) noted the importance of forces that change the geographical horizon of the business enterprise and the imperfect information about markets. He emphasized the awareness of opportunities and the lower perceived risks of FDI coming gradually together with more knowledge and experience. He did not, however, explain when foreign firms will be able to gain advantage over domestic ones and why.

A domestic firm enjoys the advantage of a more intimate knowledge of the domestic market and, in so doing, does not incur additional costs of control from foreign countries or exchange risk. The foreign firms, as Hymer (1976) eloquently explained, must have some firm-specific advantage to offset the inherent disadvantages of operating on a multinational scale. He found these advantages in market imperfections. For Hymer, the firm is an agent of market power and collusion, investing to create barriers to entry and reduce competition. To Cowling and Sugden (1987), this would lead to an anti-competitive impact on the host country (compare with Baran and Sweezy 1966; see also Lall 1976).

In sharp contrast, others started from the institutional Coasean (Coase 1937) approach on the nature of the firm, proposing that the firm is an agent of internalizing transactions, thus reducing transaction costs (see Buckley and Casson 1976; Rugman 1980; Caves 1982; Hennart 1982). In these theories, the firm is defined as an organizer of (more efficient) non-market transactions, not as one looking for market power. They emphasize the internal working of the firm.

A third approach emphasizes macroeconomic reasons, as in the earlier versions of product life cycle proposed by Hirsch (1967) and Vernon (1966) or in Aliber's (1970, 1971) stress of financial factors. Finally, some researchers attempted to explain FDI as a result of interactions in an oligopoly and intra-industry rivalry (e.g. Graham 1975, 1985). The product life cycle was true for its time, but its demise came as more firms adopted a global strategy and as the USA lost its technological hegemony.

By definition, all MNEs are engaged in FDI. Whether or not any FDI entitles the firm to become an MNE is a question of definition (for the different possible definitions, see Aharoni 1971). Since the seminal work of Franko (1976), it was convincingly demonstrated that the nationality of the home office does matter. Kojima (1978) emphasized the difference between the Japanese type of MNE – trade creating and export platform – and the trade displacing, import substitution American type of MNE. The Japanese MNEs, he explained, were oriented towards developing countries and resource development. The US MNEs were dominated by microeconomic interests. Kojima and Ozawa (1985) also claim that FDI restructures industry in different countries in accordance with comparative advantage and explain some of the moves for international sourcing (see also Kojima 1990). Other theories emphasized the role of MNEs as developers and transferrers of technology (e.g. Wells 1984). Dunning (1977, 1988a) echoed many people's feelings that there is no one dominant theory by proposing the eclectic paradigm. It suggests that the pattern, extent and growth of activities carried out by MNEs depend on three major variables: ownership-specific advantages of MNEs, *vis-a-vis* indigenous firms in the country in which they produce (or contemplate) value added activities; location-specific advantages of countries; and market internalization advantages.

Networks do not involve ownership and cannot be explained by ownership advantages. Our task is to explain the choices of the firm – not only of market or hierarchy, but of the many alternatives between these two. It is hypothesized that this choice is based on an implicit or explicit weighing of strategic and administrative advantages and drawbacks, risks and returns, and dynamic costs and benefits. A first step toward a better understanding of the issues is to analyse the different forms of collaboration.

FORMS OF INTERNATIONAL COLLABORATION AMONG FIRMS: THEORETICAL CONSIDERATIONS

Relations among individuals within an organization may take different forms. One is a hierarchy, in which those at the top enjoy a legitimate right to tell those subordinate to them what to do while the subordinates accept this authority. A voluminous literature in organization theory tells us when these conditions hold. It is generally assumed that, within a firm, property rights of owners allow these owners to give directions to their agents to the extent that, when those supposed to obey do not (shirking for example), one faces an agency cost problem. Since the seminal work of Coase (1937) in economics, following early work on the nature of the firm (e.g. Kaldor 1934; Robinson 1931, 1934), it is generally accepted that a firm may be more efficient than the market transactions if market imperfections generate transaction costs that are higher than the cost of co-ordinating the activities by internalizing the transactions under common ownership. Transaction costs were defined by Arrow (1989: 48) as 'the costs of running the economic system'. Williamson (1981: 1544) extended this to include comparative costs of planning, executing and monitoring task competition under alternative institutional frameworks. Principal–agent theory proposes a design of optimal contracts to allow the principal to evaluate and control the behaviour of an equal (see, for example, Harris and Raviv 1978, 1979; Holstrom 1979; or Shavell 1979). (For a summary of the organizational implications, see Eisenhardt 1989; Levinthal 1988.) The principal, of course, does not possess perfect information. There may also be asymmetry of risk preferences and goal incongruence between principal and agent.

In the second half of the 1980s, researchers noticed an increasing number of coalitions among manufacturing MNEs, including those competing in the same field (Mariti and Smiley 1983; Auster 1987; Contractor and Lorange 1988b; Hergert and Morris 1988; Mowery 1988; Root 1988; Link and Bauer 1989). Firms preferred coalitions to attempts to grow alone, realizing that no one company possesses the resources necessary to expand on its own. They therefore looked for 'strategic alliances' to acquire the capabilities they lacked, rather than developing the skills internally or acquiring them in market transactions (Hamel *et al.* 1989). Many of these strategic alliances were disbanded (Harrigan 1985, 1988b). Critics (e.g. Reich and Mankin 1986) feared strategic alliances were too short sighted, creating future competitors. There were also studies of hybrid organizational arrangements (Powell 1987). The major problem identified for these co-operative ventures was their long-term viability, which was prone to be broken by one party if that party saw its long-term goals – for instance, learning about some area in which its partner is strong – achieved.

Long-term contracts between parties (e.g. a supplier of an intermediate good and the producer of the final good) can reduce the costs of continual renegotiation. These long-term contracts, however, may not be honoured and vertical integration may be preferred. Therefore, when the assets have no alternative use the buyer and the seller would enjoy bilateral monopoly power. Under this condition of asset specificity, Williamson (1985) argued, vertical integration would be preferred to legal enforcement of contracts to eliminate the risk of becoming hostage to the buyer (or to the supplier).

Clearly, if individuals trusted each other they could achieve long-term co-operation without the need for a common ownership structure or even legal enforcement. Trust, on the other hand, is not the same as an agreement. One agent may trust another but feel that he or she should still receive a larger piece of the pie or that the priorities proposed by the other party are wrong. Therefore, if the sequence of work done is of an important nature, someone will have to be the final arbitrator. The source of power to achieve this status is of importance in understanding the structure of the firms. One can be the final arbitrator because of specific expertise or because of ownership rights. In some cases, ambiguity of control can be perceived as a means to engineer trust. Buckley and Casson (1988) argue that a 50:50 joint venture is purposely ambiguous in terms of control in order to engineer a spirit of co-operation.

Much of the burgeoning literature on transaction costs of markets and hierarchy does not recognize the possibility of arrangements lying between the two. Such arrangements may be termed 'quasi integration' (Blois 1972; Richardson 1972; Kono 1984) or 'relational contracting' (MacAuley 1963; Williamson 1985) or 'transorganizational systems' (i.e. groups of organizations that go in together for a common purpose; see Cummings 1984: 368).

Such relationships are said to be possible in a high-trust society. Japan and Korea are often cited as examples. In Japan, only the key processes for profit and growth are integrated (Kono 1984). A car manufacturer finds it crucial to control, within the firm, the car design and the building of the engine, but buys tyres from outside suppliers. The famed Kanban system is based on long-term co-operation with suppliers – not necessarily on contracts. In fact, this kind of arrangement is also possible under certain power relationships, for example when the supplier is extremely dependent on the buyer and would, therefore, agree to abide by the buyer's rules. Long-term sourcing relations or subcontracting are successfully used by many strong retailers, more because of their buying power than because of trust. The retailer can use many suppliers, for each one of which the retailer is almost the only market access. The same power relations exist, for example, in the car industry. A Japanese car manufacturer buys 75 per cent of the parts from outside quasi-integrated suppliers (Kono 1984).

These relationships may also be possible because of norms, reinforced by ethical standards, of a certain profession. The threat of expulsion from the profession or from a closed community may be enough to make all participants follow agreed rules and standards. There are many different ways to inflict a penalty upon a defector. An extreme one is to refuse any future trading with him. In the diamond business, for example, major transactions are based on oral agreements. The cost of not keeping such an agreement is expulsion from any future trade.

Information technology allows major changes in these relations. Computerized reservation networks bind together travel agents and airlines. Electronic data interchange (EDI) systems change the relationships between suppliers, producers and customers. In Europe, twelve of the biggest chemical companies have set up a working party to create a pan-European EDI system. Access to the network becomes crucial, for example, to become a supplier to a large firm. Value creation is based on access to networks and these networks enjoy flexible architecture. Flexibility allows changes and assembly or reassembly of components based on interaction between participants to meet changing conditions. These networks often allow vertical disaggregation. Value added depends on access to information networks. The proliferation of these interlinking networks allows each party to pursue and enhance its particular distinctive competence, and each party complements others. Any member of the network can hold in check the behaviour of other members, based on contracts or agreements. Information system networks 'are used as substitutes for [the] lengthy trust-building process based on experience' (Miles and Snow 1986: 65). The increasing use of networks may mean a fundamental change in exchange relations.

The strength of a relationship is tested at times of strain, or when a serious divergence of interests develops. An example is the growing friction between consultants and other partners in large US auditing firms. With consulting revenues rising at a faster pace than auditing and tax practice fees, coupled with the added factor of being exposed to audit liability risks, consultants feel that their compensation is not rising fast enough. Therefore they are attempting to leave the accounting firms and take their business with them.

Strain, unrest and discontent can be caused by lack of growth, by fights over power and wealth and also by disagreements on standards and norms. Such disputes may lead some firms to prefer central control through vertical integration. Others may still value more increased flexibility in an uncertain environment. Problems of strain and discontent can also result in employees leaving a firm, not necessarily an opportunistic behaviour in joint ventures. The inner working of the firm includes many 'incomplete' contracts (Williamson 1975). The employment contract, for one, does not specify precisely everything an employee has to do. Rather, it specifies a certain range of activities about which the employee agrees to surrender autonomy and accept discretion and authority of a manager. It may also specify the boundaries of this range. Many other contracts can be arranged in this way.

Organization theory conceives organizations as open systems (Thompson 1967) with an internal structure contingent upon the environment (Lawrence and Lorsch 1967). Aldrich (1979) defined the boundaries between organization and environment in terms of membership. He operationalized membership in terms of employment contracts. Those who are not members are defined as part of the environment. Lawyers may define boundaries between an organization and its environment on the basis of legal ownership. These definitions fail to explain networks or the reasons for choosing non-ownership processes. MacKenzie (1978) explicitly defined organizations in terms of an interaction pattern between a group of participants. All in all, boundaries between organizations and environments are ambiguous, fluid or arbitrarily defined (see MacKenzie 1981). Yet, managers have to make decisions on the boundaries of the firm (Teece 1986a). Organizations can also create their own environments, at least in part (Starbuck and Hedberg 1977: 250). An organization may 'attempt to design its environment to fit its present structural arrangements' (Pfeffer 1978: 142). In making these design choices, ownership is neither necessary nor sufficient to obtain control (Kuhn and Burton 1982). To be sure, an innovative firm may find it harder to convince suppliers to take risks along with it, making costly commitments to supply parts needed by the innovator only in the case of commercial success (Teece 1986b). Yet ownership by itself would not necessarily have solved such a problem.

In PBSs, the major assets are the skilled individuals, who may leave the firm. A continuum of possible arrangements therefore exists based on neither market nor hierarchy, and their nature is not necessarily specified in advance. The coalition or the network created could be extremely stable, allowing global expansion with a minimum of friction and without internalizing through ownership.

A PBS expanding globally can do this in many ways. The first and least demanding form is a *referral service*. An example is when a client of a PBS asks its consultant firm, or a bank or a lawyer, for a recommendation of a professional in another country. Referral is often done free of charge, although it may entail assembling information about service providers in other countries. When these services are frequently needed, the local PBS firm might charge the foreign firm a *referral fee* – or a fixed fee for its services in referring clients.

Another method of international expansion is the use of correspondents, as in banks. There may also be a joint venture of many firms in a specific global network, organized around a shared data base. Examples are computer reservation systems in hotels or airlines, data bases and SWIFT networks in banks. EDI systems reshaped relationships of suppliers, producers and customers in many industries. Other networks are intercorporate alliances or research and development consortia, such as ESPRIT or the Corporation for Open Systems. Networks could also be organized to include firms with different distinctive competencies, or to operate only for certain functions, e.g. data bases or training agreements. Choices of these quasi-integrated forms are a function of specific characteristics of PBSs. Firms can also move to closer collaborations by joint ventures or strategic alliances. Finally, one firm may acquire the others to form an integrated MNE. Thus, one can encounter networks, coalitions or full ownership ties.

MAJOR CHARACTERISTICS OF PROFESSIONAL BUSINESS SERVICES

PBSs are first and foremost skill intensive, rarely capital intensive. They are mostly delivered by self-employed professionals and scale is achieved by having a large number of these highly skilled participants. Further, these firms are dependent upon the continuous and loyal service of these skilled individuals. The service provider, therefore, possesses recognized *expertise,* which is attested not only by education and experience but by a licence granted by a national unit on the basis of comprehensive exams and a period of apprenticeship. Certain services can be supplied only by such licensed individuals. For example, attestation of the validity of financial statements is based, in most countries, on an audit by a certified practising accountant (CPA) (in other countries, however, Switzerland for example, there is no legal requirement to attestation by a licensed CPA). The need for a licence is widely accepted in 'old' professions such as architecture, medicine, audit or legal services. It is not paramount in 'newer' business services, for example management consulting, market research or computer-related services.

A second characteristic of some but not all professional services is that of *personal responsibility* of the service providers, who must be organized in partnership and cannot limit their exposure to the risk of negligence by using the form of a limited liability company. In some countries, a firm offering a PBS must be called by the names of its existing or first partners. A partner in a law firm must be a lawyer and may or may not be allowed to advertise.

Third, most of the services are organized and regulated not only by governments but also by professional societies and associations. These institutions often examine and approve qualified persons for their professional duties. They also design and enforce minimum standards of behaviour and of professional ethics. Recently, in the USA and to an increasing extent in the European Community (EC), professional associations standards are being relaxed. Professionals in the USA are now allowed to advertise and auditing firms are allowed to incorporate. In addition, deregulation in many service areas has eliminated or minimized many constraints and barriers to entry.

Fourth, PBSs (not unlike many other services) are intangible, non-storable and consumed when produced (although not in the same place anymore). Further, in many cases the service can be supplied only through a close interaction between professional individuals providing the service and recipients of the services, as in medical or legal services. This is what Hirsch (1989b) called the S (simultaneity) factor. In other cases the service can be supplied to a third party, e.g. auditing. Because of technological advances in computers, unity of time and place is no longer required in the supply of services. Data are now transmitted rapidly and efficiently and allow networking. The data services created the possibilities for interactive, instantaneous transactions across borders, using a transnational communication–computer system (Sauvant 1986a, b). They did away with time and space and made it possible for a service to be produced in place A and consumed simultaneously in place B.

Data services also allowed for economies of scale and specialization of operations. By reaching global economies of scale, service MNEs can get great advantages over smaller, uninational firms. Gereffi (1989) noted that the international division of labour has shifted from country-based comparative advantages in one product or another to intra-firm division of labour. The MNE can allocate skill-intensive operations to one country and low-skill labour-intensive operations to another. Today, a New York insurance firm processes claims in Ireland to take advantage of lower labour costs. The existence of information networks means that the division of labour can be achieved not within a firm but by networking.

Fifth, in most PBSs, the service is *unique*. A doctor's (or a lawyer's) advice to one person is unique under a set of circumstances – and the service is one of a kind. The result is that it is more difficult to achieve standardization of operations – at least in some services. In many services, there is no way to engage in so-called 'reverse engineering'. An 'audit trail' can be learned by apprenticeship, not by copying from a blueprint. Some PBSs are extremely customized, based on creativity, innovation or pioneering of new concepts and techniques or non-routine ways of solving a problem. Others are much more routine, based on judgement, knowledge and experience. Many are based on the availability of human resources (e.g.

to carry out a market survey) in a standard procedure but in an efficient way (Maister 1985a). Any specific firm may specialize in one of these 'three Es' (Maister 1986). Expertise is crucial when the client has high-risk, complex and unusual problems. The client wants skills and creativity from the professional, in handling the problem. The fee is usually higher and the work is that of a 'brain surgeon'. In other types of problems, termed by Maister as 'gray hair', the client looks for a firm that can bring past experience to bear in solving the problem. The third type of problems are those in which the professional business firm is expected to execute promptly and efficiently. This third type is characteristic of most of the audit function, some basic architectural designs, market research and so on.

Junior professional persons often expect to grow and become partners. This expectation imposes a necessary growth rate on the firm. The type of work done by the PBS firm would determine its economic structure, its human resources strategy, its growth strategy and its ownership structure. Thus, the more innovative firms would tend to be partnerships, with a high ratio of senior professionals and a high level of remuneration. In contrast, firms offering an efficient execution capacity would tend to be highly leveraged, with a relatively high ratio of junior professionals to partners and owners, and a lower hourly billing rate (Maister 1982, 1986). The nature of PBSs is also different, as are the relationships with customers, the way the service is delivered and arrangements with other firms.

Finally, there is a high level of uncertainty in the minds of service consumers about outcomes. When a client calls on an architect to design a building, it is virtually impossible to anticipate exactly every detail in the execution of this order. The cost may escalate unpredictably, the structure may be faulty or major repairs might be needed. An integral part of the delivery of the service is the bargaining between client and provider – and therefore investment of time by the client. These characteristics mean that PBSs face many obstacles to global operations that severely hinder, if not prohibit, creation of an integrated world market for these services or even the operation of an MNE based on full ownership.

OBSTACLES TO INTERNATIONAL OPERATIONS

Despite rising demand, many impediments prevented PBSs from becoming MNEs. Medical doctors, for example, do not work as MNEs, and several attempts to create branches of US universities failed, probably because their advantages were location specific. Other PBS operations, however, previously considered largely non-tradeable, became more and more global.

Since the beginning of the 1980s, many studies have been carried out enumerating barriers to a free trade in services. Noyelle and Dutka (1987) identified eight areas of restrictions which impede the international expansion of business service firms: (a) restrictions on local ownership and on the right of establishment, (b) restrictions on international payment transfers, (c) restrictions on the mobility of personnel; (d) restrictions on technology transfer; (e) restrictions on trans-border data flow; (f) restrictions on procurement policies; (g) local restrictions on the business scope of firms; and (h) restrictions on the use of a firm's name. Similar lists were developed by other experts (e.g. Feketekuty 1986; Rossi 1986; Peat Marwick 1986; UNCTAD 1989: 25–31; UNCTC 1989a;). While these restrictions are all domestic regulations, not necessarily intended as trade barriers, the lists of the impediments to global operations are government-imposed restrictions.

One impediment is the *degree of heterogeneity* of the service rendered. *Ceteris paribus*, the less standard the services, the more difficult is the establishment of multinational ownership advantages. Legal advice is an example of a heterogeneous and specific service. Lawyers face fundamental differences of jurisdiction. In the UK, for example, there are two different types of lawyers. In other PBSs, the major corpus of knowledge translates across borders. This is the case for medical doctors or architects. In management consulting, the principles and methods used can be largely standardized and the firm can teach all its consultants world-wide how to use and apply similar techniques. Auditing services are more standardized than legal services – each firm may use the same audit trail – but there are many differences in taxes and other legal requirements. Indeed, law firms today operate in a highly atomistic structure while auditors are extremely con- centrated. Moreover, auditing has become a more global product than law or medicine. The top ten accounting firms had 3,156 offices and affiliates worldwide in 1988. The top ten advertising firms reported a total of 840 affiliates world-wide while the top ten law firms reported only seventy-four foreign offices (UNCTC 1990b: 150).

A second obstacle is the differences between countries with regard to the granting of licences. Most countries do not recognize professional qualifications of foreigners. Therefore, these foreigners cannot provide the service. The EC Commission has issued under the 1992 programme a directive giving accountants from any EC country the right to practise in another EC nation. A British chartered accountant who moves to Germany still must demonstrate knowledge of German law and accounting practices by taking a test, but he cannot be denied the right to take the test. Other countries require a full set of exams. Moreover, six states in the USA (including North Carolina) preclude foreigners from even taking their CPA exams. Country-specific licensing, differences in legal requirements and the need for a thorough understanding of local markets mean that firms must employ locally licensed professionals.

A third obstacle, in some PBSs, is *unlimited guarantee*. The ability to incorporate firms, thus limiting the liability of their owners, has been shown in a vast number of legal records to be one of the major reasons for the growth of the large firm. Yet, the limited liability enjoyed by shareholders of public corporations is not available to some PBSs. Partners in a law firm, and in an auditing firm, are responsible for their own conduct and are therefore liable for malpractice or negligence. They have unlimited liability for any mistakes made by anyone in the firm. Passive outside investors are not allowed; all capital must come from the partners. Each partner, therefore, may face payment of all his or her personal assets in a malpractice case. The number of partners, however, in major auditing firms is very large: KMPG world-wide has about 5,500 partners, with total personnel of 63,700 in 115 countries; Arthur Andersen has 2,200 partners world-wide; Ernst and Whinney had 3,159 partners world-wide and 35,600 total personnel in eighty-nine countries at the time it merged with Arthur Young who had 2,900 partners and 33,000 total personnel in seventy-four countries. Most of these firms, however, are networks with individual ties and no unified profit pool.

The liability exposure on alleged negligent audits or malpractice can be enormous. In 1988 (Berton 1988), a US federal judge ruled that US-based accounting firms can be sued in the US courts for allegedly negligent audits in other nations. The judge ruling denied a motion by Arthur Andersen to throw out a $260 million suit made against it by the British government. The plaintiff argued that Arthur Andersen's audit of De Lorean Motors in Ireland was negligent and filed for triple damages. Of course, such claims are covered by insurance, but management consultants in these audit firms claim they should not be charged the cost of the litigation insurance.

Fourth, in some countries, the name of a firm giving legal or audit services must be that of its existing (or founding) partners and cannot be the name of an international firm. Most laws also allow only a professional to become a partner. Again, management consulting, advertising and market research are not subject to this restriction.

Fifth, government regulations limit or reduce the tradeability of many PBSs and the access to markets. In Austria, for example, the secrecy laws are very strict. A CPA partner from another country may not be able to review the work of a local CPA. In many countries, services can be supplied only by residents – not even temporary residents.

Sixth, there are differences in the degree of care taken in following certain professional standards (or in the professional standards themselves). In accounting, until the 1970s, standards were exclusively national in character and origin. In 1973, the International Accounting Standards Committee (IASC) was created to work to enhance compatibility of financial standards globally. Yet the move towards harmonization has been slow and arduous; many IASC standards simply permit conflicting alternative treatments to accommodate differences in national standards. Thus, the IASC permits both capitalization and immediate write-off to stockholder's equity of purchased goodwill. Since 1987, there have been accelerated efforts to reduce the number of permissible alternatives or at least to identify some alternatives as preferable. Still, differences in standards is one reason for increased demand for global service suppliers.

THE GLOBALIZATION OF PROFESSIONAL BUSINESS SERVICES

The globalization of PBSs has been demand driven. Professional business firms were led, perhaps reluctantly, into a multinational route in order to serve best their important multinational clients. In the USA in the 1870s, 'Undoubtedly, increased British investments, which required close scrutiny given the wild, free-wheeling business environment in the United States in the 1880s, brought English professional accountants to the United States' (Previts and Merino 1979: 137).[1] Since the end of the nineteenth century, auditors 'followed a parallel path to the evolution of the businesses which they served' (Jones 1981: 108). Later, in particular after 1950, firms 'have come under growing pressure to follow their transnational clients, wherever the latter have chosen to go and do business' (UNCTC 1990b: 145).

Several studies have demonstrated that banks follow their customers abroad so that they can service their business needs fully (Brimmer and Dahl 1975; Gray and Gray 1981; Ball and Tschoegl 1982; Yannopoulos 1983; Nigh *et al.* 1986; Goldberg and Johnson 1990). Law firms are expected to be proficient in international tax implications and advertising firms may be called to launch global advertising campaigns. A PBS MNE could offer a certain standard of service and enjoy a higher reputation; in addition, risk-averse clients would prefer such firms ('we employed the best engineering consultant') in order to reduce risk.

MNEs would not always want their professional service firms to be global; they may opt for a local supplier who is familiar with the peculiar conditions of each separate market. A producing MNE may pick-and-choose the best firm in each country (Radway 1990). MNEs do not usually acquire other inputs, e.g. computer paper, from global firms on a global order. The major competitive advantage of a PBS is its implicit guarantee of a high level of quality across all nations. In auditing, for example, an MNE may require common standards of auditing from its various subsidiaries, and therefore would be willing to pay a higher fee for auditing by the same firm world-wide. Globalization is easier when the PBS firm can standardize operations (Porter 1990, following Levitt 1976).

In some cases, e.g. architects and design engineers as well as construction contractors, the international expansion was a result of growing
demand from newly independent nations that launched ambitious development projects but lacked the expertise in designing and managing them.
Falling workloads at home pushed many to look for opportunities overseas
and these opportunities escalated as a result of the petro-dollar availability,
mainly in the Middle East but also in Latin America.

The demand for the supply of global services created opportunities for
international expansion. Yet the obstacles discussed above made it
extremely difficult to operate a global firm. The solution has been either a
creation of joint ventures (or coalitions) or, more often, global co-
ordination without ownership ties but by a network.

In the production of goods, MNEs are clusters of firms incorporated
under the laws of different countries, all of which are wholly or partially
owned subsidiaries of a parent firm. This type of MNE is the one studied in
the past by legions of scholars in international business. The expansion of
so-called service MNEs is, on the other hand, often an expansion of a
network of several autonomous partnerships. Each partnership gives up
some of its autonomy to achieve minimum common standards and to gain
more work and reputation. These network arrangements are also common
in hotels, retailing or food outlets in which franchising is common. The
MNE sells a package of management know-how and marketing technology
– maintaining a common standard of service, cleanliness or way of cooking.
These values are infused to each franchisee who benefits from the
reputation of the firm and from access to its international reservation
system. There are many other examples of networks. Holders of credit
cards travel internationally, thereby enhancing the value of the card if it can
be used world-wide. These credit card firms established and maintained a
multinational network of establishments honouring the card. Banks also
maintain a world-wide network of automated teller machines. In all of the
above cases, the advantages of multinational operations are based not on
ownership but on networking.

EXPLAINING COALITIONS OF PROFESSIONAL BUSINESS
SERVICE FIRMS

Management has to use scarce managerial talents effectively. Quasi-
integration, standardization, procedure manuals, full disclosure, shared
information systems and peer reviews may be better means of controlling
those variables which are essential to overall performance than internalizing or integration. While networking may have originally been a
means of overcoming obstacles to international operations, it has become a

major new tool to focusing on variables, allowing value added to increase. It created a new era in which markets have become less essential than belonging to a network and firms' boundaries are being increasingly altered without hierarchical changes. Networking has also reduced the importance of size and has allowed much more flexibility as a means of coping with uncertainty. Arm's length transactions among individual firms in different nations are sometimes preferred to an integrated structure within a firm, since they reduce co-ordination costs. Some of these variables are common to all PBSs. Others are industry specific. The configuration of advantages varies because of the degree of heterogeneity of the service, the degree of professional responsibility, the specific difference between countries' laws, cultures and norms and the relative size of firms.

When unlimited liability is not legally required, the ability to use a world-wide pool of experts reduces the risk of world-wide operations which, along with the reputation of a large MNE, explains the creation of one world-wide firm with fully owned subsidiaries. These subsidiaries can then rely on the world-wide experience of the firm in tackling problems and borrow personnel temporarily. Further, they can tap capital from outsiders and are not limited to the funds generated by the partnership, as auditing firms are (a point which consultants in these firms complain about). Indeed, management (and engineering) consulting firms tend to be organized more in the 'classical' MNE cluster of subsidiaries, as are some specific niches in other services such as global advertising.

Ownership of subsidiaries (as opposed to the network arrangement) is more likely when all of the following occur.

1 The system can be standardized.
2 There are significant economies of scale.
3 The home country firm is an exclusive owner (or at least a better supplier) of certain technologies, know-how or contacts with governments crucial for multinational operations (as in the case of design engineering work tied into aid funds).
4 No host country firms exist in the area with the specific knowledge required.
5 The home country firm deems central control to be essential, e.g. local firms may not have sufficient expertise and the home country firm dominates others in size and expertise.
6 A minimum efficiency scale can be reached by each subsidiary.
7 There is a frequent need to transfer temporarily professionally skilled individuals from one country to another.

When the above conditions are not fulfilled a coalition may be preferred. Coalitions may allow a firm to reap benefits it cannot obtain by arm's length transactions, mergers or international development. These benefits include economies of scale or scope, access to knowledge when there are asymmetries between firms, risk reduction and shaping a firm to compete with another and on what basis. These benefits are weighed against the costs of co-ordination, erosion of competitive position and creation of an adverse beginning position. Both benefits and costs are likely to change over the life of the coalition (for a detailed analysis, see Porter and Fuller 1986). Coalition may also be preferred when two or more firms want to experiment with co-operation on a limited scale.

Networks have been analysed to a lesser degree than ownership and coalitions. They are more flexible and their architecture can be changed more easily. They allow flexibility in the face of uncertainty. They are an easier form of co-operation among firms of equal size or experience. In fact, most economic activities can be carried out by loosely coupled trans-organizational systems – or networks. *Prima facie*, they are preferred to ownership ties as they take less effort in co-ordination and allow much more flexibility by changing architecture. Since all participants gain by participating in the network, they prefer to co-operate. Co-operation, however, is not automatically guaranteed and defection could always be a problem. It is therefore of utmost importance for all concerned to feel that they gain by co-operation, and to structure *ex ante* rules that would ensure it (Axelrod 1984; Oye 1986).

Two major problems are faced by networks: (a) making sure that each local autonomous firm, in exchange for access to clients, gives the right priority to serving the client and ensuring minimum standards of quality; (b) achieving optimal distribution of benefits (clients, knowledge transfer, reputation – and the resulting profits) and costs. Since no one local firm alone can achieve these goals, the creation of a network is a feasible solution. The network does not have to be integrated into one firm, even in the case of asset specificity, because behaviour can be controlled by professional ethics standards. However, when these two problems are deemed insoluble, the firm would not join a network.

Some characteristics of a successful network are true in all PBSs. Competitiveness of all PBSs depends very much on accumulated knowledge, skills and reputation, and on a presence in all major markets. Independent firms operating in different markets can increase their total revenues if they co-operate in referring clients to each other. In some cases, these firms may be called by a common name, even though they do not share common ownership, liabilities or profits. By using the same world-wide name, local partnerships gain in reputation, allowing each local organization to get more work by referral from foreign sources, or even locally, being perceived then as a firm which maintains high standards and a high level of expertise. To protect this reputation, there would have to be an agreement on minimum standards to be adhered to by all members of the autonomous organizations network.

In all PBSs, a key factor of success is the skill of the professional. Management would have to create a network allowing affiliation of the best professionals. Much attention would be paid to training, motivation and giving incentives. However, reduced or poor quality in one country could damage the reputation of the firm in all parts of the world; there is therefore an important externality problem in reputation. All PBS MNEs and global networks would therefore be designed to enhance quality and control throughout the operations of such networks. They would also ensure on-time delivery. Quality and delivery enhance reputation. Quality monitoring is achieved by allowing power of inspection to other parts of the firm, for example through peer review. 'Peer' means equal, not hierarchy, and quality does not have to be controlled by a central office. The review is made by persons from other countries, not necessarily from 'headquarters', and since all participants in the network share an interest in maintaining minimum standards of quality, they would allow peer reviews. They all need to get the benefit of a brand name to avoid losing their reputation because of a scandal. Reputation is a means of signalling quality and, since size is often seen as signalling quality assurance, large networks have an important advantage. There is the added difficulty, in most PBSs, for customers to enforce contingent contracts, depending on observations as to the actual delivery of the services. Another important variable would be the degree of standardization possible.

The network can avoid, forestall or obviate serious problems of co-ordination (and the risk of negligence resulting in malpractice suits). In spite of being able to insure against malpractice, the cost of this insurance could be higher for world-wide partnerships. Further, the local partners may also be willing to pay for training of their personnel in a centralized training place. Thus, in most networks, each one of the local participants pursues its particular distinctive competence but also consents to some of the following:

1 to work (and charge fees, but also pay referral fees) on cases referred by other organizations in the network;
2 to refer work in other countries to sister organizations in the network;
3 to maintain minimum standards of professional work;
4 to be subject to periodical reviews to maintain quality;
5 to send partners or professional workers to be trained in certain methods by other parts of the organization.

Almost all PBS firms stop at this stage. Theoretically, the next step is an *international* partnership, in which the profits are shared world-wide. Such an arrangement, however, also means that these partners have unlimited liability for work done internationally. Arthur Andersen is the only PBS firm of its type that is said to be a full international partnership. Historically, Arthur Andersen

> had preferred to enter into agreements with overseas practices that would represent them in particular countries. . . . [Later Arthur Andersen] gradually severed all its existing agreements with other national practices. This move was stimulated by a desire to maintain strong central control over accounting standards and procedures and led to an effective dissolution of the firm's existing international network of offices. Therefore it was not until 1955 that Arthur Andersen opened an overseas office in its own name.
>
> (Daniels *et al.* 1989: 90–1)

Since then, the firm grew, mainly by buyouts of existing national practices. The close centralized approach of Arthur Andersen is not typical. A possible explanation for this strategy is that the firm gets more of its income from consulting (40 per cent compared with less than 20 per cent in other auditing firms). However, in 1955, the organization did not obtain 40 per cent of its revenues from consulting. A senior partner of the firm, in a private correspondence, felt that it was important to ensure that each client be treated equally any place throughout the world. Senior partners in the firm believed that it was critical to have common training and methodology. It was also believed that a system of different profit pools and different financial incentives within the network or partnership may not ensure preferential treatment to multinational clients. Obviously, certain factors are more important in one type of PBS than in others. Thus, in some PBSs financial resources are a key factor, e.g. banks find it necessary to merge to maintain international competitiveness. In others, consistency must be assured. Thus, auditing firms services are used by third parties, be it the government, the stockholders or the banks, who must use consistent rules. Lawyers or medical doctors, on the other hand, service clients alone and, in these cases, consistency is less important. One result is a quest for a common set of policies, procedures and performance measures. It may well be that incentives will have to be tied to the achievement of co-operation.

In design engineering firms, the major advantage for multinational operations might have been reliance on government financing or tie-ins to government aid (Strassmann and Wells 1988: 179). In contrast, lawyers are employed because of their skills, experience and contacts to deliver on time and provide quality services. However, when the legal question crosses international barriers and becomes very specialized, as in international tax or international acquisition, clients may prefer a domestic firm to a multinational one. Moreover, an *ad hoc* network may be a better method of providing the international service than the cumbersome organization of an integrated MNE, for which, in addition, one has to guarantee a certain scale. Further, the capability and credibility of individual law offices may be easier to recognize, by prospective clients, if a loose network is maintained.

In civil engineering, technology is universal and very little technological advantage is possible. Still, one may have advantages in management methods or in specialized construction, such as large fuel-cell power plants or hazardous waste management technology (Strassmann and Wells 1988: 36), or in project management of a large project. Large architectural consulting firms operate abroad by temporarily moving professional workers. In these instances, wholly owned subsidiaries were set up abroad to manage the project. Later they might have continued and won more contracts from local clients. 'Forty per cent of the firms in Seymour's international sample entered foreign markets to undertake work for home country clients' (Seymour 1986: 163–4, as quoted in Strassmann and Wells 1988: 227).

CONCLUSIONS

PBS firms have been facing rising demands for global operations. The globalization of the market increased customers' needs for service to a wide range of services offered globally. Accounting firms, for example, went through a series of attempted mega-mergers to be able to give their large multinational clients world-wide services. The EC streamlined regulations of PBS firms and the professional bodies looked for more harmonization.

PBSs are also very heterogeneous. Lawyers must be specialists in legal systems that are very different in different countries. Architects have to be aware of local constraints, although their profession is more international. Dentists do the same type of work world-wide. Certain professionals must be licensed by their national association and/or by government. Others do not need such a licence. Some PBSs are allowed to incorporate, limiting their liability, while others cannot. The customer in some cases is an individual, in others a firm, and in the case of auditors, the whole community of existing and potential stockholders. For all of these firms, the major assets are human resources. These professionals must have incentives to join the firm and to continue to work for it long term. However, they are vulnerable to possible withdrawal of key personnel who might take business and expertise with them. This vulnerability increases with expansion into foreign, often unknown, markets. In foreign markets, firms may prefer and often are forced by legal requirements to acquire local skills or capabilities. This could be done by an acquisition of an existing firm, by merger, by a joint venture or by an agreement with another local firm on the mutual supply of services.

The analysis of this chapter shows that many benefits can be achieved and many costs avoided by not imposing ownership. When legal liabilities are unlimited, it becomes desirable to restrict the degree of integration to less than a full partnership. If the firm does not have many clients in a certain country, agreement on partial co-operation may become a less risky means of entry.

Network management must ensure that variables crucial to success are controlled. Other variables may then be left to be managed by local firms or by market transactions. Co-operation often entails exchange of mandate from clients. In order to achieve co-operation, methods must be devised to guarantee quality and ensure standardization of methods and procedures and on-time delivery of services. These goals can be achieved by training, by the creation of agreed manuals for the whole network and by peer reviews. Costs of training could be covered by individual firms for their own staff and minimum standards could be enforced by a committee of experts carrying out the peer review; the international committee can then ensure the rest of the KFS, covering its costs by levying contributions, royalties or 'taxes' on each independent part of the network.

In PBSs, there is generally a very high degree of interaction between client and service provider and a high level of customization. In the case of a global MNE, a client must be willing to pay more for a service from an MNE than from a domestic supplier. In fact, a PBS competes simultaneously in two markets, the market for human resources and the market for clients. The great challenge in managing these firms is the ability to balance the two. Further, the PBS ensures uniformity of services and, in order to achieve this uniformity, training is needed together with loyalty. Understanding how PBS firms operate globally, how the various network firms co-operate and how they leverage their human resources is interesting in itself. It also tells us a lot about how firm-specific advantages are achieved. Most importantly, it shows us how management decides on the boundaries of the firm when coalitions or networks are preferred to ownership and how they are managed. It is likely in the future that networks may become the common form of organizational structure, allowing international interaction, not limited to any specific market place.

NOTE

1 After Barrow, Wade, Guthrie & Co., the first US auditing firm, was formed in 1883, several more firms were opened, often by British persons. Thus, Price Waterhouse was a British firm, and it opened a branch in the USA in 1890 under

the names of two partners (Jones, Caesar & Co). Arthur Young arrived from Glasgow and James Marwick from Scotland. Others, such as Haskins and Sells, were two Yankees, as were the two brothers Ernst. Arthur Andersen worked for Price Waterhouse and created his own firm in Illinois, in 1908, while continuing to teach at Northwestern University. The British chartered accountants took effective control of the American Association of Public Accountants and hostility surfaced between them and the native born accountants. Thus, US auditing firms started as having different organizations with no common ownership – in Great Britain and in the USA – and their governance structure was drawn accordingly. This type of governance has been the bud of the networks of today.

9 The impact of bargaining and negotiating on the globalization of professional service firms

Karin Fladmoe-Lindquist

INTRODUCTION

Professional services are an increasingly important segment of the internationalization of the service sector. However, unlike the more visible consumer services of fast-food restaurants and hotels which may be reasonably standardized, professional services are typically very knowledge intensive. Furthermore, professional services are more likely to be mobile and may be provided independently of the specific corporate structure (Nusbaumer 1987b).

BARGAINING AND CULTURE

The professional service characteristics of personal contact between client and provider and the long-term buyer–seller relationships (Richardson 1987) that are necessary to reduce client uncertainty and improve quality control result in a continual process of negotiation between client and provider. The client negotiates with a representative of the service company. This representative, who acts as an agent of the firm, has wide discretion due to the complexity of professional service provision. For example, auditing involves continuous decisions on what operations should be examined closely. Likewise, marketing and advertising involve creative and analytical negotiations on scale, design and implementation of advertising campaigns.

The complexities of provider–customer interaction in professional services become multicultural and multidimensional at the international level. The internationalization of the professional service firm increases the risks to the firm regarding client uncertainty and quality control. The highly interactive client–provider provision system means that professional service firms must respond more quickly to their clients. As a result, the professional service firm has less time for organizational learning and adjustment to different cultural norms compared with more traditional goods-producing firms (Enderwick 1989).

The reduced learning time is further complicated by the fact that standards for quality control are culturally determined parameters (Casson 1987). Under these conditions, it is possible for all-important process errors to be committed without fully understanding the error itself or its long-term implications for the firm. The international business literature is full of anecdotes regarding fatal interaction errors unwittingly made by business people unfamiliar with local cultural norms. As a result, critical mistakes in dealing with clients may occur early and damage much needed local credibility.

This credibility is critical to the success of any service firm (Zeithaml 1990). A reputation for reliability is especially important for international service firms that do not have the long-term relationships in a particular community that can build trust between manager, service provider and customer. A history of long-term interactions between client and provider and provider and manager builds trust and confidence for all three parties. The clients believe *ex ante* that they will receive quality service and the manager believes *ex ante* that the provider will deliver quality service to the client.

Professional service firms are also subject to substantial amounts of local control and regulation regarding provider credentials and qualifications (Enderwick 1989). For example, local labour content laws may require that a specific percentage of an advertising team be local professionals. Legal and accounting practices are subject to substantial amounts of local licensing requirements (Noyelle and Dutka 1987). Local knowledge of national regulatory and market conditions plays a significant role in the success of the professional firm in the international market (Richardson 1987).

The internationalization of the professional service firm affects both the client–provider and the provider–manager interaction. Such interaction relies on the different parties being able to communicate their needs and interests clearly to each other. However, cultural diversity makes communication more difficult. Different cultural groups perceive, interpret and evaluate the world differently (Adler 1991). This affects the ability of the client and the professional service provider to reduce uncertainty easily and to come to agreement regarding the provision of the professional service. It also affects the ability of the manager to communicate with and evaluate the local professional service provider. The ability of service management to provide the necessary leadership for quality service may be hindered by problems in cross-cultural communications. Ultimately, the cost of the transaction for all parties rises as the difficulty of cross-cultural communication increases.

There is empirical evidence that the cultural differences between the bargainers can affect the outcomes of negotiations. A study by Brandt and Hulbert (1976) of sixty-three multinational enterprises (MNEs) and their Brazilian subsidiaries found significant differences in the communication practices between the managers of the different cultural groups (i.e. American, European and Japanese). They suggested that the communication of information plays a crucial role in the co-ordination of multinational operations and the implementation of strategy. Harnett and Cummings' (1980) research found that the effects of culture alone on bargaining behaviour was not clear. However, differences between the countries and the clustering of scores on the Personality Attitude Schedule suggest that differences do exist between managers from different countries. Graham (1985) has conducted extensive research on the bargaining behaviours of American, Japanese and Brazilian businessmen. His findings indicate that there are substantial communication differences between the three groups. Such differences include the level of initial offer, initial concessions, interruptions and the use of silence in discussions. His research, however, only focused on negotiations between bargainers of the same culture.

More recently, international bargaining research has begun to examine intercultural bargaining behaviour. Graham and Andrews (1987) investigated how cultural variation affected negotiation outcomes in face-to-face situations. They found that there was a significant decrease in the number of new alternative solutions considered and a lowering of the number of mutual solutions that were acceptable to both parties. Finally, Adler and Graham (1989) found that negotiators do modify their negotiating behaviour when shifting from intra-cultural situations involving managers of their own cultures to cross-cultural situations involving managers of different cultures. Interestingly, the Americans in the sample typically modified their behaviour the least when negotiating with a different cultural group. They were most likely to use the same negotiating approaches regardless of the cultural orientation of the other party.

In summary, the business of professional services involves high levels of client and management uncertainty. The globalized professional service firm must rely on its negotiating agents to behave in the best interests of the firm, not only technically but also culturally. The effect of 'personality intensiveness' takes on an international inter-cultural dimension that can make or break the globalized professional service firm. In addition, the greater the distance from the home office, the harder it is for management to provide the type of positive leadership that is central to maintaining quality service by the immediate providers (Zeithaml 1990). The organizational form choice, such as a network or a wholly owned subsidiary, may affect the ability of management to maintain quality control and to reduce client uncertainty. The next section presents the theoretical framework and develops several propositions that may be used to investigate this question.

TRANSACTIONS COSTS FRAMEWORK

The customization of professional services and the necessary knowledge gap between client and provider create a situation of significant asset dedication and information asymmetry that gives rise to uncertainty for both the client and the managers of the professional service provider. As a result of these conditions, transactions cost analysis (TCA) provides a useful framework for examining the organizational choice of the globalized professional service firm. The organizational choice that is the focus of this chapter is the international network. An international network is a complex arrangement involving two or more firms operating in two or more countries without formal equity arrangements.

There has been substantial research on the question of the organizational choice of the multinational firm (Hennart 1982; Casson 1987; Rugman 1987; Dunning 1989a). This research stream has its origins in the seminal work of Coase (1937) and is more fully discussed by Aharoni in Chapter 8. However, despite the extensive theoretical and empirical work concerning the multinational firm, the multinational professional service firm has received less attention.

Broadly, TCA focuses on the costs of bargaining and negotiating and the resulting organizational choices by a firm (Casson 1987). The central issue in TCA is whether a particular activity is more efficiently performed within an organization or by the market place. In essence, the question of TCA rests on the most efficient governance structure for a set of activities (Williamson 1985).

Williamson (1985) describes three key determinants of the cost of a transaction. These are asset specificity, uncertainty and frequency. Of these three dimensions, asset specificity is considered to be the most important. The critical test of asset specificity rests on the question of whether or not the assets involved in the transaction are shifted easily to alternative uses. As the potential for asset specificity rises, the possibility of a bilateral trading relationship increases along with the resultant costs, primarily as a result of opportunism by either party. Uncertainty, the second point, increases the costs for the contracting groups to pursue a transaction with a fully specified contract. Frequency, the third dimension of TCA, involves the number of discrete interactions involved in a particular activity and affects the possibility of creating non-standard governance structures to reduce costs.

The delivery of professional services involves a classic bilateral trading relationship with high uncertainty and frequent interaction even after a contract for service is signed. The nature of professional services does not permit the initial negotiation of complete or even reasonably partial contracts. Often, important information is only available during the contract execution stage and cannot be inexpensively forecasted. As a result, service contract execution operates in a climate of information asymmetry and uncertainty that gives rise to the use of bargaining by either party as *ex post* adjustments to the contract are needed (Williamson 1985). The frequency with which bargaining occurs in the contract execution stage affects the transaction costs and allows firms to use alternative governance approaches such as networks. This is true of the interactions between client and provider as well as the interactions between provider and manager. The more frequent the interactions, the more likely that the costs of non-standard governance structures are recoverable (Williamson 1985).

Typically, TCA examines the polar choices of market or hierarchy. However, there is growing interest in organizational forms that fall outside these two alternative choices (Powell 1987, 1990; Johanson and Mattson 1988; Hansen and Wortman 1989). The concept of networks has been used to describe long-term relationships between two or more independent firms (Thorelli 1986). Johanson and Mattson (1988) describe networks as a set of relationships among firms that are interdependent. Such networks are considered to be particularly useful when there is a need for timely and reliable information (Powell 1990). They avoid the organizational complications of bureaucratic structures than can hinder the transmission of information and inhibit flexible responses to changing market conditions.

Williamson (1975) refers to such organizations as intermediate or hybrid forms that lie between the firm and the market. This hybrid view has been challenged by Powell (1990) who suggests that the concept of a mixed mode is not helpful nor historically accurate and only serves to de-emphasize the importance of examining collaborative forms of organizations. The network is an important organizational form that deserves to be considered as an independent alternative.

There has been some empirical work investigating networks. Acheson's (1985) examination of the Maine lobster market concluded that the identity of the transacting parties did matter, that continuity was valued and that local information was very important to the functioning of the system. His research further indicated that there were several factors that inhibited firms from fully internalizing the different activities. These barriers included monitoring problems, the value of independence to the fishermen and a concept of territoriality. Eccles (1981) investigated the homebuilding construction industry. His findings indicate that construction projects involve a unique combination of labour and materials that must be used at the site and that the co-ordination of the different work groups is a complex task. Traditional firm or market arrangements do not meet the needs of managing the diverse needs of different labour specialties such as carpenters, bricklayers, electricians and plumbers. As a result, the use of quasi-firm arrangements has evolved to manage the construction process.

PROPOSITIONS

Given a situation of incomplete contracts under conditions of high uncertainty, information asymmetry and frequent interaction, several propositions are advanced. These focus on the three principal types of uncertainty that are central issues in professional services: management uncertainty (i.e. quality control), contract uncertainty (i.e. incomplete contracts) and client uncertainty. A summary of each proposition follows the discussion.

MANAGEMENT UNCERTAINTY

A central issue in the management of professional service firms is the problem of quality control. The immediate professional service providers work under conditions (i.e. unsupervised, either alone or in teams) that hinder the ability of managers to evaluate the quality of effort fully. Knowledge gaps and information asymmetry between the management and the service provider create additional managerial uncertainty. The immediate providers are the professionals in the 'trenches' and they frequently have more information regarding the progress of a contract than do the managers and supervisors. As a result, managers must rely on the professionals' self-policing efforts for quality control (Mills 1986).

When professional service firms globalize, the problem of quality control by managers is aggravated by physical distance and cultural differences. The standard approach of professional service firms to manage quality control is to control the recruiting and hiring processes tightly (Lebell 1973). It is suggested that the best way to manage quality is to hire the 'right' people. At the international level, the recruiting, hiring and supervising processes of local professional providers becomes very costly as the home office attempts to understand complex local standards and procedures (Enderwick 1989). Specifically, differences in perceptions of quality, bargaining practices, local laws and communication patterns will increase the problem of monitoring and evaluating the activities of the professional service provider.

As a result, international professional firms may search for alternative organizational arrangements, such as networks, that allow them a presence in a foreign market, but do not incur the complex transactions costs associated with quality control and monitoring of professional service providers from a distance. Network arrangements allow the host country office the flexibility and autonomy to institute the appropriate recruiting and monitoring arrangements for quality control. They also transfer the burden of the risk of quality failure to the local office. This transfer of accountability creates incentives for the local office to maintain quality control methods and provide leadership.

Proposition 9.1

The greater the difficulty of monitoring quality control by the home country professional service manager, the more likely that network arrangements will be used by globalized professional service firms. This network structure permits leadership and hiring practices to occur at the level closest to the professional service provider.

CONTRACT UNCERTAINTY

Professional services during contract execution require a series of adaptive, sequential decisions that cannot be perfectly forecasted and integrated into the initial contract negotiation process. As a result, contracts are necessarily incomplete and uncertain agreements that require evolution and modification during project execution. This condition gives rise to a continuous process of bargaining and negotiation as the need for modifications arises.

The necessary bargaining for contract modification is complicated by the effects of culture on bargaining behaviour. Different cultures and countries vary substantially in their views regarding the appropriate level and intensity of bargaining. Such variation in values can affect the perceived quality of the delivered service, from the perspective of the client, immediate service professional and the managers of the professional service firm (Enderwick 1987). The amount and quality of the subsequent bargaining contributes to the overall transaction costs of project execution and the efficacy of specific types of contracts (Williamson 1985).

As a result, the organizational choice of networks may make a substantial difference to the ability of the globalized professional service provider to bargain easily and effectively. The immediate provider needs to be able to make the necessary adjustments on the spot to meet the demands of the clients without continual reference to some supervisor a great distance away. Frequent interruptions in negotiations to acquire either information or authorization from the home office may adversely affect the confidence of the client regarding the qualifications of the service provider and their ability to deliver the professional service satisfactorily. The placement of liability on the host country office moves the responsibility for bargaining and negotiating to those who are most directly involved and who should best understand local norms regarding bargaining.

Proposition 9.2
The more frequent the bargaining in the execution of the professional service, the more likely that network arrangements will be used by international professional service firms.

CLIENT UNCERTAINTY

Client uncertainty poses the third concern for international professional service firms. Typically, clients prefer to be able to reduce their uncertainty through personal interaction with the service providers and the use of local agents (Kotler and Bloom 1984). At the international level, this means that professional service firms benefit most from having a local presence and service providers with whom clients can interact. A service provider that is not available for advice and consultation reduces the effectiveness of the professional service. Part of what clients purchase is the process of interaction (Maister 1982). This process includes advice, reassurance, support and personal involvement. Both distance and culture can reduce the effectiveness of the desired interaction.

One method that clients use to reduce uncertainty is evaluation of the service provider by the amount of experience that the professional service firm has in dealing with particular problems. The evaluation of experience clearly needs to have host country referral points, otherwise it becomes meaningless. For example, for a European client, the University of Tokyo may have far less significance as a signal of competence than it would within Japan. Likewise, technical expertise is more credible if the projects and the previous clients are familiar. As a result, international professional service firms need either to hire individual providers with the required local credentials or to develop network arrangements with other firms that already have such credentials. Firms with long-term standing in the community may have a substantial edge over newcomers with no history (Grönroos 1990).

Additionally, professional service clients need to have some assurance that the providers are accountable if the service quality is inadequate or if some type of follow-up action is necessary. Affiliation with a local firm, or at least the use of the name of a local firm, may increase confidence and reduce client uncertainty. Network arrangements and local affiliations signal to clients that the international professional service firm is available and easily accessible if problems arise and imply a commitment to the ongoing interaction process. As a result, internationalized professional services may find that it is not to their advantage to appear to be too new or too distant. Otherwise, the internationalized professional service firm may discover that the costs of developing a market presence become very high as they incur necessary trust-building transactions (Williamson 1985).

Proposition 9.3
The greater the client uncertainty regarding the behaviour of the immediate professional service provider, the more likely that network arrangements will be used by international professional service firms. Network arrangements provide the requisite local credentials to firms that are either too new or too distant to assure clients of their competence.

SUGGESTIONS FOR EMPIRICAL TESTS

Within specific industries, such as advertising, accounting and construction, there has been progress in examining the internationalized professional service firm. However, there are few cross-industry studies within professional services. As a result, research findings tend to be industry specific without advancing the broader understanding of the similarities and differences among the professional service industries.

It is important to examine the question of organizational choice for professional service firms empirically. The framework for evaluating contractual choices advanced by Casson (1987) provides one approach for testing the propositions discussed earlier. This framework operates at four general levels of characteristics that include the nature of the advantage, the nature of the firm, the nature of the industry and the nature of the countries. Each of these four areas has several specific sub-characteristics that are important to firms evaluating the different contractual arrangements.

The issue of management uncertainty is affected by the nature of the countries and the behaviour of the international professional service provider. Specific country characteristics that would affect this issue include the different perceptions of quality, the different bargaining practices, the different host country laws and the difficult communications as a result of different interaction patterns.

The nature of the industry is clearly a relevant factor in managing contract uncertainty. The degree to which quality is difficult to judge will vary among the different professional services, as will the degree to which contracts are difficult to specify *ex ante*. For example, professional services that focus on highly technical innovations and solutions will experience more difficulty in specifying a contract *ex ante* than will a firm that specializes in the procedure type of project that has a more clearly defined solution.

Finally, the nature of the advantage of the international professional service firm affects the issue of client uncertainty. The experience of the firm and its service providers are definite firm level advantages in professional services, along with work organization and management abilities. Fundamentally, these are the sources of competitive advantage for professional service firms.

One of the difficulties with research on international service firms, however, is the availability of and access to information. Network arrangements are typically non-equity contractual arrangements. As such, they do not need to disclose important information regarding their structures and agreements that would be helpful in understanding the globalization efforts of professional services. Furthermore, there are difficulties in comparing information from different countries because of differences in sectoral definitions. Despite these problems, the growth of globalized professional services makes research in this area critical.

CONCLUSIONS

Professional services by nature must deal with high levels of uncertainty, incomplete contracts, information asymmetry, frequent bargaining and bilateral negotiating. These problems are complicated by the cultural effects on the bargaining and negotiating that are necessary to the adjustment of incomplete contracts. The choice of governance structure is not a cut and dried issue and must be carefully chosen to facilitate the reduction of managerial uncertainty, client uncertainty and contractual uncertainty.

10 Risk-sharing incentive contracts: on setting compensation policy for expatriate professionals in a foreign operation

Zur Shapira

The problem of compensation and incentive contracts is difficult. Analysing it in an international context makes it even more complicated. This chapter addresses the issue of compensating expatriate professional managers. The chapter is conceptual and advances a theoretical perspective based on considerations of risk taking. Naturally, such analysis does not include some other variables which may be useful in analysing other aspects of the problem. The chapter starts by introducing the uniqueness of internationally traded services and its implications for various forms of dealing with overseas clients. Next, literature describing incentive contracts and risk sharing is briefly surveyed. Then a model is offered to analyse the compensation of expatriate professional managers within the general framework of agency theory. Finally, some possible extensions of the model are discussed.

Globalization of services

Several authors have discussed aspects of internationally traded services as opposed to goods. On the one hand, the invisibility of traded services may confound the discussion (Feketekuty 1988). On the other, services comprise a large and growing part of the gross national product of industrialized countries. It also makes a significant part of international trade and reached an estimated $560 billion in 1989 (see GATT 1989). Indeed, the estimate may be even higher as a significant part of trade in goods is actually trade in services (see Chapter 5). While international trade in services can take on different forms, the analysis in this chapter focuses on the case of multinational corporations who play a key role in that domain.

A multinational corporation which is headquartered in one country and offers services in another country may choose to do so in one of the following ways:

1 It can establish a local office in the country where services are rendered.
2 It can provide services through a local contractor.
3 It can form a partnership with a local business.
4 It can sell its services to foreign customers from its home country office.

Several variables can affect the choice of a multinational corporation regarding the ways it renders its services; amongst them are considerations of cost and effectiveness. Are there differences between a business services multinational corporation and a corporation that deals with manufacturing? In a sense, a business services multinational corporation may be more flexible than its manufacturing counterpart. An automotive multinational corporation that manufactures cars in a foreign country needs to have a physical presence in that country. A marketing corporation which markets agricultural products in different countries may also need a physical presence in the form of distribution centres and warehouses. Does a consulting firm specializing in marketing or management need to have a physical presence in the country where its customers are? An initial response may be negative, as the consulting firm may have its consultants sit in its headquarters in country X while providing the services to its clients in country Y. This can be done by using telephones or electronic means such as facsimile machines and electronic mail. The framework advanced in this chapter suggests some variables which affect the company's choice of using such means versus establishing a physical presence in a foreign country.

There are various patterns of co-operation in international services. Banks tend to use corresponding banks. However, attempts to globalize banking services appear not to be too attractive for many US banks who reduce the number of their overseas branches (Kraus 1990). Several consulting firms prefer to have actual subsidiaries. While many factors such as tradition and culture may affect such a decision, it appears that risk tendencies may be one of the determinants of the organizational form of international trade in services. This chapter examines the possible role of risk taking in that respect.

Incentives and risk sharing

The relations between risk sharing and incentives is a problem that has been analysed by economists in different domains such as insurance (Arrow 1965; Raviv 1979) and compensation (Stiglitz 1975). The latter became a salient topic in the 1980s when leveraged buyouts and mergers and acquisitions led to rethinking the classical relation of ownership and control (Jensen 1989).

In classical approaches to risk taking, decision-makers are assumed to be risk averse in general (Arrow 1965). Recent developments in behavioural decision theory propose that risk tendencies may vary as a function of reference points. If outcomes are non-negative people are assumed to behave in a risk-averse manner. The obverse is assumed for non-positive outcomes (Kahneman and Tversky 1979). Current work suggests that, in evaluating decision alternatives, managerial risk tendencies are partially determined by their focus of attention. That is, focusing on a *performance target* may lead to different risk tendencies in evaluating a particular alternative, than if the focus is on *survival* (March and Shapira 1992).

Managerial incentives and risk taking

In purchasing a certain security the buyer/owner shares the risk with the company whose stock he or she bought. If the price goes up he gains and if it goes down he loses. Managers who are compensated by salary only do not share the risk of the owners. This may create a conflict between owners and managers. Indeed, some of the arguments favouring stock options for managers are based on precisely such arguments. That is, the conflict between a manager (an agent) and an owner can be reduced if a significant part of the manager's compensation is tied to the company's performance.

Two issues cloud the above picture. First, there is a rather complicated problem of the measurement of managerial performance. Second, it appears that managers are much more worried about real losses than about opportunity losses (Shapira 1993). Hence, managers may not be attracted by fully shared (riskwise) incentive contracts. If they choose some kind of employment contract they may seek a better cushion against failure than if they started their own business. This may be even more pronounced when an incentive contract is set in a company that trades services internationally.

A FRAMEWORK FOR SETTING COMPENSATION POLICY

The framework is developed within the agency theory perspective (Jensen and Meckling 1976). The thrust of this approach is that there are differential risk tendencies between an owner on the one hand and a manager (agent) on the other. A manager behaves in a way that maximizes his own utility function; however, it may not coincide with the wants of the owners. A major ingredient of the agency perspective is the limited way in which an owner can monitor the performance of his agent. A possible solution to the apparently divergent utilities and the lack of proper monitoring is the setting of incentive contracts. If a significant part of the manager's renumeration is tied to the company's performance, a large part of the conflict is reduced.

Consider the case of a multinational corporation that is looking to start trading in services in a different country. Suppose the company deals with managerial consultation and has no experience in the specific country. In that respect the company faces a lot of uncertainty and risk. Research in behavioural decision theory pointed at the degree to which risk is related to perceived control. Langer (1975) has shown that people develop a (faulty) sense of control that helps them deal with risky situations. Shapira (1993) found that managers make a sharp distinction between gambling and managerial risk taking. The latter has been identified by managers as a situation in which control can be exerted.

Uncertainty and physical presence

An element that increases the feeling of control in uncertain situations is being at the site where action is taking place. This may refer to an individual manager as well as to a business firm. Thus, several US law firms feel that they need a physical presence in Tokyo and so do several investment banking firms. On the other hand, if the nature of international trade is such that most activities can be handled through standard operating procedures then no physical presence is needed. Several activities carried between banks fall in the latter category. Thus, uncertainty and perceived control are major determinants of the physical presence in a foreign operation. For simplicity we consider the case of a multinational corporation that deals with management consultation.

Proposition 10.1

If a multinational corporation in the management consultation business is about to start providing services in a foreign country, the more uncertain and risky the situation is perceived to be, the more the company will tend to have some form of physical presence in the foreign country.

The form and degree of presence is not easily defined. Suffice it to say that at least the head of the foreign operation would be an expatriate.

RISK SHARING AND COMPENSATION: A MODEL

In a risky situation, there is a partial correlation between action and outcomes. Consider the case of a selection task (Einhorn and Hogarth 1978), which was extended to the case of project selection by Galai and Shapira (1985). The degree of success of a project can be only partially predicted, and hence one of two errors is likely to occur. First, some projects that were selected turn out to be failures. Second, it turns out in retrospect that some projects that were rejected would have actually been successful. In the selection decision a critical value x_c is determined such that if the *ex ante* evaluation of the project yields a value x whereby $x \geq x_c$ the project is accepted. The project is rejected if $x < x_c$. After the decision is made the project's performance is measured and a critical value y_c is determined. If the *ex post* realized value is equal to or greater than y_c the project is considered a success. It is classified a failure if the project does not reach the critical value (namely if $y < y_c$). The degree to which the *ex post* realization of the project is predicted by the selection decision is the predictive validity of the *ex ante* evaluation and can be described by the correlation coefficient R_{xy}. The situation is portrayed in figure 10.1.

Galai and Shapira (1985) further developed the above framework as a model for project selection. According to their analysis, investment in risky projects is determined by the relative utilities (or payments) of the 'positive hits' versus the two decision errors. Obviously, the degree of predictability (uncertainty) is a major factor that influences the probabilities of the two errors and hence their utilities as well.

It can be argued that a major asset of a consulting company in management is *reputation*. To that end it is argued that the degree of risk taking will be inversely related to the reputation the company has. Thus, a company with an established reputation is presumed to behave in a risk-averse manner. In Figure 10.2 a risk-averse policy is expressed by moving the decision criterion to X_{c1} on the right; conversely, a risk-seeking policy is one which is marked by moving the decision criterion to X_{c2}, on the left. As Galai and Shapira (1985) noted, moving the decision criterion reduces one error but increases the other.

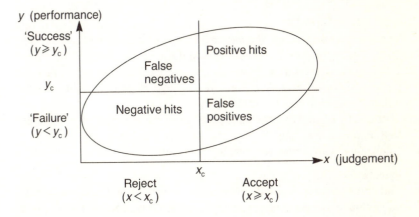

Figure 10.1 Project selection: the relations between a decision and its possible future outcomes

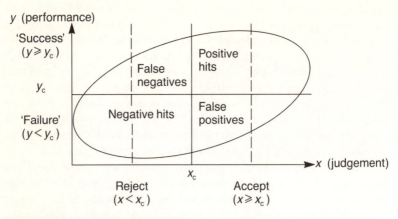

Figure 10.2 Conservative (x_{c1}) and risky (x_{c2}) decision criteria, as they differ from the 'standard' criterion x_c

In addition to moving the decision criterion on the horizontal axis, compensation policy may differ as to the sharing of profit or loss. For instance, a risk-averse company, concerned about reputation loss, may set up a very conservative cut-off point X_c. However, even though the criterion is conservative, a type I error can still occur. Since presumably the manager in the foreign country decides about new projects the company may not have control over X_c. Such control can be achieved by setting a compensation policy as follows. Let the compensation W of a manager be given by the following:

$$W = \begin{cases} K + a\,(y - y_c) & \text{if } y \geq y_c \\ K + b\,(y - y_c) & \text{if } y < y_c \end{cases}$$

where K is a basic salary. The manager receives a premium of a per cent of the profits on the project if it succeeds, and b per cent penalty if the project yields a loss. The relation between a and b reflects the degree to which the company is risk-averse. In general, if b is large relative to a, the manager will be inclined to take fewer risks.

It can be argued that the more risk-averse the company is, the more it will implement a 'larger' b in its incentive controls relative to a in comparison with a more risk-seeking company.

Proposition 10.2
The more a multinational corporation is established and has a high reputation in a foreign country, the more its incentive contracts will have an element of penalty for losses in comparison with a non-established non-reputed company.

Proposition 10.2 is advanced in a positive rather than in a normative sense. However, as noted by Baker *et al.* (1988), many companies seem to be reluctant to penalize managers and employees for poor performance. This suggests that the proposition may be interpreted in a normative manner as well.

EXTENSIONS

Other factors

Obviously, other factors come into the picture as well. The above model describes the simplest case of risk sharing, primarily from the companies' perspective. The model can be made more complex by allowing information about the probability distribution of the decision alternatives in terms of the success criterion y_c. Furthermore, instead of talking about manager's compensation one can analyse the manager's utility function as affecting his or her decisions.

The model portrays only part of the relation between a parent company and its expatriate manager(s). In particular, only monetary incentives were discussed. However, this may not apply to all companies and definitely not to all countries and cultures. For instance, while long-term monetary incentives are used in motivating US bank executives, they are almost non-existent in US based Japanese banks (Dunn 1990). Far Eastern countries such as Japan and Korea tend to place a heavy emphasis on long-term commitment and loyalty rather than on monetary incentives. The relations between risk sharing and non-monetary determinants of attracting, motivating and retaining expatriate managers should be explored. At the moment it appears that such non-monetary factors have a significant effect on expatriate managers (Korbin 1989).

Risk and the composition of executive ranks

Many foreign operations are manned by expatriates, local managers and third-country nationals. This makes the setting of incentive policy a more complicated issue. In looking at these three groups, considerations of fairness enter the equation as well. From the perspective taken in this chapter, it appears that the *less* risky the foreign operation is perceived to be by headquarters the more it will tend to have local employees and fewer expatriates. This is of course contingent on tax structures and wage levels in the different countries. In addition, sending expatriate managers to a foreign operation may reflect other interests of the parent company such as broadening the training of managers (Deutsch 1990).

Proposition 10.3

The less risky the ongoing operations of a multinational corporation in a foreign country are perceived to be (by headquarters), the less need there is for expatriate managers in this foreign operation.

Some evidence in support of this proposition comes from cases of some foreign service companies in the USA whereby, after the business is established (hence less risk is perceived to exist), the companies look for more local executives to replace their expatriate managers (Holzberger and Platte 1990).

CONCLUSION

This chapter provides a preliminary analysis of the role of risk sharing and incentive contracts in setting compensation policy for expatriate managers. The present framework was developed in a conceptual way, yet it was substantiated by interviews with several top executives from multinational corporations. These managers held top positions in the headquarters of their companies. They have also served as top expatriate managers in their companies as well. The executives emphasized the importance of risk of loss of clients and reputation as a major factor in sending expatriate managers to head their companies' operations in foreign countries.

Three propositions were made regarding the physical presence of expatriates in a foreign operation, as well as the relative 'intensity' of these expatriates in the composition of the managerial ranks. A simple preliminary model formulating the compensation policy from an agency-theory/risk-sharing perspective has been outlined. Possible extensions should attempt to include other non-monetary factors for developing a more comprehensive model of the compensation of expatriate professional managers.

ACKNOWLEDGEMENTS

Work on this chapter was done while I held the NEC Fellowship of the Center for Japan–US Business and Economic Studies, New York University. I have benefited from the comments of Yair Aharoni and John Minton on an earlier draft of this chapter. The technical assistance of Beverly Serrant is acknowledged.

11 Co-operative strategies for professional service firms: unique opportunities and challenges

Bente R. Lowendahl

INTRODUCTION

Over the last few years, a number of authors have pointed out the importance of looking into the role of co-operative ventures in the strategic management of modern firms. This is true not only in the case of domestic firms, but also – and maybe even more so – in international business (e.g. Harrigan 1985; Contractor and Lorange 1988a; Kogut 1988b; Hamel *et al.* 1989). The present chapter differs from most of the previous research on international joint ventures in several respects.

First, recent research interest in co-operative ventures, like research in international business and strategic management in general, has been predominantly focused on the issues that are of fundamental importance to *manufacturing* firms entering foreign markets. One notable exception to this is Harrigan (1985), who includes a chapter on joint ventures in service industries, but who focuses entirely on US domestic joint ventures. In the present chapter, I try to point out the key issues relevant to joint ventures between professional service firms, based on insights from an exploratory study of an engineering consulting firm established as a joint venture between twelve competing companies.

Second, the majority of the research projects on international co-operative ventures have focused on joint ventures between *partners of different national origins*, as in Root's definition:

> I define an international co-operative arrangement as any form of long-term co-operation between two or more independent firms headquartered in two or more countries that undertakes or supports a business activity for mutual economic gain.
>
> (1988: 69)

In the present chapter I focus on a joint venture where all founding partners were headquartered in the same country and continued to compete domestically; i.e. there was no foreign partner involved.

And third, the predominant emphasis has been on joint ventures between *two – as opposed to multiple – 'parent' firms*, such that the conceptual analysis may focus on the relationship between the two 'parents', the relationships of the 'parents' to the 'child', and the 'child's' relationship to its competitive environment – including its parents (Harrigan 1985). As Harrigan points out: 'A joint venture must be considered as a troika – the 'child' as well as the parents' (1985: xii). As mentioned above, the case described here involves a joint venture between as many as twelve – and later fifteen – parent partners. In the following, this joint venture will be called Alpha. The actual name of the firm is withheld in order to maintain the confidentiality of the company.

Alpha may also be unusual in that it has survived as a joint venture for more than thirty years, and at times with very high financial performance. As Kogut points out, joint ventures tend to be highly volatile legal entities: 'Joint ventures, like any form of organization, undergo a cycle of creation, institutionalization, and, with high probability, termination' (1988a: 169). Alpha has avoided termination, but – as will be explained below – has been subject to some fundamental changes over its life to date.

The chapter is organized as follows: the following section describes the focal case in terms of this theory, but also points out aspects of the case which may require an extension of this theory. The third section presents a set of tentative propositions regarding some key issues in the formation and strategic management of professional service firm joint ventures, and the fourth section provides a few concluding remarks.

CHARACTERISTICS OF THE FOCAL JOINT VENTURE

Data collection

The present chapter is based on insights gained in an exploratory case study of a joint venture – here called Alpha – formed over thirty years ago by twelve engineering consulting firms targeting international projects. Data for the study were gathered in semi-structured interviews with senior executives and other employees of Alpha as well as senior executives of some of the parent firms. The interviews typically lasted between one and three hours and focused on key issues in strategy formulation and implementation. (Please refer to the Appendix for a list of people interviewed.) Information was also gathered from parent and joint venture firm presentations, brochures, annual reports etc. The data presented here are part of a larger comparative case study focusing on the international strategic management of five international professional business service firms.

Some key characteristics of professional service firms

An underlying assumption of the research reported here is that there are fundamental characteristics that distinguish professional service firms from the firms traditionally reported in the literature. This is true not only for manufacturing firms, but also for most of the service firms described. I would argue that in many respects it is meaningless to talk about services as if they comprise a homogeneous set of firms. Table 11.1 summarizes how professional business service firms may be classified in terms of key characteristics proposed by four different authors on service marketing and management.

Table 11.1 Characteristics of professional business service firms (PBSFs)

Dimension	PBSF
Output	
Tangible versus intangible dominant	Intangible[a]
Customized versus standardized	Customized[b]
Degree of deliverer judgement	High[b]
Supply	
Constrained versus unconstrained capacity	ST: Constrained
	LT: Less constrained[b]
Resource base	People (professionals)[c]
Capital intensity	Low/Strategic decision
Number of service outlets	Low/Strategic decision[b]
Demand	
Fluctuating versus stable	Moderately fluctuating [b]
Client type (service recipient)	
People versus things	People/organizations[b]
Delivery process	
Degree of client involvement	
in problem definition	Moderate to high
in delivery	Varies
Place of interaction/delivery	'Site' or client offices[b]
Nature of interaction	
formal versus informal	Both[b]
continuous versus discrete	Discrete/*ad hoc*[b]
Simultaneity in production and consumption	Varying[d]

Sources: [a] Shostack 1977; [b] Lovelock 1983; [c] Thomas 1978; [d]Grönroos 1985
Notes: ST, short term; LT, long term.

For the purpose of the present analysis I would like to highlight the following.

1 The key strategic resource is the professionals.
2 The second most important strategic resource is the reputation of the firm and its 'experience record' (portfolio of completed projects).
3 The technology or firm 'black box' is embodied in individuals as well as processes/methods, but most of the technology is 'public domain' and common knowledge to all members of the profession.
4 Delivery is project based and *ad hoc* rather than continuous.
5 Output is highly customized and frequently requires innovative solutions, and hence operations are very hard to predefine and standardize.
6 A large part of the production and delivery process has to take place 'on site' as defined by the client.

These characteristics are likely to affect the formation, evolution and functioning of joint ventures between such firms, as will be shown below.

Characteristics of Alpha and its parents when founded

Alpha was founded in the late 1950s, at a time when the parents were all small engineering consulting partnerships dominated by strong and enthusiastic entrepreneurs. Despite the fact that they were all in the same industry, they rarely competed head-on with each other. The domestic market had been booming but reached a stagnation period, and the partner firms were looking for a way of reducing their vulnerability to demand instability without reducing the number of professional employees.

Internationalization was seen as the ideal solution, for many reasons:

1 The markets did not fluctuate simultaneously with domestic markets, which would allow for an export of excess capacity.
2 Domestic lending agencies were just starting to fund projects in Third World countries.
3 Many of the entrepreneurs leading the founding partner firms felt a strong ideological commitment to contributing to the improvement of living standards in developing countries and believed that they could make a significant difference (this is in the late 1950s and early 1960s).
4 The founding partners had a combined expertise and experience in certain technical areas which were considered first rate world-wide and which was thought to be exportable.
5 International projects were seen as a good way of attracting and keeping some of the best professionals, at a time when travelling and working overseas was seen as giving high status both socially and professionally.

Alpha was set up as a partnership of twelve equal partners, in terms of ownership as well as control. The joint venture had the mandate to market all partners internationally and to compete for overseas projects, whereas all the personnel for the projects was to be provided by the parent firms. This joint venture is a clear example of *horizontal co-operation* (Harrigan 1985), given that both the parent firms and the 'child' were competing in the same industry. It was also an example of what Lorange and Roos (1992) describe as *downstream co-operative ventures*, as the joint venture was only expected to provide marketing and distribution services to the parents.

In order to prevent Alpha from competing with its parents, the 'domain' (Levine and White 1961) of the joint venture was limited to international projects. Alpha was not allowed to compete for any domestic project, whereas the parents accepted not to undertake international operations except through the joint venture.

The stated reasons for the formation of the venture were *strategic* (Harrigan 1985): the 'child' was to build the international 'practice' of the parent firms through marketing efforts *vis-à-vis* key international clients and funding agencies in order for the parents to reap benefits from excess capacity. As a result of this, the joint venture had a maximum of organizational flexibility, but was totally dependent on its parents for its key resources: competent personnel. At the same time, this internationalization effort involved a minimum of resource investment and risk taking by each of the parents. Not only did they limit their involvement in Alpha to a one-twelfth share per partner, but they also structured the international operations as a separate legal entity with a different name from that of the parents. If a major unsuccessful project overseas should occur, the parents could let Alpha go bankrupt without risking their own reputation. Given that none of the firms had substantial international experience prior to the establishment of the joint venture, the independence of Alpha legally, reputationally and economically acted like an important 'insurance policy' for the parents.

An unstated reason for the formation of the venture may also have been *competitive*, as Alpha became the dominant competitor within the industry *vis-à-vis* domestic funding agencies. A few years later, other groups of competitors formed similar ventures in order to strengthen their competitive position *vis-à-vis* Alpha, but they never threatened its position.

Evolution of Alpha and its parents

In professional services, the key investments are typically in the *reputation* associated with the name of the firm, in the *competence* of the professionals – including the relevant international experience, and in the *networks* of relationships to clients. As mentioned above, the reputation built through the completion of projects was connected to Alpha, and the same is true for the networks of contacts to clients – especially local governments overseas and domestic and international lending agencies such as the World Bank. Similarly, the problems associated with unsuccesful projects were also linked to Alpha and not to its parents. The competence resources for the projects, however, were to remain with the parents in order to maximize the synergies for the parents and the flexibility of the 'child'.

The flexibility of the venture, in terms of very low overhead costs as all personel costs outside of projects were absorbed by the parents, was a clear strength. The same was true for its bargaining position *vis-à-vis* domestic funding agencies, which allowed Alpha to win some prestigious and profitable projects. Alpha could draw on a very large pool of professional resources (in 1988 the joint venture had a staff of slightly more than 200, but could draw on more than 2,300 professionals from the partner firms) and this fact gave it a competitive advantage relative to its smaller competitors.

The first projects were highly successful in terms of the quality of the solutions delivered and thus allowed Alpha to establish a reputation as a credible high-quality supplier of engineering services overseas. The joint venture was also able to develop personal relationships to decision-makers both with local governments in the foreign countries and with the domestic and international funding agencies. These relationships enabled the venture to win new contracts in these countries, both as their local relationships helped them gain information about new projects earlier than their competitors and as their locally experienced professionals and their favourable 'experience record' gave them a competitive advantage.

The data suggest that there may be significant first-mover advantages in this industry, in terms of the development of an 'experience record', the building of a reputation for consistently high-quality work overseas and the establishment of a network of contacts. A network of contacts may act as a barrier to new entries. Another competitive advantage is the key professional experts with the relevant international experience (referred to in the industry as 'international CVs'). Again, the firm that has had the longest international experience may also be expected to have a larger number of experts with 'international 'CVs', yet, since experts are highly mobile, this advantage may be hard to sustain over time. As one of the executives of Alpha said: 'I think we win a project based 25 per cent on the firm's reputation, 40–50 per cent on the international CVs of the professionals, and the rest is methodology, project management procedures, unique approaches etc.'

Autonomy of the joint venture

Despite its dependence on parent firm resources, Alpha evolved with substantial autonomy. The strategy was clear and simple: Alpha should market the resources of the parents and only involve a small group of staff. The strategy of Alpha was soon changed, however, without the parents intervening in this process. Two major shifts were seen early on.

First, Alpha felt uneasy about having project managers from one partner firm running entire projects in the name of all partners. This was both an issue of quality control and reputation building and an issue of budget control. The loyalty of partner-firm project managers was more to the partner firms than to Alpha and, as each partner had very little to lose from a bad Alpha project, the problems soon became obvious. The solution was for Alpha to hire Alpha project managers, which meant increasing the number of joint venture employees and expanding the scope of Alpha's operations. This strategic shift was not planned by the parents, but rather driven by Alpha's internal needs for control.

Second, the marketing focus of Alpha soon shifted from being driven by a technology (know-how) push from the parents' strengths to a market pull from the clients and in particular from the domestic lending agencies. When the clients wanted projects that the parents did not have the resources to cover, Alpha preferred to hire resources from non-parent companies. This need for additional types of know-how led to the inclusion of several new partners over the years. By 1988 there were fifteen partners, although a couple of the original partners had dropped out and new firms had been added.

Alpha grew and, as already mentioned, in 1988 they had about 200 employees, including a few offices overseas. Yet, given the original mandate of the joint venture, the focus was still on competing for and winning international projects in order to build reputation and on building 'international CVs' by sending good engineers overseas. Challenging projects both in terms of geographical location and engineering problems were sought out and a lot of pride was generated through the successful completion of these projects. But Alpha had never been set up as an independent unit intended to make profits on its own. It grew into an independent firm but had very little business orientation and only in the late 1980s was a director of finances brought in. The parents generally got their profits through the transfer pricing of professionals used on Alpha projects, whereas Alpha was basically intended to be a not-for-profit agency spending a given percentage of parent revenues from international projects on marketing and reputation building. The shift in strategy and the independence of Alpha was not followed by the required change in management, strategic planning and control processes (Lorange 1987), neither within Alpha nor between Alpha and its parents. In addition, Alpha shifted the scope of its operations but never had a strategy discussion with its parents regarding which key competence areas the venture should prioritize in their marketing efforts.

Evolution of the parent firms

At the same time as Alpha grew and prospered, the parents and the domestic industry also evolved. Some parent firms remained small specialized niche-players with a limited and focused expertise, whereas others grew large and expanded their know-how base substantially. One result of the expansion of many of the parent firms was that their broad expertise base made them overlap with the 'domains' of other partner firms. During most of the 1960s and 1970s, the domestic market grew rapidly, and there were enough projects for all to operate profitably. In the late 1970s and early 1980s, the market experienced a recession and the domestic competition became fierce. Again the parent firms wanted to export their excess capacity, but now ran into a situation where the internationalization through Alpha was felt as a constraint for many of them. Not only did they only get a one-fifteenth share of the returns on their internationalization efforts, but they also had to co-operate and share their strategic resources with competitors. More and more the issue of 'black box' protection became salient and the best people and methodologies were reserved for the domestic market, where the parent firm did not have to share the revenues with other partners.

The differences in partner-firm evolution also affected their involvement in Alpha, as some firms were almost 'sleeping partners' and had very little desire for international projects, whereas other partner firms saw Alpha as a major constraint on their own firms' internationalization efforts. A couple of partners also dropped out, as they refused to comply with the rules giving Alpha the sole right to all overseas operations.

Why did the parent firms allow Alpha so much discretion?

A number of factors are likely to have contributed to this 'uncontrolled' growth of Alpha. First, *the number of parent firms* in the venture is likely to have contributed significantly. In the early phases of Alpha's life cycle it was probably a strength for Alpha, but a complication for the parents. As many authors on co-operative strategies point out (e.g. Harrigan 1985; Lorange 1987; Kogut 1988a), one of the main threats to the survival of a co-operative venture is the high likelihood of conflicts between the parent firms leading to the termination of the venture. Lorange (1987) suggests that most 'shared' joint ventures established with (two) equally active parents tend to be dissolved unless (a) one of the partners is allowed to become dominant in the control of the venture or (b) all (both) parents allow the venture to 'grow up from a "sibling" to a full-blown workable "adult" entity' (1987: 11). Whereas the number of parent partners in this venture could easily have led to a stalemate for Alpha, in the early years of the venture the result rather seemed to be that the highly qualified managers of Alpha were given more discretion than intended. None of the parents was willing to let coalitions of their competitors dominate the management of the venture.

Second, *the nature of the key resources* of the professional service firm is likely to have contributed to the high degree of discretion of the managers of Alpha. The 'child' was seen merely as a project-getting agency for the parents, with very little value in itself, whereas each of the parents maintained control over the key resources, namely the professional employees. Hence, the parents seemed not to be very concerned with the operations of Alpha. I would also speculate that the traditional orientation of professional firms in general, and of engineering firms in particular, towards considering marketing and sales as activities of much less value than the core engineering activities (Kotler and Connor 1977), may have contributed to the willingness of the partners to leave Alpha alone. As pointed out above, several partners became a lot more concerned with, and involved in, efforts to control the joint venture when at later stages Alpha had evolved into a highly valued entity with a strong international reputation.

Similarly, I would suggest that *the project orientation* of engineering consulting firms may have contributed to the autonomy of Alpha. The parent firms were used to managing projects where the project manager would be given a high degree of discretion and responsibility for making the project succeed. They also had a lot of experience from working on joint projects with competitors, as large projects in engineering consulting frequently are won and operated by coalitions of two or more competitors – domestically as well as internationally. The easiest solution for the parents was to remain passive partners, and to let the 'project manager' – in this case the manager of Alpha – set up the organization and manage its day-to-day operations independently.

A third factor likely to have contributed to the autonomy of Alpha in the early years was *the nature of the parent firms and their managers* at the time of the founding. The parent-firm managers were strong individuals with an extremely high commitment to making Alpha succeed, and they knew and respected each other. The first manager of Alpha is also described as a strong entrepreneur, as illustrated by the following story (told independently by several employees of Alpha): 'He was sent to Ethiopia with a typewriter and an empty cigar box with two dollars in it, and told to get new projects. And he did, with great success.' When the original founders retired and more managerially oriented managers took over, consensus over the evolution of Alpha was much harder to reach. By this time, the parent firms had become fierce competitors and were not willing to let any partner or group of partners dominate the control of Alpha. Alpha was profitable and highly respected internationally and, since the conflict over control issues was never resolved, Alpha continued to be rather independent.

A fourth important factor was that most of the key *control issues* of Alpha were *related to on-site managerial control of projects* and close co-operation with local clients, and these were *far away*. Only Alpha managers supervised what went on overseas, whereas the parent-firm managers had to rely on reports from Alpha managers returning from overseas projects. Many authors on international business have emphasized the increasing difficulties arising from controlling far-away operations, culturally as well as geographically. Sophisticated control systems and routines may be required in any firm operating internationally. In a 'shared' joint venture, the control systems must be good enough to satisfy all partners – as well as the management of the joint venture (Lorange and Roos 1992). As mentioned above, the systems of Alpha were focused on quality control and project completion, but not on financial routines, bargaining on contract rates, cost control and profit generation.

Conflict and crisis

By the 1980s, Alpha had evolved into a well-established professional firm in its own right, with a strong quality reputation, highly qualified professionals and documented experience from projects in over 130 countries in all regions of the world. The 'child' had grown up and was now a highly valuable firm. I would suggest that the success of the joint venture was one of the factors that contributed to an escalating conflict between the parent firms. Conflicts between the parent firms over the right to compete for overseas projects, over Alpha's expansion into domestic projects that 'almost fell into their lap' and over the allocation of resources to the joint venture evolved into a full-blown crisis as the beloved 'child' failed significantly on two major projects. Alpha lost money in both 1986 and 1987 and, given its limited slack financial resources, had to ask its parent firms for support.

The parent firms had evolved in three different directions: some firms wanted to sell their shares and cash in a price as high as possible, other firms wanted to buy in order to expand their international operations through the control of the name, the networks and the reputation of the joint venture and a third group of firms might have been willing to sell but refused to grant their competitors the advantage following the reputation of the joint venture. The sale of a partner's share in Alpha required a majority vote by two-thirds of the owners and it turned out to be impossible to find any combination of ten firms willing to vote for the same group of partners to take over the ownership of the joint venture.

'Final' solution, the present (Autumn 1990)

Alpha desperately needed resources and the managers of both the parent firms and the 'child' agreed that a solution involving one majority partner and a few smaller partners would be the best. Several alternatives were explored and after nearly two years of negotiations seven partners sold their shares in the joint venture, giving one partner majority ownerhip. The seven partners remain minority owners but no longer have equal shares. This new Alpha was formed two years ago and major reorganizations followed. The new majority owner is certainly not a passive parent and executives say that their intention is to integrate Alpha fully with their own engineering consulting operations, which are mainly domestic and focused entirely on a single know-how base which is different from those of Alpha. The present managers of Alpha express relief that the conflict has been solved but also great concern over what such a merger may imply for the future.

In addition to the major changes in parent ownership structure and the following internal reorganizations, Alpha now faces a very different competitive arena. Several of the seven partners who sold their shares in the joint venture have joined forces and formed a potentially strong competitor within one of the joint venture's traditional core competence areas. They have also tried to convince clients that part of Alpha's reputation carries over to their new firm. Since most of the key executives of Alpha remained with the joint venture after the crisis, I would expect that the firm-specific reputation will remain with Alpha and its present owners. The reputation ('CVs') carried by the individuals no longer connected to Alpha naturally follows these professionals into the new firm.

The crisis was so recent that it is hard to know whether Alpha has reached a stable solution that will now allow for a new period of growth and profitability. Built into the final agreement between the previous and present owners was a special contract denying Alpha the right to compete domestically under the Alpha name for the first five years. This also prevents the new majority owner from competing under the Alpha name for all its domestic projects, which makes the full integration of the two firms difficult at present.

ALPHA: SUCCESS OR FAILURE?

Some tentative propositions

The previous section illustrated some fundamental characteristics of professional service firms, which may offer these firms opportunities and challenges in addition to those faced by managers of manufacturing firms trying to establish and manage international joint ventures. One first reaction to the case described here is that it seems to be so unique that it may be impossible to draw conclusions from it that are relevant to other firms. I would propose that it is the fact that it is a professional service firm which caused it to survive with such a large number of owners. In fact there are many examples of other professional service firm joint ventures which are equally strange in terms of what the theory based on manu- facturing firms would lead us to expect.

Joint venture theory emphasizes the importance of the negotiation of a formal contract or 'bargaining agreement' (Harrigan 1985) between the parent firms prior to the establishment of the joint venture and the agree- ment on a clear set of formal control systems that allow the parents to control the venture. In addition, theory emphasizes renegotiation of the agreement and adjustment of the control systems as both the parent firms and the joint venture evolve over time. The case presented here seems to violate all the advice presented in the theory, and yet Alpha survived and for nearly thirty years was highly successful both in terms of project completion and reputation building and even in terms of profitability (until recently). How could this be possible?

I suggest that characteristics both of professional service firms in general and of engineering consulting in particular create challenges for the tradi- tional theory. The fact that the key strategic resource of the firms is the expertise and experience of the professionals combined with the fact that their task is to generate innovative solutions to problems that are unique every time creates challenges for the management of these firms. Professionals are trained in a tradition where professional judgement and expertise are valued more than managerial authority. Similarly, since each situation is unique, no manager at headquarters can decide *ex ante* what will need to be decided on site. The fact that the sites are overseas is likely to increase the discretion of the project manager. These factors together have led to the development of organizational structures within engineering consulting firms where project managers have a very high degree of dis- cretion and where controls are more based on professional peer reviews than on formal management systems.

Within the engineering consulting industry, joint venture projects are very common. I would suggest that, whereas the autonomous position of the project manager seems to be required for all types of projects, it seems likely that the project manager of joint venture projects will be even more autonomous than where there is only one parent firm, since the joint venture project manager would have to refer to two or more managements for advice. The reasons why it is still possible for the project manager to carry out projects in terms of the standards established by the parent firms seem to be both that project managers typically have been with their parent firms for many years and have internalized their firm's norms and requirements, and that advice is sought with the most respected professional in any given area. This allows for the consultation of different people for different issues and for seeking advice where the best professional is expected to be found, regardless of which of the parent firms a project manager works for.

Whereas traditional joint venture theory would have suggested tighter formal controls in order to counter these strong pressures for autonomy and discretion, I would suggest that more formal controls may actually be detrimental to the functioning of professional service firms. In the best case scenario, formal controls introduce additional 'red tape', whereas the decisions are made based on advice from the professionals with the relevant expertise and experience regardless of parent firms and managerial positions. In the worst case scenario, formal reporting takes the place of informal consulting with relevant experts and both efficiency and effectiveness are likely to suffer.

Based on this discussion, the following propositions result.

Proposition 11.1
Joint ventures formed by professional service firms are likely to require less formalized bargaining agreements and less active control by parent firms in order to succeed as highly autonomous entities than joint ventures between manufacturing firms.

Proposition 11.2
In joint ventures formed by professional service firms where the project managers traditionally have and require a high degree of discretion, such as where a high degree of innovation and on-site decision-making is required, highly formalized controls are likely to reduce the efficiency and effectiveness of the operations of the joint venture.

The major challenge for the parent firms, then, is how to keep control of the joint venture such that it will function as an integrated part of the parents' strategy *without* the use of formal controls. The solution chosen in the management of projects within many single firms may be an alternative, namely an emphasis on socialization and development of project manager loyalty and on frequent interaction and informal communication between professionals. The moment Alpha was allowed to recruit and keep their own project managers, the loyalty and communication between project managers and parent firms was naturally reduced, whereas the loyalty to Alpha was increased and the communication between peers became more frequent within Alpha than between Alpha and its parent firms. The latter was further enhanced as Alpha developed a 'critical mass' of professional expertise within its boundaries. It seems likely that if the parent firms wanted to maintain control over the operations of Alpha, they would have had to prevent Alpha from establishing its own autonomous professional organization in order to force the loyalty and communication to be related to the parent firms rather than to the joint venture.

Proposition 11.3
In joint ventures formed between professional service firms where formal controls are inefficient, informal controls such as socialization and frequent informal interaction will be emphasized and facilitated in order for the parent firms to control the joint venture.

In fact, this situation was illustrated by a comment by the senior Vice President of marketing at Alpha, who talked about the '5-kilometre syndrome'; the parent firms which were located next door or even within the same building as Alpha tended to be highly involved both in project proposals and in the follow-up on projects, whereas those that were located a few miles away only got involved in a more infrequent communication.

Another major challenge to the management of professional service firms in general and joint ventures in particular, is the role of 'invisible assets' (Itami 1987) such as reputation, experience and networks of contacts to loyal clients which are accumulated over the years of operation. The fact that Alpha was set up as an independent legal entity allowed the parent firms to internationalize with much less risk both financially and reputationally. But the very establishment of Alpha also involved a decision to let the joint venture accumulate some of the invisible assets, in particular the reputation which was connected to the name Alpha. Some of the international experience was naturally accumulated by the parent firm professionals, but when Alpha started recruiting its own staff even this effect was smaller than expected. And the distribution of this experience across parent firms was highly uneven.

According to Itami (1987), the 'invisible assets' play an important role in the development of a unique competitive position in all firms, but I would suggest that in professional service firms the 'invisible assets' constitute the core of the firm's assets and are absolutely fundamental to the firm's existence. 'Invisible assets' cannot be shared between parent firms of a joint venture at a later point in time. In terms of the Alpha joint venture, the issue of a possible termination of the venture and how to share the 'invisible assets' was not discussed until the crisis became a fact. At the time of the foundation, the parent firms did not think that the joint venture might become so highly successful and that the international operations might become an important rather than peripheral part of the strategies of the parents. But at the time of the crisis, the main problem became the issue of who should be allowed to take over the name and reputation of Alpha. I suggest that a discussion and clarification of these issues at the foundation of the venture, or as early as possible after the joint venture gained momentum, might have reduced the trauma of the conflict that Alpha eventually had to go through.

Proposition 11.4
Where the benefits from a joint venture's investments cannot be shared between partners at a later stage, joint venture success is expected to increase conflicts between parent partners, unless issues of joint venture termination have been resolved prior to the formation of the joint venture.

In terms of the above discussion, it may be very hard to determine whether or not Alpha as a joint venture was a success or a failure. As an autonomous unit, it succeeded in winning major contracts and completing projects at a high quality world-wide. That way it also succeeded in building a reputation for high quality. Yet it did not succeed in controlling its financial performance well enough to avoid major problems, and its parent-firm structure and lack of internal financial controls made it impossible to accumulate sufficient slack resources to allow the firm to maintain operations without parent help in the face of the failed projects. In terms of being a tool for the internationalization of the parent firms, the opinions among parent-firm managers are mixed but mostly negative. There is no doubt that, in the early years, Alpha helped the small parent firms undertake projects overseas that they would not have been able to win and complete individually. But as the parent firms grew and Alpha became more independent, the parent firms with most international strategies wanted a larger share of their internationalization than they could get through Alpha. To them, the joint venture became a limiting factor in their internationalization, rather than a helpful strategic tool. But by that time, given the fact that the joint venture agreement did not have any termination clause in it, the parent firms that were most involved hesitated to get out of the venture as they were afraid to let their competitors gain the advantage of the name Alpha. In a sense, the very success of Alpha became its largest problem in terms of its relationship to the parent firms.

CONCLUSIONS

The present chapter has attempted to raise some of the issues that are important to the formation and strategic management of professional service firm joint ventures based on insights from an exploratory case study. The study suggests that, while many of the key issues in joint venture management are likely to be the same for professional service firms as for any other type of firm, e.g. the need to emphasize the evolutionary nature of both the 'parents'' and the 'child's' strategies, there may be aspects of professional service firms that require different approaches to the management of the venture. One key difference suggested is the fact that the strategic resources of professional service firms make decisions about their own allocation, sometimes without referring to parent-firm executives for advice. Insights from the case suggest that whereas it may be easier for professional service firms to establish autonomous ventures, joint ventures that need to be tightly integrated with 'parents'' strategies and operations may require more investment in formal agreements, venture design and tight control structures than similar ventures established by manufacturing firms.

Further research into the joint ventures of professional service firms is clearly needed. In some professional service industries joint ventures are extremely frequent, yet they often seem to be designed as *temporary* co-operative arrangements. It would be interesting to see further empirical research into the differences – if any – in longevity of joint ventures set up to be permanent across different service and manufacturing industries. Similarly, studies of how factors such as previous project management and joint venture experience affect the success of the venture might add important new insights.

The study reported here looks at only one professional service firm joint venture within a single industry. Additional research is clearly needed in order to establish whether the characteristics reported here generalize to other engineering consulting firms, firms with different home country origins and firms within other professional service industries. It may be as dangerous to assume that professional service firms form a homogeneous subset of firms as it is to assume that all service firms are homogeneous. One major difference suggested in the propositions above is the difference between professional service firms that deliver project-based services (e.g. management and engineering consulting) and firms that deliver services according to continuous contracts (e.g. auditing). Further studies of professional service firms in multiple industries may indicate other key differences that need to be explored, as well as how they affect the formation and management of joint ventures.

ACKNOWLEDGEMENTS

I thank all the professionals at Alpha who gave so much of their time to explore these and other strategic management issues with me. In particular, the President and the Vice President of marketing have both spent hours discussing and explaining key issues. Without their support, this research would have been impossible! Names of firms and individuals are withheld for reasons of confidentiality. I would also like to thank William M. Evan, Peter Lorange, Johan Roos, Harbir Singh and the participants at the conference at Duke University for helpful comments on an earlier draft of this chapter.

APPENDIX: PEOPLE INTERVIEWED AT ALPHA

Within Alpha

President and Chief Executive Officer (CEO) of Alpha
Senior Vice President Marketing, Alpha
Executive Vice President Alpha and previously president of one of the present minority partner/owner firms
Senior Vice President Alpha, competence division A
Assistant Vice President Alpha, competence group A1 (one level below Senior Vice President; division A includes two competence subgroups)
Assistant Vice President Alpha, competence group A2
Assistant Vice President Alpha, competence group B1 (division B has three competence subgroups)
Assistant Vice President Alpha, competence group B2
Senior professional Alpha, competence group B3

Present and previous owner firms

President and CEO of present majority owner firm during crisis and buyout; now director of business development of present majority owner
Previous president of one of the previous partner/owner firms and also chairman of Alpha during crisis and sell-out
President and CEO of two present minority partner/owner firms, now merged into one large firm
President and CEO of two previous partners/owners, now merged into one large firm
Previous president of founding partner firm (senior partner at the time of foundation of Alpha) which sold out in the early 1970s, wanting to internationalize independently. He was also the first chairman of Alpha.

12 Patterns of international competition in service industries: global oligopolistic reaction and national competitive advantages

Jiatao Li and Stephen Guisinger

INTRODUCTION

The international competition in service industries has received growing attention among researchers, corporate managers and policy-makers. As in manufacturing industries, most large service multinational enterprises (MNEs) compete internationally through a wide range of equity and non-equity foreign involvements such as direct investments, joint ventures or networks. Dunning (1989a) reviews the conceptual and theoretical issues in applying the eclectic theory of international production to explain the internationalization of service MNEs. Many studies of service MNEs, however, are industry or home country specific (Boddewyn *et al.* 1986) and have not examined the patterns of competition across countries. As asserted by Nigh *et al.* (1986), further research may uncover differences in the pattern of international competition for service MNEs based in different countries and in different service industries.

MNEs based in the same country may follow similar strategies in international competition. Kogut (1988c) explained country patterns in international competition as reflecting committed resources and organizational routines derived from national demand, cultural characteristics and institutional characteristics. This perspective suggests a view of international competition as an evolutionary process, which begins with firms investing in organizational and technological resources which correspond to the cultural and demand characteristics of the immediate local environment. Given the development of its skills, the international competitiveness of a firm is determined by the characteristics of demand and of oligopolistic rivalry in different national markets. The social and cultural environment influences the skills developed in a country and the competitive behaviour of national firms. These two influences generate country patterns in international competitive behaviour.

Previous studies of foreign direct investment have focused on the choices of MNEs in the manufacturing sectors either to export or produce abroad and on the significance of the variables influencing the choice of foreign location (e.g. Aharoni 1966; Horst 1972; Dunning 1973; Root and Ahmed 1978; Davidson 1980). Most of these studies suggest that the crucial variables are likely to depend on (a) the *raison d'être* for foreign direct investment (market-oriented, resources-oriented or part of a regional or global strategy); (b) the product characteristics; (c) the behaviour of competitors; and (d) the attitudes, regulations and policies of governments of host countries (Dunning 1989a).

The unique features of service industries have to be considered when analysing the international competition of firms in these industries. First, many service needs are similar among developed countries. Although the quality or variety of services varies more than that of goods, the demand for services, for example between consumers from different countries with similar levels of income, is likely to be less heterogeneous. Second, some services require simultaneous production and consumption (location-boundedness).

International involvement in services may take several forms, including foreign direct investment which embraces the sales of services produced by the foreign affiliates of MNEs (Dunning 1989a; Porter 1990). Such investment is assumed to be necessary for firms to control the way in which they utilize or acquire intangible assets across national boundaries (Dunning 1988b). For some service industries, the nature of location-boundedness makes it necessary for a parent firm to have a local facility (Boddewyn *et al.* 1986). The literature also suggests that the mode of organizing the international involvement depends first on the transaction costs involved and second on the extent and pattern of government regulations (Buckley and Casson 1976).

In this study, we empirically investigate patterns of international competition of service MNEs, encompassing firms based in different countries and nine different service industries. Hypotheses are developed based on two major theoretical arguments for the internationalization of service MNEs. The first one is the inter-firm rivalry argument. Firms in oligopolistic industries match foreign investments of competitors in major markets (Knickerbocker 1973; Graham 1978). The second argument is based on competitive advantages (Dunning 1989a; Porter 1990). These hypotheses are tested through a logistic regression model using data for 168 of the largest service MNEs in nine service industries for the two periods 1976–80 and 1980–6. All these service MNEs are based in the triad nations: Japan, Europe and the USA.

OLIGOPOLISTIC REACTION AND SERVICE
MULTINATIONAL ENTERPRISES

In previous studies international competition has frequently been characterized by oligopolistic interdependence (Hymer 1976; Knickerbocker 1973). First, studies have suggested that FDI flows and the export of manufactured goods are significantly correlated with the existence of entry barriers in the home market (Caves 1982). Second, degrees of industry concentration were also found to be correlated among developed countries (Pryor 1972). As a result, a significant proportion of world competition involves the penetration of markets by members of different national oligopolies (Erdilek 1985; Kogut 1988c).

In the context of international competition, the empirical question relates to how members of a regional oligopoly behave internationally regarding each other and how members of oligopolies in different countries behave regarding their actual or potential mutual market penetration. These patterns of competitive behaviour may reflect national traits regarding anti-trust regulations, government intervention and tolerance of competitive or co-operative behaviour. Thus, country patterns may exist in international competition (Kogut 1988c). Firms originated in countries with similar income levels and demand characteristics are likely to develop overlapping and directly competing product offerings. Thus the characteristic of consumer demand is also important in the analysis of oligopolistic behaviour.

In an oligopolistic industry, firms are few enough to recognize the impact of their actions on their rivals and thus on the market as a whole (Caves 1982). Because the firms are mutually interdependent, their behaviour will tend toward a pattern of tit-for-tat matching of investments in major markets (Knickerbocker 1973; Kogut 1988c). Foreign investment is undertaken by an oligopolist in order to 'counter, check, or forestall a move by some rival oligopolist' (E.M. Graham 1985).

Knickerbocker (1973) investigated rivalrous behaviour in FDI among US manufacturing industries. He argued that the extent of foreign investment depends on the form that oligopolistic interdependence takes in these industries. Examining the activities of established subsidiaries by 187 US MNEs in twenty-three countries over 1948–67, he found a significant relationship between industry concentration in the USA and the 'bunching' of foreign investment in a particular manufacturing industry. Flower's (1976) study also demonstrated that entry concentration rises with seller concentration in the home country and the rate differs across countries.

These studies suggest that the concept of oligopolistic reaction contributes to the explanation of firms' international expansions. Service MNEs undertake FDI in order to protect or strengthen an international market position *vis-à-vis* the major competitors. Firms in these oligopolistic industries will compete in each other's territories and thus lead to a 'follow the leader' pattern of foreign investment by service MNEs. There is a strong suggestion that large MNEs often adopt a 'follow the leader' or 'exchange of threats' strategy (Knickerbocker 1973; Flowers 1976; Graham 1978). Widespread evidence in support of this oligopolistic strategy can be found in the investment patterns of the leading oil, automobile, pharmaceutical, semiconductor and consumer electronics companies. Studies of US advertising FDI also support this hypothesis (Terpstra and Yu 1988).

Hypothesis 12.1
Foreign investment of service MNEs is positively related to the global oligopolistic reaction in the host country.

COMPETITIVE ADVANTAGES OF SERVICE INDUSTRIES

Nations differ markedly in their patterns of national competitive advantage in service industries. As international competition in services grows, national competitive advantage in services is assuming growing importance to firms and nations alike (Porter 1990). Dunning (1989a) reviews the nature of the competitive advantages of service firms and provides an extensive list of ownership, location and internalization advantages for several service industries. Service MNEs can utilize and add value to their competitive advantages via FDI, either to supply the service to local customers or to serve a regional or even a global market. In some service industries, however, the competitive advantages of foreign MNEs seeking to establish a local presence may not be as great as those of domestic companies or are insufficient to compensate for the additional costs of servicing a foreign market (Hirsch 1987a).

Kogut (1988c) proposed that, in international competition, firms exploit those skills and routines which drive their home market success. He argued that the sustainability of a firm's international competitive advantage is influenced by the conditions of appropriability. The more the advantage is embedded in specific organizational routines, the less it is diffusible among firms. The more the advantage is culturally and institutionally embedded, the less it is diffusible among countries. The international competitiveness of a firm is significantly influenced by factors such as the location-specific advantages of the home country and the properties of demand and the institutional structure among countries.

Porter (1990) defined international success by a nation's industry as 'possessing competitive advantage relative to the best worldwide competitors'. Because of the existence of protection, subsidies and differing accounting conventions, neither domestic profitability nor the existence of some exports is a reliable indicator of competitive advantage for an industry. He suggests the best measure of international competitive advantage as either (a) the presence of substantial and sustained exports to a wide array of other nations and/or (b) significant outbound foreign investment based on skills and assets in the home country.

Hypothesis 12.2
Foreign investment of service MNEs is expected to be positively related to the international competitiveness of the industry in the home country.

OTHER COUNTRY- AND FIRM-RELATED FACTORS

As suggested by studies of FDI in manufacturing industries, many other factors may also have effects on the foreign investment decision of service MNEs. We consider here five categories of country- or firm-related factors that may have significant effects on the globalization of service MNEs.

Market size

Previous studies (Scaperlanda and Mauer 1969; Dunning 1973; Agarwal 1980; Davidson 1980) have shown that the market size of the host country has a positive impact on the inflow of manufacturing FDI. This relationship has also been observed in the internationalization of multinational banks (Gray and Gray 1981; Rugman 1981), international advertising agencies (Weinstein 1977; Terpstra and Yu 1988), multinational insurance firms (UNCTC 1980; Schroath and Korth 1989) and in the location choice of offices of international companies (Dunning and Norman 1987). We would expect that foreign investment of service MNEs is positively related to the market size of the host country.

Government regulations

One of the important factors affecting the location of service activities by MNEs in recent years has been the changes in national regulatory patterns on controls and impediments of inward FDI by service MNEs (OECD 1982, 1987a; Walter 1985; UNCTC 1988). Nigh *et al.* (1986) found that the openness of the host country to new foreign branches affects the US international banking involvement in that country. In many countries, governments strictly control the extent and form of foreign involvements in service industries (UNCTC 1988). Host governments also have a variety of fiscal instruments or direct means that favour services by indigenous companies (Feketekuty 1988). Moreover, there are self-imposed barriers to entry or performance requirements in several service industries (Dunning 1989a). Thus, we would expect that foreign investment of service MNEs is positively related to the openness of the host country to the establishment of new foreign service subsidiaries in that industry.

Cultural distance

The need for local responsiveness or adaptation of services supplied by MNEs to local customers is likely to be the greatest in host countries with different cultures, tastes, living habits and industrial needs (Prahalad and Doz 1987; Dunning 1989a). The impact of culture is also expected to change over time. In the early years of international expansion, service firms followed a similar pattern to that of manufacturing firms. They first made investments in the highly developed, culturally similar areas of the world and then in the less developed and less culturally similar countries. In this study we examine the impact of cultural differences on the international behaviour of service MNEs based in the triad nations over the period (1976–86). Franko (1983) cited cultural and linguistic differences as major constraints on the internationalization of Japanese service firms. Li and Guisinger (1991) found that cultural distance has a significant impact on the failure rate of foreign subsidiaries. Thus, we would expect that cultural distance between the home and host countries has a negative impact on FDI of service MNEs. This impact may also decrease over time.

Growth of firm size

Firm size has been shown to be positively related to FDI in manufacturing (Horst 1972; Grubaugh 1987). Horst (1972) studied the relationship between a firm's decision to invest abroad and the firm's characteristics and found that firm size was the only significant factor. Firm size has also been shown to have a positive impact on the international behaviour in several service industries such as banking and advertising (Ball and Tschoegl 1982; Terpstra and Yu 1988). Since we examine the international behaviour of the top fifteen or top thirty service MNEs in nine industries we focus instead on a dynamic measure: the growth in firm size. We would expect that foreign investment of service MNEs is positively related to the growth of size of the service firms.

Home country business presence

One of the motives for the early venturing abroad of service firms has been following home country client firms. This motive has been shown in international banking (Khoury 1979; Goldberg and Saunders 1980; Ball and Tschoegl 1982; Nigh *et al.* 1986) and in the international advertising industry (Weinstein 1977; UNCTC 1979; Terpstra and Yu 1988). The early venturing abroad of insurance, banking and accounting firms was to supply foreign affiliates of MNEs with services they had previously supplied to their parent companies. These pre-established relationships give service MNEs certain competitive advantages over local service firms. With the globalization of markets, firms in other service industries have found it increasingly necessary to become multinational to win new or retain existing business (Dunning 1989a). We would expect that foreign investment of service MNEs is positively related to the home country business presence in the host country.

METHODOLOGY

We compiled data for 158 of the largest service MNEs in eight service industries for the period 1976–80 and 168 of the largest service MNEs in nine service industries for the period 1980–6 from publications of the United Nations Centre on Transnational Corporations (UNCTC 1988). The data listed the number of foreign subsidiaries each service MNE had in five host countries (regions): the USA, Canada, Japan, Western Europe and other developed countries (Australia and New Zealand) in 1976, 1980 and 1986. We focused on service MNEs based in the triad nations: Japan, Europe and the USA. Firms from these triad nations (regions) account for 95 per cent of the largest service MNEs in these nine industries. Data for 1976 and 1980 were frequently missing. We collected some of the missing data from related industry directories. Table 12.1 contains this expanded data set.

We examine whether a service MNE decides to establish a new foreign subsidiary in a host country after reviewing the effects of its own competitive advantages, the competitors' actions and other country- or firm-related factors. By formulating the issue as a decision, we use a binary dependent variable to express whether or not a service MNE increased its number of subsidiaries in a foreign country over a specific period of time. For the period 1976–80, the value of our dependent variable, foreign investment ($P[\text{FI} = 1]$), is unity if a service MNE increased its number of subsidiaries from 1976 to 1980 in a given host country and zero otherwise. We applied the same method to the data for the 1980–6 period.

Table 12.1 A summary of sample data, 1976–86

| | Number of parent service MNEs | | | | | | | |
| | 1976–80 | | | | 1980–6 | | | |
	USA	Japan	EC	Total	USA	Japan	EC	Total
Finance-related								
Insurance	13	7	9	29	14	7	9	30
Reinsurance	5	1	9	15	5	1	9	15
Trade-related								
Wholesale	–	13	3	16	–	13	3	16
Retail	18	5	6	29	18	5	6	29
Business services								
Accounting	n.a.	n.a.	n.a.		6	–	1	7
Advertising	10	2	6	18	11	2	6	19
Construction	6	8	6	20	6	8	6	20
Other services								
Publishing	8	–	5	13	8	–	5	13
Airlines	8	2	8	18	9	2	8	19
Total	68	38	52	158	77	38	53	168

Note: n.a., not available.

We constructed a new measure of the global oligopolistic reaction (OLIGOP). OLIGOP intends to capture the essence of whether other firms feel some pressure about setting up a subsidiary in a given host country. OLIGOP is measured by the following model.

$$\text{OLIGOP}_{ij} = C_{ij} / P_{ij} \tag{12.1}$$

where C_{ij} is the number of other foreign (parent) service firms with affiliates in industry i, host country j, besides the service MNE in question; P_{ij} is the total number of all foreign parent service firms that could establish affiliates in industry i, host country j, in 1976 and 1980 respectively. The measure is similar to the oligopolistic measure used by Terpstra and Yu (1988), with the extension that we consider the global oligopolistic reaction, thus more accurately reflecting the reality of global competition in service industries.

We developed a new measure for international competitiveness of service MNEs. Our international competitive index (ICI) is a synthesis of the revealed comparative advantage (RCA) index as developed by Balassa (1965; 1977b) and the intra-industry foreign direct investment (IIFDI) index as developed by Norman and Dunning (1984) and Dunning (1988). We define the international competitiveness index ICI_{ij} as

$$ICI_{ij} = (Q_{ij} - I_{ij})/(Q_{ij} + I_{ij}) \tag{12.2}$$

where Q_{ij} is the number of subsidiaries in industry i formed overseas by firms based in country j; and I_{ij} is the number of subsidiaries in industry i formed in country j by firms not based in country j.

We calculated the ICI for the nine service industries in the triad nations for both 1980 and 1986, using data from UNCTC (1988). With this ICI, we can analyse the international competitiveness of one country's service industry relative to the same industry in other countries. It should be noted that the index for international competitiveness works well under the condition that there are no government restrictions on both inward and outward foreign investment. Further research is required to refine this measure to include government restrictions.

The market size of a host country (GDP) is measured by the gross domestic product in 1976 and 1980 respectively for the two periods. The sources of these data are the World Bank (1978, 1982). The market size for Western Europe is the sum of the GDPs of the member countries. Since disaggregated data are not available for each host country in Europe, US and Japanese service firms are assumed to invest in Europe to pursue the regional strategy (the European market).

We developed an openness index (OPEN) to measure the openness of service industry i in country j to the establishment of new foreign service subsidiaries. The degrees of government controls and impediments affecting inward FDI in each service industry are estimated on an integer scale of 1–4, 1 representing industries with the most restrictive control and 4 representing industries with little or no controls and impediments on inward FDI in 1980 and in 1986. The major sources of data are OECD (1982, 1987a), with supplementary data from USTR (1984, 1986) and UNCTC (1983–8).

We drew measures of cultural distance (CD) between the home and host countries from the work of Hofstede (1980). Hofstede found that differences in national cultures vary substantially along four dimensions: uncertainty avoidance, individuality, tolerance of power distance and masculinity–femininity. Using Hofstede's indices and following the methodology of Kogut and Singh (1988), a composite index was formed based on the deviation along each of four cultural dimensions to measure the cultural distance between the home and host countries.

The growth of firm size (GSIZE) was measured by the annual growth rate in revenues of service MNEs over the two periods. Data are derived from UNCTC (1988). The home country business presence in a host country (FDI) is measured by the book value of the foreign direct investment position from the home country in 1976 and 1980 respectively. Data were collected from the US Department of Commerce (1984), OECD (1987b), UNCTC (1988) and from various sources as compiled by Dunning and Cantwell (1987).

RESULTS

We analysed the logistic regression model for firms in the overall sample over the two periods. The total number of observations for the 1976–80 period is 684 and for the 1980–6 period is 725. Separate analyses were also performed for the US, Japanese and European service MNEs.

Overall patterns of international competition

Table 12.2 shows the results of logistic regression for the overall sample. The x^2 scores of models for the two periods indicate that the models are highly significant overall, attesting to the explanatory power of the independent variables.

Table 12.2 Logistic regression estimates of service FDI determinants: overall sample

Variable	1976–80	1980–6
Constant	–3.85***	–3.30***
	(0.43)	(0.42)
OLIGOP	3.46***	2.76***
	(0.55)	(0.42)
ICI	0.33	0.40*
	(0.21)	(0.22)
GDP	0.65***	0.21**
	(0.16)	(0.09)
CD	–0.41***	–0.19*
	(0.12)	(0.11)
OPEN	0.27*	0.49***
	(0.17)	(0.16)
GSIZE	0.41**	0.12**
	(0.17)	(0.05)
FDI	–0.24	–0.72**
	(0.67)	(0.36)
X^2	143.46	197.85
Degrees of freedom	7	7
Probability value	2.5×10^{-9}	3.3×10^{-8}
Observations	684	725
Firms	158	168

Notes: *** $p < 0.01$; ** $p < 0.05$; * $p < 0.10$; standard errors in parentheses.

The degree of global oligopolistic reaction has a positive and significant impact on foreign investment of service MNEs for both periods (see Hypothesis 12.1). Our results support the hypothesis that service MNEs follow their competitors (both domestic and international) in going abroad as a defensive strategy. This is consistent with findings of oligopolistic reactions in the international behaviour of manufacturing firms (Knickerbocker 1973; Flowers 1976; Graham 1978). The continuing integration of the world economy, the globalization of markets and the improving communications technology all suggest that a firm must compete with a global strategy (Hout *et al.* 1982).

Foreign investment of service MNEs is found to be positively related to the international competitiveness (ICI) of the industry in the home country (see Hypothesis 12.2). The result is consistent for both periods, although the impact in the first period was significant only at a 0.15 level. Because we did not adjust for the effects of government restrictions on the index for international competitiveness, the index may be biased upward for countries with higher degrees of government restrictions. Because countries liberalized their restrictions in the early 1980s, the bias is reduced in the second period and the impact of national competitive advantages becomes significant.

The impact of market size of the host country (GDP) on foreign investment of service MNEs is found to be positive for both periods. This confirms the findings of previous empirical studies in single service industries (e.g. Terpstra and Yu 1988, in advertising). The results highlight the similar market-seeking behaviour of service MNEs and manufacturing firms.

For both periods, foreign investment of service MNEs is found to be positively related to the openness (OPEN) of the host country to the establishment of new foreign service subsidiaries in that industry. The liberalization in national restrictions on inward FDI during the early 1980s (UNCTC 1988) has shown a significant impact on FDI of service MNEs during the 1980–6 period.

The cultural distance CD between the home and host countries is found to have a negative impact on FDI of service MNEs for both periods. This result is consistent with studies of effects of culture on foreign entry modes (Kogut and Singh 1988) and on failures of foreign-controlled firms (Li and Guisinger 1991). We can also observe that the significance level of the cultural factors decreases over time. The impact of cultural distance is much more pronounced in the early stage of internationalization.

As in the case of manufacturing firms, the growth in the size of a service firm (GSIZE) has a positive impact on foreign investment of service MNEs. This is consistent with findings of foreign investment by manufacturing firms (Horst 1972; Grubaugh 1987). Service MNEs may have ownership advantages in competing with local firms. This result seems also consistent with Dunning's (1988b result) that intra-industry FDI is more likely when the ownership advantages are firm specific rather than country specific. Following home country client firms is a motive observed on early venturing abroad of most US service MNEs. However, our results show that home country business presence (FDI) does not have a significant impact in the first period and has a negative impact in the second period. This contradictory finding may be attributed to two factors. The first factor is the measurement and comparability of foreign investment positions across countries (Dunning and Cantwell 1987). Even though we consulted multiple data sources, data on the FDI position of each country are very incomplete and difficult to compare. The second factor is the problem of multicollinearity. As expected, the FDI position is highly correlated with the market size and other explanatory variables. This may reduce the significance level of the FDI variable as an explanatory variable.

It should be noted that these results do not conflict with the 'following the client' hypothesis. The results suggest that, although early venturing abroad of service MNEs followed their client firms, as service MNEs from the triad nations established their presence in the developed markets the motivation for new FDI shifted to serving the local market.

Regional patterns of international competition

The patterns observed in the overall analysis are obviously reflected in the results of regression analyses for the regional data, but there are a number of quite interesting differences between regions. Regional comparisons are somewhat hampered by the reduced number of observations for each region, but the results are nevertheless informative. All significant coefficients in the regional analyses have expected signs (Table 12.3).

Interestingly, global oligopolistic reaction is the only variable significant in both periods in each of the three regional models as well as in the aggregated analysis. In fact, oligopolistic market structure is the only variable common to even two of the regions. Each explanatory variable in the overall analysis is significant in one of the regions but in none of the others, suggesting quite important differences in investor motivation between regions.

In both periods, European investors appear to be positively influenced by three factors – oligopolistic market structure, the growth of their own firms and the size of foreign markets – and negatively influenced by cultural distance. In both periods, the accumulated value of foreign direct investment FDI is highly correlated with the size of foreign markets. The FDI variable was not included in the model for the second period. When we

Table 12.3 Logistic regression estimates of service FDI determinants: by regions

Variable	USA		Japan		Europe	
	1976–80	*1980–6*	*1976–80*	*1980–6*	*1976–80*	*1980–6*
Constant	−5.29***	-3.33***	−2.02	−2.68	−2.24***	−2.22***
	(0.83)	(0.66)	(8.39)	(23.2)	(0.73)	(0.60)
OLIGOP	4.87***	3.77***	3.42***	3.74***	2.45***	1.73**
	(1.19)	(0.72)	(1.06)	(1.01)	(0.95)	(0.74)
ICI	0.03	0.64*	1.57*	−0.26	−0.01	0.77
	(0.41)	(0.37)	(0.91)	(0.91)	(0.53)	(0.63)
GDP	0.34	0.01	−0.08	0.69	0.92***	0.38***
	(0.24)	(0.11)	(0.71)	(3.71)	(0.32)	(0.14)
CD	−0.74	−0.02	−2.10	−1.83	−0.67***	−0.41*
	(0.55)	(0.36)	(3.25)	(8.88)	(0.26)	(0.21)
OPEN	0.62*	0.31	0.81	1.84***	−0.27	0.26
	(0.37)	(0.29)	(0.58)	(0.68)	(0.32)	(0.24)
GSIZE	0.37	−0.21	0.47	−0.47	0.51**	0.53***
	(0.38)	(0.29)	(0.58)	(0.62)	(0.24)	(0.19)
FDI			0.65	−0.45	5.98	
			(0.96)	(2.15)	(6.13)	
X^2	61.39	93.60	42.89	63.07	54.64	67.70
Degrees of freedom	6	6	7	7	7	6
Probability value	3.7×10^{-9}	7.7×10^{-11}	1.4×10^{-5}	1.74×10^{-7}	2.3×10^{-9}	1.3×10^{-8}
Observations	272	308	152	152	260	265
Firms	68	77	38	38	52	53

Notes: *** $p < 0.01$; ** $p < 0.05$; * $p < 0.10$; standard errors in parentheses.

rerun the model without including the size of foreign market (GDP) variable, the parameter for the FDI variable becomes positive and significant for both periods.

Japanese investors in the first period appear to be driven by competitive factors – oligopolistic market structure and the index of competitive advantage. However, in the second period, the host country policy variable of openness becomes significant, while the competitive advantage index drops out. Interestingly, the cultural distance variable was not found to have a significant impact, perhaps because cultural distances between Japan and all Western countries are uniformly large. Without any variation, this variable cannot be statistically significant, even though it may have substantial explanatory power.

Interestingly, the motivation for US investors is a mirror image of the Japanese case: openness is important in the first period while the index of competitive advantage replaces it in the second period. As expected, the home country business presence (FDI) is highly correlated with the size of foreign markets and thus was not included in the model.

CONCLUSIONS

This chapter investigates two major arguments concerning the international competition of service MNEs. The first argument relates foreign investment by service MNEs to global oligopolistic reaction, where firms play a tit-for-tat game of matching foreign investments in major markets. The second argument relates foreign investment by service MNEs to the competitive advantages of service industries. In international competition firms exploit those skills and routines which drive their home market success.

We have empirically tested these hypotheses with foreign investment decisions of 168 large service MNEs based in different countries and in nine industries. The results of our tests for the two periods (1976–80 and 1980–6) suggest that foreign investment of service MNEs is positively related to global oligopolistic reaction. Firms in service industries do match foreign investments in major markets by their competitors. Thus inter-firm rivalry explanation contributes to our understanding of international competition between service MNEs.

We find that the index for international competitiveness of home industries is positively related to foreign investment decisions of service MNEs, particularly in the second period (1980–6). This suggests that over the long run the sustained competitive advantages play a major role in international competition.

We also investigated the effects of several country- or firm-related factors. Our results show that foreign investment of a service MNE is negatively related to the cultural distance between the home and host countries and is positively related to the market size of the host country, the openness of the host country to the inward FDI in services and the growth in firm size. Our results also show that service MNEs based in the triad nations already have an established presence in developed markets. Their decisions for new FDI seem to be more motivated by serving the local and other foreign customers in the host market. The patterns of international competition show quite important differences across countries. This is reflected in our analysis of factors influencing foreign investment decisions of service firms by each of the triad regions for the two periods. Oligopolistic market structure is the only variable significant in both periods in each of the three regional models as well as in the overall analysis. The results suggest important differences in investor motivation between the regions. The importance of these factors also changes over time.

Further research should extend our measures of international competitiveness to consider the effects of government restrictions. The measure for global oligopolistic reaction should also be refined to incorporate the 'urgency' of firms' counter-moves of matching foreign investment in major markets. Research examining strategies of a service MNE in countering a competitor's move by forming joint ventures, coalitions or networks would be most appropriate.

13 International competitiveness and corporate strategies in the construction services sector

Yehia Soubra *

The construction and engineering design (CED) services sector accounts for about 8–10 per cent of GDP in the industrialized countries and in such developing countries as Algeria and Yugoslavia, and about 3 per cent in less advanced countries such as Nepal and Uganda (World Bank 1984: 3, 11). It is an important generator of employment for both skilled and unskilled labour and, in some countries, constitutes a key source of foreign exchange earnings.[1] This sector contributed 9 per cent of GNP and provided employment for over 5 million persons in the USA in 1985 and accounted for 10 per cent of both GDP and employment in Japan. It is used by all countries to varying degrees as a macroeconomic management tool to rectify economic imbalances such as inflationary pressures or unemployment problems.

SALIENT FEATURES OF THE CONSTRUCTION SERVICES INDUSTRY

The construction services industry is highly fragmented. Most firms are small or medium sized and provide technical services to small residential projects and simple infrastructural facilities. In Japan there are more than 5,000,000 construction firms and in Western Europe thousands of companies operate in this sector and their individual market share in any one country does not exceed 4 per cent (Swiss Bank Corporation 1990: 4). In the USA there are over 1 million firms doing business in this sector and only a few thousand of them are engaged in international activities (Office of Technology Assessment 1987: 124–7).

Construction services consist of two main groups of services that are interrelated and equally necessary to bring an investment project from conception to realization, including operation and maintenance. The first group comprises consulting and engineering design services and the second comprises physical construction services, or what is sometimes referred to as project implementation services (Soubra 1989: 185–8).

Consulting and engineering design services

Consulting and engineering design services are knowledge-intensive services and are essential to optimize investment in all its forms, in its choice, in the technical process of its execution and in its management (Roberts 1973: 39–42). The designs and specifications that these services produce should be the least-cost and highest-productivity solutions consistent with the economic and social constraints of individual markets. Many of these services are multidisciplinary in nature, requiring general and specialized engineering and other technical and economic skills to produce the requisite outputs. The output can take different forms, ranging from drawings to general and training reports and operating manuals. Consulting and engineering design services can be classified according to the stage of development of an investment project (Araoz 1981). They would include (a) pre-investment services (e.g. opportunity studies, market studies, feasibility studies and location studies); (b) project execution services (e.g. process and product design, architectural and structural design, design and layout of machinery and equipment, purchasing, inspection and testing of materials and equipment); and (c) project implementation services (including production activities and technical and management personnel training).

Consulting and engineering design services help to determine the technological dimension of investment projects and to establish forward and backward linkages in the national economy. The interlinkages produced between these services, the local research and development activities and the capital goods sector are of particular importance. Decisions on the sources of supply of these services would also affect the procurement of construction implementation services and equipment. Mainly because of the externalities that they generate, these services have a strategic role to play in economic growth and development. They condition the provision of physical construction services through the techno-economic specification they establish for individual investment projects and elements of machinery and equipment. These services do not produce only specifications for goods and raw materials that should be used in the implementation of a given project; they also formulate criteria for the selection of contractors and raw material suppliers and often suggest modes of project financing.[2]

Apart from the interlinkages they produce within national economies, consulting and engineering design services are used as an important mechanism for the transfer of technology in all economic sectors. Through their international activities, consulting and engineering design organizations (CEDOs) have contributed to the transfer of technical knowledge between firms and countries at different levels of development. The transfer of technology through CED services has taken different forms, including (a) embodied technology transfer, namely through the provision of the services referred to above; (b) formal instruction through training courses; (c) on-the-job training; (d) collaborative management; and (e) technological information including documents and computer software.

Consulting and engineering design services can be provided by individuals acting alone, or grouped in companies or organizations that are independent or captive. Independent CEDOs that perform within an institutional framework, be it a private or a state-owned company, may be specialized or diversified services organizations. In the case of captive CEDOs, the service entities could be part of a construction firm, could be tied into a manufacturing facility or could simply operate in a department within a public organization responsible for infrastructure-related projects. Some of these CEDOs are often difficult to identify as they are labelled 'technical realization', 'engineering', 'marketing' or 'technical sales' departments. The work of those that are integrated into manufacturing facilities is generally, but not exclusively, confined to the activities of the manufacturing firms and these activities often fit within those firms' corporate strategies. Finally, CED service entities may be tied into construction firms that provide fairly comprehensive physical construction services. Here the dividing line tends to be blurred between the consulting and engineering design services subsector on the one hand and the physical construction subsector on the other. Recently, increased competition in the international engineering design services subsector has partly resulted from the development and growth of engineering and construction firms providing design-related services and of design-construct firms stimulated by increased demand for integrated/packaged CED services.

Construction services

These are the services that transform the techno-economic specifications produced by the consulting and engineering design services into physical entities such as infrastructure projects or industrial plants, including machinery and equipment. Labour, capital and raw materials are used in providing these physical construction services. In addition to skilled personnel, these services employ a fairly large proportion of semi-skilled and unskilled labour and their provision requires a much larger capital outlay than that needed by firms providing consulting and engineering design services. Construction services are generally supplied by engineering contractors in different fields of specialization, such as residential buildings, highways, bridges, power, sewerage, transportation, manufacturing etc. Consulting and engineering design services account for between 5 and 10 per cent of the cost of an investment project, the bulk of which is spent on construction services, material and equipment.

THE INTERNATIONAL CONSTRUCTION MARKET

The following review of the evolution of the international market for CED services deals separately with each of the two main groups of services discussed above. It is based on trade statistics published in a weekly magazine, *Engineering News Record* (*ENR*), as part of an annual survey covering the top 200 international design firms and the top 250 international contractors. These surveys rank the design services rendered in the export market and the contractors according to their foreign contract values. Although the data are incomplete and have some shortcomings, they are useful in so far as they give an overview of the evolution of the international market for CED services (Soubra 1989: 188–90), particularly as international business in this sector tends to be conducted mainly by a few large companies from both developed and developing countries.

Table 13.1 Regional distribution of foreign billings of the top 200 international design firms, 1986–9 (millions of US dollars)

Region	1986	1987	1988	1989[a]
Africa	855.3	948.6	824.1	937.5
Asia	982.3	1,133.6	1,152.8	2,000.0
Latin America	320.6	434.8	322.3	443.8
Middle East	907.2	742.3	808.7	803.1
Europe	313.6	531.6	621.5	1,770.0
North America	160.9	230.6	428.7	1,433.9
Total	3,539.9	4,021.5	4,158.2	7,388.3[b]

Source: *Engineering News Record* various issues
Notes: [a] The large increase in billings in 1989 reflects design-related services on industrial, petrochemical and power facilities by major US and foreign engineering and construction firms that were not included formerly among ENR's top 200 international design firms. These billings do not include design–build work (ENR 1990).
[b] Excluding the design billings of the engineering and construction firms, the total billings of the traditional design consultants for 1989 were about $4.3 billion, which represented an increase of 2.2 per cent over 1988.

Consulting and engineering design services

Regional export markets

The foreign design billings of the top 200 traditional design consultants have increased moderately from $4.15 billion to $4.3 billion. However, if the design billings of major foreign construction and engineering companies are included then the total would be around $7.4 billion[3] (Table 13.1). Foreign design billings increased in almost all geographical regions – Asia, with about $2 billion, continues to be the strongest regional market in which US, Japanese and European companies are engaged in fierce rivalry. About fifty-four US firms control 44 per cent of this market between them, followed by the British with 17 per cent and the Japanese with 10 per cent. The second regional market that has witnessed an increase in foreign design billings for the top 200 design firms is Europe, with the value of such billings amounting to $1.7 billion. Here, again, the US firms have the lion's share of this market (64 per cent), followed way behind by their British counterparts (11.2 per cent). North America, including the USA and Canada, also witnessed an increase in foreign billings for the top 200 international design firms, reaching $1.4 billion. Whereas the British firms have managed to capture over 40 per cent of the foreign design billings in the USA, US firms accounted for about 90 per cent of such billings in Canada. Finally, the Middle East experienced a decline in foreign design billings while Africa and Latin America exhibited an increase.

Competitive position of major players

US and European firms dominate the international design market. Between them they account for over 85 per cent of foreign design billings of the top 200 international design firms, with more or less equal market shares. The USA continues to be the largest individual exporter of engineering design services, accounting for over 40 per cent of the international design market in 1989. Among the European firms, those of British nationality come second after the USA, with a 16 per cent share of the international market, confirming their competitive strength and lead in Europe in this subsector over the years. While the competitiveness of Canadian and Japanese firms seems to have been eroded, with their share declining from 16 per cent to 8 per cent and from 6 per cent to 3.5 per cent, respectively, the position of German firms seems to be more or less stable (Table 13.2). Canadian firms have been less competitive, mainly in the US market, accounting in 1989 for about 16 per cent of the design billings of the top 200 design firms in this country, compared with about 62 per cent registered in 1988. Although a few companies from developing countries have appeared on *ENR*'s list of the top 200 international design firms, their international work remains very small, accounting for less than 5 per cent of total foreign design billings.

Table 13.2 Market share of international design, 1983–9 (as measured by foreign billings of the top 200 international design firms) (millions of US dollars and percentage share in parentheses) [a]

Country	1983	1984	1985	1986	1987	1988	1989 [b]
USA	1,204	1,037	1,165	918	1,042	1,039	3,228.8
	(31)	(30)	(32)	(26)	(26)	(25)	(43.5)
France	361	234	239	306	260	133	323.2
	(9)	(7)	(7)	(9)	(6)	(3)	(4.3)
FRG	253	249	230	282	356	302	452.3
	(7)	(7)	(6)	(8)	(9)	(7)	(6)
UK	592	454	463	481	451	440	1,182
	(15)	(13)	(13)	(14)	(11)	(10)	(16)
Canada	269	187	266	204	518	672	594.4
	(7)	(8)	(7)	(6)	(13)	(16)	(8)
Japan	127	166	226	221	259	257	257.4
	(3)	(5)	(6)	(6)	(6)	(6)	(3.5)
Netherlands	203	228	219	259	358	424	471.1
	(5)	(7)	(6)	(7)	(9)	(10)	(6.3)
Other countries	841	809	832	869	774	933	912.6
	(22)	(23)	(23)	(25)	(19)	(22)	(12.2)
Total	3,850	3,464	3,640	3,540	4,017	4,200	7,421.8
	(100)	(100)	(100)	(100)	(100)	(100)	(100)

Source: *Engineering News Record* various issues
Notes: [a] Total does not correspond to the sum of components because of rounding at the component level. The period 1983–9 (instead of 1980–9) has been selected for reasons of comparability of data. Whereas ENR's *Annual Surveys*, since 1983, have included the top 200 international design firms, they included only the top 150 such firms during the 1970–82 period.
[b] Foreign billings for 1989 include those of major US and foreign engineering and construction firms not included formerly among the top 200 international design firms (see footnote a in Table 13.1).

Construction services

In 1989, the value of foreign construction contracts increased by 20 per cent to $112.5 billion, the highest since 1983 but lower than the 1981 peak of $134.4 billion. This increase, which occurred for the second consecutive year, has manifested itself in additional foreign contracts for the top 250 international contractors in all geographical regions. Europe has surpassed Asia as the most attractive market with some $25.4 billion worth of foreign construction contracts, representing about 22 per cent of the total export market (Table 13.3). This region has emerged as a high-growth market for foreign construction companies with the value of international business more than doubling in the four years from 1986 to 1989 and showing an increase of more than 30 per cent in 1989 alone. This reflects the prospects of the 1993 single European market and an upward trend in construction activities.

Among the top 250 international contractors doing business in this market, twenty-two US firms control 44.5 per cent of foreign contracts between them, followed by British firms with 14.7 per cent and French firms with 10.4 per cent. US firms have also managed to dominate all the other regional export markets. In 1989, they controlled 31 per cent of the international construction business in Asia, 42.4 per cent in the Middle East, 39 per cent in Africa, 26.4 per cent in Latin America and 53.5 per cent in Canada. Japanese firms are particularly strong competitors of US firms in Asia, where they control about 27 per cent of foreign contracts. Among the top 250 international contractors that won construction contracts in the USA in 1989, there were eight British firms with a combined market share of 28 percent, eleven West German firms controlling 19 per cent of international business in this country and twenty-three Japanese firms with about an 18 per cent share of this export market.

While the top 250 international contractors won about 40 per cent of the construction contracts in Africa and 18 per cent more in North America in 1989, their international business in the Middle East and Latin America has

Table 13.3 Regional distribution of foreign construction contracts awarded to the top 250 international contractors, 1986–9 (billions of US dollars)

Region	1986	1987	1988	1989
Africa	13.1	9.0	10.1	14.3
Asia	17.3	15.5	20.5	24.5
Latin America	5.2	7.4	7.5	7.6
Middle East	16.1	13.4	17.4	17.8
Europe	11.9	17.2	19.4	25.4
North America	10.4	11.5	19.2	22.7
Total	73.9	73.9	94.1	112.5

Source: *Engineering News Record* various issues

improved only slightly. Whereas the developing countries accounted, for about 85 per cent of the international construction market in the early 1980s, the corresponding share in 1989 was less than 60 per cent. The contraction of the Middle East market, resulting mainly from the decline in oil revenues since the mid-1980s and the completion of fairly large infrastructure projects in this part of the world, together with the debt crisis that slowed investment in construction activities, mainly in Africa and Latin America, partly explain the decline of international business in the developing world where the capability built up in this sector has also meant that some construction work, mainly civil engineering, is now handled by local firms.

Competitive position of major players

The USA remains the largest individual exporter of such services, accounting for about 34 per cent of the international market, up from 27 per cent in 1988 and 24 per cent in 1987 but well below the corresponding figure of 45 per cent reached ten years ago (Table 13.4) In 1989, six of the top international firms (ranked according to their foreign contract values) were of US nationality.

European firms among the top 250 international contractors together captured 47 per cent of the export market. Of these, the French contingent seems to have been successful in maintaining its share of the market (at about 12 per cent), while Italian firms have become less competitive with their combined share declining from 14 per cent to less than 10 per cent. Moreover, the number of Italian firms ranking among *ENR*'s top 250 international contractors has continued to decline, from fifty in 1987 to forty-one in 1988 and thirty-eight in 1989.

Thirty-four Japanese firms appeared on *ENR*'s list in 1989, compared with thirty-eight in 1990. These companies seem to be attracted by the growing domestic market. Japan's Ministry of Construction had estimated that the total construction investment in fiscal 1989 would be about $482.7 billion, from which the fifty-two member firms of the Japan Federation of Construction Contractors Inc. drew most of its $147.9 billion in new contracts (*ENR* 1990a).

The top 250 international contractors include firms from developing countries such as Yugoslavia, the Republic of Korea, China, Brazil, India, Singapore, Argentina and Venezuela. Eight Yugoslav firms were on the list in 1989, with a combined market share of 0.7 per cent compared with 1 per cent in 1988 and 2 per cent in 1986. After an impressive export performance in the early 1980s, Korean firms experienced difficulties in competing in a rapidly changing international environment. In effect, the

Table 13.4 Market share of international construction (as measured by new contracts awarded to the top 250 international contractors) (billions of US dollars and percentage share in parentheses) [a]

Country	1980	1981	1982	1983	1984	1985	1986	1987	1988	1989
USA	48.3	48.8	44.9	29.4	30.1	28.2	22.6	18.1	25.9	38.4
	(45)	(36)	(36)	(31)	(37)	(35)	(31)	(24)	(27)	(34)
France	8.1	12.1	11.4	10.0	5.4	6.7	7.1	8.6	11.1	13.2
	(7)	(9)	(9)	(11)	(7)	(8)	(10)	(12)	(12)	(11.8)
FRG	8.6	9.9	9.5	5.4	4.8	5.4	5.5	5.9	8.1	8.6
	(8)	(7)	(8)	(6)	(6)	(7)	(7)	(8)	(9)	(7.7)
Italy	6.2	9.3	7.8	7.2	7.8	8.7	7.4	9.2	13.3	10.8
	(6)	(7)	(6)	(8)	(10)	(11)	(10)	(12)	(14)	(9.6)
UK	4.9	8.7	7.5	6.4	5.7	5.6	7.0	7.9	9.4	12.9
	(5)	(6)	(6)	(7)	(7)	(7)	(9)	(11)	(10)	(11.4)
Other Europe	9.2	12.6	10.3	9.1	7.2	6.2	6.7	8.9	7.3	7.4
	(8)	(9)	(8)	(10)	(9)	(8)	(9)	(12)	(8)	(6.6)
Japan	4.1	8.6	9.3	8.7	7.3	11.6	9.4	9.9	11.6	12.8
	(4)	(6)	(8)	(9)	(9)	(14)	(13)	(13)	(12)	(11.2)
Republic of Korea	9.5	13.9	13.8	10.4	6.8	4.8	2.6	2.1	1.4	–
	(9)	(10)	(11)	(11)	(8)	(6)	(4)	(3)	(2)	(–)
All other countries	9.4	10.5	8.6	7.0	5.9	4.4	5.6	3.3	6.0	8.5
	(9)	(8)	(7)	(7)	(7)	(5)	(8)	(4)	(6)	(7.5)
Total	108.3	134.4	123.1	93.6	80.5	81.6	73.9	73.9	94.1	112.5

Source: Engineering News Record various issues
Note: [a] Total does not correspond to the sum of components because of rounding at the component level.

competitiveness of Korea has been eroded with its market share constantly declining since 1983, from 11 per cent in 1983 to as low as 2 per cent in 1988 and a negligible share in 1989 (see Table 13.4). Also, the number of Korean firms on *ENR*'s list of the top 250 international contractors continued to decline from fourteen in 1986 to eleven in 1987, seven in 1988 and five in 1989. The rather poor performance of the Korean firms in the second half of the 1980s may be attributed to their slowness in adjusting to changes in the international market, as reflected in the concentration of their activities in the declining Middle Eastern market and on infrastructure-related work, although some attempts were made to provide industrial engineering services. In addition, the fierce rivalry that ensued among the Korean firms themselves in the international market, together with their weakness in arranging project financing, may have contributed to the decline of this country as a major exporter of construction services.

CORPORATE PRACTICES AND STRATEGIES

The evolution of the international market for consulting and engineering design and construction services over the past ten years and the changing competitive positions of firms and countries during this period has been accompanied by changes in corporate practices and strategies, including the conclusion of strategic alliances and new forms of collaboration among firms in the industry. Some of those alliances have been reflected in accelerated moves towards mergers and acquisitions, particularly in Europe, in anticipation of the 1993 single European market. In addition, technology-based strategies, together with corporate practices that combine finance with technical services, are shaping the conduct of international business.

Trends in co-operation agreements

Fierce competition in a low business environment during most of the 1980s has imposed further strains on the behaviour of companies in the industry. Firms reacted in different ways to this situation. Some attempted to venture into new markets, including China[4] and the USSR.[5] Others (such as Japanese construction firms) began to pay relatively more attention to their growing domestic market. Others (e.g. Korean firms), mainly the financially weak ones, could not withstand the stiff competition and withdrew from the international market, a move which may have been encouraged by the government as part of its policy of limiting the number of Korean firms operating in this market.

A trend that has emerged during the 1980s is that international firms can do better business while co-operating with each other and in association with local partners. Unlike the situation which prevailed in the 1970s, when international firms tended to provide the whole gamut of construction services for clients in foreign countries, the trend now seems to be towards co-operation between different companies and/or through subsidiaries in providing these services based on the respective strength of the parties involved. US companies, for example, have given increased attention to construction management services and less attention to construction implementation services which were either subcontracted to other firms or provided in co-operation with local firms.

The philosophy underlying this trend is the increasing recognition among international firms of the advantages of 'localization', which could mean doing business in foreign markets through, for example, subsidiaries or joint ventures. Those entities would operate more like indigenous firms and less like expatriate firms. This trend is particularly noticeable in the European and US markets. According to the fifty-six members of the Overseas Construction Association of Japan Inc. about half of the US work reported by its members in 1988 was won by local subsidiaries, compared with 29 per cent in 1987 and 27 per cent in 1986 (*ENR* 1988: 45).

The existing co-operation agreements include strategic alliances formed between companies of different nationalities which were hitherto rival competitors in their respective markets and in third markets. Examples of such co-operation agreements are the collaboration between the American firm Bechtel and the Japanese firm Kumagai Gumi in building a $170 million dam in Canada (Office of Technology Assessment 1987: 147) and the world-wide marketing agreement between the American firm Fluor Daniel and Ohbayashi, one of the largest contractors in Japan. This agreement covers potential projects located in the USA, Japan and other countries (*ENR* 1986: 36). In Asia, where Japanese and Korean firms used to be fierce competitors, they are now entering into co-operation agreements.[6] This new trend has led to a restructuring of overseas operations, more flexible loca- tional strategies and a surge of mergers and acquisitions in the industry.

Acquisitions and strategic stake purchases across national borders

As already indicated, the different forms of collaboration that have developed among construction and engineering design companies take into account the complementarities that exist among them and the specificities of the markets in which they operate. The strategies of some firms have been based on mergers and acquisitions. This is the case, for example, with international firms operating in the US market. Except for some of the

Japanese companies that prefer to set up their own subsidiaries, almost all the US volume reported by foreign contractors was won through mergers or the acquisition of US companies. German and British companies have been particularly active in this respect. This trend has accelerated in other regions to take advantage of the barrier-free global market that is in the making. In anticipation of the 1993 single European market, cross-border acquisitions, joint ventures and other partnership agreements have lately

Table 13.5 Cross-border holdings between European contractors

Company	Country	Stake in	Country	Stake %
Bouygues	France	Banco Central[a]	Spain	4
		Fercaber	Spain	70
Dumez	France	Dywidag	Germany	10
		CFE	Belgium	34
		McAlpine	UK	5
Dywidag	Germany	Dumez	France	5
Fougerolle	France	Maurice Delens	Netherlands	40
GTM Entrepose	France	Wiemer u Trachte	Germany	50
SGE	France	Norwest Holst	UK	55
		G & H Montage	Germany	100
Spie Batignolles	France	Davy Corporation	UK	14
Jean Lefebvre (GTM)	France	Probisa	Spain	14
Bilfinger & Berger	Germany	Birse Group	UK	15
Holzmann	Germany	Jotsa	Spain	50
		Nord France	France	40
		Hillen & Roosen	Netherlands	100
		Tilbury	UK	14
Dragasos	Spain	Ramalho Rosa	Portugal	75
Trafalgar House	UK	Sofresid	France	40
Huarte and Italstrade	Spain Italy	Empresa Tecnica	Portugal	100
Italstrade	Italy	Solius	Spain	100
Impresit	Italy	Hasa-Huarte	Spain	33
Ballast Nedam	Netherlands	Rush & Tompkins (parts of)	UK	–[b]
HBG	Netherlands	CEI	Belgium	100
		Nuttall	UK	100
		Kyle Stewart	UK	100
Decloedt	Belgium	Boskalls	Netherlands	10

Source: Swiss Bank Corporation and *Financial Times* 18 June 1990
Notes: [a] Owns 30 per cent of Dragados (Spain).
   [b] Bought majority of contracting business from receivers.

been increasing, particularly between European construction firms.

Table 13.5 lists most of the strategic purchases that were made in Western Europe since the beginning of 1989. It shows that European contractors have pursued this strategy to consolidate their position in this growing market. French and German contractors have been particularly active in buying stakes in each others' businesses and in other European contracting firms. Britain and Spain seem to be attractive places for other European companies to have stakes in local companies. In contrast, construction companies in France, Germany and Italy, which are family businesses with a complex share structure, have tended to be more difficult to acquire by other European companies (Swiss Bank Corporation 1990).

Technology-based strategies

Technological change, including advances in new technologies, is affecting different parts of the construction industry. The spread of computer-aided design and drafting (CADD) together with the diffusion of innovation in construction methods and materials, particularly in the industrialized countries, is altering the technological intensity of the industry. In Japan, many European countries and, to a lesser extent, the USA, efforts were made by engineering and construction firms, with government support in some cases, to promote investment in construction research and development. This investment was estimated for Japan at about 3 per cent of total industry revenues (Office of Technology Assessment 1987: 148), way above the corresponding figure of 0.4 per cent for the USA (*ENR* 1989b: 7), where some relevant research and development takes place outside the construction sector. While Japanese and European companies have placed increased emphasis on the development and diffusion of technological innovation in construction methods and materials, US firms have proved to be the leaders in computer applications in the industry, particularly in design work and construction management. In their technology-based strategies, US firms have tried to benefit from advances taking place in other industries (e.g. software) in which the USA is a leader in innovative performance. It has been estimated, for example, that the US firm Bechtel has more than ten times as many CADD workstations installed as the large Japanese engineering and construction firms (Office of Technology Assessment 1987: 139).

Despite differences in the magnitude and focus of their research and development efforts, international firms, particularly those from the high-wage industrialized countries but including construction firms from some low labour-cost developing countries and other technologically weak countries (e.g. East European countries), have updated their technology to compete against each other. However, some of these same firms tend to differ in their individual assessment of the advantages offered by some specific new technologies, such as CADD.

The experience of some firms has shown that investment in CADD has helped them to offer more options to their clients, improved draughting speed and accuracy, shortened the time required to bid on new projects and provided firms with additional flexibility to make quick adjustment to designs and drawings to suit their clients' needs. Proponents of CADD consider that this technology has generally promoted the smooth running of construction projects and design improvements (*ENR* 1990: 34–40). According to other industry sources, CADD is essentially a marketing tool (Farmer and Hall 1989: 87). It is more a matter of form than substance. They are doubtful about its cost-effectiveness (*ENR* 1990: 36).

In this connection, it may be safely said that not enough is known about the effects of CADD on competitiveness in the construction industry. Firms are still learning how to use this technology and take advantage of the opportunities it offers. Also, CADD is generally only one component in an automated information system that was adopted by some engineering services companies. The extent to which it is well integrated in the system affects the productivity gains and cost saving it may engender. This illustrates the importance of the systemic nature of the technology in the elaboration of corporate strategies.

Financing and construction services

Over the past ten years, financing has become an increasingly influential factor affecting the competitiveness of engineering and construction firms, particularly in the markets of developing countries in Latin America and Africa which have been affected by the debt crisis and by falling commodity prices. For international firms to win construction contracts in many of these countries, project financing has tended to become a requirement. Companies that could offer financing with technical services have managed to improve their position in the international market. This was the case with Italian firms in 1988. During that year, the top 250 international contractors won contractor-financed work worth $6 billion, of which about $3.2 billion was awarded to Italian firms (*ENR* 1989: 54).

The sources of financing mostly used are commercial bank loans, the contractors' government and, to a lesser extent, equity investment and countertrade. The role of international and regional financial institutions in financing construction work is also important in this regard. It may be relevant to mention here that over 40 per cent of World Bank project assistance goes to construction activities. While large developed-country construction firms have, in their strategies, attached increased importance to the project financing aspect of construction work, developing-country firms continue to be weak in their ability to raise the requisite financing at competitive rates.

PROSPECTS

The downward trend observed in the international construction market since the early 1980s seems to be decelerating and a surge in the value of foreign contracts has already begun and could continue. As already shown, international business in construction, as measured by the value of foreign contracts awarded to the top 250 international contracts, has reached $112 billion, up from $94 billion in 1988 and $73.9 in 1987 and 1986. There are indications that the construction export market may witness high growth in the next ten years. Four regional markets would seem to be the main poles around which such growth will be centred. These are Europe, Asia, North America and the Middle East. Preparations for the 1993 single European market of 320 million people are beginning to fuel international competition in construction services. They have already encouraged moves towards mergers and acquisitions and the setting up of joint ventures in the industry. This trend is likely to accelerate with the ongoing efforts within the European Community to harmonize building standards, testing and certification procedures. Since the formation of a European market would require a wide network of transport infrastructures, additional construction work has been created or is planned mainly for civil-engineering-related services.

The channel tunnel is one example of a large infrastructural project on which work has progressed markedly. New roads and highway projects are planned in Spain, France and Italy during the next ten years, together with further development of railways linking different European countries (Swiss Bank Corporation 1990: 12-13). Fierce competition is likely to develop in this attractive market, mainly between US, European and Japanese firms.

Asia would seem to be another growth market, offering new opportunities for international construction firms. It is estimated that the value of construction projects in Southeast Asia will increase by 20 per cent a year over the next ten years, with more than $300 billion worth of new contracts. A substantial part of that is likely to be spent on infrastructure-related work to support the surge in industrial activities in this rapidly growing region (*Financial Times* 18 June 1990).

Indonesia and Thailand appear to be promising markets in this respect. In Indonesia, banking credits for construction projects rose to $6 billion in

1989 from $4.5 billion in 1986; and in Thailand the value of total construction was $8.5 billion, representing 12 per cent of GDP (*Financial Times* 18 June 1990). Malaysia is also planning to spend about $30 billion on government projects in its 1991–5 development plan (*Financial Times* 11 May 1990). China has attracted a large number of construction firms in the past and is likely to continue to be a targeted market. However, the provision of financing and technology would continue to be part of the requirements to win construction contracts in this country.

Japan is also spending huge sums on construction work to develop its own infrastructure. The Japanese government estimates that its investment in new infrastructure work in the 1980s and 1990s will be around $4 trillion (at 1980 prices) (*The Economist* 29 April 1989: 76). To this should be added the construction-related expenditure originating in the rapidly growing private sector. This lucrative market continues to be relatively closed to foreign contractors, although steps have been taken recently by the Japanese government to allow such contractors, mainly those from the USA, to tender for some public construction contracts. This seems to have occurred as a result of US pressure threatening the use of retaliatory trade sanctions against this country. While the economy in Japan is witnessing a rapid growth and the construction market is expanding, severe labour shortages constitute a major macroeconomic problem confronting the nation. The problem is compounded by the difficulties of local firms, including construction companies, in making use of foreign labour (mainly from other Asian countries such as the Philippines, Thailand, Korea and Pakistan) in the design and execution of investment projects. This has been influenced by the restrictive emigration policy of the government whose objective is to preserve the cultural homogeneity and social harmony in the country.

The fairly large North American construction market, particularly that of the USA, offers good business prospects for international and particularly European and Japanese companies. The acquisition of US companies is a trend that is likely to continue to characterize the strategy of foreign firms in this market.

The Middle East seems to be emerging once again as another growth market for international construction firms. As already mentioned, the value of construction contracts awarded in this market to the top 250 international contractors has been declining during most of the 1980s. However, a resurgence of the market began in 1988 with such contracts rising by about 30 per cent and remaining more or less stable in 1989. More recently, multi-billion dollar projects seem to have been awarded to inter- national firms in the region, principally by Saudi Arabia. These projects, aimed at renovating and expanding oil and gas facilities in the country, could cost more than $45 billion over nine years (*ENR* 1990b). These huge projects, however, are becoming rare in the region where demand has been increasing for maintenance work for the fairly large infrastructural projects built in the 1970s. Their implementation, however, could be delayed because of the Gulf crisis that hit the Middle Eastern region in August 1990.

As regards Eastern Europe, international firms are in the process of learning how to do business in this region, where financing is likely to be one of the major factors affecting their competitiveness. Some efforts have been made to identify partners in these countries with whom international firms can work on construction projects. While many Western construction firms are eyeing this new market, they tend to be cautious in their attitude to it and in their investment decisions. With respect to East Germany, these firms seem to be more forthcoming, particularly after the decision to unify East and West Germany was taken.[7] Poland, which has developed a certain export capability in construction services, could offer partnership possibilities for international firms to work in the domestic market or in other East European markets. Finally, the USSR is a potential market whose evolution and opening up may be followed closely by foreign construction companies.

To take advantage of the opportunities offered by the changes occurring in the global market place, international construction companies are likely to pursue a mixture of technology-based and locational strategies to suit different markets. Emphasis is expected to be placed on technology strategies based on the increased use and improved application of computers, further development and adoption of automated construction methods and new construction materials. These strategies would essentially aim to reduce labour and material costs, improve the quality of construction services and allow firms to adapt rapidly to changing market conditions.

Locational strategies are likely to be more flexible and increasingly used by firms to penetrate new markets and/or consolidate their positions in existing ones, which could necessitate different structures to overseas operations. Relocation of certain production activities to offshore sites to take advantage of low labour cost, availability of skilled personnel and proximity to markets would continue to be an attractive option to international firms.

Financing has become more of an integral component of the strategies of these firms, particularly in the heavily indebted developing countries of Africa and Latin America, as well as China and East European countries. The combination of project financing with construction services has become a strategic factor affecting the competitive advantage of firms in the international market. Together with accelerated moves towards mergers, acquisitions and joint ventures and the increased diffusion of new technology in the industry, it has contributed to the creation of a new business environment that offers opportunities and presents challenges to construction and engineering services firms, particularly those from developing countries, in attempting to increase their participation in world trade.

NOTES

* Member of the UNCTAD secretariat. The views expressed are those of the author and do not necessarily reflect those of the UNCTAD secretariat. The designations employed and the presentation of material do not imply the expression of any opinion whatsoever on the part of the secretariat of the United Nations concerning the legal status of any country, territory, city or area, or of its authorities, or concerning the delimitation of its frontiers or boundaries.

1 The total foreign exchange earnings from overseas construction by firms from the Republic of Korea amounted to $11billion during 1978–85, which accounted for more than 50 per cent of the commodity trade deficit of this country during the same period (Sooyong 1988).
2 According to one study that examined large projects in the 1970s, up to 80 per cent of projects by firms from the Federal Republic of Germany have been awarded to construction firms from that country. The corresponding figures are 63 per cent for Japan and 50 per cent for France and Italy (see Murphy 1983: 138).
3 To account better for the volume of foreign design billings *ENR* has included US and foreign engineering and construction firms in its top 200 ranking for 1989. Their billings represent only design and design-related services and do not include design–build work (*ENR* 1990: 47).
4 In 1988, China was considered the most popular market where eighty-five of the top 250 international contractors were working (*ENR*, 1989a).
5 Of the $7.5 billion in contracts won by the top ten contractors active in Europe in 1987, about $3 billion were for work for the USSR (*ENR* 1988).
6 As an example, Maeda Construction Corporation from Japan signed a regional agreement with Ssangyong Construction from Korea (*ENR*, 1990c).
7 Fluor Daniel Inc. from the USA entered into a co-operation agreement with Ingenieurbetrieb Anlagenbau (Leipzig), the largest engineering and construction services firm in East Germany, to benefit from its extensive knowledge of the local market (*ENR* 1990d).

14 Business co-operation with Eastern Europe: problems and perspectives

Viktor Vlasek

The political, economic and social changes in Eastern Europe are occurring at such a pace that it is difficult enough for the citizens of this region to follow them, not to mention the foreigner. The later the changes in particular countries started, the higher their rate of development. That is, what happened in Poland over ten years took ten weeks in the German Democratic Republic and ten days in Czechoslovakia.

But the euphoria over the decay of a hated totalitarian system is over and we woke up to everyday reality, full of complex political, economic, social, ecological, national and religious problems that grew and ripened for the last forty years under cover of the official illusion of the always successful socialist state. These problems were labelled as remnants of the past or 'insignificant troubles' of socialist growth and their solution was either postponed or completely neglected.

THE COMMUNIST INHERITANCE

In order to present briefly the extent of inherited problems, I shall mention the most important from an economic point of view.

1 Severely distorted prices that often have no relation to the value or scarcity of goods. In the totalitarian system prices were used only for controlling the material flow in industries and for the creation of quasi- equilibrium in the supply–demand for consumer goods. Consequently, this led to inefficient allocation of resources, to rigidities and to bottle- necks because false prices gave incorrect signals to the economy and its efficiency.
2 Centralized decision-making which transformed the enterprises to obedient executives of central planning institutions without any degree of economic freedom. This in turn created huge inflexible production units unable to act independently in the market economy.

The present industrial structure is characterized predominantly by state ownership and a relative paucity of small and medium-sized firms. Such a structure generates lack of competition, limited product variety and an overall rigidity in industrial production.

3 A non-existing or underdeveloped economic, legal, commercial, banking etc., infrastructure. The planned economy centrally decided all important economic issues and distributed almost all material, financial and goods streams. There was therefore little or no need for institutions without which the market economy cannot exist (e.g. banks, stock exchange, tax office, commercial courts etc.).

4 An ill-defined structure of property rights. Within the last forty-five years the state nationalized almost all the means of production, as well as a large part of housing, without keeping an accurate record of this process. As a result, the almighty state is the ill-defined possessor of almost all of the national wealth. The socialist slogan 'Everything belongs to everybody' means in fact that nothing belongs to anybody.

I could go on lamenting about out-of-date production equipment, foreign trade oriented exclusively to the USSR etc. But the aim of this exposé is not to cry over spilt milk, but rather to outline some important features of the economic landscape of Eastern Europe.

POSSIBLE CHANGES

With some differences in time, rate and intensity, all the states of Eastern Europe are trying to change their economic image. The common goal is economic transformation, moving these economies from relatively inefficient, centrally planned systems marked by lack of incentives and distorted price structures and quantity allocations to more efficient market-oriented systems based on competitive prices. Generally speaking, the assumed goal is to move the economy to a higher welfare equilibrium with as little transitional cost as possible.

Since no general formal theory of such a transition exists the approaches of particular countries differ – we speak about Polish, Hungarian or Czechoslovak models. An analysis of these models is beyond the framework of this particular chapter. Let us leave to history the final assessment of which one will prove itself the most efficient and concentrate here on one problem of the transition.

After the disappearance of the symbolic Iron Curtain and the destruction of the Berlin Wall, there are no barriers between the former communist countries and the rest of the world. At the same time the present Comecon system practically broke down, leaving the member countries in a very difficult situation. An illustration of the extent of this problem is that in 1988 Czechoslovak exports to Comecon countries were 73 per cent realized with a complicated system of bilateral trade (clearing) agreements based on non-convertible currency.

Given this context, there is only one reasonable solution to the problem: a dramatic extension of economic co-operation with the part of the world which we used to call Western or capitalist countries (the latest term is non-socialist countries). Having arrived at this conclusion about the solution, we then invented the magic formula for it: the joint venture. This will be discussed further, but in order to present the core of this chapter I shall first make brief reference to another topic.

PROFESSIONAL SERVICES IN EASTERN EUROPE

In the centrally planned economies the professional services either did not exist or existed on a small scale, often hidden under cryptic names. A broad network of research institutes existed controlled by the state, ministries or enterprises which provided mostly engineering, technical and management services. The marketing services were hidden under the name of market research, but in fact there was not much use for this service in the distribution economy where the problem is not so much selling but getting the goods. There was no need for auditing, legal or financial services and advertising services were at a minimum level.

Suddenly, the need for these services has appeared and the existing organizations or newly constituted firms (mostly private but also newly constituted state organizations) are trying to meet new demands.

The staffs of these firms are mostly well educated and perfectly informed about the local context but have little or no experience in the demanded services. They try to overcome this gap by intensive study in various educational courses organized by local universities and other institutions, often in co-operation with Western firms, universities or consulting companies.

A positive role in this field is being played by Czech and Slovak emigrés returning from working abroad to visit or re-emigrate, and attempting to use their experience in support. The main problem is that the difference between the free market economy and the local economic system is so deep that the experience cannot be used directly but must essentially be transformed to the local conditions. Any foreign financial expert, for instance, knowing the economic situation of a capitalist firm would fall into despair over Czechoslovak records. They would not find any land in the balance sheet, there is no cash flow account etc. The enterprises' accountancy would seem completely untransparent. The Czechoslovak legal jungle is so dense that even local lawyers often lose their way in it. The sources of information are dispersed in many, often quite unpredictable, institutions. (A small illustration from daily life exemplifies this: if you want to buy or sell a second-hand car in Prague, you will find information in the directory under the firm 'Klenoty', which means jewellery!).

These few examples demonstrate the necessity of co-operation between Western firms dealing with professional services and local partner firms in Eastern Europe. This co-operation would be mutually useful – the local firm will provide the necessary information transformed into an understandable form for the Western partner who in turn will provide the know-how. This would be the first stage. Should this co-operation be successful (and I hope it will be in most cases), the local firms would be integrated into large international companies by way of the East European magic formula – the joint venture.

JOINT VENTURES AND THEIR PROBLEMS

The 'joint venture' (or 'common enterprise' or 'mixed company' as it is called in particular countries) is one of the instruments for the opening of our economies to the world. It is, by definitions which differ slightly in different countries, a branch organization of two enterprises, one of which is local and the other foreign. The foreign enterprise brings, besides capital, the know-how (and in production units the technology). The local firm brings labour, the market and some specialized part of the know-how.

The institution of the joint venture was introduced to the states of Eastern Europe only a few years ago in reaction to the failure of the socialist development model. It is considered as a means of quiet development towards a new hopeful economic order whose feature and theory is not yet clear. It is expected that the marriage between Eastern and Western firms will bring a whole range of advantages:

1 it should support technical innovation, which has been neglected for a long time;
2 it should improve the quality of products and their parameters and design;
3 it should increase productivity by the better use of capital and labour;
4 it should modernize management methods which at present are often elementary, especially in marketing, accountancy and production control.

The founding of new firms as joint ventures is also desirable from a social welfare standpoint, although the beneficial effect of joint ventures is frequently exaggerated. Experience from Hungary, Poland and Czechoslovakia suggests that care should be exercised when infusing foreign capital into existing firms.

The main problem encountered in these countries is that existing firms are sold (often by self-interested managers) at prices that may not reflect their market value. This is a sign of incompetence or lack of control on the part of the relevant governments rather than malevolence on the part of Western investors. Nevertheless, subsequent attempts by the domestic authorities to recontract may negatively affect the working relationship and discourage further inflows of foreign capital. The present situation shows that, in spite of some exemplary success, the number of joint ventures remains rather limited. There were 580 in 1989, with the impact on the economy of these countries still being very small. In Poland they represented only 1.3 per cent of industrial production in 1988. The negotiations are complicated and the signed agreements are often realized only after some delay.

But the existing obstacles can be surmounted. Because all foreign firms will have to face up to these obstacles, the following is a list of the most important.

Ideological obstacles Despite the positive political development there remains the dual image of joint ventures. For many people fed for decades with Marxist–Leninism doctrines, any co-operation with the capitalist devil seems dangerous. Others, with strong nationalist feeling, are afraid of a cheap trade-off of the national wealth to the capitalist West.

Inertia of management structures The rigidity of a centralistic mechanism characteristic of East European economies, such as planning, state monopoly of foreign trade and the administrative character of control instruments (prices, currency exchange rates, state subsidies etc.) is deeply, if subconsciously, in the minds and behaviour of management staff. It will take a long time to be rid of this completely – it may be a question of the next generation.

Legal limitations Defining the 'rules of the game' is essential for reducing uncertainty and providing an environment that is conducive to economic decision-making. The laws on enterprise, property rights, banking, taxation, foreign investment etc. are indispensable elements of a well-designed economic structure. The legal fuzziness reigning in this field until now was substituted in all the East European countries by an excess of new laws and regulations, often not linked together and still being revised. This is a very inconvenient situation since, from an economic standpoint, simplicity and clarity are very beneficial features of a legal framework. In countries with complex economic laws and regulations, economic agents tend to waste time and other resources to achieve legal compliance. Complex legal systems also induce firms to seek legal exceptions and contribute to unproductive rent-seeking activities and corruption.

Lack of institutions and authorities   The foreign firm may be shocked by the undeveloped banking system and the inexperience of only recently constituted institutions like tax offices, commercial courts or the still non-existent institutions such as a stock exchange and land and real-estate agents. Some problems will be caused by an insufficient and/or inefficient infrastructure – telephone networks, roads etc.

Labour   Labour, and particularly human capital, is the principal asset of the East European economies. As in the rapidly growing Far-Eastern economies, labour input could serve as the engine of economic growth – if appropriately deployed. Arrangements are made to design labour laws and institutions in order to provide the labour force with appropriate protection while also introducing the much needed incentives for effort and quality work. The developing industrial relations system will be characterized by the already emerging economically oriented trade unions and some form of worker–management participation in large firms. By reducing industrial conflict, both institutions should contribute to a greater worker identification with the firm and thus increase labour productivity.

The East European labour power generally is well educated and skilled with a high degree of flexibility. The problem will be in efficient control of this labour power and in finding the right incentives to get similar production effects as in Western countries, taking into account local social law, limitations in the ways of remuneration and, last but not least, usage. A solution can be found, but the problem must be carefully studied and a large element of tact, patience and sensitivity will be necessary in order to find the overall national access which will allow the solution to be brought into perspective.

Convertibility of local currencies   The situation differs in East European countries. Full convertibility has been achieved (in a very specific way) only by the former German Democratic Republic; almost full convertibility exists in Hungary and Poland (they have paid for it with high inflation). The transition in Czechoslovakia has not been realized, but most probably a slightly limited convertibility of the Czechoslovak crown will be introduced on 1 January 1991. It is necessary to enable capital inflow and technology transfer. These inflows and transfers are desirable because they modernize the economy, help reallocate resources in the economy and reduce the adjustment cost (in terms of unemployment etc.) of the economic transition.

Closely connected with convertibility is the profit repatriation of foreign firms, but this should cause no trouble in the near future, because, as shown above, the crucial problem of convertibility must be solved by the end of this year. Incidentally, for Czechoslovakia's largest trading partner, the USSR, it is a condition that all trade in 1991 shall be conducted in hard currency only.

Small financial advantages Western partners considering settling in East Europe will compare the proposed financial advantages (credits, subsidies, land grants, tax allowances etc.) with conditions offered by Western or developing countries with low wages – e.g. Portugal, Ireland or Tunisia. They will often find our conditions insufficient (for local governments do not take this competition into account), but through negotiations these advantages can often be extended.

This brief list of problems (which is far from complete) should not create the opinion that a joint venture with an East European country is possible only in a few extraordinary cases. It is intended only to give a realistic picture of the present situation (which is still changing) and limit the sometimes exaggerated hopes of firms on both sides. Joint ventures are certainly no all-round medicine for all the disorders of the East European economies, but given realistic access they could provide good solutions for some particular problems.

The following is advice for those who will dare to enter this business.

1 Give profound study to feasibility, the legal framework, the financial conditions, the market etc. The study of existing joint ventures will provide valuable information. Study the aims and aspirations of a future partner, their needs, possible alternatives and the characteristics of the firm. During this phase, the assistance of a local consulting firm is probably vital. It not only can provide the necessary information but in addition can reveal features beneath the surface of the facts presented. What is more, it can explain why the facts are as they are.

2 Be ready to accept a compromise between conflicting ambitions. In order to recognize and understand the opinion of a partner ground work preparation is required. Both sides must achieve mutual advantage from a good association – any attempt to skim all the cream from the milk is the surest way to ruin an association.

3 Have mutual trust and confidence. Even the most scrupulously prepared agreement will not endure if it is not based on a solid agreement between partners with an anticipated openness that will

allow the inevitable problems to be overcome. After all, the joint venture is only one of the many possible forms of co-operation between East and West. The spirit of co-operation is certainly more important than the legal framework. The scale of joint ventures is usually rather small and their impact on the state economy not too great, but it can be expected that their number and impact will increase with the opening up of East European countries to the world economy.

CONCLUSION

The states and people of Eastern Europe are at a historical crossroads. After all their experience with a totalitarian system Eastern Europe certainly knows what it does not want for the future. But what it does want is not so easy to say. We are looking for a new face for society – socially fair and economically efficient.

There is much enthusiasm for capitalism in East European countries because of its economic success – but the problem is that any precise copying of successful existing patterns could appear misleading. Capitalist states are developing and we must take into account the deep and fast moving changes currently appearing in the 'western' systems of free market economies.

We have to look forward in the short term, which means surviving changed conditions with a minimum loss of living standards, but also recognize that within the next ten to twenty years we shall have to compete under new conditions of accelerated economic integration, production, business and service globalization.

Science and technology in the form of high technology and intellectual know-how will present themselves as the most efficient form of capital.

The basic trends of this new phase of economic order are as follows:

1 a transition from standard mass production to production according to the individual orders of the final user;
2 the elimination of differences between owners and employers;
3 the diminishing of differences between managers and workers;
4 the introduction of democratic market principles within enterprises etc.

The human brain will become more important than natural resources, and human aspirations and deeds will become stronger than the tyranny of political and social institutions.

God help us with a successful landing in the harbour of this new, better world.

15 Globalization of professional business services and Eastern Europe

Jan Maciejewicz

In this chapter the meaning of globalization of professional services to the East European economies is discussed. Recent changes taking place in this region are reviewed. In particular, the developments in the area of professional services in Eastern Europe during the past few years are described and a general overview is given of the most important limitations still existing in the region. The nature and scope of interactions between the globalization process and internal economic forces in Eastern Europe, in particular in the area of services are also examined. Some comments on the possible future involvement of Eastern Europe into this process of globalization are presented in the last part of the chapter.

INTRODUCTION

Recent years have witnessed a considerable increase of international trade in services which made it an attractive topic for policy-makers and analysts. Technological advances, in particular in the area of information technology, tend to increase the tradeability of many services. At the same time, however, services are heavily regulated industries in most countries which constitutes a visible barrier to the expansion of international production and trade in services.

Trade in services is now one of the major issues being discussed within the Uruguay Round of multilateral trade talks as well as within the EC 1992 programme and in numerous bilateral and plurilateral arrangements and agreements. East European economies have been somehow in the shadow of these dynamic developments in international production and trade in services, though their attitude towards this sector of the economy seems to be changing in the past few years. This last trend, in turn, is closely related to the huge and complex process of transition from closed to open societies and from a command-type economy to a market-driven economy.

Services still constitute a moderate part of the economic activities in

East European countries. The structure of service industries prevailing in those countries is rather traditional, with the majority of activities being performed by the trade, construction and transportation sectors. Contribution of services to national income is fairly differentiated in individual countries of the region, ranging from around one-quarter to slightly over one-third of the total. The most service-oriented economies are those of Hungary and Poland. Other countries clearly lag behind in this respect.

However, the recent trends towards the globalization of many types of service industries have an important impact on the development of those industries within the region. These trends, together with the vast changes in the East European economies, form both a challenge and a threat for the said countries. Major issues appearing in this broader context include the following:

1 the meaning of globalization of professional services to the economies of Eastern Europe;

2 major challenges and threats as caused by the process of globalization, and

3 possible ways of integration of East European countries into the world service economy.

These issues will be addressed below.

PROFESSIONAL SERVICES IN EASTERN EUROPE

Eastern Europe is now fully engaged in a fundamental political reorganization whose economic effects have already begun to be felt, particularly through a greater reliance on market rather than administrative or command-type disciplines. Marketization of the East European economies means also a greater openness and exposure to foreign competition.

One of the major instruments adopted by all countries in the region is the introduction of laws permitting joint ventures with the participation of foreign companies. This is supplemented by a strong move towards privatization and the break-up of monopolistic structures. These legal and institutional changes would require considerable foreign aid for their effective implementation and, which seems equally important, a demand for increased foreign investment, training and other forms of economic cooperation. This process has already started and is expected to continue in the long-term perspective.

East European economies have been rather slow in developing the infrastructure of their professional services. This relates both to the internal and external competitiveness of those countries. Past developments in many accredited types of professional services, like accounting, auditing or legal services, have isolated the countries in the region and made them different from the rest of the world. Obviously, this has led to the creation of different standards from those prevailing in the world market and consequently, has been a factor limiting external co-operation in these services. Also, the majority of professional services have not gone through the process of externalization in the past and were usually performed as in-house activities. Thus, the economies of scale have not been enjoyed by many of the service industries which, in turn, hampered their development and scope for possible impact on the rest of the economy. In particular, this related to such services as accounting and auditing, management and engineering consulting services, software and computer-related services as well as printing and publishing services. The level of externalization of these services has been exceptionally low and most industrial and service companies have had their own branches rendering these services on an in-house basis.

Weak developments in the area of professional services in Eastern Europe stem not only from the lack of externalization or the consequent lack of economic conditions and incentives for growth of local professional firms. An important factor has been the slow development and limited absorption of information technology within the region. Professional services depend markedly on information technology which enables economies of scale and increased tradeability of these services. Thus, the low level of diffusion of information technology has been a crucial factor limiting both the quantity and quality of services rendered. In particular, it has been important in such areas as telecommunication, financial or computer-related services, whose development is closely related to the use of information technology. Moreover, a lack of modern and efficient telecommunication networks and financial institutions has a serious bearing on the efficiency of other service and industrial sectors (Table 15.1).

The major way to overcome these deficiencies in the short and medium term has been the introduction of relevant foreign investment laws in all countries in the region. The number of foreign investment ventures in these countries is soaring. For instance, in September 1990 there were 2,000 in Poland. Most of these establishments are small and medium-sized companies, operating in the manufacturing sector.

The analysis of 761 joint companies established in the course of 1989 indicates that 272 of them, or 35 per cent, were operating in the services sector (Table 15.2). Data on these companies were gathered from the data bank of the Polish Agency for Foreign Investments. Many joint ventures indicated several areas of their activities and only the main one has been chosen for the present analysis. Thus, almost half of the companies analysed are operating in the business services area. Transportation,

222   *Jan Maciejewicz*

Table 15.1 Availability of telephone service in selected markets, 1988

Country	Telephone main lines per 100 inhabitants	Waiting list for main lines (thousands)
Western Europe		
Sweden	66	n.a.
Switzerland	54	8
FRG	46	26
France	45	28 (1986)
UK	39	0
Italy	35	119
Spain	28	578
Portugal	18	178
Asia–Pacific		
Japan	41	66 (1986)
Singapore	35	0.07
Eastern Europe		
Yugoslavia	14	538 (1984)
Czechoslovakia	14	n.a.
Hungary	8	n.a.
Poland	8	2,189

Source: International Telecommunication Union 1990
Note: n.a., not available.

tourism and construction were jointly representing the other half of the joint ventures in the services sector.

Engineering and consulting services represented almost 40 per cent of all joint companies established in the business services sector. German, US and Swedish partners were dominating in this respect. Joint ventures in the area of engineering and consulting services were usually engaged also in manufacturing activities. Additionally, they constituted a major source of technological and organizational skills being acquired by the Polish counterparts in the process of mutual co-operation.

Another important area of foreign capital involvement in the Polish services sector has been software and computer-related services. The major motivation for foreign companies to enter these business services has been the existence of highly skilled human resources in Poland. Most of the software services produced by the established joint ventures are being exported to Western markets. Out of twenty companies, more than half have their foreign partners in Germany and the USA.

Table 15.2 Numbers and sectoral and geographical breakdown of joint ventures in the services sector established in Poland in 1989

Service category	Total	Country						
		FRG	USA	Sweden	Austria	UK	France	Other
Transportation	71	40	2	8	3	2	–	16
Tourism	37	18	–	4	4	1	1	9
Construction	26	13	1	2	2	1	–	7
Financial	2	–	1	–	–	–	–	1
Other	7	1	–	–	1	–	2	3
Business services	129	39	22	10	10	7	6	35
Rental and leasing	10	5	2	–	1	–	–	2
Real estate	2	–	1	–	–	–	–	1
Legal	1	–	–	–	–	–	–	1
Accounting and taxation	2	–	–	–	–	–	–	2
Management	12	4	1	3	1	1	1	1
Engineering and consulting	51	15	9	5	3	2	2	15
Research and development services	3	1	–	–	–	–	–	2
Software services	20	7	4	–	2	2	1	4
Exhibition management	2	–	–	–	–	–	–	2
Printing and publishing	15	5	4	2	2	–	1	1
Total	272	111	26	24	20	11	9	71

Source: Author's calculations based on data supplied by the Agency for Foreign Investment.
Note: The total number of joint ventures analysed was 761.

An equally important role seems to be played by joint companies established in the area of printing and publishing, management, advertising and rental and leasing services. The most important partners were again West German, US and Swedish companies.

Visibly less important areas of foreign service companies' involvement have been legal, accounting and auditing, market research or real-estate services. However, during the last few months some major multinational corporations have entered the Polish services market. In the advertising services field, the leading world company, Saatchi and Saatchi, signed an agreement in April 1990 with a Polish counterpart. In the accounting, auditing and management consulting services, all the 'Big Six' have recently established their branches in Poland. These examples indicate also the possible future direction of developments of business services in Poland. The involvement of foreign capital in these developments seems to be increasing and exerting a profound impact on technological upgrading of the services and their greater integration with world standards and markets.

GLOBALIZATION OF PROFESSIONAL SERVICES – CHALLENGES AND THREATS FOR EASTERN EUROPE

Services constitute an important supportive activity to industry. Thus, the process of globalization of markets forms a driving force for increased demand for certain services. It is particularly true in the case of business services which follow their manufacturing multinational clients world-wide. An example of such a pattern includes the internationalization of leading management consulting firms, law companies and many financial institutions. But this pattern occurs most visibly in the retail and wholesale trade as well as in the hotel industry, where internationalized branching is a major factor leading to large economies of scale.

The chain of interconnections is especially complex in mutual links between merchandise trade and service transactions. The increase in world trade in goods stimulates the expansion of services, which are related to this trade. Consequently, when the initial growth of merchandise exports is strong and long enough, it may result in a growing demand for means of transportation, data processing, telecommunication equipment and services and the like.

There also exist mutual links between different types of traded services. The most obvious one is that the development in technology increases the tradeability of services. Thus, more and more services are being sold internationally as a package, as certain types of services fulfil a transport-ation function for many others. This increased tradeability stems mainly from the far-reaching changes taking place in information and communi-cation technology.

Professional business services constitute one of the most rapidly growing segments of internationally traded services. They comprise a range of licensed and non-licensed industries which require large inputs of knowledge in order to start and operate the business. The process of growth of professional firms is thus usually a long-term phenomenon. Firms operating in this area gain company-specific know-how and organizational and marketing skills through their various activities in the market, which is in most cases governed by competition rules. It is then natural for those firms to be closely linked to their corporate clients and, consequently, to change the profile of their business in parallel with the changes taking place in local and international markets.

One of the new features of the world economy in the last few years is the emergence of Eastern Europe as a location for international investments. From the point of view of professional business firms the East European market has two dimensions. The first one relates to the natural extension of activities to cover new clients in the region. The second relates to the necessity to serve old clients, usually multinational giants, who 'go east' and establish their presence in these newly opened markets. These two dimensions should be looked at closely in order to get the proper understanding of the meaning of globalization of professional services to the East European economies.

Major professional business firms have recently started their expansion to the East European market, auditing and management consulting firms at first. All 'Big Six' companies are already established in Hungary, Poland and Czechoslovakia. This process is somewhat slower in relation to the Soviet Union. Other areas of professional business services in the region are considerably less penetrated by foreign investors owing to the lack of appropriate regulations and unfavourable economic conditions prevailing in relevant industries. In particular, this relates to telecommunication and financial services. The only exceptions here are Hungary and Poland, where the regulatory situation has recently been changed in order to attract foreign investments in these areas. Moreover, some new measures are to be introduced in order to create better conditions for sustained growth of the sectors.

The extension of activities of professional business firms to include Eastern Europe has a number of barriers and limitations. In the case of auditing and management consulting firms, the major obstacle is the different accounting code in these countries. The code is much more complicated and detailed than the Western standards in this area. However, all countries in the region have undertaken efforts to introduce new standards coherent with those prevailing in the West. In Poland, the new code, based on the EC standards, will become effective from the beginning of 1991. Other countries in the region are also changing their respective regulations.

Another major problem relates to the existing gap in the level of prices between Eastern Europe and the developed market economies. The level of fees charged by the Western professional business services firms considerably exceeds existing levels in Eastern Europe. This gap makes foreign professional firms somewhat incompatible with the expectations of potential East European clients. Obviously, the transformation of the economies in the region towards market-oriented economies is rapidly narrowing the gap in income levels. During this transitional period, the strategy of multinational professional firms is clearly based on two major assumptions. The first may be characterized as a long-term approach based on considerable discounts to the fee levels normally levied. This approach takes into account the fact that there is a large amount of specificity in the transitional markets of Eastern Europe and therefore in the short and medium term professional firms should become better acquainted with the markets in order to be well established by the end of the transitional period.

The second element of the strategy relates to the strong reliance of the professional firms on foreign-aid funds. The competition to get East European projects financed from those funds is fierce as they enable compensation for the losses stemming from the discounts referred to earlier.

Another dimension of professional firms' expansion to Eastern Europe relates to the necessity to serve existing, multinational clients who establish their activities in the region. At present, the level of foreign investment in Eastern Europe is still modest, though there is a visible upward trend in this respect. One interesting indicator of future possible developments in this area is the result of a survey conducted by one of the largest professional firms, DRT International. In September 1990, the company revealed a global survey on 'Corporate investment plans for Eastern Europe'. The survey covered 128 clients of the firm with turnovers in excess of $1 billion in thirteen major market economies. All polled multinationals show strong interest in investing in Eastern Europe.

The most favoured countries for investment are former East Germany, Hungary and the Soviet Union. Poland and Czechoslovakia are still lagging behind as a location for large investments. Joint ventures are the most usual type of planned investment of big multinationals, which may be the result of both legislative incentives for this type of co-operation in Eastern Europe and existing resources in the region that enable joint business with local firms.

The majority of planned investments originate in Western European companies. North American and Far East investors are planning a long-term strategy towards Eastern Europe. It is interesting to note that for multinationals from outside Europe the most important reason for not investing in Eastern Europe is the minor role that this region plays in their current business strategy and the lack of an adequate infrastructure. West European multinationals view prohibitive regulations in Eastern Europe as a major reason for not investing.

Summing up, both dimensions of professional firms' expansion to Eastern Europe indicate that it is going to be a long-term process, though the decision to establish a presence in the region has already been taken by the majority of the 'Big Six' corporations. Their involvement in the economic restructuring of Eastern Europe may apparently speed up the process of change and may be a factor encouraging and facilitating foreign direct investments. Global corporations may have a greater confidence in well-known auditing and management consulting companies when they invest in unknown markets. Thus, foreign professional firms seem to be in a better competitive position than local consulting companies *vis-à-vis* multinational clients. However, globalization of professional business services brings about various positive results for the long-term development of local expertise in this area.

PROSPECTS AND CONCLUSIONS

Services are becoming a growing concern in the economies of Eastern Europe. This is, first of all, an inevitable outcome of the economic changes currently under way in the region. In the market-oriented economies which are emerging from those changes, services should gain a new impetus for growth. This process will obviously be supported by a visible, greater openness of these economies through more internal competition and learning-by-doing effects. In consequence, professional firms from the region may soon increase their share in the international market for business services considerably. Co-operation with big multinational professional business companies will be an important factor facilitating the achievement of the above objective.

Globalization of professional business services, and in particular the extension of professional firms' activities to Eastern Europe, will move the steady process of upgrading the economic infrastructure in the region forward. In the short and medium term, the most viable impact may take place in the telecommunication and financial services sectors. These two sectors are experiencing vast and rapid changes in all countries of the region. The monopolies that existed in these areas in the past are being replaced by a more competitive environment, mainly through deregulation policies. Foreign operators are playing a crucial role in this respect, both in the telecommunication sector and in the banking sector.

Deregulation policies in major industrial countries and in all East European economies seem to be under way. Developments in information technology and growing activities in offshore financial markets are already allowing for global operations of large multinational corporations. The governments are clearly forced by these developments to deregulate or re-regulate their national service markets. The 1990s will most probably be a time of further change in this direction. This relates both to multilateral and plurilateral efforts to liberalize the world services trade and to the initiatives undertaken by individual governments. The Uruguay Round of multilateral trade negotiations on trade in services, free trade bilateral services agreements, the single market initiative, including the area of service industries within the EC, and the numerous deregulation or liberalization steps undertaken by individual countries in selected service sectors are all examples of a new trend towards a rapidly changing international trade regime. Therefore, changes taking place in Eastern Europe are coinciding with major trends in the world economy, including the process of globalization of professional services and relevant adjustments in East European economies.

Thus, there is every indication that the mood of experiment which now pervades a large part of Eastern Europe will give plenty of scope for new ways of producing, using and trading services. This leads to the conclusion that it might result in a burst of innovations in different types of services originating in Eastern Europe, caused by the necessity to tackle emerging problems. In consequence, it may increase the motivation of Western partners to enter into various co-operation agreements with East European service firms.

In parallel with the existing interest of some East European countries in establishing economic co-operation with OECD, it might be necessary for them to regulate certain economic activities according to the rules coherent with the OECD practice. The same is true of co-operation based on agreements signed between East European countries and the EC. All these new undertakings are important factors in strengthening the process of the coming together of East European economies to the world economy. The strong emphasis on the service sector will be marked during the last stages of this process.

Lastly, it should be noted that the greater involvement of East European economies contains not only challenges, but also threats. Weakly developed local markets for professional business services may not be solid ground for learning-by-doing or technology transfer processes, usually associated with the presence of large multinational professional firms. Thus, the governments of the countries in the region have a crucial role to play in these important processes.

16 The global expansion of Japanese financial service firms: role of domestic economic and regulatory policies

Raj Aggarwal

INTRODUCTION

The cold war between the USA and the Soviet Union finally appears to be over but Japan seems to have emerged as the victorious party. While the now exhausted protagonists invested a large proportion of their savings and other resources on maintaining a high level of military preparedness, the Japanese continued to save at phenomenally high rates and invest in new machines, education and commercial research. Consequently, Japanese commerce and finance are now healthy, strong and positioned for further growth while the Soviet economy faces major problems and the future prosperity of the US economy is threatened by the large amounts of foreign and domestic debt capital that have been used to maintain its recent prosperity.

Such changes in the commercial and financial standings of nations do not seem to be a new phenomenon. While Italian banks dominated global commerce four hundred years ago and Dutch banks had their heyday about two hundred years ago, the British dominated global finance and commerce for the hundred or so years until the first World War. US companies and banks then took over the task of providing leadership and financing for global trade. This US hegemony of global finance was first challenged (briefly) by petroleum-exporting Arab nations in the 1970s and is now under increasing assault by Japan.

These changes in national prominence in global finance are reflected in the activities of their financial institutions. For example, the largest banks in the world in the fifteenth and sixteenth centuries were Italian. More recently, in 1908, six of the top ten banks globally were British. By 1970, six of the top ten were US banks. By 1990, of the largest ten banks in the world, seven were Japanese, two were French and only one was American. According to data released by the Bank for International Settlements (BIS) in its 1990 annual report, Japanese banks accounted for 38 per cent of international bank assets while US banks accounted for only 14 per cent. Do these changes in the global rankings of US and Japanese banks reflect the historical trend of continuing westward shift in the global economic centre of gravity?[1] Does the evolving orientation of the global economy mean that the US dominance of global commerce and finance is going to be replaced for the foreseeable future by the ascent of the Japanese?

In this chapter the recent international expansion of Japanese financial institutions is described and the consequences of this Japanese expansion for the international financial system and for financial institutions based in other countries are considered. These issues have become particularly relevant as international trade in financial services has become increasingly important.

THE JAPANESE FINANCIAL SYSTEM AND ITS ECONOMIC ROLE

Japan has now overtaken the USA as the major international creditor while the USA has slipped to being the largest debtor nation in the world. Inward foreign portfolio investments into the USA have exceeded outward portfolio investments since 1983 and the net foreign direct position of the USA has also been negative since 1988. These trends are widely expected to continue at least in the short term with a further improvement of the Japanese position and a deterioration of the US position. Unsurprisingly, Japanese financial firms are emerging as particularly strong competitors in global financial markets. It seems that Japanese financial firms are taking advantage of their access to inexpensive and plentiful capital in their domestic market to expand successfully in global markets.

The global expansion of Japanese financial firms has been closely related to the increased importance of Japan in the global economy and to the high per capita level of financial resources available domestically to Japanese institutions. A large proportion of Japanese economic growth and of the international expansion of Japanese firms can be traced to the advantages derived from the high rate of domestic savings in Japan. The rise of Japan in the global economy may be based primarily on the willingness of the Japanese people to work incredibly hard, save phenomenal amounts of their incomes, sacrifice and focus on the success of their economic group and maintain a relatively low standard of living. Thus, as discussed further below, it seems that the high level of work ethic among its population, supplemented by a high savings rate and low expenditures on defence and social services have been the cornerstones of the rapid growth of the Japanese economy and of its increasing influence in the world economy.

Finance in Japanese economic growth

In sharp contrast to the situation in the Western industrialized economies, Japanese government regulation of the financial sector and other government economic policies seem to have been designed to work closely with the private sector to ensure high savings rates and to support significantly the positive feedback loops that further enhance the positive economic effects of these policies. As explained below, the economic effects of such government policies in Japan are leveraged because of the non-equilibrating and expansionary effects of the positive feedback loops.

According to Nagourney (1988), for the 1983–6 period the ratio of gross savings to GNP was 31.5 per cent for Japan while comparable figures for West Germany, the UK and the USA were 23.6 per cent, 17.7 per cent and 14.5 per cent respectively. On the other hand, Japanese defence spending is kept at about 1 per cent of GNP while comparable figures for other countries are much higher (6 per cent of GNP for the USA). Similarly, as indicated in Table 16.1, Japanese expenditure on transfer payments, such as for welfare and for other government consumption, are a far smaller proportion of GNP than are similar figures in other industrial countries.

The Japanese government traditionally has actively encouraged a high savings rate by allowing significant amounts of interest income to be tax-free and by providing other tax advantages to savers. The savings rate is also enhanced by the Japanese practice of paying a significant proportion of compensation in two semi-annual lump-sum bonuses. In addition, with the relative lack of mortgage financing or other consumer credit or of well-funded retirement schemes or other social safety nets, the Japanese savings rates indeed have to be relatively high.

The beneficial effects of the high savings rate in Japan are further enhanced by other policies and practices designed to make the high savings rate easier to achieve. The Japanese ability to create high levels of savings with low overhead spending on defence and social services also makes possible a high rate of investment in capital goods and consequent high rates of growth in worker productivity and in the economy. These increases in worker productivity and, thus, wage rates help make the high savings rate easier to maintain. The high savings rate also means lower interest rates which help justify the Japanese company focus on long-investment-horizon activities and on market share gains. If higher rates of return are associated with these longer-term strategies they will also enhance the Japanese ability to maintain high savings rates. Thus, government policies that encourage high savings rates, low interest rates and high rates of investment in capital goods are supported by a number of positive feedback loops that make these processes self-reinforcing. Given the learning curve and

Table 16.1 Economic characteristics of selected major countries

Country	GNP		Expenditures as percentage of GNP			Density per square kilometre habitable			Land as percentage of national wealth
	$ billion	Per capita	Government consumption	Defence	Capital formation	Exports	Population	GNP ($ million)	
USA	4,881	19,813	20.6	6.4	15.0	7.4	54	1.1	24.2
Japan	2,867	23,382	9.6	1.0	28.9	12.8	1,523	35.5	66.2
UK	837	14,658	20.8	4.7	16.9	26.3	365	5.2	2.3
West Germany	1,208	19,741	19.7	3.0	19.4	31.6	384	7.6	
France	948	16,962	19.3	4.0	19.3	20.9	165	2.8	10.4

Source: Keizai-Koho Center 1990

entry-barrier-based strategic advantages of being an early mover in most industries, these Japanese government policies also provide Japanese firms with critical advantages in global markets.[2]

In addition to the easy availability of funds resulting from the high savings rate and appropriate government policies in Japan, the rapid managed rise of the Japanese yen also has had major strategic implications. Because of the managed nature of a great deal of Japanese external trade, the rise of the yen has not reduced US imports from Japan or increased US exports to Japan as may have been expected in a free market economy. However, as Kester and Luehrman (1989) note, the lower dollar reduces the relative ability of US firms in the newer or 'sunrise' industries to develop, acquire and maintain strategic foreign investments that may provide a head start in developing technologies, market shares and other options for future growth. Therefore, while a lower dollar may make firms in mature US industries more price competitive, it reduces the competitive ability of US firms in other more profitable industries where there is extensive non-price competition. In contrast, the rise of the yen makes US companies, technology, real estate and other productive assets, including options for future growth in the US and global markets, relatively inexpensive for Japanese acquirers. Thus, the global rise of Japanese financial prowess has also been supported by the recent rise in the value of the yen (see Kester and Leuhrman 1989).

Similarly, the international expansion of Japanese firms has also been assisted by the relatively high stock and land prices in Japan (for details see Cutts 1990; Fingleton 1990). The total capitalization of the Tokyo Stock Exchange has grown at about 25 per cent per year in the 1980s in terms of the yen and at even higher rates when measured in terms of US dollars. While the total capitalization figures are not strictly comparable because of extensive cross-holdings and thus double counting in Tokyo, it was being widely contended at the end of the 1980s that the Tokyo Stock Exchange had become the largest stock exchange, having overtaken the New York Stock Exchange.[3] While Japanese stock prices are often depicted in some parts of the press as fragile and prone to a crash, other parts of the press contend that the market is stronger than it may seem based on US or Western standards. The unusually high price to earnings (P/E) ratios in Tokyo in the latter half of the 1980s were noted to be well above comparable US ratios. However, it has also been widely contended that these differences can be accounted for by differences in expected growth rates, differences in accounting standards, such as the use of accelerated depreciation and reserve accounts, exclusion of the incomes of subsidiaries and the low valuation of hidden assets such as land and shares of other companies that lead to low estimates of reported income and reported book values.

However, the rapid rise in Japanese P/E ratios in the second half of the 1980s seems to be related to the rise of Japanese land prices during the same period.[4]

As an example of the high land prices in Japan, in late 1988, an 80 per cent mortgage on Tokyo real estate alone would have been enough (at $7.7 trillion) to purchase *all* the land in the USA (at $3.7 trillion) and *all* the publicly listed companies in the USA (at $2.6 trillion). While land prices in Japan can be expected to be somewhat higher than in the USA and other countries because of the high intensity of its usage as indicated by the GNP per unit of land in Japan (see Table 16.1), it seems that recent increases leading to the unusually high land prices in Japan may have resulted from the deregulation of financial markets in the mid-1980s and by unusually restrictive tax and zoning laws in Japan.[5] High land prices in Japan also seem to have a wider economic impact. For example, as indicated above, because many Japanese companies carry significant amounts of land that is undervalued in their balance sheets, high land prices is one reason given to justify the high P/E multiples and the high stock prices in Japan. In addition, high Japanese land prices have also been advanced as a reason for the rapid increase in Japanese investment in US real estate ($16.54 billion in 1988), especially in Hawaii and the West Coast.[6]

The role of Japanese financial structure

The global expansion of Japanese financial institutions and other companies may also benefit from the unique aspects of Japanese finance. There is considerable literature that emphasizes the cultural and social embeddedness of business relations and the differences between Western and Japanese mores and norms. This literature contends that Japanese culture and economic structure drives Japanese business strategy and makes it very different from that in the USA.[7] Japanese patterns of financing, production, distribution, investment and trade are different from those in Western industrialized countries. For example, a large number of Japanese companies are organized into large but loosely co-ordinated business groups known as the Keiretsu. Japanese corporate debt is mostly in the form of bank borrowings while a significant proportion of US corporate debt is in the form of public debt securities.[8] As discussed below, these and other differences in financial market structure and institutional arrangements lead to differences in corporate behaviour such as reduced reliance by Japanese firms on external capital markets for funding capital expenditures and the use of higher levels of debt by Japanese firms compared with their Western counterparts.

Compared with their US or British counterparts, Japanese financial institutions are characterized by fairly high degrees of concentration and by close business ties with industrial groups, including cross-ownership and membership on each others' boards of directors. While the pre-Second World War Ziabatsu, with hierarchical and vertical control structures, were broken up, they have been replaced by Keiretsu groups of companies with co-operative and horizontal, but nevertheless effective, group structures.[9] For example, presidents of companies and financial institutions in each Keiretsu business group typically meet monthly to discuss business strategies.

Compared with their counterparts in other Western industrial nations, Japanese corporations have closer relationships with their lead banks and longer term relationships with their suppliers and customers which are usually anchored by extensive cross-holdings of equity. A group-owned city bank usually acts as the lead or 'main bank' for the industrial companies that belong to a Keiretsu, ensuring that funds continue to be available to such companies regardless of temporary, seasonal or cyclical variations in the flow of funds. This stability in bank financing means that Japanese companies can safely manage much larger proportions of debt in their capital structure than their Western counterparts can (Aggarwal 1990). Hoshi *et al.* (1990) show that the role of Japanese banks in providing stable financing to group companies reduces the cost of financial distress for such companies and is associated with higher levels of performance among them.

The 'main banks' in Japan also act as board representatives of the large proportion of ownership typically held by the members of the Keiretsu and seem to provide opportunities for economies in monitoring activities related to overcoming information and incentive problems typically associated with arm's length market transactions.[10] As indicated by Ballon and Tomita (1988: 109), financial institutions and other business corporations held 66.3 per cent of the outstanding equity of an average Japanese company listed on the Tokyo Stock Exchange in 1985. An implication of this group structure of Japanese business may be the relative ease with which groups of Japanese financial firms can formalize their existing co-operative ties to form universal banks as the Japanese financial structure is formally deregulated.

Hodder (1990) contends that the close monitoring provided by the main bank reduces the need to issue costly new equity and may thus give such Japanese companies a cost of capital advantage. Further, as indicated earlier, most of this debt is in the form of bank loans and Japanese companies do not seem to rely on public capital markets to fund much of their capital expenditures. It has been shown (Myers and Majluf 1984; Jensen 1986) that because of agency, information and other transactions costs, firms are likely to invest more, especially if they do not have to raise funds from external financial markets. In recent years, Japanese firms have raised only 6–8 per cent of the required funds from public capital markets while banks provided about 40 per cent of such funds, with the rest coming from internal sources (Tamura 1988).

There are many other differences in the Tokyo and New York financial markets. These differences include institutional and seasonal differences, such as the annual rise of the yen in March and the preponderance of a 31 March fiscal year-end, differences in the attitudes towards insider trading and differences in the float of stock available for public trading because of long-term corporate cross-ownership.[11] Many of these differences further discourage the use of the external financial markets by Japanese corporations.

Thus, Japanese managers can and do pursue corporate goals that are different from and take a longer term view than those pursued by American managers. For example, in evaluating new investments the most important goal for US managers is return on investment while Japanese managers take a longer view and consider their most important goal as increased market share.[12] As this discussion indicates, Japanese financial institutions play a very important role in ensuring that Japan's high savings rate is deployed appropriately to support corporate policies consistent with a high rate of economic growth. Government regulation can therefore be expected to be an important influence on the operation of Japanese financial institutions.

The regulatory environment of Japanese financial firms

The Japanese financial system consists of three layers, the regulatory authorities, public financial institutions and private financial institutions. The Ministry of Finance and the Bank of Japan are the two major regulatory agencies. In spite of recent deregulation of the financial sector, the Japanese economy still retains an active and large institutional structure for public finance that includes the Japan Development Bank, the Post Office Savings Bank and a number of other public financial institutions as shown in Figure 16.1. Private financial institutions are still characterized by strict demarcations between banking, securities activities and other financial firms. As Figure 16.1 shows, there are three types of commercial banks: city banks, regional banks, and foreign banks. Among the specialized institutions are the long-term credit and trust banks and financial institutions to serve small businesses and particular industries. The last category of private financial institutions consists of insurance companies, securities houses and housing finance companies.

The Japanese financial system is undergoing rapid changes as deregulation is extended to additional sectors. The government controlled interest

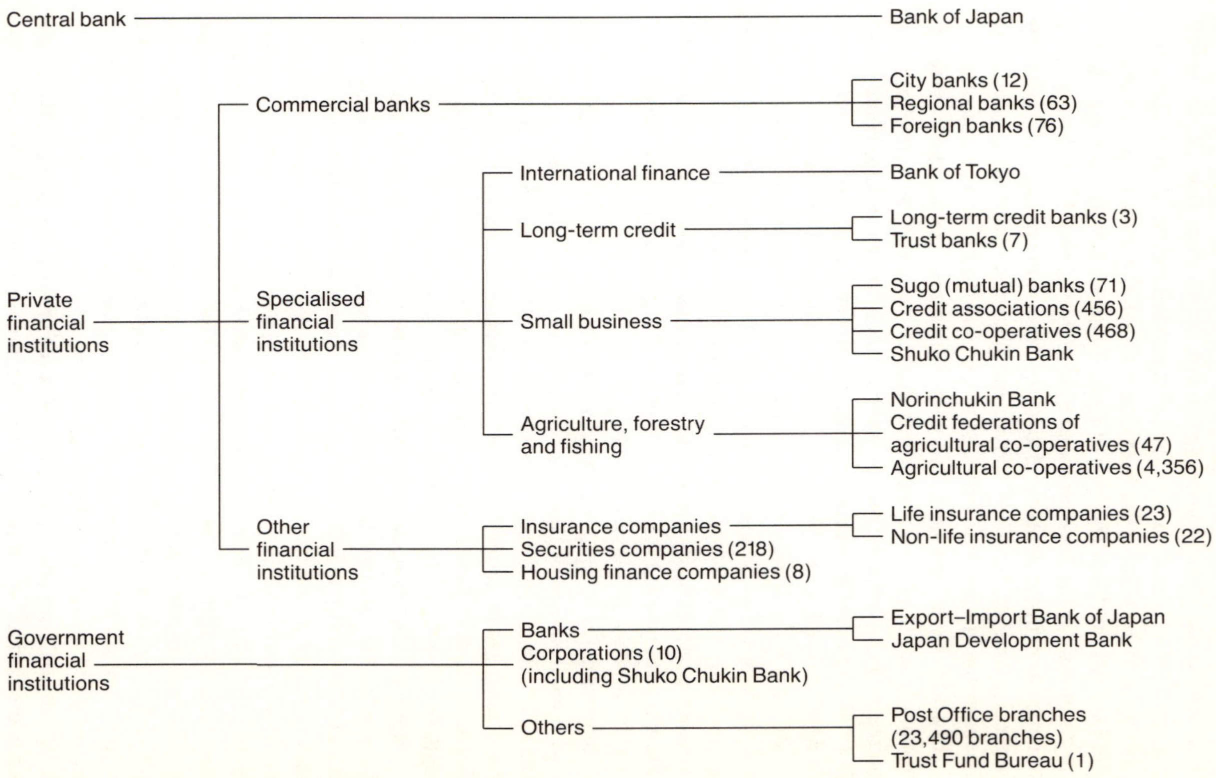

Central bank —— Bank of Japan

Private financial institutions

Commercial banks
- International finance —— Bank of Tokyo
- City banks (12)
- Regional banks (63)
- Foreign banks (76)

Specialised financial institutions
- Long-term credit
  - Long-term credit banks (3)
  - Trust banks (7)
- Small business
  - Sugo (mutual) banks (71)
  - Credit associations (456)
  - Credit co-operatives (468)
  - Shuko Chukin Bank
- Agriculture, forestry and fishing
  - Norinchukin Bank
  - Credit federations of agricultural co-operatives (47)
  - Agricultural co-operatives (4,356)

Other financial institutions
- Insurance companies
  - Life insurance companies (23)
  - Non-life insurance companies (22)
- Securities companies (218)
- Housing finance companies (8)

Government financial institutions
- Banks
  - Export–Import Bank of Japan
  - Japan Development Bank
- Corporations (10) (including Shuko Chukin Bank)
- Others
  - Post Office branches (23,490 branches)
  - Trust Fund Bureau (1)

Figure 16.1 Structure of the financial sector in Japan

Source: Wathen 1986

rates and therefore the allocation of capital during most of the first thirty years of the post-Second World War era. Since foreign operations were severely limited, Japanese financial institutions were segmented according to the domestic markets served. The system began to change in 1975 with the need to finance large government deficits following the 1973 oil price increase. An active secondary market in government bonds was allowed to develop as was a parallel market in short-term bond repurchase instruments (the Gensaki market). The availability of free market interest rates led to large outflows from the banks which were then allowed to sell short-term money market instruments to raise funds.[13] In a study of twenty-seven large banks, Pettway *et al.* (1988) document that these domestic deregulatory moves in Japan raised the riskiness of the stocks of these Japanese banks.

In addition, as Japanese financial institutions are forced to rely increasingly for funding on securities markets owing to the deregulation of interest rates, restrictions on international transactions are also being lifted. In 1980, Japan made a major change in its foreign exchange control law, changing it from 'restriction in principle, freedom only as an exception' to 'freedom in principle, restrictions only in exceptions'. With these deregulatory moves, Japan not only allowed foreign financial firms to enter the Japanese market but, in addition, the government has allowed Tokyo to become an increasingly important international financial centre with the external yen bond and syndicated loan markets growing to rival the external markets in other currencies including the US dollar.

Interestingly, in spite of these major changes in the regulatory and market environment of Japanese financial institutions, the market shares of Japanese savings held until recently by the different types of institutions has remained remarkably steady. As indicated in Table 16.2, only the shares accounted for by life insurance and investment companies have changed to increase slightly over the last decade.

However, this stable situation may soon be changing with the increasing deregulation of financial markets. For example, not only are domestic interest rates rising to international levels, Japanese banks now have to pay market rates for over 70 per cent of their deposits (in 1990) while this proportion was only 37 per cent in 1988. Since the BIS allowed Japanese banks to count 45 per cent of their unrealized gains on holdings of corporate stock as part of their capital, any declines in Japanese stock prices puts pressure on Japanese banks to increase their profitability to meet the BIS minimum capital ratio targets.[14] At the beginning of the 1990s most banks in Japan are considering possible mergers in order to survive in an era of deregulated interest rates. For example, the 452 'Shinkin banks' or credit co-operatives, as well as the 3,600 'Nokyo' or farmer's co-operatives, are considered prime candidates for consolidation over the next few years. For

Table 16.2 Distribution of Japanese savings

	March 1978		March 1983		June 1988	
	Savings (trillion yen)	Percentage share	Savings (trillion yen)	Percentage share	Savings (trillion yen)	Percentage share
Deposits	119.8	49.5	174.4	45.8	250.1	42.4
of which banks	55.2	22.8	80.0	21.0	121.4	20.5
Post Offices	45.0	18.6	78.1	20.5	119.0	20.1
Trusts	14.0	5.8	21.2	5.5	29.1	4.9
Bonds	23.1	9.5	34.6	9.1	48.7	8.2
Investment policies	4.6	1.9	7.8	2.0	38.5	6.5
Insurance policies	35.6	14.7	64.8	17.0	107.7	18.2
Total	242.0	100.0	380.9	100.0	593.1	100.0

Note: Stocks are based on the market value of listed stocks.
Source: *The Banker* January 1989

similar reasons, but at the other end of the scale, the recent merger between the Kyowa and the Saitama banks was preceded by the merger of the Mitsui and the Taiyo Kobe banks that created one of the largest banks in Japan.

In addition, as Japan's population ages, much growth can be expected in the area of pension fund management and there are likely to be significant challenges to the dominant position in this area currently held by life insurance companies and trust banks. Japan's social expenditures are expected to grow as a proportion of its GDP from 15.4 per cent in 1980, to 21.9 per cent in 2000 and 27.1 per cent in 2010, with pensions accounting for 4.2 per cent, 10.4 per cent, and 14.3 per cent of the GDP respectively.[15] While there are a number of securities trading houses in Japan, the big four – Nomura, Nikko, Diawa and Yamaichi – dominate with upwards of 60 per cent of the trading volume and total assets among Japanese firms in that industry. However, Japan's insurance companies also see themselves as major forces in institutional money management. The twenty-four life insurance firms in Japan have been growing rapidly, having tripled their 1980 total assets to over 80 trillion yen in 1988. The thirteen listed non-life insurance companies have also grown similarly.

As this discussion indicates, Japanese financial institutions face a number of domestic strategic challenges as a result of the recent deregulation of Japanese financial markets. While the global expansion of Japanese financial institutions is influenced by these domestic developments, such expansion is also influenced by global economic forces.

GLOBAL EXPANSION OF JAPANESE FINANCIAL FIRMS

According to the sixtieth annual report of the BIS issued in June 1990, Japanese firms acted as lead managers for 39 per cent of all Euro-bond issues in 1989. The same report indicates that the Japanese share of international bank assets had risen by December 1989 to 38.3 per cent, with the next largest country, the USA, accounting for only 14.2 per cent. These figures were only 26.1 per cent for Japan and 21.9 per cent for the USA as of December 1985. In recent years, about 30 per cent of Japanese bank assets have been located outside Japan (Terrell *et al.* 1989). Table 16.3 provides another illustration of the global expansion of Japanese banks. As this table indicates, Japanese banks have a significant presence in all the major financial centres with major operations in the USA, the UK, Hong Kong, Singapore, Switzerland and Australia. It is estimated that the share

Table 16.3 Japanese banks abroad

Country	Subsidiary	Branch	Agency	Total
Australia	21	0	0	21
Bahrain	1	0	0	1
Belgium	6	7	0	13
Brazil	3	1	0	4
Canada	11	0	0	11
Cayman Islands	1	10	0	11
China	1	3	0	4
France	0	7	0	7
Germany (West)	0	11	0	11
Hong Kong	3	24	0	27
India	0	1	0	1
Italy	0	3	0	3
Korea (South)	0	11	0	11
Luxembourg	7	0	0	7
Netherlands	4	0	0	4
Panama	2	5	0	7
Singapore	0	22	0	22
Spain	0	4	0	4
Switzerland	22	0	0	22
Taiwan	0	1	0	1
UK	6	23	0	29
USA	1	30	2	33
Total	89	163	2	254

Source: *The Banker* April 1989

of domestic banking assets accounted for by Japanese financial institutions now amounts to 8 per cent for the USA, 25 per cent for California and 23 per cent for Britain.[16]

Domestic and international merger and acquisition activity by Japanese firms is increasing. In 1984, Japanese companies concluded 140 mergers and acquisitions transactions with an average size of 5.4 billion yen and with foreign acquisitions accounting for 23.2 per cent of the total. These figures have grown to 555 transactions, 10.5 billion yen and 56.8 per cent respectively. Japanese banks and other financial institutions share this rising Japanese tendency to engage in domestic and international mergers and acquisitions.[17] Table 16.4 summarizes Japanese acquisitions of US financial institutions in the 1980s.

Table 16.4 Selected Japanese investments in US financial firms in the 1980s

Date	Investor	Investment	Amount [a]
February 1981	Sanwa Bank	First City Bank of Rosemead	28
July 1981	Mitsui Bank	Manufacturer's Bank	173
September 1981	Bank of Tokyo	California Bank	30
April 1983	Fuji Bank	Walter E. Heller Group	425
September 1984	Mitsubishi Bank	Bank of California	282
November 1984	Sanwa Bank	Continental Leasing (IL)	56
June 1985	IBJ	J.H. Schroeder B&T	n.a.
February 1986	Sanwa Bank	Lloyds Bank of California	263
August 1986	Sumitomo Bank	12.5% of Goldman Sachs	500
October 1986	IBJ	Aubrey Lanston Bond Dealer	234
March 1987	Nippon Life	13% of Shearson Lehman	538
October 1987	A Consortium	Securities of Bank America	350
November 1987	Yasuda Life	25% of Paine Webber	300
February 1988	Bank of Tokyo	Union Bank of Los Angeles	759
May 1988	Fuji Bank	24.9% of Kleinwort Securities	40
June 1988	Sanwa Bank	80% of Brophy Knight Secs.	75
June 1988	LT Credit Bank	Greenwich Capital Markets	144
July 1988	Nomura Securites	20% of Wasserstein Parella	100
July 1988	Yamaichi	25% of Lodestar	n.a.
July 1988	Yamaichi	Interlink Fund	100
September 1988	Dai Ichik	20% of LaSalle Group	n.a.
December 1988	Nikko	20% of the Blackstone Group	100
February 1989	Tokoi Insurance	40% of First Insurance	29
March 1989	Yamaichi	20% of Lodestar Corp	25
August 1989	DKB	60% of CIT Leasing	1500
September 1989	Diawa Bank	Lloyds of US Retail Bank	1600
October 1989	Tokoi Corp	10% of Delaware Corp.	42

Source: Various news accounts, compiled by the author
Note: [a] All amounts are in millions of US dollars; n.a., not available.

Table 16.5 Japanese investment in foreign securities by type of investor (billions of US dollars)

	1983	1984	1985	1986	1987 [a]
Commercial banks	1.8	4.5	12.6	23.1	24.8
	(13.7%)	(16.5%)	(22.6%)	(22.7%)	(29.8%)
Trust banks	1.5	4.1	12.8	28.9	17.3
	(11.4%)	(15.2%)	(23.0%)	(28.3%)	(20.9%)
Insurance companies	4.8	6.4	8.0	20.7	16.8
	(36.9%)	(23.6%)	(14.4%)	(20.3%)	(20.3%)
Investment trusts	0.3	2.5	3.3	19.1	10.0
	(2.1%)	(9.1%)	(6.0%)	(18.7%)	(12.1%)
Others	4.2	8.9	16.8	16.5	15.0
	(31.7%)	(32.8%)	(30.3%)	(16.2%)	(18.1%)
Securities companies	0.5	0.7	2.0	−6.4	−0.9
(own account)	(4.2%)	(2.8%)	(3.7%)	(−6.2%)	(−1.1%)
Total	13.1	27.0	55.6	102.0	83.0
	(100.0%)	(100.0%)	(100.0%)	(100.0%)	(100.0%)

Source: *JEI Report 35A* 16 September 1988
Note: [a] January–September. Some short-term securities transactions are included, making data not comparable with the relevant balance of payments statistics.

As Table 16.5 indicates, international portfolio investments by Japanese financial institutions have grown very rapidly in recent years. Japanese commercial banks, trust banks, and investment trusts have been particularly aggressive in this regard. In addition to Japanese banks, a number of other Japanese investment management firms also expect to participate in this growing global market. The larger Japanese insurance companies are already experienced in international money management, averaging over 10 per cent of their assets in foreign securities. A number of these insurance companies have also begun to make overseas acquisitions to position themselves better for institutional money management in Japan. For example, Nippon Life acquired a 13 per cent stake in Shearson Lehman, Yasuda Mutual Life an 18 per cent stake in Paine Webber and Sumitomo Life a 15 per cent stake in Ivory and Sime of Scotland.[18]

Financial markets value Japanese financial firms highly and expect them to continue to grow in importance and global market share. As shown in Table 16.6, by the end of the 1980s Japanese financial firms were larger in market value than US financial firms and their value rivaled industrial companies globally. According to this table, twenty-five Japanese financial firms are valued higher than any US financial firm. One consequence of these higher valuations of Japanese financial firms is that they enjoy high credit ratings and can raise capital in the USA and international markets at lower rates than US financial firms can. This high valuation and easy access to US and other capital markets gives Japanese banks an important advantage in their quest for global markets. Poulsen (1986) documents that 'Japanese banks use the United States as an alternative source of funds during periods of tight credit in Japan'.

As this brief discussion indicates, just as British and US banks did before them, Japanese banks are now also becoming multinational. They are doing so because they need new growth markets as domestic growth is limited. They also go overseas to continue to serve their clients as Japanese industrial corporations become increasingly multinational. Goldberg and Saunders (1981) and Hultman and McGee (1989) indicate that Japanese banking presence in the USA is positively related to the level of Japanese foreign direct investment (FDI) in the USA and to the dollar value of the yen. As with banks from Western nations in earlier times, Japanese banks can exploit their superior knowledge of and contacts with their home-based multinational corporations. As Tschoegl (1983) contends, Japanese banks can also take advantage of economies of scale as they continue to grow through multinational expansion. Finally, Japanese banks are also engaging in international expansion for other traditional reasons such as risk diversification (Aggarwal and Durnford 1989) and the ability to exploit internationally high domestic market to book ratios (Aliber 1984). Marr *et al.* (1989) indeed show that the easy availability of capital seems to give Japanese bankers a significant competitive edge in global markets. Thus, in addition to the need to deploy surpluses of domestic funds, Japanese banks seem to have many of the same reasons for multinational expansion as did British and American banks for their multinational expansion in earlier times. Because of the fundamental nature of these reasons for the multinational expansion of Japanese banking, the phenomenon is unlikely to be short lived.

A STRATEGIC ANALYSIS OF JAPANESE FINANCIAL INSTITUTIONS

The development of strategic responses to the global expansion of Japanese financial firms depends on an analysis of the nature of the markets for financial services and on an analysis of the relative strengths and weaknesses of the Japanese competitors especially as they adjust to changes in the global economy. This section presents a brief review of these issues to develop and suggest a useful paradigm for assessing competitive strategies.

Table 16.6 Financial firms among the *Business Week* Top 1,000

Name	USA								Japan								Name
	Rank	MV	P/B	P/E	INC	Assets	ROE	IND	Rank	MV	P/B	P/E	INC	Assets	ROE	IND	
American Express	101	11,382	2.0	23	530	99,470	8.8	62	2	68,787	11.1	160	425	292,147	6.9	61	Sumitomo Bank
American Intl Group	124	9,269	1.9	8	1042	27,910	19.1	63	4	63,252	10.7	80	757	315,714	13.4	61	Dai-ichi Kengyo Bank
Citicorp	161	7,550	1.0	LOSS	-1140	203,600	NEG	61	5	62,810	10.2	93	661	284,550	11.0	61	Fuji Bank
J.P. Morgan	188	6,502	1.4	52	83	74,010	2.6	61	8	56,116	6.3	26	2,167	27,869	24.5	62	Nomura Securities
General Re	236	5,281	2.1	10	499	9,438	19.8	63	9	55,890	12.5	122	448	237,361c	10.3a	61	Industrial Bank of Japan
Aetna Life & Casualty	262	4,999	0.8	6	871	72,750	13.1	61	10	55,806	9.6	71	767	256,857a	13.5	61	Mitsubishi Bank
Farmers Group	337	4,119	2.7	16	247	3,462	16.7	63	11	51,422	9.8	75	670	254,402a	13.1	61	Sanwa Bank
March & McLeman	353	3,970	5.0	13	302	1,634	38.2	63	16	32,775	8.5	80	336	151,531	10.6	61	Long-Term Credit Bank Jpn[a]
Security Pacific	371	3,861	1.3	LOSS	-11	72,840	NEG	61	18	31,282	8.5	84	361	188,605	10.1	61	Tokai Bank
American General	372	3,855	0.9	8	563	28,010	11.1	63	19	30,246	8.3	62	405	185,430	11.3	61	Hitsui Bank[a]
Cigna	396	3,640	0.7	6	719	53,490	11.8	63	22	28,346	9.4	54	481	96,841	17.4	62	Mitsubishi Trust/Bnkng[a]
PNC Finanacial	402	3,613	1.7	14	256	36,500	12.2	61	23	26,366	9.2	52	465	91,827	17.5	62	Sumitomo Trust/Bnkng[a]
Travelers	407	3,602	0.8	11	374	50,160	7.2	63	26	25,299	9.7	115	211	7,139	8.4	64	Mitsubishi Estate
CNA Finicial	423	3,501	1.1	8	393	19,560	15.1	63	30	23,594	4.7	20	1,192	35,106	23.9	62	Daiwa Securities
Banco One	493	3,028	1.8	12	209	17,370	16.8	61	32	22,456	7.7	88	250	20,632	8.7	63	Tokio Marine & Fire
Student Laon Mktg Asso.	505	2,973	6.3	18	181	22,860	35.9	62	34	21,484	6.1	57	441	148,884	10.7	61	Bank of Tokyo
Wells Fargo	512	2,954	1.6	43	51	44,180	3.8	61	36	20,847	5.7	20	1,056	20,096	29.1	62	Nikko Securities
Fed. Natl Mortgage	513	2,951	1.9	8	376	100,400	24.0	62	45	18,748	6.9	57	249	155,282	12.2	61	Taiyo Kobe Bank[a]
Bankers Trust NY	564	2,679	0.9	LOSS	1	56,520	NEG	61	47	18,101	8.6	50	349	76,265	17.4	62	Mitsui Trust & Banking
Merrill Lynch	570	2,663	0.9	27	68	53,010	3.4	62	49	17,610	4.2	18	1,000	16,801	23.9	62	Yamaichi Securities
USF & G	590	2,536	1.7	9	265	10,140	19.5	63	56	16,425	6.6	64	217	90,612b	10.3b	61	Daiwa Bank
Chubb	644	2,321	1.2	7	330	8,609	17.1	63	59	16,068	7.9	75	177	103,247	10.5	61	Nippon Credit Bank[a]
Chase Manhattan	656	2,296	0.7	LOSS	-895	99,130	NEG	62	69	14,226	7.8	46	259	68,605	17.0	62	Yasuda Trust & Banking[a]

Company								
Continental Corp.	668	2,267	0.9	13	221	12,150	7.1	63
Geico	725	2,072	3.1	11	178	2,846	28.6	63
1st Insterstate Bankcorp.	732	2,039	1.0	LOSS	-556	50,920	NEG	61
First Wachovia	743	2,004	1.5	11	177	19,340	14.2	61
St Paul	751	1,968	1.2	6	324	8,399	18.5	63
Barnett Banks	753	1,955	1.5	10	196	23,450	15.3	61
Household intl	759	1,944	1.3	9	222	16,980	20.4	62
Lincoln National	768	1,926	0.8	9	237	18,000	8.9	63
NCNB	786	1,849	1.2	9	167	28,910	12.9	61
Great Western Finan.	792	1,837	1.0	10	210	28,630	9.5	61
Bank of Boston	823	1,745	1.1	99	20	34,120	1.1	61
Bank America	832	1,717	0.7	LOSS	-955	92,830	NEG	61
Safeco	855	1,644	1.1	7	253	6,615	16.4	63
Aon	867	1,608	1.4	10	156	7,084	13.9	63
NBD Bancorp.	868	1,608	1.3	10	162	23,350	12.6	61
First Chigcago	883	1,567	1.1	LOSS	-571	44,210	NEG	61
Chemical New York	892	1,539	0.5	LOSS	-854	60,560	NEG	61
CoreStates Financial	905	1,502	1.5	9	162	14,590	17.6	61
H.F. Ahmanson	907	1,502	0.8	11	200	30,510	7.8	61
Citizens & Southern	923	1,468	1.4	9	158	20,440	14.6	61
Manufacturers Hanover	937	1,435	0.7	LOSS	-1140	73,350	NEG	61
Capital Holding	971	1,361	1.2	11	171	10,380	11.5	63
Fireman's Fund	974	1,355	1.1	6	301	9,602	17.8	63

Company								
Kyowa Bank[a]	97	11,649	5.4	43	216	97,161	12.4	61
Mitsui Real Estate Dev.	99	11,558	5.4	66	170	13,314	8.3	64
Bank of Yokohama[a]	113	10,434	5.6	74	130	75,274[c]	7.6	61
Yasuda Fire & Marine[a]	175	6,971	6.0	61	100	14,882	9.9	63
Hokkaido Takushoku Bank[a]	195	6,391	4.4	52	110	68,165	8.5	61
Taisho Marine & Fire[a]	220	5,679	5.3	51	96	10,300	10.5	63
Shizuoka Bank[a]	223	5,585	3.5	47	106	36,521	7.4	61
Sumitomo Marine & Fire[a]	227	5,516	6.0	56	87	9,156	10.6	63
Sumitomo Realty & Dev.	357	3,952	3.0	48	76	5,096	6.1	64
Orient Finance[a]	394	3,661	2.6	36	97	3,4394	7.2	62
Nippon Fire & Marine[a]	439	3,389	5.0	45	67	7,538	11.0	63
Nippon Shinpan	492	3,030	2.4	32	92	34,074	7.6	62
Tokyu Land	539	2,798	4.4	204	13	3,956	2.2	64
Daikyo Kanko[a]	611	2,454	3.5	38	63	7,046	9.3	64
Orient Leasing	876	1,580	1.7	17	91	21,112[a]	10.1[b]	62
Hitachi Credit	904	1,511	2.0	48	31	4,430	4.2	62

Notes:

a   Based on non-consolidated results.
b   Based on consolidated earnings per share and non-consolidated book value per share.
c   Total assets based on interim rather than year-end balance sheet.

Source: Business Week 1988

Macroeconomic challenges for Japanese financial institutions

Like other Japanese firms, Japanese financial institutions face a number of challenges in adjusting to the major changes forthcoming in the domestic Japanese economy. Japan must not only contend with significant changes in the global economy and its role in it, but must also simultaneously cope with internal demographic, social and economic changes. It is not clear how long the Japanese consumer will continue to make the sacrifices required to maintain high growth rates, especially as succeeding generations move away from traditional values to adopt values that are more Western or American. Further, the proportion of the aged in Japan is rising rapidly with negative implications for Japan's overall savings rate and for the proportion of its GNP that must be devoted to social programmes. Because of its already relatively advanced technological level, the Japanese economy may no longer just be able to borrow or copy foreign technology and may have to spend more on research and development. Further, Japan's new generation is developing work habits and loyalties different from its parents. Gains from economic development are now becoming more difficult to distribute evenly and currently seem to be going disproportionally to those that own land or stocks. Combined with an inadequate, and in some cases corrupt, political system, social and political harmony may be difficult to maintain.[19]

Japan's export surplus has been making its future increasingly dependent on the economic performance of the rest of the world. While Japan has been exporting goods and services it has been accumulating financial assets in return. These Japanese goods and services are being consumed by global consumers while domestically the Japanese have maintained high prices and a relatively low level of consumption. However, Japan's accumulated financial assets are denominated in US dollars and other Western currencies and are vulnerable to losses in value because of inflation and currency devaluation in the USA and other Western economies. Further, the Japanese economy is becoming more open to international influences and Japanese businesses must learn to operate efficiently outside Japan. Japanese firms and managers must make the transition from an export-based economy to one based on FDI where they have to learn to work with and as a part of the non-Japanese world. However, because of the global importance of Japanese finance and business, how the Japanese handle these domestic and international challenges is of great interest to the rest of the world.

Strengths and weaknesses of Japanese financial firms

As discussed earlier, Japanese financial firms have many strengths in the global market place. First, they are fairly well capitalized with good continuing access to inexpensive new capital. Second, they are well supported by members of their industrial group, the other companies in their Keiretsu. In developing their international business, Japanese banks can exploit their close ties with their traditional customers as these large Japanese companies themselves become global corporations. Third, perhaps because of their low cost of capital and thus their low discount rates, they can and often do take the long view in developing and implementing their growth strategies.

However, Japanese banks may also have significant weaknesses. First, Japan may not be able to continue to generate surplus savings for its financial institutions for too much longer as the demographic changes already under way result in an increasingly larger proportion of aged in the population. As discussed earlier, habits of hard work and thrift may be weakening especially among the new generation in Japan. This shortcoming may be compounded as Japanese banks do not seem to react quickly to changes in the economic environment. For example, in spite of the availability of large pools of funds domestically until recently, as documented in Aggarwal and Baker (1984), Japanese banks shared in the widespread mid-1980s decline in capital ratios among large banks internationally. In order to raise capital, Japanese banks have recently sought further deregulation in the form of permission to sell securitized assets. In spite of their relatively high credit ratings, Japanese banks often pay more for inter-bank funds in the USA than do comparable domestic banks (Holand 1990: 1, 32). Further, as Table 16.7 indicates, Japanese banks have not been able to avoid the Third World debt problem as such lending constitutes a significant proportion of their equity for a number of Japanese banks.

Second, Japanese financial institutions are unused to providing value to retail customers. Traditionally, their operating procedures and pricing structures have often subsidized their large customers at the expense of their small and retail customers. For example, during the 1980s bull market, individual Japanese investors were net sellers of securities each year, while in 1990 with the 40 per cent drop in the Nikkei average they emerged as net buyers. As individuals continue to decline as traders of securities (22.4 per cent of trades in 1988 versus 69.1 per cent in 1949) in Japan, the securities industry is considering the steps it should take to lure them back.[20]

Third, the high degree of homogeneity in Japanese society may limit the ability of Japanese firms to manage their foreign operations. It seems that Japanese banks overseas have not been able to overcome cultural barriers as they continue to serve primarily other Japanese customers. For example, of the $307 billion in US assets of Japanese bank branches, about a third are owed to entities in Japan and another third to Japanese companies in the

Table 16.7 Third World loan exposure of Japan's commercial banks (billiions of yen at 30 September)

Bank	1987	1988	1989	March 1988 Assets (%)	Equity (%)
Bank of Tokyo	639.6	679.1	663.1	3.21	146.5
Dai-Ichi Kangyo	406.4	346.6	361.3	0.75	36.6
Sumitomo Bank	411.5	391.2	379.5	0.85	39.6
Fuji Bank	326.1	335.3	329.3	0.72	29.4
Mitsubishi	346.5	376.1	349.7	0.80	35.0
Sanwa Bank	330.5	322.5	320.8	0.76	34.6
Tokai Bank	296.5	304.6	278.6	1.00	48.8
Mitsui Bank	215.2	197.7	198.4	0.77	37.5
Taiyo Kobe	173.1	169.9	162.2	0.74	40.2
Daiwa Bank	96.9	98.1	88.8	0.68	27.1
Kyowa Bank	90.5	91.5	91.6	0.67	29.5
Saitama Bank	99.8	102.2	89.9	0.78	34.4
Hokkaido Taku	106.6	105.8	100.0	1.06	52.4
Average				0.93	42.7

Sources: *Economist* 14 March 1987; *JEI Report 35A 16 September 1988; Euromoney* February 1990; *New York Times* 29 April 1990

USA. The operations of Japanese banks and securities firms in the USA have suffered numerous setbacks. The problems faced by Fuji Bank in returning its Walter E. Heller affiliate have been widely discussed in the press and recent reports indicate that the Wall Street operations of the big four Japanese securities firms have had to release employees and have been suffering significant losses.[21]

Fourth, because of the globalization of many product and financial markets and the size and global influence of the Japanese economy, Japanese policies now have global consequences and often provoke opposing responses. Therefore, the recent emergence of Japan as a major global economic power poses many challenges not only for the rest of the world but also for Japanese managers and policy-makers. Japan must adjust to its new position in the global economy while preparing to meet its many domestic challenges. Thus, Japanese managers and policy-makers must cope simultaneously with changes in the global economy and with demographic, social and economic changes within Japan.

Strategic markets for multinational financial firms

In view of the importance of the economics of information and of business diversification, possible activities of multinational financial firms can be classified along two dimensions that measure the diversity of customers and the geographic diversity of operations. Along each of these two dimensions a firm's activities can be depicted as having three major levels. In terms of product diversity, such firms can provide retail or wholesale services or they can specialize in particular product niches. In terms of geographic diversity, a firm can be a multinational firm with operations in most major and many minor national markets, an international firm with operations only in a few selected foreign markets or a firm with operations only in the domestic market. Thus, the strategies followed by a financial services firm can be categorized into one or more of the nine cells of such a three by three matrix. Figure 16.2 summarizes this matrix of nine possible market strategies.

These nine strategic market categories can apply to each type of financial firm regardless of its industry classification, i.e. whether it is engaged in depository activities, securities management and trading or in the provision of insurance services. The appropriate strategic response of a particular financial services firm will depend on its industry classification, industry structure and the nature of the competitive response evoked, as well as on the gap between its existing and desired location(s) in the nine cell market matrix. In order to understand and develop an optimum strategic response for a given multinational financial firm, these strategic

Figure 16.2 Strategic matrix of markets: MN, multinational niche; IN, internatioinal niche; DN, domestic niche; MW, multinational wholesale; IW, international wholesale; DW, domestic wholesale; MR, multinational retail; IR, international retail; DR, domestic retail

issues must be addressed specifically for each firm in the light of the economics of international expansion in the financial intermediation industry discussed earlier in this chapter, and on the strengths and weaknesses of the competition.

As prior discussion has indicated, Japanese financial institutions have many strengths in global markets that seem to originate in their domestic environment of benign government policies, high savings rates, the Keiretsu group structure and high rates of international expansion by their Japanese client corporations. However, Japanese financial institutions also face significant challenges in global markets. They lack significant experience with retail markets for consumers and businesses, especially (but not just) outside Japan. They also lack significant experience in implementing strategies based on non-price competition for servicing non-Japanese firms.

Thus, it seems that the Japanese multinational financial firms are likely to be stronger as competitors in the top left-hand corner of the market classification matrix in Figure 16.2, i.e. in the markets for financial services that have low customer diversity but have high geographic diversity. Japanese financial institutions are likely to have the lowest level of competitive advantages in domestic retail banking. As a matter of fact, so far there do not seem to be any instances of success by the Japanese in such retail markets while they have been strong competitors in the various aspects of wholesale and niche banking. Nevertheless, with more experience Japanese financial institutions should be able to overcome many of these disadvantages. If the experience of Japanese companies in automobiles and consumer electronics is any guide, Japanese financial institutions should continue to be very significant competitors in global financial markets.

CONCLUSIONS

The causes and consequences of the recent international growth of Japanese financial institutions and the challenges this growth poses for US and other Western multinational financial firms have been described and analysed in this chapter. The analysis suggests that while Japanese financial institutions have some significant advantages in their access to relatively easy and inexpensive financing and close relationships with Keiretsu firms, they also suffer from some disadvantages as they prepare to compete in global financial markets. These disadvantages stem primarily from their limited experience with highly competitive retail banking and from demographic, social and deregulatory changes within Japan. Therefore, it seems clear that while US financial institutions and businesses face a serious challenge from well-financed and patient Japanese counterparts, Japanese financial institutions are by no means omnipotent as they face a number of challenges both at home and abroad. Multinational financial institutions from other countries should be able to take advantage of these factors to develop appropriate strategies to compete successfully with Japanese financial institutions for global markets.

ACKNOWLEDGEMENTS

The author would like to thank the Edward J. and Louise E. Mellen Foundation for research support, Tamir Agmon, Doug Foster, Art Noetzel, David Schirm and participants in the Duke conference for useful comments and Alex Deluna, Tom Rechin and John Stenger for research assistance.

NOTES

1 See Aggarwal (1986) for details of the continuing westward shift in the global economic centre.
2 Another possible implication of these high-savings-rate-based Japanese policies for economic growth is that the particular set of management policies followed by Japanese companies may have few, if any, lessons for managers in other countries. It is possible that the current Japanese success may be based primarily on nothing more than the Calvinistic values of thrift and hard work that seem to have consistently produced the same results in the past. It should be noted that American management techniques enjoyed global fame as being the best approach to management in the post-Second World War period when the USA enjoyed global economic hegemony (the causes for which were also, in hindsight, mostly unrelated to management techniques). Thus, Japanese management techniques may be less important in explaining the success of Japanese firms than the process of generating and deploying the high level of savings in Japan. It should be noted that in this process, Japanese financial institutions serve the very important economic role of managing and directing Japanese savings to their corporate users.
3 According to McDonald (1989), corporate cross-holdings of equity in Japan account for about one-quarter of Japan's reported market capitalization.
4 For discussions of the unusually high P/E ratios in Japan see, for example, Ballon and Tomita (1988) and Wakasugi (1988). For the strong relationship between Japanese P/E ratios and land prices see, for example, page 81 of the 1989 annual report of the Basel, Switzerland, based BIS.
5 For an excellent discussion of this viewpoint, see Fingleton (1990) and Cutts (1990).
6 See Ohmae (1988) for the figures relating to the value of Tokyo real estate and its ability to purchase US companies. The $16.54 billion figure for the Japanese investment in US real estate is from a study by Kenneth Leventhol and Company, accountants in Los Angeles, as cited in Rundle (1989). Additional details of the Japanese investment in US real estate are provided in Dervan (1987) and Tsui (1987).
7 For a review of these issues see, for example, Granovetter (1985), Wolferen

(1989) and others. These differences often lead to misunderstandings and problems between Japan and its trading partners. As an example, while the USA notes that Japanese exports to the USA persistently exceed Japanese imports from the USA, the Japanese note that the Japanese buy the same volume of goods produced by US companies and their Japanese affiliates as does the USA of goods made by Japanese companies and their US affiliates. For details see Weekly and Aggarwal (1987: 151–5).

8 These differences are not well explored in the published literature and differences in Japanese and Western finance are not widely understood in spite of a growing list of popular (e.g. Wright and Pauli 1987; Powell 1988; Viner 1988) and academic (e.g. Feldman 1986; Thorn 1987; Ballon and Tomita 1988) books on various aspects of Japanese financial markets.

9 It should be noted that these Japanese business group arrangements, or Keiretsu, are not much different from power sharing business groups of otherwise independent businesses in many other countries such as West Germany, France, South Korea or India. Nevertheless, the prevalence of large business groups in these countries also may mean that the business sector is able to influence public policy significantly with even further reductions in the environmental risk faced by these large firms. For further details on the co-ordination role of the industrial groups see, for example, Ballon and Tomita (1988), Gerlach (1987), and Gato (1982).

10 See, for example, Hoshi, *et al.* (1989), Gerlach (1987) and Sheard (1989).

11 For details see, for example, Aggarwal *et al.* (1989), Ballon and Tomita (1988), Feldman (1986), Thorn (1987), Wakasugi (1988) and Wright and Pauli (1987).

12 For details of these differences in Japanese and US corporate goals, behaviour and debt ratios see, for example, Ballon and Tomita (1988) and Wakasugi (1988).

13 According to Ropoport (1990): 'Early this year Japanese banks were paying competitive market rates for 55 per cent of their funds compared to 10 per cent five years ago.'

14 Because of the late 1990 decline of the stock market, credit ratings of Japanese banks began to suffer. See *The Economist* (1990j) and Evans (1990).

15 Based on a study by the International Monetary Fund as cited in *The Economist* (1988b).

16 The figure for California is from Zimmerman (1989) while the other figures are as reported in Kotkin (1988).

17 The mergers and acquisition figures are from Lee (1989). The increasing focus of Japanese banks on overseas growth is discussed in Hashimoto (1986) and in Chowdhury (1989).

18 *The Economist* (1988a). Also see Holloway (1987).

19 For details of the high costs of products and services in Japan see, for example, *The Economist* (1989) and for the nature of the Japanese political system see, for example, Wolferen (1989).

20 See *The Economist* (1990k) and Chandler (1990).

21 For details see, for example, Choy (1989).

17 Globalization of banking services: Canada's strategies in the Triad

Alan M. Rugman and Andrew Anderson

INTRODUCTION

In this chapter we develop a framework to examine the operations and strategies of the Canadian banks when entering or expanding in a foreign market. We draw on Casson's definitional framework (1989) of a multinational bank. This definitional framework permits a distinction between those banks which engage in international banking activities but have none or only marginal physical assets abroad and those banks which engage in some international banking functions as a subset of their overall activity but which also own and operate at least one banking operation in a foreign country. The latter set of banks we refer to as MNBs. For example, a Japanese bank buying foreign securities in the USA or lending to a Third World government may be engaged in international banking but is not necessarily an MNB unless it owns operations in the foreign country. In this chapter we explore current banking activities in Canada and set banking strategies against competitors based in the USA, Japan and the European Community (EC). This leads to possible strategic directions that Canadian MNBs may take in the near future in these triad areas.

PLANNING BANK STRATEGIES

To analyse the positions of the Canadian MNBs and their foreign subsidiaries we shall use the framework of Figure 17.1. This figure separates the structure and strategy of a bank in its various international markets. We shall examine each of the four areas of 'strategy' outlined in the figure. These include the competitive advantages/disadvantages, the positioning of the bank in the foreign market, the types of delivery systems and the types of products. Each of these strategic decision areas is dependent on structure and vice versa. In many cases the structure will be determined by the strategy initially adopted by the Canadian MNB. While Figure 17.1 uses a hierarchical approach, the framework of analysis should actually be viewed as a continuous flow of information up and down the decision system. This will become clearer as we proceed with our analysis.

In a very large and legally fragmented institutional environment, like the USA and perhaps to a much lesser extent Canada, 'regional operations' might be substituted for 'foreign operations'. In the case of the EC, as the EC's banking laws become increasingly homogenized a bank strategist there will eventually be examining 'regional operations' when considering other EC operations. The various laws which operated to maintain the separation of the national markets in the twelve member countries of the EC will eventually disappear. Cultural barriers in the EC may not, however, disappear as quickly. This will result in the necessity for some type of continued regional strategic analysis for banks operating in the EC.

For the present analysis, however, we shall start by assuming that homogeneity exists in general in the 'domestic operations' of the countries

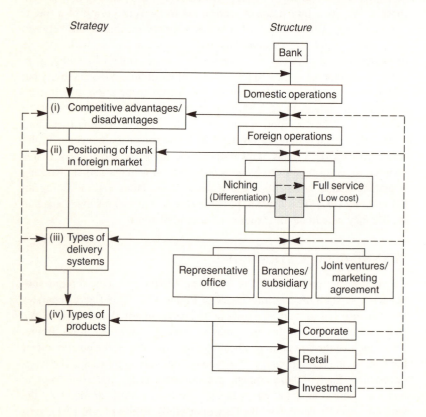

Figure 17.1 Planning international bank strategies

or areas that are examined. These include Canada, the EC and Japan. In the case of the USA we need to take account of the stratified nature of its banking system.

Competitive advantages and disadvantages

The first step in assessing the potential of a Canadian bank to enter or expand into a foreign market is to examine the competitive framework of its domestic operations in Canada. It is necessary to take into account both the foreign-specific advantages (FSAs) and the country-specific advantages (CSAs) that the bank can utilize in building its competitive advantage. It is also necessary to take into account any perceived disadvantages that the bank may be facing in its home market *vis-à-vis* both external markets and the domestic market. Regardless of whether the Canadian bank is already situated in some manner in the foreign market, it will still have to analyse its competitors in that market. This will involve an analysis of two types of competitors; first, domestic or home country competitor banks or other financial intermediaries and, second, foreign target market competitor banks or financial intermediaries. These are illustrated in Figure 17.2.

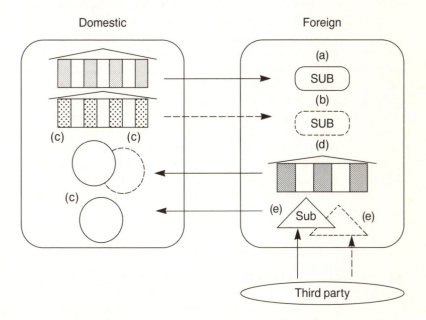

Figure 17.2 Competitors to examine in the domestic and foreign markets: . . . , potential competitor; —-, competitor

Domestic competitors consist of (a) home country domestic market incumbents, i.e. those domestic banks of the home country that entered the foreign market first; (b) planned home country domestic market entrants, i.e. domestic competitors that are considered to be potential entrants in the near future to the foreign target market; and (c) third-party banks in the home market operated from the target foreign market. These include competitors that have moved into the home country's domestic market, i.e. either subsidiaries of the domestic banks in the planned foreign target market or third-country banking operations that are run out of the planned foreign target market.

Foreign target market competitors consist of (a) domestic incumbents, i.e. the foreign country's own domestic banks; and (b) third-party domestic market incumbents, i.e. any third-country competitors located in or perceived to be considering entry in the short run to the planned foreign target market.

The two types of competitors cannot be ignored, since the strategic decision to impinge on a competitor(s) market is likely to result in one (or more) of three types of responses that could have an impact in the foreign target market or spill over from the foreign target market into the home country's domestic market. These include primarily a pro-active or reactive strategy. A pro-active strategy could result in a price war on competitors' similar or even diverse product offerings in either the foreign or domestic markets. A reactive strategy could also occur whereby the competitor, facing a possible perceived out-gunned situation from the new entrant, withdraws from the market or consolidates its position by producing fewer product offerings, i.e. becoming even more specialized as a niche player. It is also necessary to be aware of government reaction which could result in a zero-action strategy by the bank's potential competitors. An example of a zero-action strategy is where the foreign bank competitor gives deference to anti- competition laws. In this situation any activity which could be seen as an attempt to limit entry to a non-competitive market might result in some type of an anti-competition response from the foreign or even domestic govern- ment; therefore the foreign competitor(s) deliberately decide to ignore the new entrant to their market.

Positioning the bank in the foreign market

Once the domestic strengths of the bank and its competitors have been assessed, the bank has to make the decision as to where to position itself in the market as either a niche player or a full-service operator. This will differ according to which national market the bank is entering or even which part of a national market a bank is entering. It will also require an evaluation of the sovereignty issues outlined previously, since the bank's ability to be licensed in certain activities is dependent on the particular 'national' laws in existence in the foreign market. A niche player would be offering one or more very specialized services to a limited client group, thereby, it is hoped, making it difficult for competitors to enter the market or even forcing competitors to exit the market. A full service bank would be one which offers a large range of services to a broad range of clients, where most of those services would face some degree of competition. Normally a full service bank would be servicing the corporate, retail and investment markets. While it would not necessarily be engaging in international trans- actions, it probably will be, owing to the nature of the products it would have to offer its international corporate clients and private investment clients. This will depend on whether it decides that it will service more than only its new foreign target market domestic clients.

The niching versus full service decision is more one of deciding which clients it would be better at servicing than one of which products to service those clients with. However, the two areas of decision are entwined and a product decision further down the decision hierarchy may negate or require changes in the 'clients to be serviced with' decision.

Types of delivery systems

Based on the decision as to which clientele group(s) the bank will service, it will then have to decide on the type of delivery system that will serve that group or those groups best. There are three possible delivery systems available to the bank: (a) a representative office or offices; (b) branches in some type of a subsidiary arrangement; and (c) a joint venture or marketing agreement with a bank or another intermediary that can sell the bank's service(s).

A representative office is normally the cheapest and easiest way to service a foreign market. It is the most constraining, however, with regard to which clients and ultimately what products may be offered in the domestic foreign target market. A representative office is normally associ- ated with a strict niching policy of servicing a limited clientele base. In most cases this will consist of the home-country based firms, i.e. not necessarily multinational enterprises (MNEs) but those firms which require limited foreign market presence for some types of services. It may also consist of some limited service to individuals but in general any such activity is secondary to the decision to operate a representative office in the foreign market.

The decision to establish a branch network through a subsidiary relation- ship is primarily dependent on the decision to become a full-service bank.

This would normally mean the acceptance of retail deposits. Without having access to a fairly large source of capital the bank would face pricing pressures on the loans that it would be able to make and would therefore be out-competed by banks and other types of deposit-taking institutions that are already established in the foreign target domestic market with a large customer savings base to draw on.

A subsidiary type delivery system has the disadvantage of being expensive to establish. Starting a branch network from scratch involves high transaction costs on information about the foreign market (location and competitors), supply networks and overhead capital. It may also take a long time to establish customer loyalty which would affect the bank's ability to make loans or gather savings. Another key consideration is cultural adaptation to the accepted way of doing business in the home country's bank versus the foreign operations. This would be of concern in the purchase of a ready-made domestic foreign target market financial operator.

The purchase of a ready-made retail network would require careful consideration as to why the financial institution is for sale. The bank may be buying a foreign operation that is already culturally un-adaptive and may face wider problems in the quality of its managers and lending staff as well as a poor asset base to liabilities. The benefits gained from an initially cheaper purchase price versus the higher cost of establishing a retail network from scratch may be lost if considerable resources have to be spent on rebuilding the foreign operation both in capital and customer-trust terms. Banking is a service industry which involves high trust between individuals. That trust relationship may be more expensive to buy back under a bad corporate name than developing a bank and its image from scratch. For an earlier, though still relevant, discussion of the benefits of trying to achieve market growth through *de novo* (internal) expansion versus expansion by (external) merger, with regard to banking in the USA, see Cohen and Reid (1966). These ideas may be even more apt for banks planning cross-border acquisitions.

The option for a bank which wants to engage in a broader customer base but does not have the resources (expertise) or capital resources to expend on a full-service facility is to form a joint venture or have a marketing agreement with a financial intermediary. This intermediary does not have to be a bank but could be a firm with the necessary market delivery system. For example, it could be an oil company which has a credit-card network or a department-store chain. In all cases the bank is prepared to sacrifice some of its profits and independence in order to gain the (brand name) delivery system. A marketing agreement or joint venture may result in the problem of knowledge (expertise) dissipation. In this case the partner may eventually develop enough knowledge that it could eventually become a competitor.

A classic example of a bank attempting to enter a restrictive market is the strategy adopted by Citibank in order to enter and gain market share in the Japanese market. An entrant to this market faces the dual restrictions on market access of culture and of restrictive Japanese financial regulations on foreign banks' entry. The latter aspect is facing increasing pressures for reductions by American trade negotiators seeking broader market access to financial services in Japan. Citibank was initially denied approval in 1986 to purchase the financially troubled 100 branch Heiwa Sogo mutual bank in Tokyo. However, while rebuffed, Citibank was not finished. In order to gain wider distribution for its products it reached a joint venture marketing arrangement to provide foreign-remittance services through some 2,000 branches of the Japanese postal-savings system. Further, Citibank is trying to gain access to the BANCS ATM network with its 20,000 machines that are operated by the large Japanese commercial banks. It is also seeking to obtain an agreement to assist Mitsubushi Bank with new product and strategy developments in order for Mitsubushi to take better advantage of Japan's increasingly deregulated financial markets (*The Economist* 1990f).

Types of products

The decisions made as to the types of products a bank can offer are continuous over the lifetime of the bank's foreign operations. Various products will be required in order to service the three major client markets or groups: (a) corporate customers; (b) retail customers; and (c) investment customers. In many cases the distinctions between these groups are now becoming blurred.

The bank is constrained by its initial decision on whether to be a niching or full-service bank and by the type of delivery system it has chosen. If at this stage in the decision process the types of products that are available are considered, upon examination, to be non-competitive, it may require a re-evaluation of the type of delivery system or initial positioning decision, i.e. perhaps the decision to forgo a full-service capability and become a niche player needs to be reconsidered. Similarly, if dissipation of a customer base is occurring through the lack of a product which requires another financial intermediary to handle it, the bank, in order to develop and market that product, may have to make the decision to become a full-service (wider-service) player.

As can be seen, the linkages between product, physical structure and operating strategy are very closely linked in a bank's decision process. The product is the final arbiter of that process, since it is what the bank will earn its profits and pay its shareholders from. Outmoded or non-competitively priced or delivered products or services will eventually combine (or succeed individually) to undermine the competitiveness of even the largest bank if permitted to continue unchecked. The strategy formulation process is designed not only to develop new products or services but also to maintain a continual check and verification system (monitoring process) on how well products and services already offered by the bank are doing. This function is often overlooked in the desire to be the first on the block with a new product. New products, however, will not necessarily overcome losses and problems that have developed owing to the poor sales or mismanagement of older products. The bank has to evaluate why each product or service fails if the strategy formulation process is truly to work.

OPERATIONS AND POSSIBLE STRATEGIC CHANGES IN CANADIAN BANKS IN THE TRIAD AREAS

We are now prepared to examine the operations and strategies Canadian MNBs will face at the macro-level when expanding or moving into the triad markets of the USA, Japan and the EC. While this section generalizes a country's banks and their foreign operations by lumping them together and thereby eliminating micro-variables, it still captures the CSAs or disadvantages of the domestic or home country. For simplification we assume that all banks which originate from one country will face generally similar CSAs or disadvantages. As a cautionary note, however, the CSAs or disadvantages within a country will have different degrees of impact on various banks in the home country.

Figure 17.3 permits us to capture the areas of operation of a country's group or groups of banks and their client servicing strategy of niching or full service. The horizontal axis indicates whether the banks are multi-national or domestic in their level of operations. Those banks operating in the left-hand side of a main quadrant in the matrix are domestic in operating level, while those on the right-hand side are multinational in scope. At the same time the horizontal axis also permits us to show whether the domestic operations are servicing only domestic clients, only international clients or a combination of the two. If the banks were located in the far left-hand side of the left half of the matrix it would indicate that they are servicing primarily domestic customers (A). Similarly, if they were located on the far right-hand side (the centre line) of the left half of the matrix they would be primarily servicing international clients (B). This idea also applies to the servicing of domestic and international clients in the right half quadrant of the matrix.

The vertical axis of the matrix indicates whether the banks have adopted a niching or full-service strategy in the type of client service strategy adopted by the bank for its Domestic and/or international area of

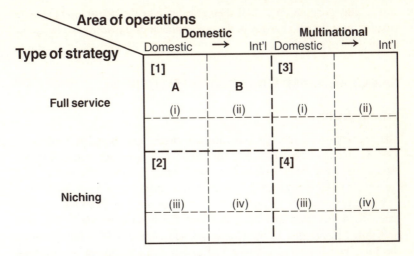

Figure 17.3 Operations and strategy of the world's banks

operations. Those banks in the top half of the matrix have adopted a full-service strategy, i.e. one of servicing corporate, retail, and investment clients. Those banks located in the bottom half of the matrix have adopted a niching strategy, whereby they are principally concentrating on servicing clients in only one or a few of the major client functional areas. This group could extend to non-banks that offer financial services.

The matrix therefore shows us the position of four types of banks: (a) domestic, full service; (b) domestic, niching; (c) multinational-full service, and; (d) multinational-niching. It also permits us to examine eight sub-categories of service by type of clientele, i.e. domestic versus international, or two in each quadrant of (a) domestic, full service; (b) international, full service; (c) domestic, niching; and (d) international, niching.

It is important to realize that none of the four main quadrants or the eight sub-quadrants of the matrix in Figure 17.3 is superior to another. A group of banks located in different quadrants may all be successful banks. Similarly, a bank or group of banks located anywhere in the matrix may be completely unsuccessful. The success or failure of a bank or banks located in one of the four quadrants is dependent, as already indicated, on the products offered and their competitive nature in the market that they are sold in. This will be dependent on the level of resources and autonomy allocated by the bank to permit its representative office, branch or subsidiary to compete in that sector. For the present time we shall assume that the bank has made a calculated decision to be in a particular quadrant (market) and therefore has allocated sufficient resources and autonomy to sustain this position. We shall therefore analyse the possible changes in position given other changes in the environment or the desire to change its initial level of commitment.

CANADIAN-BASED FINANCIAL INSTITUTIONS

Present position

The breakdown of the top 200 financial institutions based in Canada in 1989 is given in Table 17.1. For convenience in assessing their role in our model they have been divided into three areas: 'banks', 'like banks', and 'other'. In 1989 there were fifty-one 'banks' made up of eight Schedule 1 or Canadian controlled banks; forty-two Schedule 2 or foreign-controlled banks; and one merchant bank that was Canadian controlled. The eight Schedule 1 banks plus the merchant bank had assets of C$483 billion, while the forty-two Schedule 2 banks had assets of C$52 billion, giving total assets of C$535 billion. Approximately 9.8 per cent of the total 'bank' groups assets were foreign owned in 1989.

There were also sixty-three 'like banks', or 'near banks', operating in Canada in 1989. These included twenty trust companies all domestically owned and twenty credit unions also domestically owned. Most of the trust companies operate branch networks in various parts of Canada, while some of the larger trust companies have also acquired foreign holdings. The trust companies in Canada clear their demand instruments (cheques) through one of the eight large banks. The trust companies make up over half the assets in the 'like bank' category: C$135 billion of a total of C$203 billion in assets, or 62 per cent. There were also twenty-two companies that engaged in other types of lending, including twelve lending institutions, eight leasing finance companies and two acceptance companies. There was also one venture capital company. Approximately 7.5 per cent of the 'like banks' were foreign controlled in 1989.

In the third category, of 'other', there were eighty-six institutions that are now permitted to engage in some of the activities that were traditionally the reserve of the Schedule 1 and 2 'banks'. These include thirty-four life-insurance firms, fourteen management companies, ten investment dealers, twenty-six property and casualty insurance companies and two mutual fund companies. The life insurance companies have approximately 42 per cent of the assets of the Schedule 1 banks – C$200 billion. However, it can be assumed that a large proportion of these assets are not used in direct competition with the 'banks', but are used instead to provide the types of services traditionally provided by these companies. This would apply similarly to the property and casualty companies and the mutual fund

Table 17.1 The top 200 financial institutions in Canada in 1989[a]

Class	No.	Canadian assets	No.	Foreign assets	No.	Total assets	Percentage foreign controlled	No. over C$1 billion in assets	Largest firm's assets	Smallest firm's assets
Banks										
Schedule 1 banks	8	477,391	0	0	8	477,391	0.00	7	114,660	341
Schedule 2 banks	0	0	42	52,242	42	52,242	100.00	16	6,138	299
Merchant banks	1	5,333	0	0	1	5,333	0.00	1	5,333	5,333
Sub-total	9	482,724	42	52,242	51	534,966	9.77	24	–	–
Like Banks										
Trust companies	20	134,540	0	0	20	134,540	0.00	12	39,826	368
Lending institutions[b]	10	43,177	2	3,364	12	46,541	7.23	11	9,212	379
Credit unions	20	17,649	0	0	20	17,649	0.00	4	3,894	316
Leasing finance	7	6,626	1	4,608	8	11,234	41.02	3	4,608	293
Acceptance corporations	1	338	1	8,360	2	8,698	96.11	1	8,360	338
Venture companies	1	295	0	0	1	295	0.00	0	295	295
Sub-total	59	202,625	4	16,332	63	218,957	7.46	31	–	–
Other										
Life insurance companies	27	190,895	7	9,490	34	200,385	4.74	23	25,953	329
Management companies	13	195,089	1	2,605	14	197,694	1.32	12	44,358	409
Investment dealers	8	17,698	2	3,693	10	21,391	17.26	7	5,617	404
Property and casualty	13	11,243	13	10,027	26	21,270	47.14	4	2,559	306
Mutual fund companies	2	3,320	0	0	2	3,320	0.00	2	2,051	1,269
Sub-total	63	418,245	23	25,815	86	444,060	5.81	48	–	–
Total	131	1,103,594	69	94,389	200	1,197,983	7.88	103	–	–

Source: The Financial Post 1990a
Notes: [a] Assets in C$000,000.
[b] Other than banks.

firms. The management companies involve some double counting since a number of these firms are the owners or holding companies of trust or other companies, since the trust companies' assets are often consolidated with the management firms. For example, Trilon Financial owns Royal Trustco Ltd, while CT Financial Services owns Canadian Trustco Mortgage Company and other subsidiaries.

The seventy-four Canadian-owned financial institutions with assets of more than C$1 billion in 1989 include seven large federally chartered banks which operate as full-service banks and whose shares are widely distributed. Their combined assets in 1989 were C$477 billion or 42 per cent of all financial institutions with C$1 billion or more in assets. They include the Royal Bank of Canada, the Bank of Nova Scotia, the Bank of Montreal, the Canadian Imperial Bank of Commerce, the National Bank of Canada and the Laurentian Bank of Canada. The ten largest financial institutions in Canada are given in Table 17.2. They control 57 per cent of the total assets of all Canadian-controlled financial institutions of C$1,104 billion in 1989. The rest of the financial firms consist of niche players in various specialized markets.

There were twenty-eight foreign players in Canada with assets of more than C$1 billion in 1989. These included sixteen niche banks, two lending companies and one leasing finance company. Some of the foreign-owned banks and lending companies operate limited branch networks with the most extensive branch network belonging to a management company, Household Financial Corporation of Household Finance in Chicago, principally a loans company. There are three banks from the USA, Switzerland and France, two banks from Hong Kong, Japan and the UK and one from West Germany. One area that has a lot of foreign companies operating in it is in the property and casualty business, where approximately 50 per cent of the firms in Canada are foreign controlled: C$10 billion of C$21 billion.

The ten largest foreign financial firms in Canada in 1989 are given in Table 17.3. These ten firms have 45 per cent of the assets of all foreign-controlled financial firms in Canada in 1989. They consist of five 'banks', one life-insurance company, one acceptance company, one management company (finance company), one securities house and one loans company. The largest single firm is General Motors Acceptance Corporation. Similar to Ford Credit Canada Ltd, these 100 per cent US-owned firms have been in Canada a long time and niche themselves primarily as credit providers for car purchases. The largest foreign 'bank' in Canada is Hongkong Bank of Canada, which when combined with Lloyds Bank of Canada easily makes it the largest foreign-controlled financial institution in Canada in 1989.

Table 17.2 Ten largest Canadian financial institutions by assets, 1980 and 1989

Rank, 1989	Institution	Assets 1989 (C$000,000s)	Rank, 1980	Assets 1980 (C$000,000s)	Percentage change in assets, 1980–9	Rank
1	Royal Bank of Canada	114,660	1	62,884	45.16	6
2	Canadian Imperial Bank of Commerce	100,213	2	55,428	44.69	7
3	Bank of Nova Scotia	81,001	4	43,176	46.70	5
4	Bank of Montreal	78,921	3	48,842	38.11	8
5	Toronto-Dominion Bank	63,069	5	33,842	46.34	4
6	Trilon Financial Corporation[a]	44,358	n.a.	n.a.	n.a.	n.a.
7	Royal Trustco Ltd	39,826	8	8,274	79.22	1
8	Caisse de depot et placement du Quebec	37,493	7	11,749	68.66	2
9	Mouvement des caisses Desjardine[b]	37,283	n.a.	n.a.	n.a.	n.a.
10	National Bank of Canada	33,927	6	16,464	51.47	3
	Top ten's assets (%)	630,751 (57)				
	Remaining assets (%)[c]	472,843 (43)				
	Total assets (%)	1,103,594 (100)				

Source: *Financial Post* 1981, 1990a
Notes: a First appeared in 1983
b First appeared in 1982.
c Total sample by the *Financial Post* of 200 financial firms; 131 Canadian controlled.
n.a., not applicable.

Table 17.3 Ten largest foreign financial institutions in Canada by assets, 1980 and 1989

Rank, 1989	Institution	Assets, 1989 (C$000,000s)	Rank, 1980	Assets, 1980 (C$000,000s)	Percentage change in assets, 1980–9	Rank
1	General Motors Acceptance Corporation	8,360	1	2,420	245.45	3
2	Hongkong Bank of Canada [a, b]	6,138	n.a.	n.a.	n.a.	n.a.
3	Citibank Canada[c]	5,274	n.a.	n.a.	n.a.	n.a.
4	Ford Credit Canada Ltd	4,608	2	990	365.45	1
5	Lloyds Bank of Canada[a, b]	4,544	n.a.	n.a.	n.a.	n.a.
6	Prudential Assurance Group of Companies[d]	3,332	n.a.	n.a.	n.a.	n.a.
7	Barclays Bank of Canada	2,730	3	812	236.21	4
8	Household Financial Corporation Ltd	2,605	7	577	351.47	2
9	Burns Fry Ltd[d]	2,402	n.a.	n.a.	n.a.	n.a.
10	Swiss Bank Corporation (Canada)[c]	2,376	n.a.	n.a.	n.a.	n.a.
	Top ten's assets (%)	42,369 (45)				
	Remaining assets (%)[e]	52,020 (55)				
	Total assets (%)	94,389 (100)				

Source: The Financial Post 1981, 1990a
Notes: [a] Owned by Hongkong & Shanghai Banking Corporation.
[b] Did not appear until 1982 listings.
[c] Did not appear until 1981 listings.
[d] Did not appear until 1989 listings.
[e] Total sample by the *Financial Post* of 200 Financial institutions, 69 foreign controlled.
n.a., not applicable.

The operations of the various groups of banks in Canada are depicted in Figure 17.4, which has the same quadrants as Figure 17.3. The seven large banks A(D) and some of the larger trust companies with international operations, are located in quadrant 1(ii). Most of the foreign banks F(I) are niche players principally involved in larger domestic commercial loans and servicing their international corporate clientele. They appear in the middle right of quadrant 2(iii)–(iv). One major exception that is developing is the Hong Kong Bank of Canada (with parent assets of $130 billion) which recently acquired Lloyds Bank and its retail branches for $190 million. With 104 branches, $10.5 billion in assets and 3,000 employees the Hongkong Bank is an important player on the West Coast and Vancouver's largest financial corporation based in that city (Schreiner 1990). It has also become Canada's seventh largest bank. In Figure 17.4 it appears to the right of the foreign banks with a distinctively domestic appearance. The remaining Canadian and foreign-owned financial institutions B(D) appear toward the upper left in quadrant 2(iii), i.e. most of their operations are

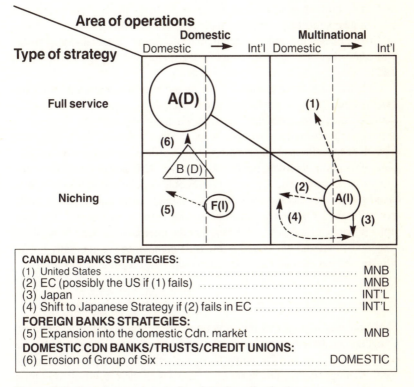

Figure 17.4 Operations and strategies of the Canadian banks

niched with some players moving into more than one niche but as a group they are not yet considered to be full service in their scope of operations. Similarly, most of their business is serving the domestic customer with a more limited orientation toward international transactions.

Table 17.4 lists the foreign operations of the Canadian-based financial institutions in the US, Japan and the EC in 1988 (the last year for which all the countries' data were available for the same year). The figures for the EC only include the UK, West Germany and France. These three countries, however, account for the bulk of Canadian financial institutions activities in the EC. From Table 17.4 it can be seen that the major Canadian players in the 'triad' are the large Schedule 1 chartered banks in Canada and one trust company, the Royal Trust Bank. Similarly, the securities houses' operations are interlinked with the large integrated bank, since most of the large companies were acquired by those institutions following the first round of deregulation of financial markets in Canada. Those financial institutions that are most likely to be 'multinational' in their operations are found within the boxes. They are primarily the Schedule 1 chartered banks and their brokerage and securities houses. In 1988 they accounted for sixty-nine operations and 6,404 employees in the main 'triad' areas. These are by no means the only foreign operations of the Canadian-based financial companies but they do account for the majority of foreign operations in 1988.

The international operations of the large Canadian chartered banks and trust companies, A(I), are located in quadrant 4(iv). This depicts that, while some of their foreign-owned subsidiaries have assumed the function of servicing the domestic customer base in other countries, as a group the Canadian subsidiaries and/or representative offices are still limited to principally handling international transactions for their parent companies' operations in Canada. The Bank of Nova Scotia's operations in the Caribbean stand out as an example of a domestic foreign customer servicing bank, even if many of those customers originally come from Canada. The dark linkage line does indicate, however, that the international operations of the Canadian chartered banks and a few trust companies are generally one of MNBs, i.e. that they do have extensive ownership considerations abroad.

Four potential directions in international strategy for Canadian banks

Five potential changes in the direction of the domestic (home country) Canadian chartered banks and trust companies' foreign operations are depicted in Figure 17.4 including four international strategies. The foreign banks that operate in Canada are also shown with their resulting long-term strategies. Each of these strategies will now be examined in detail.

Table 17.4 Foreign operations of Canadian financial institutions in the USA, Japan and the EC[a], 1988

	USA		Japan		EC		Total	
	No. of operations	No. of personnel	No. of operations	No. of personnel	No. of operations	No. of personnel	No. of operations	No. of personnel
Banks and trust companies								
CIBC (see 1 below)	12	1,291	1	55	3	670	16	2,016
Bank of Montreal (see 2 below)	4	532	1	50	3	334	8	916
Bank of Nova Scotia (see 3 below)	9	400	1	50	2	350	12	800
Toronto Dominion Bank	1	494	1	50	1	150	3	694
Royal Bank of Canada (see 4 below)	1	350	1	60	3	154	5	564
National Bank of Canada	4	280	1	21	2	47	7	348
Royal Trust Bank	–	–	–	–	1	245	1	245
Bank of Montreal Trust Co.	1	23	–	–	–	–	1	23
Canadian Laurentian Bank	–	–	1	12	–	–	1	12
Mercantile Bank of Canada	1	n.a.	–	–	–	–	–	–
Total	33	3,370	7	298	15	1,950	55	5,618
Securities houses								
4 RBC Dominion Securities	–	–	1	10	1	220	2	230
1 Wood Gundy	–	–	1	18	2	195	3	213
3 Scotia Mcleod	–	–	1	15	2	124	3	139
Richardson Greenshield	1	94	–	–	2	22	3	116
2 Nesbitt Thomson	–	–	–	–	2	35	2	35
Buma Fry (and Timmins)	1	3	–	–	1	30	2	33
1 CIBC	–	–	–	–	1	30	1	30
2 B of M Capital Markets	–	–	–	–	1	25	1	25
Midland Doberty	–	–	–	–	2	20	2	20
Levesque, Beaubier Geoffrion	–	–	–	–	1	10	1	10
Merrill Lynch Canada	–	–	–	–	1	3	1	3
Total	2	97	3	43	16	714	21	854

Source: The banker 1989a–f
Note: [a] Includes the UK, the FRG and France.

Strategy 1: Competing as a full-service MNB

The first strategy shifts the foreign operations of the large Canadian chartered banks or trust companies into becoming full-service MNBs. This will most likely require large expenditures of money by the Canadian parent banks and a long-term commitment to their foreign operations. This strategy may be most relevant for the USA where state barriers are gradually being eroded (Compton 1987). For example, California is due to permit inter-state banking starting in 1991 (*The Economist* 1990e). In order to service a large broadly located customer base, the long-term development of a branch network is necessary for any growth potential. This is particularly relevant in view of the disappearance of the demarcation lines that have traditionally separated commercial banking from deposit institutions and investment banking, as well as the insurance business (*The Economist* 1990h).

It may be predicted that over time many bank retail customers in the USA will demand that their financial institution be able to deliver on a large variety of their banking needs. This could arise as an outgrowth of the trend to all-under-one-roof retail shopping that is occurring in other areas. If this does occur, this aspect of consumer preference will combine with prudence on behalf of financial institutions that engage in risk reduction of their asset base, particularly mortgages, by also engaging in commercial banking and ultimately in investment banking, though there is disagreement on whether the staid, conservative commercial banks are particularly compatible with the more entrepreneurial investment banks that are perpetually seeking new deals (Chu 1988a, b).

One of the six large Canadian chartered banks, however, believes that it can develop an internal culture which combines the attributes necessary in both a commercial and investment banker. The Toronto Dominion Bank was the only major Schedule 1 bank in Canada not to purchase a brokerage house in order to enter the securities field. The Chairman of the bank believes that in the long run this approach will pay-off owing to the eventual merger between the banking and securities industries. This will leave banks that purchased securities houses with excess capacity that will be costly to resolve. By developing slowly and building internally on its well-educated bank staff (all but one of its executive Vice Presidents have Masters degrees in Business administration along with 15 per cent of its 4,000 managers, compared with only 5 per cent of the Royal Bank of Canada's 8,500 managers), the Toronto Dominion Bank may be able to develop an entrepreneurial culture in its bankers.

Servicing a larger customer base has the benefit of spreading the operating costs of a large branch network over a broader range of products and clientele groups, rather than over a narrowly serviced clientele base with limited financial product or services lines that could restrict profits during economic down-turns (Wilcox and Rosen 1988). In order to develop this broad-service branch network the Canadian financial institutions would have to be prepared to decentralize their decision-making apparatus, with most of the authority for operations being left to their US operation. A centralized decision-making process from Canada would probably suffer from a lack of ability to transfer culturally adaptive products to the US market, as well as, in general, the flexibility and responsiveness necessary to deal with a non-homogeneous customer base between Canada, the USA and their respective regions.

In terms of a strategy for the large Canadian banks that may best service the USA, they appear to stand well poised to move into the northern USA with the eventual demise of the National Bank Act of 1933 (Glass–Steagall Act) (see Duncan and Jolly 1988). Combined with both a broad-based experience in servicing many branches across an extremely large country and a heterogeneous industrial and resource mix, the Canadian chartered banks have both the knowledge and skills to take advantage of such a similarly large diversified market in the USA. However, as long as the USA limits inter-state banking, then it may be more appropriate for the larger Canadian banks to restrict themselves to niche banking by servicing corporate clients in the USA that do business in Canada (this is depicted in the second strategy).

Experience with the savings and loans (SLs) crisis in the USA, particularly in the southern states, would seem to suggest that the Canadian banks should be wary of purchasing ready-made full-service facilities in the USA. In most cases an undervalued bank would probably reflect poorly secured long-term assets. These would require a great deal of staff time and capital to solve. However, much of the problem in the US SLs industry may be localized in different regions of the USA, or even to particular banks, but the overall problem of the crisis on investment in the industry would help to pull down the price of the assets of banks which under normal circumstances would be good investments. This would make some SLs assets a bargain for foreign banks willing to move into the US market.

The availability of good banks, or their assets to purchase, may dry up owing to the increasing degree of bank consolidation and merger activity presently being undertaken in the USA by the larger American banks. This can be seen in the growth of the super-regionals in the USA over the last ten years (*The Economist* 1990a, g). For example, the rapid growth of North Carolina's NCNB with extensive operations in Texas, South Carolina and Florida made it the only top ten bank outside of New York or California. This is a major achievement given the SLs problem in the southern states (Hector 1990).

One shortcoming that will retard the ability of the Canadian banks to do business in the USA is the relativly sophisticated nature of US banking competition that has developed over the last hundred years owing to extensive state and federal regulatory control. US financial institutions have developed a myriad of new financial products, beginning with the certificate of deposit in the early 1960s in order to offer their clients higher deposit rates. While the Canadian banking industry has competed on product offerings and not price it is questionable whether competition has been as intense as in the USA. Chant (1988: 98–9) indicates that this type of product competition has been relatively absent from the oligopolistic Canadian financial market. In order to overcome this detriment to operating in the US market, Canadian banks will have to be prepared to spend heavily on financial product design if they want to remain competitive. This is particularly true of developing electronic delivery systems and integrating them with the human dimensions of the service function (Feuchtwanger 1988), as well as developing more extensive fee-based lines of products and services (Binner 1988).

All is not wrong with the Canadian banks and their adoption of new technology. Some of the larger Canadian chartered banks have been initiators by adopting the latest in technology. A number of recent examples stand out. The Canadian Imperial Bank of Commerce has started a pilot project for a consumer telephone banking system in London, Ontario (CIBC Link-up). The first use by a financial institution of satellite technology occurred when the National Bank of Canada launched its satellite communications system that links 145 retail branches with its Montreal-based head office (*Toronto Star* 1990). Similarly, the Toronto Dominion Bank has spent the last six years developing a computer system that permits all product information on a customer to be maintained in one place for access by all its branches.

Strategy 2: A specialized services niche market MNB

The second strategy is one of expanding into the foreign domestic market, perhaps by servicing a broader range of clients, i.e., broadening the operations of the foreign base, but still being a specialized player compared with the larger full-service banks in the area. This strategy may be appropriate for the soon to be unified national markets of the EC. After 1992 a single, easily obtainable licence will be made available to all European banks. This will permit a bank to open branches in all twelve markets without having to obtain permission in each market or to allocate specific capital to each branch (Carletti and Aaronson 1989).

It may be worthwhile for Canadian banks to partially buy their way into the more unified financial market through the purchase of smaller European financial operators that service a broader clientele base, particularly the smaller firms in the EC that have not yet developed a loyalty to a larger EC-based bank. This should overcome the dual problem in the EC of: (a) a tightly linked corporate-bank operating structure in some markets (particularly in West Germany and increasingly in France) and (b) cultural barriers between the interaction of Canadian bank personnel with EC bank personnel and corporate treasurers. An example of the intricacies of the industrial web is the $6 billion worth of industry acquired by Deutsche Bank in West Germany, including a 28 per cent stake in Daimler-Benz, West Germany's biggest corporation. Similarly, it handles a quarter of the country's securities trading. This type of financial power would be no match for the Canadian banks, which in their own domestic market are restricted from acquiring production assets. Yet, Deutsche Bank may not have a strong advantage in the rest of the EC since it has not concentrated on the broad European or international markets (Carletti and Aaronson 1989).

By buying into a reputable and ready-built bank–corporate network, with the ability to expand by servicing small EC firms that may not yet be served within one of the larger corporate–bank relationships, the Canadian subsidiary will garner quicker market presence and ready-made customers which otherwise would take many years to develop.

For banks or trusts already involved in subsidiary operations in the national markets of the EC this type of strategy could in general be ignored, unless the subsidiary has been returning few if any profits to the bank and retrenchment is therefore required by returning to more profitable types of operations. This could involve selling the subsidiary and retreating to a limited branch or representative office arrangement. This would involve a type 3 strategy that we discuss next. It could even mean exiting the market. This option was taken by RBC Dominion Securities Ltd (a subsidiary of the Royal Bank of Canada) when it decided to shut down its UK stock broker-age operations, Kitkat & Aitken, and its UK market making subsidiary, RBC Kitkat, owing to the over-capacity problem in the industry. RBC Dominion International would continue to operate in the underwriting and trading of Canadian shares and Euro-Canadian bonds the trading of Canadian federal and provincial bonds, and international corporate-finance activities.

According to Melly (1990), the common thread running through all the activities of the Canadian banks and securities houses in London is some reliance on the home North American market. For example, the Royal Bank of Canada has sold its French, West German and Belgium commercial and retail banking operations while its RBC Dominion Securities Inc. unit has been made the management hub of all the Royal's investment banking operations outside Canada. The Bank of Montreal, through its US subsidiary Harris Bancorp Inc. of Chicago, has niched towards its North American commercial customers interested in doing business in the EC. The Canadian Imperial Bank of Commerce, while still being a niche player, has moved more aggressively in Europe. It has set itself up as an indigenous European institution providing some account facilities for key North American clients, but principally developing specialist niches in energy project finance, communications and infrastructure lending, arbitrage and acquisition financing. One major exception appears to be Royal Trustco Ltd, which has been in London since 1929, and has turned to targeting the financial active entrepreneur, someone who wants to use his money to develop new business and therefore needs more than a standard portfolio management of wealth.

The more niche-oriented, profit-seeking strategies of the Canadian banks in Europe may put them in good stead over the five to ten year period following 1992. According to *The Economist*, the pan-European strategy will be very difficult to achieve, even for the large well-capitalized national banks in the EC. Retail banking in the EC is dominated by a clutch of the biggest banks. Also, it is a brand-conscious high-volume business where economies of scale matter (*The Economist* 1990c). In some cases, however, financial products travel badly, while in others, e.g. life insurance, car loans and credit cards, they travel well. Citicorp has shown itself adept in the USA at using electronic networks and direct mail to build a large banking franchise on the back of a credit-card network. This strategy may be particularly useful for the EC. Except for the largest of banks a financial supermarket approach to Europe could mean financial disaster. One EC bank that has done very well by specialized niching is France's Compagnie Bancaire which in general has steered clear of bank networks. With its seven slim subsidiaries free to chart their own innovative strategies the bank has maintained a 12 per cent capital adequacy ratio when many of its larger competitors have trouble reaching the mandatary 8 per cent (*The Economist* 1990: 89–90). Canadian banks may do well to follow this approach in the EC.

Strategy 3: Retrenchment from being an MNB

Strategy 3 is basically a retrenchment strategy. In this case the Canadian chartered banks' foreign operations (representative offices or branches) would increase their reliance and consolidation in servicing a tighter niche foreign market, primarily through the export of banking services. This strategy may be more relevant in Japan or Eastern Europe where there is still the necessity of servicing Canadian corporate clients overseas and where future potential warrants a market presence. Also, the branch office(s) can overcome what is the hardest part of operating in Japan, a cultural unwillingness to do business with foreigners. With a long-term presence in Japan being built up with Japanese personnel, Canadian banks could expect to see these cultural barriers eroded. This approach is similar to the one required in the EC, but over a much longer term, by eventually servicing unattached smaller firms in Japan. If Canadian banks take this route they will have to be prepared to offer the same type of strong industry–bank partner relationship that the Japanese banks at present do, i.e. one that may return relatively few profits over the short haul in Japan.

A note of caution about operating in Japan is necessary. As the Japanese market barriers between the financial and equity markets break down, the Japanese market may become very competitive, thereby returning few, if any, profits. This happened also in the broker–dealer function in London after the Big Bang (see Channon 1988: 60). However, in order to carry on business in the more profitable areas a Japanese market presence is necessary, particularly as Japanese corporations show continued reluctance to deal with foreign banks for the majority of their banking requirement even while located in foreign markets. This problem may in the long run work itself out as Japanese firms become more globalized. However, this may be of little comfort to non-Japanese banks over the short to medium run as they face increased competition from the Japanese subsidiaries in their own domestic markets.

Strategy 4: Variable niche MNBs

The type 4 strategy requires operating between strategies two and three. For some product lines it may be worthwhile developing a larger profile in the domestic industry, while for other products it could involve only selling them as an international bank. This strategy may develop in the EC owing to the consolidation by the larger EC-based banks, post 1992. In this case the EC may be too large for a Canadian financial company to cover fully, particularly if limited funds are available. An EC strategy for a Canadian bank or trust may then, for example, concentrate on having full-service operations in key cities throughout the EC, and only those types of products that could be serviced by electronic means outside the key areas. This strategy represents a geographical niche in branch location, a full-service product spectrum within those centres, and a niche strategy outside the major banking national centres.

This strategy would be quite complicated to operate. It is different from what exists today since the EC strategy would be directed from one capital centre of operations in the EC, i.e. London or Frankfurt, and not from a myriad of capitals as is at present required. Yet, scale economy products would be marketed from the centre while products that are unique in national taste to one operational area would be marketed from that base. In effect this would require extensive loosening of control from the centre in order to operate an economy of both scale and scope operation. This is represented in Figure 17.1 by the shaded area between niching and full service.

The competitors' strategies

Strategy 5: The Elimination of Foreign Restrictions

On 21 November 1988 the Canadian government passed an Order in Council approving a banking licence for American Express. American Express Bank of Canada will operate without branches by using the existing network of automated teller machines (ATMs). This was a result of the larger Canadian banks denying Amex access to their ATM network. The large Canadian banks have been upset by this owing to the fact that Amex is not a bank in the USA. Also it operates in some fields denied to Canadian banks including insurance and retail sales. Finally, the same access is denied to Canadian banks that want to do business in the USA by the Glass–Steagall provisions, (see *Globe and Mail* 1990). This frontal attack on the Canadian banks has come at the end of a process that has gradually liberalized the Canadian domestic market to access by foreign banks.

Amex's expansion into Canada is not particularly different from the other foreign banks' entry strategies to the extent that the majority of the foreign banks have concentrated in serving niche markets or, after having tackled the large Canadian banks by trying to serve as a full-service bank, by retreating into niche strategies. As already mentioned the Hongkong Bank of Canada has been successful in Canada primarily through its astute operations and the purchase of a Canadian branch network by acquiring financially troubled, smaller Canadian banks. This case is the exception, however. More representative of the foreign banks' operations in Canada is the strategy adopted by BT Bank of Canada, which has successfully niched in the securities business and in fact has sold its retail banking network and credit-card business. Similarly, the giant mutual fund company, Fidelity Investments of Boston, is looking at the Canadian market owing to the free trade agreement and the good market opportunities for investment in Canada. Canada has begun to mark a turnaround for many of the foreign banking operations. For example, in the first quarter of 1990 the fifty-seven foreign bank subsidiaries showed a marked increase in net income of 40.6 per cent. In contrast, net income at the large chartered Canadian banks rose by just 1.4 per cent (see *The Financial Post* 1990b). This may also be a problem owing to the absolutely smaller asset base of the foreign bank subsidiaries.

While in absolute terms the operations of the foreign banks in Canada remain small, it can be expected that with further international deregulation they will continue to push into some of the more traditional areas that the chartered Canadian banks used to serve. Their ability to form full branch networks, however, given the geographical size of Canada and the already well entrenched large branch networks of the big six Canadian banks, means that they are unlikely ever to become a dominant force in the Canadian banking environment unless some radical changes occur, which is extremely unlikely at this time.

Strategy 6: the elimination of domestic restrictions

The big Canadian chartered banks have been extending their product and services domain in recent years. They have entered the securities business with partial deregulation and appear likely to be permitted to enter the fiduciary business by purchasing trust companies. In fact the Royal Bank has not even waited for the proposed changes in the Bank Act to take place but has bought the International Trust Company of Canada (Hemeon 1990). However, Canadian banks are still not allowed into two businesses that they would like to be in: car leasing (Amex had to get out of the leasing business in order to become a Canadian bank) and the sale of life insurance (Simon 1989).

The life-insurance companies in Canada, however, have been encroaching on the banks by entering the commercial-term loan field (McNish 1990). For example, Mutual Life of Canada is the leading corporate lender in the insurance sector. As other insurers enter the field they will also find themselves in direct competition with the major chartered banks. The insurance companies, while at present small in the term loan business, have an advantage in their ability to lend long term, twenty years or more, owing to their extensive deposit base in the form of insurance premiums. In the long run they could become formidable opponents and erode the low profit margins that already exist in the commercial loans sector.

The large chartered Canadian banks have also been more active in promoting mutual funds. The Bank of Nova Scotia, the Royal Bank and the Bank of Montreal all formed investment management subsidiaries in 1988, handling the banks mutual funds as well as portfolio management services. Gradually, as the market barriers between the different financial sectors weaken and disappear, the larger Canadian chartered banks and trust companies will find their position eroded by the smaller domestic financial firms and non-traditional sources of competition. If allowed to operate by the same rules as their competitors the larger banks will be well able to maintain their sovereign position, though perhaps a bit diminished. If they are restricted at the same time as other players are being allowed to compete in their traditional areas of operations, the larger Canadian chartered banks and trusts could then find themselves in a very weakened state.

CONCLUSIONS

In this chapter we have outlined at an industry level the possible strategies that can be followed by the various financial industry players in Canada, both in the domestic Canadian economy and in the triad markets of the USA, Japan and the EC. In order to operate as MNBs in the triad regions the Canadian banks are going to have to be prepared to be nationally responsive to the sovereign interests of the governments in those areas. This will require the transfer of authority lower down in the organizational hierarchy and into the foreign operations of the Canadian MNBs. This in turn will require more independent and better educated bankers. As the regulatory barriers between the different types of banking activities decline, and as competition increases, it can also be expected that commercial bankers are going to have to become more entrepreneurial and risk taking in their outlook if they are to capture or maintain foreign market share.

Operating from a small domestic market relative to the other triad members the large chartered Canadian banks will be well placed to develop strategies that focus on a number of financial areas rather than by trying to develop into MNBs with full service facilities world-wide. This follows from the more limited number of MNEs that are domestically resident in Canada versus the much larger numbers based in the US, Japan or the EC. How the Canadian government and provincial governments permit competition to improve and increase in Canada will be equally important as how successfully it permits Canadian banks to compete as MNBs. If the new Canadian financial regulations grant access to previously forbidden areas of operation and activities, without granting similar changes to larger Canadian chartered banks, these banks could then find that their domestic base has been eroded compared with the domestic base of their competitors found elsewhere in the triad.

Without a strong domestic base to operate and compete from, Canada could find itself with a smaller number of global banking players. A failure to have Canadian MNBs could directly harm Canadian multinational corporations (MNCs) and their ability to compete globally, if Canadian MNCs find it increasingly difficult to obtain services from foreign-owned MNBs during periods of recession or capital crunches. If the foreign MNBs favour their own domestic firms to the detriment of their foreign customers, i.e. Canadian ones, Canada's interests abroad or even domestically could suffer.

In an ideal world it should make little difference where the MNB was originally domiciled. Instead, the choice of which bank to use should be dependent only on the quality and price of the service that the MNB is able to offer. This, however, is more theory than reality and the country of ownership is still an important consideration for firms when deciding on their overall financial requirements. To this end, Canadian banks have already slipped down the global scale of banks internationally, probably resulting in Canadian firms seeking a larger proportion of their financial requirements from foreign-based MNBs, particularly for expansion abroad or in areas considered too risky by Canadian MNBs. This should certainly not be further encouraged by domestic policies that hinder the large banks and make them even more internationally non-competitive. For example, Canadian banks have lost out on financing deals owing to regulations in the securities field.

To the extent, however, that Canada's large banks seek protection in order to maintain their oligopolistic position in the domestic market, or at least what is now left of that position, Canadian financial regulators should permit as much international competition to enter the domestic Canadian market as possible. They should be careful, however, in making sure that they do not over-extend the types of market access provisions to the foreign banks in the Canadian market that Canadian banks do not receive abroad. In the long run, if Canada's large chartered banks are going to succeed, or even remain in the running as globalized financial institutions, along with their counterpart MNBs in the EC, USA or Japan, then efficient domestic financial services laws need to be maintained and the Canadian government and the industry itself need to lobby for and obtain efficient international rules on banking and other financial services.

ACKNOWLEDGEMENTS

We would like to thank Dr Yair Aharoni for hosting the workshop on services at Duke University and Dr Kalman J. Cohen, Distinguished Bank Professor, Fuqua School of Business, for his insightful comments and suggestions on this chapter.

18 The internationalization process in professional business service firms: some tentative conclusions

Yair Aharoni

INTRODUCTION

In 1940, Colin Clark (p. 34) noted that the 'economics of tertiary industry remains to be written'. Hill, in 1977 (p. 336), found the 'complete neglect of services in economic theory is almost incredible given the role of services in contemporary economics'. In the 1980s, the neglect is in the process of being redressed but many questions are still unanswered, both when these firms are looked at as black boxes and when the inner operations of the firms are considered.

The participants in the conference all stressed the importance of understanding the distinctions between 'goods' and 'services'. Despite much effort, these distinctions are still not very clear. Many of the services are embodied in goods but are also sold separately. Design activities is one example. A designer may work as an independent. Alternatively, a designer may be an employee of a firm. In the first case, the work will be recorded as a 'service', in the second as 'goods'. This point is repeatedly made by different authors and many attempts have been made to offer different definitions of services and to draw boundaries between goods and services. Stigler's observation from 1956 that there seems to be 'no authoritative consensus on either the boundaries or classification of the services industries' (Stigler 1956: 47) still holds true. (For a summary of the many definitions and classifications, see Grönroos (1990: 26–35).) Moreover, the exact definition of a profession still has to be agreed on. Yet it is generally agreed that we live in a service society and that the rules of this society have to be understood.

It is also clear that our knowledge of certain service firms is quite embryonic. Most academic work on services and on their globalization seems to have been done by marketing experts (for early contributions see Wilson 1972; Kotler and Bloom 1984) who increasingly emphasize the importance of quality and the need to reduce perceptual gaps between service suppliers and receivers (see Brown *et al.* 1991; Zeithaml *et al.* 1991). What emerged from our conference was a montage of a wide variety of issues and points of view. Several participants attempted to look at the phenomenon of services in general. Much less was distilled about the specific forces related to the professional business firm. To some extent, of course, these professional business service (PBS) firms share characteristics with other firms. Indeed, several participants stressed the need to build the theory of the global PBS as an extension of the tested theories they, and others, developed to explain goods-producing multinational enterprises (MNEs). Clearly, for any firm, the advantages of operating beyond national borders must exceed the additional costs of doing so. Therefore the PBS global firm may be seen as a special case of the goods-producing MNE. The global PBS must be able to internalize operations across national borders so that the co-ordination of activities within one operation unit is more efficient than market activities between different ownership units. Indeed, transaction costs economics was used to explain multinational banks (Grubel 1977; Gray and Gray 1981).

It is also evident that some service firms followed goods-producing MNEs (on banks, see Channon 1988: ch. 6). For many PBS firms, the need to serve multinational clients is said to have been a major reason for international expansion. The demand pull also created a perceived necessity to build or acquire subsidiaries abroad to facilitate their firm-specific advantages (FSAs) rather than move persons from headquarters on a temporary assignment. PBS firms may also be perceived as a means to reduce the problem of asymmetric information. The uncertainty as to the outcome of a service transaction entails a preference for firms with a reputation and a proven track record and thus allows these firms to have specific ownership advantages. At the same time, there seems to be very little advantage stemming from economies of scale.

DIFFERENCES

One difference between other MNEs and PBS firms is that the international expansion of PBS firms is much more strongly influenced by different regulatory and licensing environments. It may well be that one reason for the widespread operations of multinational management consulting firms is the relative lack of such differences in regulation. Moreover, management consultants do not have to be licensed. They can also incorporate, reducing the risk to any individual partner. It may also be that management is perceived as a US-developed craft and a US origin is seen as providing credible quality signals. Thus, heterogeneous regulatory and institutional environments may reduce the ability to achieve FSAs to allow multinational operation. Further, the regulatory environment means that PBS multinational firms face different hurdles from other MNEs in international operations. Whether or not harmonization and mutual recognition will eliminate this problem remains to be seen. Even if they do, one major distinction of PBS firms will remain – that they are totally dependent on the skills of the professionals. A PBS firm enjoys very few economies of scale. The economies of scope it can achieve by producing closely related services are also limited by the ability of professionals to learn from each other and to co-operate. Information technology may make it is easier to reduce the per-unit cost of a service by offering similar services. Still, since the major assets of a PBS walk home every night, much depends on the ability of the firm to recruit, organize, train and motivate professionals. Without such an ability the firm would be unable to signal quality and reputation and thus would not be able to be successful. Whether or not an ownership structure is indispensable or whether different pools of professionals participating in a network is sufficient is a fascinating question for further research. A related question is the degree to which innovation may create FSAs in a PBS. Clearly, a global PBS necessitates the skills of organizational learning, which is stressed for 'transnationals' by Bartlett and Ghoshal (1989). Internationalization strategy, as shown by Carman and Langeard (1980), is much riskier for a service firm than for a manufacturer of physical goods. The service firm is allowed a much shorter time for learning and getting used to the new market. It has to start producing its service all at once, maintaining direct contacts with its customers. For a PBS firm, added complications are different licensing arrangements and different regulations.

All told, the discussion in the conference clearly shows that our knowledge of the strategy, structure and means of creating FSAs of an international PBS firm are at the embryonic stage. Much more research effort is needed to allow more definite conclusions on any of the topics discussed in the conference.

FUTURE RESEARCH AREAS

Four major research areas should be stressed. The first is broadly related to the inner workings of the service firms and organization design issues. How do these firms process information effectively? How is a network managed? How will the characteristics of the PBS firms and the key success factors faced by them affect their choices with regard to ownership and to control. Will the future see more networking, strategic alliances and co-operative ventures arrangements rather than firms connected by ownership ties? A related question is the complex relationships between professional standards, enforced by various professional organizations and the increased possibility of competition. The trade-off between these two is regarded differently not only in different countries and cultures but also by different professional associations.

A second area of research is in the interaction between political and economic issues. The role of government in regulating services has undergone a major revolution recently. The degree to which even more deregulation is possible, or the possibility of mutual recognition as in the EC, has to be researched. More generally, the trade-offs between economic forces leading to a growing demand for globalization and political realities, as well as cultural traditions looking for differences between nations and a different distribution of benefits, must be carefully studied. It is useful to learn also who is regulated: the service activity, the service provider or the movement of the service provider.

A related question is the possibility of an operation of a Gresham law of professional standards. Thus, the Securities and Exchange Commission (SEC) in the USA has maintained very high levels of reporting requirements relative to other countries. Could the globalization of markets mean that firms would tend to register their shares in places where the reporting requirements are the least stringent – followed by growing pressures on government to relax standards? Research should also be related to possibilities of reaching an international agreement on PBS trade, investment and movement of labour.

The impact of data movement issues on new economies of scale and of scope as well as on international trade is a third major area for research. Many service industries tend to enjoy much higher levels of economies of scale. The most extreme example is in restaurants, not in PBSs. Those used to be Ma and Pa operations. Today – with the help of franchising and of computers – they have become huge global firms on a world scale, as in the case of rental cars, hotels or airlines, e.g. with instantaneous guaranteed systems of reservations. Data services accelerated the possibilities of international trade in services. It also made networking a very important organizational means of achieving these advantages.

Fourth, PBS firms depend on highly skilled persons to execute the work. The importance of recruiting, developing, educating and maintaining the loyalty of the professionals who will be supplying the services cannot be overstated. Research on human resource management should allow academics to help managers in achieving better selection methods in recruiting, more efficient training, greater socialization, better career design and higher levels of loyalty. Note that technology is transferred by training efforts. Firms want to ensure that those trained will remain. They also hope to inculcate a similar culture and ways of operation among their many employees in different countries.

It would also be important to try and show how much of the differentiation and firm-specific advantages in the goods sector are in actual fact a result of services embodied in the goods. Much of the goods reputation, after all, is really a result of delivery commitments, information provided to customers, customer support staff and other kinds of services.

With the many changes in technology, one relevant question for research is the degree to which the professional business firm, under constant pressure for lower costs, would move from being a highly customized skill-intensive operation to what Roger Schmenner (1986) called a 'service factory' and what Levitt (1972) called the 'production line approach' (see also Levitt 1976). It may well be that globalization of PBS operations is still at an embryonic stage. It is not a necessary condition for success and only a few firms may choose to follow this path. In a global industry, a firm must operate globally in order to survive. In PBSs, most firms are local. There are only a handful of firms that decided to expand globally, because they had to serve multinational clients or owing to an idiosyncratic decision of a top manager. The internationalization of PBS firms was to a great degree demand driven. Firms that had no choice but to follow their clients or lose them were mainly auditing firms, much less so legal services. Indeed, there is a major difference in the degree of concentration of different PBSs. Yet, even in auditing where the concentration is highest, there are many small firms serving domestic markets. Moreover, some international PBS firms serve a specific niche. All in all, PBS firms were rarely able to expand into new areas based on reputation and thus achieve economies of scope. In advertising, for example, the attempts to sell 'one-stop shopping' to clients has faltered. Firms are still not sure how to achieve a corporate culture that will dominate diverse professions with different belief systems from different countries but also from different professions. Many firms are still groping for means to cross-refer clients and find it difficult to achieve the level of stability enjoyed by goods-producing MNEs. Unlike goods, professionals can – and sometimes do – walk away from the firm, not infrequently taking clients with them. It is also much more difficult to maintain consistency in service quality.

More research is needed about the reasons for the differences in the magnitude of multinational operations of firms in different PBSs. Why is it that most universities did not become multinationals? What, then, explains the great success of Berlitz all over the globe? Why do auditors and management consultants operate globally while most law firms and all dentists are local? Why are some PBSs (real-estate agents, lawyers) compensated on a basis of commission while others are paid for time? What are the key factors of success for such firms? Are these key factors similar across professions or not?

There are many more interesting research questions that could be added, such as the degree to which some professional services (e.g. engineering design) influence the sourcing of a project, or the applicability of general rules and theories of trade and investment to PBSs. All in all, the globalization of services opens many vistas for important work. Understanding PBS MNEs may also enable us to assess how universal and generally applicable are our theories on the trade and investment in goods.

References

Acheson, J. M. (1985) 'The Maine Lobster Market: Between Market and Hierarchy', *Journal of Law, Economics, and Organization* 1 (2): 385–98.

Adler, N. J. (1991) *International Dimensions of Organization Behavior*, Boston, MA: PWS-Kent.

Adler, N. J. and Graham, J. L. (1989) 'Cross-cultural Interaction: The International Comparison Fallacy', *Journal of International Business Strategy* 20 (3): 515–37.

Agarwal, J. P. (1980) 'Determinants of Foreign Direct Investment: A Survey', *Weltwirtschaftliches Archiv* 116 (4): 739–73.

Aggarwal, R. (1986) 'Managing for Economic Growth and Global Competition: Strategic Implications of the Life Cycle of Economics', in R.N. Farmer (ed.) *Advances in International Comparative Management*, vol. 2, Greenwich, CT: JAI Press, pp. 19–44.

—— (1990) 'Capital Structure Differences Among Large Asian Companies', *ASEAN Economic Bulletin* 7 (1): 39–53.

Aggarwal, R. and Baker, J. C. (1984) 'Variations and Trends in Capital Ratios of Large Banks', *Akron Business and Economic Review* 15 (2): 25–32.

Aggarwal, R. and Durnford, J. (1989) 'Market Assessment of International Banking Activity: A Study of U.S. Bank Holding Companies', *Quarterly Review of Economics and Business* 29 (1): 58–67.

Aggarwal, R., Rao, R. P. and Hiraki, T. (1989) 'Skewness and Kurtosis in Japanese Equity Returns: empirical evidence', *Journal of Financial Research* 12 (3): 74–82.

Aharoni, Y. (1966) *The Foreign Investment Decision Process*, Boston, MA: Harvard Graduate School of Business Administration.

—— (1971) 'On the Definition of the Multinational Enterprise', *Quarterly Review of Economics and Business* 2 (3): 27–37.

Akehurst, G. and Gadrey, J. (eds) (1987) *The Economics of Services*, London: Frank Cass.

Aldrich, H. E. (1979) *Organizations and Environments*, Englewood Cliffs, NJ: Prentice Hall.

Aliber, R. Z. (1970) 'A Theory of Foreign Direct Investment', in C. P. Kindleberger (ed.) *The International Corporation: A Symposium*, Cambridge, MA: MIT Press, pp. 17–34.

—— (1971) 'The Multinational Enterprise in a Multiple Currency World', in J. H. Dunning (ed.) *The Multinational Enterprise*, London: Allen & Unwin, pp. 49–56.

—— (1983) 'Money, Multinationals and Sovereigns', in C. P. Kindleberger and D.

B. Andresch (eds) *The Multinational Corporation in the 1980s*, Cambridge, MA: MIT Press, pp. 245–59.

—— (1984) 'International Banking: A Survey', *Journal of Money, Credit and Banking* 16 (4), part 2: 661–78.

Anderson, J. B. (1990) 'Compensating Your Overseas Executives, Part 2: Europe in 1992', *Compensation and Benefits Review* 22 (4): 25–35.

Araoz, A. (1981) *Consulting and Engineering Design in Developing Countries*, Ottawa: IDRC.

Arkell, J. and Harrison, I. S. (1987) *A Sectoral Study on the Relevance of the OECD Conceptual Framework to International Trade in Consultancy Services*, Paris: OECD.

Arrow, K. J. (1965) *Aspects of the Theory of Risk Bearing*, Helsinki: Yrjo Jahnssonis Saatio.

—— (1989) 'The Organization of Economic Activity: Issues Pertaining to the Choice of Market vs. Non Market Allocation', in US Joint Economic Committee, *The Analysis and Evaluation of Public Expenditure: The PPB System*, Washington, DC: Government Printing Office.

Ascher, B. and Whichard, O. G. (1987) 'Improving Services Trade Data', in O. Giarini (ed.) *Emergence of the Service Economy*, Oxford: Pergamon Press, pp. 255–81.

Auster, E. R. (1987) 'International Corporate Linkages: Dynamic Forms in Changing Environments', *Columbia Journal of World Business* 22 (2): 3–6.

Axelrod, R. M. (1984) *The Evolution of Cooperation*, New York: Basic Books.

Baker, G., Jensen, M. and Murphy, K. (1988) 'Compensation and Incentives: Practice vs. Theory', *Journal of Finance* 43: 593–616.

Balassa, B. (1965) 'Trade Liberalization and "Revealed" Comparative Advantages', *The Manchester School* 33 (2): 99–123.

—— (1977a) 'Stages Approach to Comparative Advantage', *Staff Working Paper*, Washington, DC: World Bank.

—— (1977b) ' "Revealed" Comparative Advantage Revisited: An Analysis of Relative Export Shares of the Industrial Countries 1953–1971', *The Manchester School* 45 (4): 327–44.

Ball, C. A. and Tschoegl, A. E. (1982) 'The Decision to Establish a Foreign Bank Branch or Subsidiary: An Application of Binary Classification Procedures', *Journal of Financial and Quantitative Analysis* 17 (3): 411–24.

Ballon, R. J. and Tomita, I. (1988) *The Financial Behavior of Japanese Corporations*, Tokyo: Kodansha International.

The Banker (1989a) 'Foreign Banks; Tokyo', February.

—— (1989b) 'Foreign Banks; New York', June.

—— (1989c) 'Foreign Banks; Other U.S. Offices', June.

—— (1989d) 'Foreign Banks; West Germany', September.

—— (1989e) 'Foreign Banks; London', November.

—— (1989f) 'Foreign Financial Institutions; France', December.

Bar, F. and Borrus, M. (1987) 'From Public Access to Private Connections: Network Policy and National Advantage', *BRIE Working Paper 28*, September.

Baran, P. A. and Sweezy, P. M. (1966) *Monopoly Capital*, New York: Monthly Review Press.

Bartlett, C. and Ghoshal, S. (1989) *Managing Across National Boundaries: The Transnational Solution*, Boston, MA: Harvard Business School Press.

Barton, J. H. (1986) 'Negotiation Patterns for Liberalizing International Trade in

Professional Services', *Barriers to International Trade in Services*, Chicago, IL: University of Chicago Legal Forum.

Basche, J. R. (1986) *Eliminating Barriers to International Trade and Investment in Services*, New York: Conference Board.

Berton, L. (1988) 'Accounting Firms Can Be Sued in US Over Audits Done Abroad, Judge Says', *The Wall Street Journal*, 10 March: 10.

Bhagwati, J. N. (1984) 'Splintering and Disembodiment of Services and Developing Nations', *The World Economy* 7 (2): 133–44.

—— (1987a) 'Trade in Services and the Multilateral Trade Negotiations', *World Bank Economic Review* 1 (4): 549–69.

—— (1987b) 'International Trade in Services and Its Relevance for Economic Development', in O. Giarini (ed.) *The Emerging Service Economy*, Oxford: Pergamon Press for Services World Forum, Geneva, pp. 3–34.

—— (1988a) *Protectionism*, Cambridge, MA: MIT Press.

—— (1988b) 'Services', in J. M. Finger and A. Olechowski (eds) *The Uruguay Road: A Handbook for the Multilateral Trade Negotiations*, 2nd printing, Washington, DC: The World Bank, pp. 207–16.

Binner, B. C. (1988) 'INVEST: The Full-Service Brokerage Approach', in M. Coler and E. Ratner (eds) *Financial Services: Insiders Views of the Future*, New York: New York Institute of Finance, pp. 77–92.

Bishko, M. J. (1990) 'Compensating Your Overseas Executives, Part 1: Strategies for the 1990's', *Compensation and Benefits Review* 22 (3): 33–43.

Blois, K. J. (1972) 'Vertical Quasi-Integration', *Journal of Industrial Economics* 20 (3): 253–72.

Bloom, P. N. (1984) 'Effective Marketing of Professional Services', *Harvard Business Review* 62 (5): 102–10.

Boddewyn, J. J., Halbrich, M. B. and Perry, A. C. (1986) 'Service Multinationals: Conceptualization, Measurement and Theory', *Journal of International Business Studies* 17 (3): 41–57.

Boyd-Barrett, O. (1989) 'Multinational News Agencies', in P. Enderwick (ed.) *Multinational Service Firms*, London and New York: Routledge, pp. 107–31.

Brandt, W. K. and Hulbert, J. M. (1976) 'Patterns of Communications in the Multinational Corporation: An Empirical Study', *Journal of International Business Studies* 7 (1): 57–64.

Brazil, Government of, *et al.* (1990) *Structure of a Multilateral Framework for Trade in Services*, #MTN.GNS/W/95 (26 February).

Bressand, A. (1989) 'Access to Networks and Services Trade: The Uruguay Round and Beyond', in UNCTC, *Transnational Corporations, Services and the Uruguay Round*, New York: UNCTC, pp. 215–48.

Bressand, A. and Nicolaïdis, K. (1988) 'Les Services au Coeur de l'Economie Relationnelle', *Revue d'Economie Industrielle* 43 (1): 141–63.

—— (eds) (1989) *Strategic Trends in Services: An Inquiry in the Global Services Economy*, New York: Harper and Row.

—— and —— (1991) 'European Integration in a Networked World Economy', in W. Wallace (ed.) *The New Dynamics of European Integration*, London: Pinter Publishers for the Royal Institute of International Affairs, pp. 27–50.

Brimmer, A. and Dahl, F. (1975) 'Growth of American International Banking: Implications for Public Policy', *Journal of Finance* 30 (2): 341–63.

Brooke, M. Z. and Holly, J. (1980) 'International Management Contracts', in L. Otterbeck (ed.) *The Management of Headquarters–Subsidiary Relationships in*

Multinational Corporations, New York: St. Martin's Press, pp. 297–317.

Brown, S. W., Gummesson, W., Evardsson, B. and Gustavsson, B. (eds) (1991) *Service Quality Multidisciplinary and Multinational Perspectives*, Lexington, MA: Lexington Books.

Buckley, P. J. (1987) 'Tourism: An Economic Transaction Analysis', *Tourism Management* 8 (September): 190–4.

—— (1988) 'The Limits of Explanation: Testing the Internalization Theory of the Multinational Enterprise', *Journal of International Business Studies* 19 (2): 181–93. Reprinted in P. J. Buckley (1989) *The Multinational Enterprise: Theory and Applications*, London: Macmillan.

—— (1989) *The Multinational Enterprise: Theory and Applications*, London: Macmillan.

Buckley, P. J. and Casson, M. (1976) *The Future of the Multinational Enterprise*, London: Macmillan.

—— and —— (1985) *The Economic Theory of the Multinational Enterprise: Selected Papers*, London: Macmillan.

—— and —— (1988) 'A Theory of Cooperation in International Business', in F. Contractor and P. Lorange (eds) *Cooperative Strategies in International Business*, Lexington, MA: Lexington Books, pp. 31–53.

Burgess, J. (1989) 'Global Offices on Rise as Firms Shift Service Jobs Abroad', *Washington Post*, 20 April: E1.

Burghleman, R. A. (1983a) 'Corporate Entrepreneurship and Strategic Management', *Management Science* 29 (12): 1349–64.

—— (1983b) 'A Process Model of Internal Corporate Venturing in Diversified Major Firms', *Administrative Science Quarterly* 28 (2): 223–44.

Business Week (1986) 'A Scramble for Global Networks', 21 March: 140–8.

—— (1988) 'The Global 1000', 18 July: 137–86.

Cameroon, Government of, *et al.* (1990) *Multilateral Framework of Principles and Rules for Trade in Services*, #MTN.GNS/W/101 (4 May).

Campayne, P. (1990) 'The Impact of Multinational Banks on the International Location of Banking Activity', University of Reading, mimeo.

Cantwell, J. A. (1988) 'The Contribution of Recent Foreign Direct Investment in Services to a Changing International Division of Labour', *University of Reading Discussion Papers in International Investment and Business Studies* 117 (May): 28.

Carietti, S. and Aaronson, S. (1989) 'Which Banks Can Bank on 1992?', *The Bankers Magazine*, July–August: 20–7.

Carman, J. M. and Langeard, E. (1980) 'Growth Strategies for Service Firms', *Strategic Management Journal* 1 (1): 7–22.

Carr-Saunders, A. M. and Wilson, P. A. (1964) *The Professions*, London: Frank Cass.

Casson, M. (1982) 'Transaction Costs and the Theory of the Multinational Enterprise', in A. M. Rugman (ed.) *New Theories of the Multinational Enterprise*, New York: St. Martins Press, pp. 24–43.

—— (1983) *The Growth of International Business*, London: Allen & Unwin.

—— (1987) *The Firm and the Market*, Cambridge, MA: MIT Press.

—— (1989) 'The Economic Theory of Multinational Banking: An Internalization Approach', *Discussion Paper 133*, series B, vol. II, Department of Economics, University of Reading.

—— (1990a) *Enterprise and Competitiveness*, Oxford: Clarendon Press.

—— (1990b) 'Beyond Internalization', paper presented to Academy of International Business Annual Conference, Toronto.

—— (ed.) (1990c) *The Multinational Enterprise*, Cheltenham: Edward Elgar.

Caves, R. E. (1974) 'Causes of Direct Investment: Foreign Firms' Shares in Canadian and UK manufacturing industries', *Review of Economics and Statistics* 56 (3): 279–93.

—— (1982) *Multinational Enterprise and Economic Analysis*, Cambridge: Cambridge University Press.

Caves, R. E., Porter, M. E. and Spence, M. (1980) *Competition in the Open Economy: A Model Applied to Canada*, Cambridge, MA: Harvard University Press.

Chandler, A. D. J. (1962) *Strategy and Structure: The History of American Industrial Enterprise*, Cambridge, MA: MIT Press.

—— (1977) *The Visible Hand: The Managerial Revolution in American Business*, Cambridge, MA: Harvard University Press.

Chandler, C. (1990) 'Tokyo Panel Seeks to Lure Individual Investors to Stocks', *Wall Street Journal* 16 November: C11.

Channon, D. F. (1988) *Global Banking Strategy*, Toronto: Wiley, reprinted 1990.

Chant, J. F. (1988) *The Market for Financial Services*, Vancouver, BC: Fraser Institute.

Chase, R. B. (1978) 'Where Does the Customer Fit in a Service Operation?', *Harvard Business Review* 56 (6): 137–42.

—— (1981) 'The Customer Contact Approach to Services: Theoretical Bases and Practical Extensions', *Operations Research* 29 (4): 698–706.

Cho, K. R. (1985) *Multinational Banks: Their Identities and Determinants*, Ann Arbor, MI: University of Michigan Research Press.

Chowdhury, A. (1989) 'Banks See Future Growth in Foreign Pastures', *Asian Finance* August: 39–44.

Choy, J. (1989) 'The Global Money Centers: Competition and Cooperation', mimeo, *Report 14A*, April, Washington, DC, Japan Economic Institute.

Chu, F. J. (1988a) 'The Myth of Global Investment Banking (Part I)', *The Bankers Magazine*, January–February: 58–61.

—— (1988b) 'The Myth of Global Investment Banking (Part II)', *The Bankers Magazine*, May–June: 62–5.

Clark, C. (1940) *The Conditions of Economic Progress*, London: Macmillan.

Cline, W. R. (1983) '"Reciprocity": A New Approach to World Trade Policy?', in W. R. Cline (ed.) *Trade Policy in the 1980s*, Washington, DC: Institute for International Economics, distributed by MIT Press, Cambridge, MA, ch. 4.

Coase, R. H. (1937) 'The Nature of the Firm', *Economica, New Series* 4 (16): 386–405.

Coats, A. W. (1985) 'The American Economic Association and the Economics Profession', *Journal of Economic Literature*, XXIII (4): 1697–727.

Cohen, K. J. and Reid, S. R. (1966) 'The Benefits and Costs of Bank Mergers', *Journal of Financial and Quantitative Analysis*, 1 (4): 15–57.

Collier, D. A. (1985) *Service Management: The Automation of Services*, Reston, VA: Reston Publishing.

Commins, K. (1990) 'Arthur Andersen Signs Deal to Audit Books in Soviet Union', *Journal of Commerce*, 20 June: 4A.

Committee on Invisible Exports, various years, *World Invisible Trade*, London.

Compton, E. N. (1987) *The New World of Commercial Banking*, Lexington, MA: Lexington Books.

Cone, S. M. III (1986) 'Government Trade Policy and the Professional Regulation of Foreign Lawyers', *Barriers to International Trade in Services*, Chicago, IL: University of Chicago Legal Forum.

Contractor, F. J. and Lorange, P. (1988a) 'Why Should Firms Cooperate? The Strategy and Economics Basis for Cooperative Ventures', in F. J. Contractor and P. Lorange (eds) *Cooperative Strategies in International Business*, Lexington, MA: Lexington Books, pp. 3–30.

—— and —— (eds) (1988b) *Cooperative Strategies in International Business*, Lexington, MA: Lexington Books.

Coulbeck, N. (1984) *The Multinational Banking Industry*, London and Sydney: Croom Helm.

Cowell, D. W. (1984) *The Marketing of Services*, London: Heinemann.

Cowling, K. and Sugden, R. (1987) *Transnational Monopoly Capitalism*, Brighton: Wheatsheaf.

Crenshaw, A. B. (1990) '3 Law Firms Consider Joining Forces in Europe', *Washington Post*, 17 May: C1.

Cummings, T. (1984) 'Transorganizational Development', *Research in Organizational Behavior*, New York: JAI Press.

Cutts, R. L. (1990) 'Power From the Ground Up: Japan's Land Bubble', *Harvard Business Review* 68 (3): 164–72.

Daniels, P. W. (1982) *Service Industries: Growth and Location*, Cambridge: Cambridge University Press.

—— (1985) *Service Industries: A Geographical Appraisal*, London: Methuen.

Daniels, P. W., Thrift, N. J. and Leyshon, A. (1989) 'Internationalization of Professional Producer Services: Accountancy Conglomerates', in P. Enderwick (ed.) *Multinational Service Firms*, London and New York: Routledge, pp. 79–106.

Davidson, W. H. (1980) 'The Location of Foreign Direct Investment Activity: Country Characteristics and Experience Effects', *Journal of International Business Studies* 11 (2): 9–22.

Davis, E., Hanlon, G. and Kay, J. (1990) 'Internationalization in Accounting and Other Professional Services', paper from Proceedings of the British Academy of Management Association Meetings, Glasgow (September).

Deardroff, A. V. (1985) 'Comparative Advantage and International Trade and Investment in Services', in R. M. Stern (ed.) *Trade and Investment in Services: Canada/U.S. Perspectives*, Toronto: Ontario Economic Council, pp. 39–71.

DeGeus, A. P. (1988) 'Planning as Learning', *Harvard Business Review* 66 (2): 70–74.

De Haricourt, R. (1990) 'Joint Ventures between East European Countries and West: A Medicine or a Deception', paper for the Czechoslovakia Chamber of Commerce, Prague.

Dervan, R. (1986) 'Japanese Investors Dominate Action From Overseas', *National Real Estate Investor*, September: 61–72, 146.

Deutsch, C. (1990) 'Getting the Brightest to go Abroad', *New York Times*, 17 June.

Disstler, C. (ed.) (1987) 'La Deréglementation Dans les Années 1980s', *Le Communicateur*, Numéro Special, July.

Douglas, S. and Rhee, D. K. (1989) 'Examining Generic Competitive Strategy Types in US and European Markets', *Journal of International Business Studies*, 20 (3): 437–64.

Drake, W.J. and Nicolaidis, K. (1992) 'Ideas, Interests, and Institutionalization:

"Trade in Services" and the Uruguay Round', *International Organization* 46 (1): 37–100.

Duncan, C. N. and Jolly, B. O. Jr. (1988) 'Banks in the Securities Business: A Regulatory Primer', in M. Coler and E. Ratner (eds) *Financial Services: Insiders Views of the Future,* New York: New York Institute of Finance, pp. 100–17.

Dunn, B. (1990) 'Cultures Clash on Pay', *American Banker,* 27 July: 15A.

Dunn, J. (1983) 'Country Risk: Social and Cultural Aspects', in R. R. Herring (ed.) *Managing International Risk,* New York: Cambridge University Press, pp. 139–67.

Dunning, J. H. (1973) 'The Determinants of International Production', *Oxford Economic Papers* 25 (3): 289–335.

—— (1977) 'Trade, Location of Economic Activity and the MNE: A Search for an Eclectic Approach', in B. Ohlin, P.-O. Hesselborn and P. M. Wijkman (eds) *The International Allocation of Economic Activity,* London: Macmillan, pp. 395–418.

—— (1981) *International Production and the Multinational Enterprise,* London: Allen & Unwin.

—— (1988a) 'The Eclectic Paradigm of International Production: An Update and a Reply to Its Critics', *Journal of International Business Studies* 19 (1): 1–31.

—— (1988b) *Explaining International Production,* London: Unwin Hyman.

—— (1989a) *Transnational Corporations and the Growth of Services: Some Conceptual and Theoretical Issues,* UNCTC Current Studies Series no. 9, New York, United Nations.

—— (1989b) 'The Theory of International Production', in K. Fatemi (ed.) *International Trade: Existing Problems and Prospective Solutions,* New York: Taylor & Francis, pp. 45–84.

—— (1992) 'The Competitive Advantage of Countries and the Activities of Transnational Corporations', *Transnational Corporations,* 1 (1): 135–68.

Dunning, J. H. and Cantwell, J. (1987) *The IRM Directory of Statistics of International Investment and Production,* London: Macmillan.

Dunning, J. H. and McQueen, M. (1981) 'The Eclectic Theory of Production: A Case Study of the International Hotel Industry', *Managerial and Decision Economics* 2 (4): 197–210.

Dunning, J. H. and Morgan, E. V. (1971) *An Economic Study of the City of London,* London: Allen & Unwin.

Dunning, J. H. and Norman, G. (1987) 'The Location Choice of Offices of International Companies', *Environment and Planning* 19 (5): 613–31.

Eccles, R. G. (1981) 'The Quasifirm in the Construction Industry', *Journal of Economic Behavior and Organization* 2 (3): 335–57.

The Economist (1988a) 'Japan's Bustling Beginners', 2 April: 73.

—— (1988b) 'Survey of Japanese Finance', 10 December: 22.

—— (1988c) 'A Tongue-Twister for 1992', 16 July: 43.

—— (1989) 'The Pricey Society', 9 September: 21–4.

—— (1990a) 'Super-Regionals Lead in the National Banking Race', 17 March: 73–4.

(1990b) 'GATT Brief: Centre Stage for Services?', 5 May: 88–9.

—— (1990c) 'Europe's Banks Reach for an Uncertain Future', 26 May: 83–4.

—— (1990d) 'Peru's Lection: A Script That Went Wrong', 16 June: 46.

—— (1990e) 'Bank of America and Wells Fargo: A Lovable Pair, in their Different Ways', 30 June: 77.

—— (1990f) 'Citibank in Japan: A Tale of Tellers in Distant Places', 7 July: 77–8.

—— (1990g) 'New York's Banks: Huddled Masses', 7 July: 76–7.

—— (1990h) 'Banking and Insurance in America: Crossing the Delaware', 14 July: 81–2.

—— (1990i) 'Parental Responsibility', 8 September: 73.

—— (1990j) Japanese Banks: Back to the Streets', 3 November: 97–8.

Edwards, R. (1990) 'World's Workers Still Chained – to Home Country', *Wall Street Journal*, 16 April: 12A.

Einhorn, H. J. and Hogarth, R. M. (1978) 'Confidence in Judgement: Persistence of the Illusion of Validity', *Psychological Review* 85 (5): 395–416.

Eisenhardt, K. M. (1989) 'Agency Theory: An Assessment and Review', *Academy of Management Review* 14 (1): 57–74.

Enderwick, P. (1987) 'The Strategy and Structure of Service Sector Multinationals: Implications for Potential Host Regions', *Regional Studies* 21 (3): 215–23.

—— (ed.) (1989) *Multinational Service Firms*, London: Routledge.

—— (1990) 'The International Competitiveness of Japanese Service Industries, A Cause for Concern?', *California Management Review* 32 (4): 22–37.

Engel, M. (1985) 'Doctors With Revoked Licenses Set Up Practice in Other States', *Washington Post*, 28 April: A20.

ENR (Engineering News Record) (1986) 3 March: 36.

—— (1988) 7 July, 221 (1): 40.

—— (1989a) 13 July, 223 (2): 45.

—— (1989b) 28 September, 223 (13): 7.

—— (1990a) 7 June, 224 (23): 15.

—— (1990b) 6 July, 224 (27): 8.

—— (1990c) 6 July, 224 (27): 24.

—— (1990d) 6 July, 224 (27): 29–33.

—— (1990e) 2 August, 225 (5): 47.

Erdilek, A. (ed.) (1985) *Multinationals as Mutual Invaders: Intra Industry Direct Foreign Investment*, London: Croom Helm.

Erramilli, M. K. and Rao, C. P. (1990) 'Choice of Foreign Entry Modes by Service Firms: Role of Market Knowledge', *Management International Review* 30 (2): 135–50.

European Communities (1990) *Draft General Agreement on Trade in Services*, #MTN.GNS/W/105 (18 June).

Evans, J. (1990) 'IBCA Downgrades the Credit of Six Large Japanese Banks', *American Banker*, 6 November: 8.

Farmer, J. and Hall, N. F. (1989) 'The Impact of CADD on Consulting Engineering Firms: a Survey of CADD Users and Non-Users', *Service Industries Journal*, 9 (4): 87.

Fatemi, K. (ed.) (1989) *International Trade: Existing Problems and Prospective Solutions*, New York: Taylor & Francis.

Feketekuty, G. (1986) 'Trade in Professional Services: An Overview', *Barriers to International Trade in Services* 1, Summer, Chicago, IL: University of Chicago Legal Forum.

—— (1988) 'International Trade in Services: An Overview and Blueprint for Negotiations', Cambridge, MA: American Enterprise Institute and Ballinger.

Feketekuty, G. and Hauser, K. (1985) 'Information Technology and Trade in Services', *Economic Impact* 52: 22–8.

Feldberg, G. H. (1990) 'Japan's Foreign Lawyers Find Barriers at the Bar', *Japan*

Economic Journal, 14 July: 10.

Feldman, R. A. (1986) 'Japanese Financial Markets', Cambridge, MA: MIT Press.

Feuchtwanger, J. B. (1988) 'Delivering Financial Products to the Consumer', in M. Coler and E. Ratner (eds) *Financial Services: Insiders Views of the Future*, New York: New York Institute of Finance, pp. 195–206.

Financial Post (1981) 'Financial, Insurance and Real Estate Rankings', 75 (24): 115–17.

—— (1990a) 'The Other 500: Financial Services', 84 (20): 130–9.

—— (1990b) 'Foreign Bank Income Soars', 31 May.

Financial Times (1985) 'Disharmony Among EEC Professions', 4 April: 10.

—— (1988) 'Dismantling the Barriers to an EC-Wide Education', 8 August: 4.

Finger, M. J. and Olechowski, A. (eds) (1987) *The Uruguay Round: A Handbook on the Multilateral Trade Negotiations*, Washington, DC: World Bank.

Fingleton, E. (1990) 'Eastern Economics', *Atlantic Monthly*, October: 72–85.

Flowers, E. B. (1976) 'Oligopolistic Reactions in European and Canadian Direct Investment in the U.S.', *Journal of International Business Studies* 7 (2): 43–55.

Fortune (1982) 'Biggest Ad Agency', 1 November: 67.

Foxall, G. (ed.) (1985) *Marketing in the Service Industries*, London: Frank Cass.

Franko, L. G. (1976) *The European Multinationals: A Renewed Challenge to American and British Big Business*, Greenwich, CT: Greylock.

—— (1983) *The Threat of Japanese Multinationals: How the West Respond*, New York: Wiley.

Gadrey, J. (1990) 'L'Internationalisation des Services Personnels et Collectifs et le Developpement Economique en Europe de l'Ouest et de l'Est', unpublished paper.

Galai, D. and Shapira, Z. (1985) 'Project Selection, Errors, Compensation and Incentives', paper presented at the SPUDM conference, Helsinki, Finland.

Galante, S. P. (1984) 'Japan–US Ad Agency Attempts to Go Global', *Wall Street Journal*, 20 April: 26.

Gato, A. (1982) 'Business Groups in a Market Economy', *European Economic Review* 26 (1): 53–70.

Gatsios, K. and Seabright, P. (1989) 'Regulation in the European Community', *Oxford Review of Public Policy* 5 (2): 37–60.

GATT Group Negotiations on Services (1989) 'Elements for a Draft Which Would Permit Negotiations to Take Place for the Completion of All Parts of the Multilateral Framework', MTN.GNS/28 (18 December).

—— (1990) 'Draft Multilateral Framework for Trade in Services', MTN.TNC/W35 (14 September).

GATT Secretariat (1989) *Elements for a Draft Which Would Permit Negotiations to Take Place for the Completion of All Parts of the Multilateral Framework*, #MTN.GNS/28 (18 December), Geneva: GATT.

GATT Trade Negotiations Committee (1989) 'Mid-Term Meeting', MTN.TNC/11 (21 April).

Gereffi, G. (1989) 'Rethinking Development Theory: Insights from East Asia and Latin America', *Sociological Forum* 14 (4): 505–33.

Gerlach, M. (1987) 'Business Alliances and the Strategy of the Japanese Firms', *California Management Review* 30 (1): 126–42.

Gershuny, J. (1978) *After Industrial Society? The Emerging Self-Service Economy*, London: Macmillan.

Gershuny, J. and Miles. I. (1983) *The New Service Economy: The Transformation of Employment in Industrial Societies*, London: Frances Pinter.

Ghoshal, S. (1987) 'Global Strategy: An Organizing Framework', *Strategic Management Journal* 8 (5): 425–40.

Giarini, O. (1985) *The Consequences of Complexity in Economics: The Vulnerability, Risk and Rigidity Factors in Supply in the Science and Praxis of Complexity*, Tokyo: United Nations University, pp. 133–48.

—— (ed.) (1987) *The Emerging Service Economy*, Oxford: Pergamon Press for Services World Forum.

Gibbs, M. (1989) 'Means to Enhance the Competitive Position and Export Capacity of Service Industries of Developing Countries', in UNCTC, *Services and Development: The Role of Foreign Direct Investment and Trade*, New York: UNCTC, pp. 104–7.

Gibbs, M. and Hayashi, M. (1989) 'Sectoral Issues and the Multilateral Framework for Trade in Services', in UNCTAD, *Trade in Services: Sectoral Issues*, New York: UNCTAD, pp. 1–48.

Giersch, H. (ed.) (1987) *Free Trade in the World Economy*, Tübingen: J. C. B. Mohr.

—— (ed.) (1988) *Services in World Economic Growth*, Tübingen: J. C. B. Mohr.

—— (ed.) (1989) *Services in World Economic Growth: Symposium 1988*, Tübingen: J. C. B. Mohr.

Globe and Mail (1990) 'Technicalities Stall Licence for Controversial Amex Bank', 7 April: B3.

Goldberg, L. G. And Saunders, A. (1980) 'The Causes of U.S. Bank Expansion Overseas', *Journal of Money, Credit and Banking* 12 (7): 630–43.

Goldberg, L. G. and Saunders, A. (1981) 'The Determinants of Foreign Banking Activity in the United States', *Journal of Banking and Finance* 5 (1): 17–32.

Goldberg, L. G. and Johnson, D. (1990) 'The Determinants of US Banking Activity Abroad', *Journal of International Money and Finance* 9 (2): 123–37.

Goode, W. (1957) 'Community Within a Community: The Professions', *American Sociological Review* 22 (April): 194.

Goold, M. and Campbell, A. (1988) *Strategies and Styles*, Oxford: Basil Blackwell.

Graham, E. M. (1975) 'Oligopolistic Imitation and European Direct Investment', Ph.D. dissertation: Harvard Graduate School of Business Adminstration.

—— (1978) 'Transatlantic Investment by Multinational Firms: A Rivalistic Phenomenon?', *Journal of Post-Keynesian Economics* 1 (1): 82–99.

—— (1985) 'Intra-industry Direct Foreign Investment, Market Structure, Firm Rivalry and Technological Performance', in A. Erdilek (ed.) *Multinationals As Mutual Invaders: Intra-Industry Direct Foreign Investment*, London: Croom Helm, pp. 67–87.

Graham, J. (1985) 'The Influence of Culture on the Process of Business Negotiations: An Exploratory Study', *Journal of International Business Studies* 16 (1): 81–96.

Graham, J. L. and Andrews, J. D. (1987) 'A Holistic Analysis of Japanese and American Business Negotiations', *Journal of Business Communication* 24 (4): 63–77.

Granovetter, M. (1985) 'Economic Action and Social Structure: The Problem of Embeddedness', *American Journal of Sociology* 91 (3): 481–510.

Gray, H. P. (1983) 'A Negotiating Strategy for Trade in Services', *Journal of World Trade Law* 17 (5): 337–88.

—— (1987) *International Trade in Services: For Distinguishing Features*, Troy, NY: Rensselaer Polytechnic Institute.

—— (1990) 'The Role of Services in Global Change', in J. H. Dunning and A. Webster (eds) *Structural Change in the World Economy*, London and New York: Routledge, pp. 67–90.

Gray, H. P. and Gray, J. M. (1981) 'The Multinational Bank: A Financial MNC?', *Journal of Banking and Finance* 5 (1): 33–63.

Green, P. L. (1990) 'U.S. High-Tech Companies Ready to Serve Europe', *Journal of Commerce*, 28 August: 4A.

Grönroos, C. (1980) 'An Applied Service Marketing Theory', *Working Paper 57*, Helsinki: Swedish School of Economics and Business Administration.

—— (1982) *Strategic Management and Marketing in the Service Sector*, Research Report 8, Helsingford: The Swedish School of Economics and Business Administration.

—— (1985) *Strategic Management and Marketing in the Service Sector*, Lund: Studentlitteratur.

—— (1990) *Service Management and Marketing: Managing the Moments of Truth in Service Competition*, Lexington, MA: Lexington Books.

Grubaugh, S. G. (1987) 'Determinants of Direct Foreign Investment', *Review of Economics and Statistics* LXIX (1): 149–52.

Grubel, H. G. (1968) 'Internationally Diversified Portfolios: Welfare Gains and Capital Flows', *American Economic Review* 58 (5): 1299–314.

—— (1977) 'A Theory of Multinational Banking', *Banca Nazionale del Lavoro Quarterly Review* 123 (December): 349–64.

—— (1987) 'All Traded Services are Embodied in Materials or People', *World Economy* 10 (3): 319–20.

—— (1989) 'Multinational Banking', in P. Enderwick (ed.) *Multinational Service Firms*, London and New York: Routledge, pp. 61–78.

Guile, B. R. (1988) *Technology in Services: Policies for Growth Trade, and Employment*, Washington, DC: National Academy Press.

Guile, B. R. and Quinn, J. B. (eds) (1988) *Managing Innovation: Cases from the Service Industries*, Washington, DC: National Academy Press.

Gummesson, E. (1978) 'Toward a Theory of Professional Service Marketing', *Industrial Marketing Management* 7 (2): 89–95.

Hamel, G. and Prahalad, C. K. (1985) 'Do You Really Have a Global Strategy?', *Harvard Business Review* 63 (4): 139–48.

Hamel, G., Doz, Y. L. and Prahalad, C. K. (1989) 'Collaborate With Your Competitors and Win', *Harvard Business Review* 67 (1): 133–9.

Hampden-Turner, C. (1990) *Charting the Corporate Mind*, Oxford: Blackwell; New York: The Free Press.

Hansen, E. L. and Wortman, M. S. (1989) 'Entrepreneurial Networks: The Organization *in Vitro*', Proceedings for the Academy of Management, Washington, DC, August 13–16: 69–73.

Harnett, D. L. and Cummings, L. L. (1980) *Bargaining Behavior: An International Study*, Houston, TX: Dame Publications.

Harrigan, K. R. (1985) *Strategies for Joint Ventures*, Lexington, MA: Lexington Books.

—— (1988a) *Managing Mature Business*, Lexington, MA: Lexington Books.

—— (1988b) 'Strategic Alliances and Partner Asymmetries', in F. Contractor and P. Lorange (eds) *Cooperatives Strategies in International Business*, Lexington, MA: Lexington Books, pp. 205–26.

Harris, M. and Raviv, A. (1978) 'Some Results on Incentive Contracts with

Applications to Education and Employment, Health Insurance and Law Enforcement', *American Economic Review* 68 (1): 20–30.

—— and —— (1979) 'Optimal Incentive Contracts with Imperfect Information', *Journal of Economic Theory* 20 (2): 231–59.

Hashimoto, S. (1986) 'International Financial Market Makes Way for Japanese Banks and Securities Firms', *Business Japan*, May: 31–3.

Hector, G. (1990) 'The Brash Banker Who Bought Texas', *Fortune*, 27 August: 54–62.

Helpman, E. and Krugman, P. R. (1985) *Market Structure and Foreign Trade: Increasing Returns, Imperfect Competition and the International Economy*, Cambridge, MA: MIT Press.

Hemeon, J. (1990) 'Royal Bank Buys Trust Firm Preparing for New Bank Era', *Toronto Star*, 12 June.

Hennart, J.-F. (1982) *A Theory of Multinational Enterprise*, Ann Arbor, MI: University of Michigan Press.

—— (1990) 'The Transaction Cost Theory of the Multinational Enterprise', In C. Pitelis and R. Sugden (eds) *The Nature of the Transnational Firm*, London and New York: Routledge, pp. 81–116.

Hergert, M. and Morris, D. (1988) 'Trends in International Cooperative Agreements', in F. Contractor and P. Lorange (eds) *Cooperative Strategies in International Business*, Lexington, MA: Lexington Books, pp. 99–109.

Herring, R. J. (1983) *Managing International Risk*, New York: Cambridge University Press.

Heskett, J. (1986) *Managing in the Service Economy*, Boston, MA: Harvard University Press.

Hill, T. P. (1977) 'On Goods and Services', *Review of Income and Wealth* 23 (4): 315–38.

Hill, C. W. L., Hwang, P. and Kim, W. C. (1990) 'An Eclectic Theory of the Choice of International Entry Mode', *Strategic Management Journal* 11 (2): 117–28.

Hindley, B. (1988) 'Service Sector Protection: Considerations for Developing Countries', *World Bank Economic Review* 2 (2): 205–24.

Hindley, B. and Smith, A. (1984) 'Comparative Advantage and Trade in Services', *The World Economy* 7 (4): 369–89.

Hirsch, S. (1967) *Location of Industry and International Competitiveness*, Oxford: Oxford University Press.

—— (1976) 'An International Trade and Investment Theory of the Firm', *Oxford Economic Papers* 28 (2): 258–70.

—— (1987a) *International Transactions in Services and in Service-Intensive Goods*, Tel Aviv: Tel Aviv University.

—— (1987b) *The Internationalization of Israel's Electronics Industry*, Tel Aviv: The Jerusalem Institute of Management.

—— (1989a) 'International Transactions Involving Interactions: A Conceptual Framework Combining Goods and Services', in H. Giersch (ed.) *Services in World Economic Growth*, Tübingen: J. C. B. Mohr.

—— (1989b) 'Services and Service-Intensity in International Trade', *Weltwirtschaftliches Archiv* 125 (1): 45–59.

Hladik, K. J. (1985) *International Joint Ventures*, Lexington, MA: Lexington Books.

Hodder, J. E. (1990) 'Is the Cost of Capital Lower in Japan?', *Journal of Japanese and International Economics* 5 (1): 167–75.

Hoekman, B. M. and Leidy, M. P. (1991) 'Antidumping for Services?', in P. K. M. Tharakan (ed.) *Policy Implications of Antidumping Measures*, Amsterdam: North-Holland, pp. 77–97.

Hofer, C. and Schendel, D. (1978) *Strategy Formulation: Analytic Concepts*, St Paul, MN: West Publishing.

Hofstede, G. (1980) *Culture's Consequences*, Beverly Hills, CA: Sage Publications.

Holand, K. (1990) 'Japanese Banks Pay a Premium for Fed Funds', *American Banker*, 5 November: 1, 32.

Holloway, R. (1987) 'Awaiting the Second Tsunami: A Tide of Japanese Money Sweeps Over the World', *Far Eastern Economic Review*, 17 December: 59–61.

Holstrom, B. (1979) 'Moral Hazard and Observability', *Bell Journal of Economics* 10 (1): 74–91.

Holzberger, G. and Platte, J. (1990) 'A Rocky Road to Hiring Foreign Talent', *American Banker*, 27 July: 12A.

Horst, T. E. (1972) 'Firm and Industry Determinants of the Decision to Invest Abroad: An Empirical Study', *Review of Economics and Statistics* 54 (3): 258–66.

Hoshi, T., Kashyap, A. and Schaferstein, D. (1989) 'Bank Monitoring and Investment: Evidence from the Changing Structure of Japanese Corporate Banking Relationships', *Working Paper 3079*, National Bureau of Economic Research.

——, —— and —— (1990) 'The Role of Banks in Reducing the Cost of Financial Distress in Japan', *Working Paper 3435*, National Bureau of Economic Research, September.

Hout, T., Porter, M. E. and Rudden, E. (1982) 'How Global Companies Win Out', *Harvard Business Review* 60 (5): 98–108.

Hultman, C. W. and McGee, L. R. (1989) 'Factors Affecting the Foreign Banking Presence in the U.S.', *Journal of Banking and Finance* 13 (3): 383–96.

Hymer, S. H. (1976) *The International Operations of National Firms: A Study of Direct Foreign Investment*, Cambridge, MA: MIT Press.

Imai, K., Nonaka, I. and Takeuchi, H. (1985) 'Managing the New Product Development Process: How Japanese Companies Learn and Unlearn', in K. Clark, R. H. Hayes and C. Lorenz (eds) *The Uneasy Alliance*, Boston, MA: Harvard Business School, pp. 337–76.

Inman, R. (ed.) (1985) *Managing the Service Economy: Prospects and Problems*, Cambridge: Cambridge University Press.

International Telecommunication Union (1990) *Yearbook of Public Telecommunication Statistics*, 17th edn, Geneva: ITU.

Itami, H. (1987) *Mobilizing Invisible Assets*, Cambridge, MA: Harvard University Press.

Jain, S. C. (1989) 'Standardization of International Marketing Strategy: Some Research Hypotheses', *Journal of Marketing* 53 (1): 70–9.

Japan Economic Journal (1984) 'Specialized Consulting Firms Help Start-ups Going International', 4 September: 24.

Jarillo, J. C. (1988) 'On Strategic Networks', *Strategic Management Journal* 9 (1): 31–41.

Jensen, M. C. (1986) 'Agency Costs of Free-Cash Flow, Corporate Finance, and Takeovers', *American Economic Review* 76 (3): 323–9.

—— (1989) 'Eclipse of the Public Corporation', *Harvard Business Review* 67 (5): 61–74.

Jensen, M. C. and Meckling, W. H. (1976) 'Theory of the Firm: Managerial Behavior, Agency Costs, and Ownership Structure', *Journal of Financial Economics* 3 (4): 305–60.

Johanson, J. and Vahlne, J.-E. (1977) 'The Internationalization Process of the Firm: A Model of Knowledge Development and Increasing Foreign Market Commitments', *Journal of International Business Studies* 8 (1)L 23–32.

Johanson, J. and Mattsson, L.-G. (1988) 'Internationalisation in Industrial Systems – A Network Approach', in N. Hood and J.-E. Vahlne (eds) *Strategies in Global Competition*, Kent: Croom Helm for the Institute of International Business, Stockholm School of Economics, pp. 287–314. Reprinted in M. Casson (ed.) (1990) *Multinational Corporations*, Vermont: Elgar Publishing.

Johnson, H. G. (1970) 'The Efficiency and Welfare Implications of the International Corporation', in C. P. Kindleberger (ed.) *The International Corporation*, Cambridge, MA: MIT Press, pp. 35–56.

Jones, E. (1981) *Accountancy and the British Economy 1840–1980: the Evolution of Ernst & Whinney*, London: Batsford Books.

Kahneman, D. and Tversky, A. (1979) 'Prospect Theory: An Analysis of Decision Under Risk', *Econometrica* 47 (2): 263–91.

Kaldor, N. (1934) 'The Equilibrium of the Firm', *Economic Journal* 44 (173): 60–76.

Kanter, R. M. (1983) *The Change Masters: Innovation and Entrepreneurship in the American Corporation*, New York: Simon & Schuster.

—— (1989) *When Giants Learn to Dance*, New York: Simon & Schuster.

Katouzian, M. A. (1970) 'The Development of the Service Sector: A New Approach', *Oxford Economic Papers* 22 (3): 362–82.

Kay, J. and Vickers, J. (1988) 'Regulatory Reform in Britain', *Economic Policy* 3 (2): 285–351.

Kay, J. and Posner, M. V. (1989) 'Routes to Economic Integration: 1992 in the European Community', *National Institute Economic Review* 129 (August): 55–68.

Kay, N. M. (1991) 'Multinational Enterprise as Strategic Choice: Some Transaction Cost Perspectives', in C. N. Pitelis and R. Sugden (eds) *The Nature of the Transnational Firm*, London and New York: Routledge, pp. 137–54.

Keizai-Koho Center (1990) *Japan 1991*, Tokyo: The Center.

Kennessey, Z. (1987) 'The Primary, Secondary, Tertiary and Quaternary Sectors of the Economy', *Review of Income and Wealth* 33 (4): pp. 359–85.

Kester, W. C. and Luehrman, T. A. (1989) 'Are We Felling More Competitive Yet?' The Exchange Rate Gambit', *Sloan Management Review* 30 (2): 19–28.

Khoury, S. J. (1979) 'International Banking: A Special Look at Foreign Banks in the U. S.', *Journal of International Business Studies* 10 (3): 36–52.

—— (1980) *Dynamics of International Banking*, New York: Praeger.

Klein, W. (1982) 'The Modern Business Organization: Bargaining Under Constraints', *Yale Law Journal* 91 (8): 1521–64.

Knickerbocker, F. T. (1973) *Oligopolistic Reaction and the Multinational Enterprise*, Boston, MA: Harvard University Press.

Kobrin, S. J. (1989) 'Expatriate Reduction in America Multinationals: Have We Gone Too Far?', *TLR Report* 27 (1): 22–9.

Kogut, B. (1983) 'Foreign Direct Investment as a Sequential Process', in C. P. Kindleberger and D. B. Audretsch (eds) *The Multinational Corporation in the 1980s*, Cambridge, MA: MIT Press, pp. 38–56.

—— (1985) 'Designing Global Strategies: Profiting from Operational Flexibility', *Sloan Management Review* 26 (4): 27–38.

—— (1988a) 'A Study of the Life Cycle of Joint Ventures', in F. J. Contractor and P. Lorange (eds) *Cooperative Strategies in International Business*, Lexington, MA: Lexington Books, pp. 169–85.

—— (1988b) 'Joint Ventures: Theoretical and Empirical Perspectives', *Strategic Management Journal* 9 (4): 319–32.

—— (1988c) 'Country Patterns in International Competition: Appropriability and Oligopolistic Agreement', in N. Hood and J.-E. Vahlne (eds) *Strategies in Global Competition*, London: Croom Helm, pp. 315–40.

—— (1989) 'A Note on Global Strategies', *Strategic Management Journal* 10 (4): 383–90.

Kogut, B. and Kulatilaka, N. (1988) 'Multinational Flexibility and the Theory of Foreign Direct Investment', Reginald Jones Center, *Working Paper 88/10*, Philadelphia, PA: Wharton School, University of Pennsylvania.

Kogut, B. and Singh, H. (1988) 'The Effect of National Culture on the Choice of Entry Mode', *Journal of International Business Studies* 19 (3): 411–32.

Kojima, K. (1978) *Direct Foreign Investment: A Japanese Model of Multinational Business Operations*, London: Croom Helm.

—— (1982) 'Macroeconomic versus International Business Approach to Direct Foreign Investment', *Hitotsubashi Journal of Economics* 23 (1): 1–19.

—— (1990) *Japanese Direct Investment Abroad*, Mitaka, Tokyo: International Christian University.

Kojima, K. and Ozawa, T. (1985) 'Toward a Theory of Industrial Restructuring and Dynamic Comparative Advantage', *Hitotsubashi Journal of Economics* 26 (2): 135–45.

Kolari, J. and Zardkoohi, A. (1987) *Bank Costs, Structure, and Performance*, Lexington, MA: Lexington Books.

Kono, T. (1984) *Strategy and Structure of Japanese Enterprises*, Armonk, NY: Sharpe.

Kotkin, J. (1988) 'A Yen for Lending', *Inc.*, April: 107–10.

Kotler, P. (1980) *Principles of Marketing*, Englewood Cliffs, NJ: Prentice Hall.

Kotler, P. and Bloom, P. N. (1984) *Marketing Professional Services*, Englewood Cliffs, NJ: Prentice Hall.

Kotler, P. and Connor, R. A. Jr. (1977) 'Marketing Professional Services', *Journal of Marketing* 41 (1): 71–6.

Kraus, J. (1990) 'U. S. Banks Retreat from Global Ambitions', *New York Times*, 27 July: 1.

Kravis, I. B. (1985) 'Services in World Transactions', in R. P. Inman (ed.) *Managing the Service Economy: Prospects and Problems*, Cambridge: Cambridge University Press, pp. 135–60.

Kravis, I. B. and Lipsey, R. E. (1988) 'Production and Trade in Services by U.S. Multinational Firms', National Bureau of Economic Research, *Working Paper* 2615.

Kravis, I. B., Heston, A. W. and Summers, R. (1983) 'The Share of Services in Economic Growth', in F. G. Adams and B. G. Hickman (eds) *Global Econometrics: Essays in Honour of Lawrence R. Klein*, Cambridge, MA: MIT Press, pp. 188–218.

Kuhn, A. J. and Burton, R. M. (1982) 'Choosing the Environment for Managerial Control: General Motors in the 20's', unpublished paper.

Labaton, S. (1988) 'Now, Global Law Firms, As U.S. Skills Are Sought', *New York Times*, 12 May: A1.

Lall, S. (1976) 'Theories of Direct Foreign Private Investment and Multinational Behavior', *Economic and Political Weekly* 11 (31–3): 1331–48.

Langer, E. (1975) 'The Illusion of Control', *Journal of Personality and Social Psychology* 32 (2): 311–28.

Lawrence, P. R. and Lorsch, J. W. (1967) *Organization and Environment*, Boston, MA: Harvard University Press.

Lebell, D. (1973) *The Professional Services Enterprise: Theory and Practice*, Sherman Oakes, CA: Los Angeles Publishing Company.

Lee, J. R. and Walters, D. (1989) *International Trade in Construction, Design, and Engineering Services*, Cambridge, MA: American Enterprise Institute/Ballinger Publications.

Lee, P. (1989) 'Today the Friendly Offer, Tomorrow the Hostile Bid', *Euromoney*, August: 48–57.

Leveson, I. (1985) 'Services in the U.S. Economy', in R. Inman (ed.) *Managing the Service Economy: Prospects and Problems*, Cambridge: Cambridge University Press, pp. 27–48.

Levine, S. and White, P. E. (1961) 'Exchange as a Conceptual Framework for the Study of Interorganizational Relationships', *Administrative Science Quarterly* 5 (March): 583–601.

Levinthal, D. (1988) 'A Survey of Agency Models of Organization', *Journal of Economic Behavior and Organization* 9 (2): 153–85.

Levitan, S. A. (1985) 'Services and Long-Term Structural Change', *Economic Impact* 52: 29–32.

Levitt, T. (1972) 'Production Line Approach to Service', *Harvard Business Review* 50 (5): 41–52.

—— (1976) 'The Industrialization of Services', *Harvard Business Review* 54 (5): 63–74.

Li, J. and Guisinger, S. (1991) 'Comparative Business Failures of Foreign-Controlled Firms in the United States', *Journal of International Business Studies* 22 (2): 209–24.

Link. A. N. and Bauer, L. L. (1989) *Cooperative Research in U. S. Manufacturing*, Lexington, MA: Lexington Books.

Lorange, P. (1987) 'Cooperative Strategies: A Challenge in Multinational Management', in P. Lorange and J. Roos (eds) *The Challenge of Cooperative Ventures*, Stockholm: Institute of International Business, Stockholm School of Economics, pp. 1–22.

—— (1988) 'Creating Win–Win Strategies from Joint Ventures', *Working Paper 88–103*, Philadelphia, PA: Wharton School, William H. Wurster Center for International Management Studies.

Lorange, P. and Roos, J. (1992) *Strategic Alliances: Formation, Implementation, and Evolution*, Cambridge, MA: Blackwell.

Lorenzoni, G. (1988) *The Benetton Case*, London Business School Centre for Business Strategy (case).

Lorenzoni, G. and Ornati, O. A. (1988) 'Constellations of Firms and New Ventures', *Journal of Business Venturing* 3 (1): 41–58.

Lovelock, C. H. (1983) 'Classifying Services to Gain Strategic Marketing Insights', *Journal of Marketing* 47 (3): 9–20.

—— (1984) *Services Marketing*, Englewood Cliffs, NJ: Prentice Hall.

—— (1988) *Managing Services: Marketing, Operations, and Human Resources*, Englewood Cliffs, NJ: Prentice Hall.

MacAuley S. (1963) 'Non-contractual Relations in Business: a Preliminary Study', *American Sociological Review* 55 (February): 58.

MacKenzie, K. D. (1978) *Organizational Structures*, Arlington Heights, IL: AHM Publishing.

—— (1981) 'Concepts and Measures in Organization Developments', in J. D. Hogan (ed.) *Dimensions of Productivity Research*, vol. 1, Houson, TX: American Productivity Center, pp. 233–304.

Macmillan, I. C. and Day, D. L. (1987) 'Corporate Ventures into Industrial Markets: Dynamics and Aggressive Entry', *Journal of Business Venturing* 2 (2): 29–39.

Magee, S. P. (1977) 'Information and Multinational Corporations: An Appropriability Theory of Direct Foreign Investment', in J. Bhagwati (ed.) *The New International Economic Order*, Cambridge, MA: MIT Press, pp. 317–40.

Maister, D. H. (1982) 'Balancing the Professional Service Firm', *Sloan Management Review* 24 (1): 15–28.

—— (1984) 'Profitability: Beating the Downward Trend', *The American Lawyer*, July/August: 6–9, Reprinted in the *Journal of Management* 1 (4): 39–44.

—— (1985a) 'Firm Management', *Public Relations Journal*, August: 15–18.

—— (1985b) 'The One Firm: What Makes It Successful', *Sloan Management Review* 27 (1): 3–13.

—— (1986) 'The Three E's of Professional Life', *Journal of Management Consulting* 3 (2): 39–44.

Mallampally, P. (1990) 'Professional Services', in P. A. Messerlin and K. P. Sauvant (eds) *The Uruguay Round: Services in the World Economy*, Washington, DC: The World Bank and the United Nations Centre on Transnational Corporations, pp. 99–104.

March, J. G. and Shapira, Z. (1987) 'Managerial Perspectives on Risk and Risk Taking', *Management Science* 33 (11): 1404–18.

—— and —— (1992) 'Variable Risk Preferences and the Focus of Attention', *Psychological Review* 99 (1): 172–83.

Mariotti, S. and Cainarca, G. C. (1986) 'The Evolution of Transaction Governance in the Textile-Clothing Industry', *Journal of Economic Behavior and Organization* 7 (4): 351–74.

Mariti, P. and Smiley, R. H. (1983) 'Cooperative Agreements and the Organization of Industry', *Journal of Industrial Economics* 31 (4): 437–51.

Marr, M. W., Rogowski, R. W. and Trimble, J. L. (1989) 'The Competitive Effects of U.S. and Japanese Commercial Bank Participation in Eurobond Underwriting', *Financial Management* 18 (4): 47–54.

McCulloch, R. (1987) 'International Competition in Services', *Working Paper 2235*, National Bureau of Economic Research.

McDonald, J. (1989) 'The Mochiai Effect: Japanese Corporate Cross-Holdings', *Journal of Portfolio Management* 16 (1): 90–4.

McGee, J. and Howard, T. (1986) 'Strategic Groups: Theory Research and Taxonomy', *Strategic Management Journal* 7 (2): 141–60.

McManus, J. (1972) 'The Theory of the International Firm', in G. Paquet (ed.) *The Multinational and the Nation State*, Ontario: Collier-Macmillan, pp. 66–93.

McNish, J. (1990) 'Insurers Getting into Loan Game: Industry Moves Toward Banking', *Globe and Mail*, 18 June: B1.

Melly, P. (1990) 'Canadian Firms Slim Down and Play the Niches', *Globe and Mail*, 12 April: B21–2.

Messerlin, P. A. (1990) 'The European Community', in P. A. Messerlin and K. P.

Sauvant (eds) *The Uruguay Round: Services in the World Economy*, Washington, DC: The World Bank and the United Nations Centre on Transnational Corporations, pp. 132–49.

Messerlin, P. A. and Sauvant, K. P. (eds) (1990) *The Uruguay Round: Services in the World Economy*, Washington, DC: World Bank and the United Nations Centre on Transnational Corporations.

Miles, R. F. and Snow, C. C. (1986) 'Network Organizations: New Concepts for New Forms', *California Management Review* 28 (3): 62–73.

Millerson G. (1964) *The Qualifying Associations*, London: Routledge & Kegan Paul.

Mills, P. (1986) *Managing Service Industries*, Cambridge, MA: Ballinger.

Mills, P. and Margulies, N. (1980) 'Toward a Core Typology of Service Organizations', *Academy of Management Review* 5 (2): 255–66.

Mintzberg, H. (1978) 'Patterns in Strategy Formation', *Management Science* 24 (9): 934–48.

Mintzberg, H. and Waters, J. A. (1985) 'Of Strategies Deliberate and Emergent', *Strategic Management Journal* 6 (3): 257–72.

Mowery, D. C. (ed.) (1988) *International Collaborative Ventures in U.S. Manufacturing*, Cambridge, MA: Ballinger.

Mundheim, R. H. and Ehrenhaft, P. (1984) 'What is a "Subsidy"? A Discussion Paper', in D. R. Wallace, F. J. Loftus and V. Z. Krikorian (eds) *Interface Three: Legal Treatment of Domestic Subsidies*, Washington, DC: The International Law Institute, pp. 95–108.

Murphy, K. J. (1983) *Macroproject Development in the Third World*, Boulder, CO: Westview.

Myers, S. and Majluf, N. (1984) 'Corporate Financing and Investment Decisions When Firms Have Information That Investors Do No Have', *Journal of Financial Economics* 13 (2): 187–221.

Nagourney, S. H. (1988) *International Strategy: Japan*, New York: Shearson Lehman Hutton.

National Journal (1990) 'Free the Lawyers', 12 May: 1133.

Nees, D. B. (1986) 'Building an International Practice', *Sloan Management Review* 27 (2): 15–26.

Nelson, M. M. (1990) 'Five EC Nations Agree to End Controls on Immigration, Travel Among Them', *Wall Street Journal*, 14 June: A11.

Nelson, R. R. and Winter, S. G. (1982) *An Evolutionary Theory of Economic Change*, Cambridge, MA: Belknap Press of Harvard University Press.

New York Times (1989) 7 April: D1.

Nicholas, S. J. (1983) 'Agency Contracts, Institutional Modes, and the Transition to Foreign Direct Investment by British Manufacturing Multinationals Before 1939', *Journal of Economic History* 43 (3): 675–86.

Nicolaïdis, K. (1987) 'Contractors vs Contactors: Towards an Integrated Definition of "Trade in Services"', *Working Paper*, prepared for UNCTAD, November.

—— (1988) 'Liberalization vs Deregulation: Old Synergies, New Dilemmas', *Project Promethée Perspectives* (5), Paris, Match.

—— (1989) 'Mutual Recognition: The Next Frontier of Multilateralism?', *Project Promethée Perspectives* (10), Paris, June.

Nicolaïdis, K. and Braunschvig, D. (1989) 'Connecting to 1992: All You Need is a European Profile', *Project Promethée Perspectives* (9), March: 25–30.

Nigh, D., Cho, K. R. and Krishnan, S. (1986) 'The Role of Location-Related Factors

304   References

in U.S. Banking Involvement Abroad: An Empirical Examination', *Journal of International Business Studies* 17 (3): 59–72.

Nonaka, I. (1988) 'Creating Organizational Order Out of Chaos: Self Renewal in Japanese Firms', *California Management Review* 30 (3): 57–73.

Norman, G. and Dunning, J. H. (1984) 'Intra-industry Foreign Direct Investment: Its Rationale and Trade Effects', *Weltwirtschaftliches Archiv* 120 (3): 522–40.

Norman, R. (1984) *Service Management*, New York: Wiley.

Normile, D. (1989) 'Foreign Architects Are Going to Town in Tokyo', *Japan Economic Journal*, 16 September: 9.

Noyelle, T. (1989) 'Business Services and the Uruguay Round Negotiations on Trade Services', in UNCTAD, *Trade in Services: Sectoral Issues*, New York: UNCTAD, pp. 309–63.

Noyelle, T. and Dukta, A. B. (1987) *International Trade in Business Services: Accounting, Advertising, Law, and Management Consulting*, Cambridge, MA: Ballinger/American Enterprise Institute.

Nusbaumer, J. (1987a) *The Services Economy: A Lever to Growth*, Boston, MA: Kluwer Academic.

—— (1987b) *Services in the Global Market*, Boston, MA: Kluwer Academic.

OECD (1982) *Controls and Impediments Affecting Inward Direct Investment in OECD Member Countries*, Paris: OECD.

—— (1987a) *Controls and Impediments Affecting Inward Direct Investment in OECD Member Countries*, Paris: OECD.

—— (1987b) *Recent Trends in International Direct Investment*, Paris: OECD.

Offices of Technology Assessment (1987) *International Competitiveness in Services: Banking, Building, Software, Know-how*, Washington, DC: US Government Printing Office, ch. 4.

Office of the US Trade Representative (1986) *Foreign Trade Barriers*, Washington, DC: US Government Printing Office.

Ohlin, B., Wijkman, P. M. and Hesselborn, P.-O. (eds) (1977) *The International Allocation of Economic Activity*, London: MacMillan.

Ohmae, K. (1988) 'Low Dollar Means U.S. Has Become Bargain Basement', *Wall Street Journal*, 30 November: A18.

—— (1989) 'The Global Logic of Strategic Alliances', *Harvard Business Review* 67 (2): 143–54.

Ott, M. (1987) 'The Growing Share of Services in the US Economy – Degeneration or Evolution?', *Federal Reserve Bank of St. Louis Review* 69: 5–22.

Oye, K. A. (ed.) (1986) *Cooperation Under Anarchy*, Princeton, NJ: Princeton University Press.

Ozawa, T. (1985) 'On New Trends in Internationalization: A Synthesis Toward a General Mode', *Economic Notes* 1: 5–25.

Parsons, T. (1968) 'Professions', in *International Encyclopedia of the Social Sciences*, vol. 12, New York: Macmillan, pp. 536–47.

Paschale, R. T. (1984) 'Perspectives on Strategy: The Real Story Behind Honda's Success', *California Management Review*, 26 (3): 47–72.

Peat Marwick (1986) *A Typology of Barriers to Trade in Services*, Brussels: EEC Commission, December.

Perlmutter, H. (1969) 'The Tortuous Evolution of the Multinational Enterprise', *Columbia Journal of World Business* 4 (1): 9–18.

Pettway, R. H., Tapley, T. C. and Yamada, T. (1988) 'The Impact of Financial

Deregulation Upon Trading Efficiency and the Levels of Risk and Returns of Japanese Banks', *The Financial Review* 23 (3): 243–68.

Pfeffer, J. (1978) *Organizational Design*, Arlington Heights, IL: AHM Publishing.

Pine, A. (1990) 'Japanese Agents of Influence', *Los Angeles Times*, 30 January: 1.

Polman, D. (1990) 'U.S. Political Consultants Export Skill Overseas', *Journal of Commerce*, 18 July: 5A.

Porter, M. E. (1980) *Competitive Strategy: Techniques for Analyzing Industries and Competitors*, New York: Free Press.

—— (ed.) (1986) *Competition in Global Industries*, Boston, MA: Harvard Business School Press.

—— (1990) *The Competitive Advantage of Nations*, New York: The Free Press.

Porter, M. E. and Fuller, M. B. (1986) 'Coalitions and Global Strategy', in M. E. Porter (ed.) *Competition in Global Industries*, Boston, MA: Harvard Business School Press, pp. 315–44.

Poulsen, A. B. (1986) 'Japanese Bank Regulation and the Activities of U.S. Offices of Japanese Banks', *Journal of Money Credit and Banking* 18 (3): 366–73.

Powell, J. (1988) *The Gnomes of Tokyo*, New York: Dodd, Mead.

Powell, W. W. (1987) 'Hybrid Organizational Arrangements: New Form or Transitional Development?', *California Management Review* 30 (1): 67–87.

—— (1990) 'Neither Market Nor Hierarchy: Network Forms of Organization', *Research in Organizational Behavior* 12, Greenwich, CT: JAI Press, pp. 295–336.

Prahalad, C. K. and Doz, Y. L. (1987) *The Multinational Mission: Balancing Local Demands and Global Vision*, New York: The Free Press.

Previts, G. J. and Merino, B. D. (1979) *A History of Accounting in America: An Historical Interpretation of the Cultural Significance in Accounting*, New York: Wiley.

Pryor, F. (1972) 'An International Comparison of Concentration Ratios', *Review of Economics and Statistics* 54 (2): 130–40.

Quimpo, M. G. (1990) 'Telemarketing Scams Reach Overseas', *Washington Post*, 12 July: E1.

Quinn, J. B. (1980) 'Strategies for Change: Logical Incrementalism', Homewood, IL: Dow Jones Irwin.

Quinn, J. B. and Pacquette, P. C. (1990) 'Technology in Services: Creating Organization Revolutions', *Sloan Management Review* 31 (2): 67–78.

Quinn, J. B., Doorley, T. L. and Pacquette, P. C. (1990) 'Technology in Services: Rethinking Strategic Focus', *Sloan Management Review* 31 (2): 79–87.

Radway, R. J. (1990) 'Selecting and Managing Local Lawyers', in F. Ghadar, P. D. Grub, R. T. Moran and M. Geer (eds) *Global Business Management in the 1990s*, Washington, DC: Beacham Publishing, pp. 104–8.

Raviv, A. (1979) 'The Design of an Optimal Insurance Policy', *American Economic Review* 69 (1): 84–96.

Reich, R. B. and Mankin, E. D. (1986) 'Joint Ventures With Japan Give Away Our Future', *Harvard Business Review* 64 (2): 78–86.

Rice, R. (1990) 'Firm Sees Fresh Fields in Frankfurt', *Financial Times*, 8 October: I12.

Richardson, G. B. (1972) 'The Organization of Industry', *Economic Journal* 82 (327): 883–96.

Richardson, J. B. (1987) 'A Sub-Sectoral Approach to Services' Trade Theory', in O. Giarini (ed.) *The Emerging Service Economy*, Oxford: Pergamon for Services World Forum, Geneva, pp. 59–82.

Riddle, D. I. (1986) *Service-Led Growth, The Role of Service Sector in World Development*, New York: Praeger.

Riddle, D. I. and Brown, K. J. (1988) 'From Complacency to Strategy: Retaining World Class Competitiveness in Services', in M. K. Starr (ed.) *Global Competitiveness*, New York: W.W. Norton, pp. 239–70.

Rimmer, P. J. (1988) 'Internationalization of Engineering Consultancies – Problems of Breaking into the Club', *Environment and Planning A*, 20 (6): 761–88.

Roberts, J. (1973) 'Engineering Consultancy, Industrialization and Development', *Journal of Development Studies* 9 (1): 39–42.

Robinson, E. A. G. (1931) *The Structure of Competitive Industry*, London: Nisbet.

—— (1934) 'The Problem of Management and the Size of the Firm', *Economic Journal* 44: 242–57.

Roos, J. (1989) *Cooperative Venture Formation Processes: Characteristics and Impact on Performance*, Doctoral dissertation, Institute of International Business, Stockholm School of Economics.

Root, F. R. (1987) *Entry Strategies for International Markets*, Lexington, MA: D.C. Heath.

—— (1988) 'Some Taxonomies of International Cooperative Arrangements', in F. J. Contractor and P. Lorange (eds) *Cooperative Strategies in International Business*, Lexington, MA: Lexington Books, pp. 69–80.

Root, F. R. and Ahmed, A. A. (1978) 'The Influence of Policy Instruments on Manufacturing Direct Foreign Investment in Developing Countries', *Journal of International Business Studies* 9 (3): 81–93.

Ropoport, C. (1990) 'Tough Time for Japan's Banks', *Fortune*, 16 July: 66–9.

Rossi, F. A. (1986) 'Government Impediments and Professional Constraints on the Operation of International Accounting Organizations', *Barriers to International Trade in Services*, Chicago, IL: University of Chicago Legal Forum.

Roth, W.-H. (1988) 'The European Economic Community's Law on Services: Harmonization', *Common Market Law Review* 25, Amsterdam: Kluwer Academic, pp. 35–94.

Rugman, A. M. (1979) *International Diversification and the Multinational Enterprise*, Lexington, MA: Lexington Books.

—— (1980) 'Internationalization as a General Theory of Foreign Direct Investment: A Re-Appraisal of the Literature', *Weltwirtschaftliches Archiv* 115 (2): 365–79.

—— (1981) *Inside the Multinationals: The Economics of Internal Markets*, New York: Columbia University Press.

—— (1987) 'Multinationals and Trade in Services: A Transaction Costs Approach', *Weltwirtschaftliches Archiv* 123 (4): 651–67.

Rundle, R. L. (1989) 'New Japanese Investment in Real Estate in U.S. Might Have Peaked Last Year', *Wall Street Journal*, 8 March: A2.

Sagari, S. B. (1990) 'U.S. Direct Investment in the Banking Sector Abroad', *World Bank Economic Review* (forthcoming).

Sampson, G. P. And Snape, R. H. (1985) 'Identifying Issues in Trade in Services', *The World Economy* 8 (2): 171–81.

Sapir, A. (1982) 'Trade in Services: Policy Issues for the Eighties', *Columbia Journal for World Business* 17 (3): 77–83.

Sapir, A. and Lutz, E. (1980) 'Trade in Non-Factor Services: Past Trends and Current Issues', *World Bank Working Staff Paper 410*, August, Washington, DC: World Bank.

—— and —— (1981) 'Trade in Services: Economic Determinants and Development Related Issues', *World Bank Working Staff Paper 480*, August, Washington, DC: World Bank.

Sauvant, K. P. (1986a) *International Transactions in Services: The Politics of Transborder Data Flows*, Boulder, CO: Westview.

—— (1986b) *Trade and Foreign Direct Investment in Data Services*, Boulder, CO: Westview.

—— (1989) 'Foreign Direct Investment and Transnational Corporations in Services', in UNCTC, *Services and Development: The Role of Foreign Direct Investment and Trade*, New York: UNCTC.

—— (1990) 'The Tradability of Services', in P. A. Messerlin, and K. P. Sauvant (eds) (1990) *The Uruguay Round: Services in the World Economy*, Washington, DC: World Bank and the United Nations Centre on Transnational Corporations, pp. 114–22.

Sauvant, K. P. and Zimny, Z. (1985) 'FDI and TNCs in Services', *The CTC Reporter* 20 (August): 24–8.

Scaperlanda, A. E. and Mauer, L. J. (1969) 'The Determinants of U. S. Direct Investment in the E.E.C.', *American Economic Review* 59 (4), part 1: 558–68.

Schmnenner, R. W. (1986) 'How Can Service Business Survive and Prosper?', *Sloan Management Review* 3 (27): 21–32.

Schreiner, J. (1990) 'Bank Chairman Is Skilled Negotiator', *The Financial Post*, 7 March: 19.

Schroath, F. W. and Korth, C. M. (1989) 'Managerial Barriers to the Internationalization of U.S. Property and Liability Insurers: Theory and Perspectives', *Journal of Risks and Insurance* 56 (4): 630–48.

Schumpeter, J. A. (1934) *The Theory of Economic Development*, Cambridge, MA: Harvard University Press.

Schwartz, E. (1990) 'Legal Revisions Threaten U.S. Law Firms in France', *Washington Post*, 12 July: E1.

Self, R. (1985) 'Issues of Transnational Legal Practice', *The University of Michigan Yearbook of International Legal Studies*, vol. 7, University of Michigan Law School, pp. 269–76.

Seymour, H. (1985) 'International Investment in the Construction Industry: An Application of the Eclectic Approach', *University of Reading Discussion Papers in International Investment and Business Studies* 87 (July).

—— (1986) 'International Investment in the Construction Industry', Ph.D. Thesis, University of Reading.

—— (1987) *The Multinational Construction Industry*, London: Croom Helm in association with Metheun.

Shamia, D. D. and Johnson, J. (1987) 'Technical Consultancy in Internationalization', *International Marketing Review*, Winter: 20–9.

Shapira, Z. (1993) *Managerial Risk Taking*, New York: Russell Sage Foundation, in press.

Shavell, S. (1979) 'Risk Sharing and Incentives in the Principal and Agent Relationship', *Bell Journal of Economics* 10 (1): 55–73.

Sheard, P. (1989) 'The Main Bank System and Corporate Monitoring and Control in Japan', *Journal of Economic Behavior and Organization* 11 (4): 399–422.

Shelp, R. K. (1981) *Beyond Industrialization: Ascendancy of the Global Service Economy*, New York: Praeger.

—— (1983) *Trade in Services: The Central Trade Issues of the 80s*, International

Symposium on Service Activities in Advanced Industrial Societies, 6–8 June, Switzerland.

Shostack, G. L. (1977) 'Breaking Free From Product Marketing', *Journal of Marketing* 41 (2): 73–80.

Simon, B. (1989) 'Fear of Flying: Canada's Big Six Banks Are Afraid Their Traditional Dominance of Financial Services May Be Under Threat', *The Banker*, May: 87–8.

Siniscalco, D. (1989) 'Defining and Measuring Output and Productivity in the Service Sector', in H. Giersch (ed.) *Services in World Economic Growth: Symposium 1988*, Tübingen: J. C. B. Mohr, pp. 38–57.

Smith, A. D. (1972) *The Measurement and Interpretation of Service Output Changes*, London: Report carried out on behalf of the National Economic Development Office.

Snape, R. H. (1990) 'Principles in Trade in Services', in P. A. Messerlin and K. P. Sauvant (eds) *The Uruguay Round: Services in the World Economy*, Washington, DC: World Bank and the United Nations Centre on Transnational Corporations, ch. 1.

Sooyong, K. (1988) 'The Korean Construction Industry as an Exporter of Services', *World Bank Economic Review* 2(2): 225–40.

Soubra, Y. (1989) 'Construction and Engineering Design Services: Issues Relevant to Multilateral Negotiations on Trade in Services', in UNCTAD, publication *Trade in Services: Sectoral Issues*, New York: UNCTAD.

Starbuck, W. H. and Hedberg, B. T. (1977) 'Saving an Organization for a Stagnating Environment', in H. B. Thorelli (ed.) *Strategy + Structure = Performance: The Strategic Planning Imperative*, Bloomington, IN: University of Indiana Press, pp. 249–58.

Stern, R. (ed.) (1985) *Trade and Investment in Services: Canada/U.S. Perspectives*, Toronto: Economic Council.

Stevens, M. (1981) *The Big Eight*, London: Macmillan.

Stigler, G. J. (1956) *Trends in Employment in the Service Industries*, Princeton, NJ: Princeton University Press for the National Bureau of Economic Research.

Stiglitz, J. E. (1975) 'Incentives, Risk, and Information: Notes Toward a Theory of Hierarchy', *Bell Journal of Economics* 6 (2): 552–79.

Stopford, J.M. and Baden-Fuller, C. W. F. (1990) 'Corporate Rejuvenation', *Journal of Management Studies* 27 (4): 377–98.

Stopford, J. M. and Wells, L. T. (1972) *Managing the Multinational Enterprise*, London: Longman.

Strassmann, W. P. and Wells, J. (eds) (1988) *The Global Construction Industry: Strategies for Entry, Growth and Survival*, London and Boston: Unwin Hyman.

Swiss Bank Corporation (1990) *The European Contractors*, London, June: 4.

Tamura, T. (1988) *Japan's Financial Markets* 29, Tokyo: Fair Facts Series.

Teece, D. J. (1984) 'Economic Analysis and Strategic Management', *California Management Review* 26 (3): 87–110.

—— (1986a) 'Firm Boundaries, Technological Innovation, and Strategic Management', in L. G. Thomas (ed.) *The Economics of Strategic Planning*, Lexington, MA: D. C. Heath, pp. 187–99.

—— (1986b) 'Profiting from Technological Innovation: Implications for Integration, Collaboration, Licensing and Public Policy', *Research Policy* 15 (6): 285–305.

—— (1986c) 'Transactions Cost Economics and the Multinational Enterprise', *Journal of Economic Behavior and Organization* 7 (1): 21–45.

Terpstra, V. and Yu, C.-M. (1988) 'Determinants of Foreign Investment of U.S. Advertising Agencies', *Journal of International Business Studies* 19 (1): 33–46.

Terrell, H. S., Dohner, R. S. and Lowrey, B. R. (1989) 'The U.S. and U.K. Activities of Japanese Banks: 1980–1988', *International Finance Discussion Paper 362*, Board of Governors of the Federal Reserve System, September.

Thomas, D. R. E. (1978) 'Strategy is Different in Service Businesses', *Harvard Business Review*, 56 (4): 158–65.

Thomas, L. G. (ed.) (1986) *The Economics of Strategic Planning*, Lexington, MA: D. C. Heath.

Thompson, G. R. and Stollar, A. J. (1983) 'An Empirical Test of an International Model of Relative Tertiary Employment', *Economic Development and Cultural Change* 31 (4): 775–85.

Thompson, J. D. (1967) *Organizations in Action*, New York: McGraw-Hill.

Thorelli, H. B. (1986) 'Networks: Between Markets and Hierarchies', *Strategic Management Journal* 7 (1): 37–51.

Thorn, R. S. (1987) *The Rising Yen*, Singapore: Institute of Southeast Asian Studies.

Tichy, N. and Charan, R. (1989) 'Speed, Simplicity, Self Confidence', *Harvard Business Review*, September–October.

Timberlake, C. (1990) 'Rapid Growth Goes Awry for Saatchi and Saatchi', *Washington Post*, 28 January: H3.

Toronto Star (1990) 'National Bank Expands in Toronto', 30 March.

Trondsen, E. and Edfelt, R. (1987) 'New Opportunities in Global Services', *Long Range Planning* 20 (5): 53–61.

Tschoegl, A. E. (1983) 'Size, Growth, and Transnationality Among the World's Largest Banks', *Journal of Business*, 56 (2): 187–201.

Tsui, J. F. (1987) 'The Japanese Yen for U.S. Hotels', *Cornell H.R.A.Quarterly*, August: 16–19.

Tucker, K. and Sundberg, M. (1988) *International Trade in Services*, London and New York: Routledge.

Tumlir, J. (1985) 'Protectionism: Trade Policy in Democratic Societies', Washington, DC: American Enterprise Institute for Public Policy Research.

UNCTAD (United Nations Committee on Trade and Development) (1984) *Services and Development Process, UNCTAD Secretariat*, paper presented for the 29th Session of the Trade and Development Board, 10 September, Geneva.

—— (1985) *Production and Trade in Services: Policies and Their Underlying Factors Learning upon International Service Transactions*, New York: UNCTAD.

—— (1989) *Trade in Services: Sectoral Issues*, New York: United Nations.

UNCTC (United Nations Centre on Transnational Corporations) (1979) *Transnational Corporations in Advertising*, New York: United Nations, sales no. E.79.II.A.2.

—— (1980) *Transnational Reinsurance Operations*, New York: United Nations.

—— (1981) *Transnational Banks: Operations, Strategies and Their Effects in Developing Countries*, New York: United Nations, sales no. E81.II.A.7.

—— (1983–8) *National Legislation and Regulations Relating to Transnational Corporations*, vols I–VI, New York: United Nations.

—— (1984) *Transnational Corporations and Transborder Data Flows: Background and Overview*, Amsterdam and New York: Elsevier North-Holland.

—— (1988) *Transnational Corporations as World Development Trends and Prospects*, New York: United Nations, sales no. E88.II.A.7.

—— (1989a) *Foreign Direct Investment and Transnational Corporations in Services*, New York: United Nations, sales no. E.89.II.A.1.

—— (1989b) *Services and Development: The Role of Foreign Direct Investment and Trade*, New York: United Nations.

—— (1989c) *Transnational Corporations in the Construction and Design Engineering Industry*, New York: United Nations, sales no. E89.II.A.6.

—— (1990a) 'Transnational Corporations in the International Computer Service Sector', *Technical Paper*.

—— (1990b) *Transnational Corporations, Services and the Uruguay Round*, New York: United Nations, sales no. E90.II.A.11.

United States (1989) *Agreement on Trade in Services*, MTN.GNS/W/75 (17 October).

United States Department of Commerce (1984) *International Direct Investment: Global Trends and the U.S. Role*, Washington, DC: US Government Printing Office.

United States Trade Representative's Office (1981) *Impediments to Trade in Services*, Washington, DC: January.

—— (1984) *United States National Study on Trade in Services*, a submission by the US Government to the GATT, Washington, DC: USTR.

—— (1986) *Report on Foreign Trade Barriers*, Washington, DC: USTR.

USCOTA (United States Congress, Office of Technology Assessment) (1986) *Trade in Services: Exports and Foreign Revenues – Special Report*, Washington, DC: US Government Printing Office, OTA-ITE-316.

—— (1987) *International Competition in Services: Banking Building Software Know-How* . . . Washington, DC: US Government Printing Office, OTA-1TE-328, July.

Vernon, R. (1966) 'International Investment and International Trade in the Produce Cycle', *Quarterly Journal of Economics* 80 (2): 190–207.

—— (1983) 'Organizational and Institutional Responses to International Risk', in R. J. Herring (ed.) *Managing International Risk* (New York: Cambridge University Press, pp. 191–216.

Vickers, J. and Yarrow, G. (1988) *Privatization: An Economic Analysis*, Cambridge, MA: MIT Press.

Viner, A. (1988) *Inside Japanese Financial Markets*,Homewood, IL: Dow Jones Irwin.

Vollmer, H. M. and Mills, D. L. (1966) *Professionalization*, Englewood Cliffs, NJ: Prentice Hall.

Wakasugi, T. (1988) *Report on Japan's Stock Price Level*, Tokyo: Japan Security Research Institute.

Walter, I. (1985) *Barriers to Trade in Banking and Financial Services*, London: Trade Policy Research Center.

—— (1988) *Global Competition in Financial Services: Market Structure, Protection, and Trade Liberalization*, Cambridge, MA: American Enterprise Institute/Ballinger.

Walter, I. and Smith, R. C. (1989) *Investment Banking in Europe: Restructuring for the 1990s*, Oxford: Blackwell.

Wathen, J. C. (1986) 'Towards the Year 2000 – Japan's Emerging Role in World Finance', *Midland Bank Review*, Summer: 20–4.

Weekly, J. K. and Aggarwal, R. (1987) *International Business: Operating in the Global Economy*, Hinsdale, IL: Dryden.

Weinstein, A. K. (1977) 'Foreign Investments by Service Firms: The Case of Multinational Advertising Agencies', *Journal of International Business Studies* 8 (1): 83–92.

Wells, L. T. (1984) *Technology Crossing Borders: The Choice, Transfer and Management of International Technology Flows*, Boston, MA: Harvard University Press.

Wilcox R. and Rosen, D. (1988) 'Marketing Financial Services: Competition Heats Up as Restrictions Cool Down', in M. Coler and E. Ratner (eds) *Financial Services: Insiders Views of the Future*, New York: New York Institute of Finance, pp. 207–17.

Williamson, O. E. (1975) *Markets and Hierarchies: Analysis and Antitrust Implications*, New York: The Free Press.

—— (1981) 'The Modern Corporation: Origin, Evolution, Attitudes', *Journal of Economic Literature* 19 (4): 1537–68.

—— (1985) *The Economic Institutions of Capitalism: Firms, Markets, Relational Contracting*, New York: The Free Press.

Wilson, A. (1972) *The Marketing of Professional Services*, London: McGraw-Hill.

Wolf, M. (1987) 'Differential and More Favorable Treatment of Developing Countries and the International Trading System', *World Bank Economic Review* 1 (4): 647–68.

Wolferen, K. van (1989) *The Enigma of Japanese Power*, New York: Alfred A. Knopf.

World Bank (various years) *World Development Report*, Washington, DC: World Bank.

Wright, R. and Pauli, G. A. (1987) *The Second Wave: Japan's Global Assault on Financial Services*, New York: St. Martin's Press.

Yannopoulos, G. N. (1983) 'The Growth of Transnational Banking', in M. Casson (ed.) *The Growth of International Business*, London: Allen & Unwin, pp. 236–57.

Zeithaml, V., Parasuraman, A. and Berry, L. L. (1985) 'Problems and Strategies in Services Marketing', *Journal of Marketing* 49 (2): 33–46.

—— and —— (1990) *Delivering Quality Service: Balancing Customer Perception and Expectations*, New York: The Free Press.

Zimmerman, G. C. (1989) 'The Growing Presence of Japanese Banks in California', *Federal Reserve Board of San Francisco Economic Review* 3, Summer: 3–17.

Index